4·30-70

The Hard-to-Employ: European Programs

The Hard-to-Employ:
European Programs

Beatrice G. Reubens

FOREWORD BY Eli Ginzberg

Columbia University Press
New York and London   1970

This report was prepared for the Manpower Administration, U.S. Department of Labor, under research contract Numbers 26231-26244 authorized by Title I of the Manpower Development and Training Act. Since contractors performing research under Government sponsorship are encouraged to express their own judgment freely, the report does not necessarily represent the Department's official opinion or policy. Moreover, the contractor is solely responsible for the factual accuracy of all material developed in the report.

Reproduction in whole or in part permitted for any purpose of the United States Government.

1534812

For Ned and Peggy

Foreword | by Eli Ginzberg

For most of two decades American scholars and policymakers concerned with manpower have been engaged in a pilgrimage to Sweden, which was the originator and fountainhead of what has come to be called "active manpower policy." From the Secretaries of Labor to predoctoral candidates, the stream of American visitors has flowed toward Stockholm. But an important anomaly must be noted. The articles and books published by the visitors after their return have been few and far between, especially if the count is limited to those with scholarly pretensions. The presumption is that briefness of visit, barriers of language, and differences in environment made it difficult even for the observer with insight to come away with more than impressions. There were, of course, occasional exceptions to this generalization.

Dr. Beatrice Reubens' book, *The Hard-to-Employ: European Programs,* is unique, for she has studied the manpower experience not only of Sweden but also of eight other European countries: the United Kingdom, France, Italy, West Germany, the Netherlands, Belgium, Norway, and Denmark. And, after spending over a year in the field she took time to read, assimilate, and synthesize the large body of materials that she had accumulated about the far-flung programs aimed at assisting the hard-to-employ and to evaluate the extent to which they met their specific goals of contributing to the national objective of keeping the unemployment rate as low as possible. Hers has been a study in depth in which nothing has been taken for granted.

Dr. Reubens' interest goes beyond the legislation and the formal policies and programs focused on the problems of the hard-to-employ. She has done this—and in detail—but this was not her primary aim. Dr. Reubens has probed behind the sometimes spare, often elaborate, structures to discover whether and to what extent the objectives of the several efforts were in fact realized. It is safe to say that what she has done and with such thoroughness is not likely to be repeated in the near future. Hers is a truly definitive effort. There will, of course, come a time, after the economies of western Europe undergo further changes and the manpower problems and policies are accordingly transformed, when another major inquiry such as Mrs. Reubens carried out should be undertaken anew. But until then her effort is likely to stand alone.

Dr. Reubens begins her inquiry by raising a basic question. Why do certain people encounter difficulties in getting and holding jobs in an economy which is characterized by a continuing high level of demand for manpower? The fact that during most of the last two decades western Europe enjoyed a high level of employment which led to the planned importing of labor provided an ideal environment for studying the problems of the hard-to-employ. Her study suggests that no matter how high the level of demand for labor, there will always be some workers who because of physical, mental, emotional, or personality characteristics encounter difficulties in their job hunt, and others may have difficulty because of location, technological change, or other environmental circumstance.

After exploring the origin of the problem, Dr. Reubens adds that for reasons of history, geography, and politics these several western European countries have been concerned with the shaping of policy to keep the number of the hard-to-employ as low as possible. They are concerned with adding to their manpower supply, but they are also committed to a philosophy which holds that every person has the right and the need to work and it is the duty of the state to be responsive to these imperatives. Dr. Reubens' book presents a detailed explanation of the range of policies and programs that the several governments have pursued, such as counseling workers, subsidizing employers, creating special jobs, instituting preventive measures—all aimed at discharging this acknowledged responsibility.

The beginning of wisdom in all programming aimed at the hard-to-employ is to identify and counsel them effectively, and in her second chapter Dr. Reubens calls attention to the elaborate efforts that several countries make to this end. She calls attention specifically to the cooperation that is required between the employment officer and the social welfare and medical personnel who are often involved in assisting the peripheral workers to improve their prospects.

Dr. Reubens reviews some of the principal services that these countries provide to heighten the employability of the hard-to-employ. In western Europe, heavy reliance is placed on rehabilitative units and work-training centers where the clientele are tested as to the level of skill which they are able to acquire. Others are offered opportunities to participate in one or another type of more elaborate vocational training courses where the goal is to provide workers with higher-level skills. Some reliance is also placed on training hard-to-employ workers within industry.

As an outgrowth of World War I, Great Britain, France, Belgium, Germany, Luxembourg, and Italy have passed special legislation to assist in the reemployment of disabled veterans who had served in the military. With this legislation as a base, the large countries of western Europe have relied to a considerable extent on quotas and reservations for helping to place the handicapped in employment. Dr. Reubens estimates that over two-million persons have been placed in jobs through this approach, but she points out the drawbacks to a quota or reservation system that is not geared to rehabilitative programs, training, and adaptation of the work place.

The hard-to-employ presumptively are high-cost labor. Hence it is not surprising to learn from Dr. Reubens' review that several countries have resorted to financial incentives in the form of wage subsidies or tax incentives to encourage employers to hire these workers in spite of their low productivity. She found, however, that for the most part the incentives have not been sufficient to overcome employer resistance.

Two other financial approaches are reviewed: the first is a regional subsidy to employers to expand employment in a depressed area, and the other relates to special loans to the hard-to-employ to encourage self-employment. It is Dr. Reubens' considered opinion that to date these several financial dimensions have been less effective than the quota system.

Another effort to help the hard-to-employ to return to work is through the creation by government of special jobs. Here too the reading is mixed. The difficulties of determining the type of jobs that are best suited and the further difficulties of creating them at the right place in the right number assure that this approach can succeed only if there are strong commitment and able administration. In several western European countries both have existed, and as a consequence this avenue of attack on social pathology has had modest but significant success.

Distinct from efforts in these countries to assist the hard-to-employ back into jobs are various policies and programs focused on keeping the hard-to-employ at work, speeding their reemployment, or providing them with special financial assistance if they are forced to withdraw from the labor market.

Among the several devices that have gained some support, largely through the combined efforts of government and trade unions, are those which encourage employers to find a suitable job for a man who is no longer able to cope with his previous assignment. This pressure on employers is intensified by the various hurdles that have been erected by law, trade union arrangements, and public opinion in the way of the dismissal of workers who are likely to experience difficulties in becoming reemployed.

There are limits, however, to the use of strong-arm measures to force employers to retain workers in the face of falling demand. Hence many supplemental measures have been devised to assist the hard-to-employ to keep their jobs. Work sharing is one preferred approach. Another approach is the placing of special orders in the private market by government in periods of slack demand. Another related method is the release of special funds for public construction in periods of weak private demand which assists a wide band of workers to remain employed—those engaged in building activities as well as those who provide building materials. Another approach relates to special reconversion allowances to moderate complex market and technological disarrangements such as have been occurring as a result of the movement toward European economic integration.

The exigencies of economic development are such that some dislocations in the employment structure are an inevitable consequence of progress. But it is not inevitable that modestly endowed workers who have been holding jobs will be thrown out of work and because of their handicaps will become part of the pool of the hard-to-employ. There are policies and programs that can keep their numbers to a minimum.

Advance warning by the employer to government agencies can provide important lead time for the agencies to explore alternatives, specifically the finding of new jobs for those who will eventually be let out. Apparently in several European countries the business risks of early disclosure have been kept within bounds by the secrecy observed by the government with respect to this privileged information.

Related approaches involve special subsidies such as lowered contributions for social security from employers who are willing to hire a designated group of workers who otherwise would have no jobs. Special allowances for retraining them is another method that has found favor.

Still another method is mobility allowances to the displaced workers to assist them in relocating. On occasion a large-scale effort at industrial reconversion has taken place when a major employer, finding that he must shut down his operations, has taken the lead to attract new industry and has helped to retrain his work force for the new openings.

No matter how imaginative the proposals, it is not always possible for government, even with the active cooperation of employers and trade unions, to assume that some workers will not lose their jobs or that they will not encounter difficulties in finding new ones. While monetary compensation is seldom the equivalent of a job, it can, and has, been used to moderate the losses that workers experience when they become unemployed.

Three related approaches have been used. One has been supplemental or improved unemployment benefits so that the worker does not have to manage on what are often quite small governmental benefits. Second, in several countries recourse has been had to lump sum payments for a worker who has lost a job which is being eliminated so that he has no prospect of regaining it. He is therefore compensated, sometimes fairly liberally, for his "property rights" in a job.

The potentially most interesting effort has been the development of the "pre-pension." When a worker of 55 or 60, especially one who has been in a highly specialized field such as coal mining, loses his job and has little prospect of getting another it may be both more economic and more humane to provide special financial benefits to carry him until he reaches pensionable age rather than to attempt to relocate and retrain him.

In brief, the foregoing suggests some of the major policies and programs on behalf of the hard-to-employ that Dr. Reubens has systematically reviewed in the nine western European countries. While the story that she has to tell is interesting and significant in its own terms, it has more than one lesson for the United States, where we have confronted the problem of the hard-to-employ since 1963. Once again I can hope to call attention to only a few areas of tangency.

Before delineating the specific approaches that might be copied in whole or in part by the United States as it seeks to make inroads into the multimillion pool of hard-to-employ, it would be well to sketch briefly the principal differences between the socioeconomic and cultural conditions of western Europe and of the United States and the solutions that each has favored.

These are some of the characteristics of the American scene that are unique: large racial and ethnic minorities (about thirty million) which have been only partially integrated into the economy and society and who are handicapped in their educational preparation for employment; an advanced technology which has placed a premium on reliable workers so that American industry by law and custom is disinclined to train or hire young people in their teens; a highly educated female population with an increasing disposition to accept employment either part-time or full-time, who do not insist on jobs which will fully utilize their skills or potential and who therefore represent a source of supply which is a major alternative to hard-to-employ males; a bifurcation of many metropolitan centers into an inner ring where the poor are concentrated and an outer ring where many blue-collar and service jobs are being expanded. However, because of lack of suitable transportation and housing discrimination it is difficult for the marginal urban workers to get these suburban jobs which they could perform effectively.

While the level of welfare and related social services varies widely throughout the United States, it is likely that in the more liberal northern and western states there is less pressure on those who receive public assistance to find a job than there is in western Europe. The recent amendments (December 1967) to encourage people on welfare to undertake training which will fit them for jobs is a belated recognition of the shortcomings in the welfare system which have resulted in ever larger numbers of people on the welfare rolls despite continuing prosperity.

Finally, the sheer size of the United States and the necessity for cooperation among federal, state, and local governments in implementing various manpower policies creates additional difficulties. It is much easier for Sweden, with a homogeneous population that is smaller than that of New York City, to fashion and implement effective manpower policies than for the United States, which is twenty-five times as large.

Despite these basic differences in cultural integration, the level of technological sophistication, the size of the reserve female labor force, the splintering of the metropolitan labor market, the loose ties between the welfare system and the placement of the unemployed in jobs, and finally the differences that stem from size alone, we cannot assume that the United States can learn nothing from the efforts of western European countries to place a high proportion of their hard-to-employ in employment.

With respect to all of the possible actions noted below, we acknowledge that it will be difficult to implement them in the United States at the present time or in the near future. However, they have sufficient potential for good to warrant serious concern and experimentation.

First there is the arena of preventive actions which suggest that corporations, in cooperation with unions, do more to make room within their own establishments for workers who if dismissed would find it difficult to be reabsorbed. And in states where business has a working relationship with the Employment Service it might be possible to institute an early warning system. At a minimum this should be possible where a prospective decline in employment will result from a reduction or termination of a federal contract.

Another type of preventive action would be a study by different levels of government of how to schedule construction to moderate the substantial seasonal swings which now characterize the industry. In its 1968 amendments to the Manpower Development and Training Act, Congress instructed the Secretary of Labor to study this long-neglected issue.

We have long had "set-asides" in the letting of federal contracts to help increase the level of employment in areas of substantial unemployment. But, as an address by the former Secretary of Defense suggested, there are many additional opportunities for using the large economic resources of the Department of Defense to achieve important civilian objectives. Presumably more could be done with respect to stimulating employment in the distressed areas if this were considered a high-priority objective.

With respect to direct efforts to place the hard-to-employ in employment, the federal, state, and local governments might borrow from European countries the use of reservations and quota systems. This would mean that with respect to the large number of jobs which governments directly control—some ten million—certain ones with modest skill requirements would be reserved for handicapped persons in search of employment. The next step that government might take would be to require that those from whom it purchases goods or services become part of such reservation-quota systems. Finally, different levels of government might require all employers with a work force above a minimum size to help in the employment of the hard-to-employ by accepting a limited number.

The pros and cons of this approach must be discussed thoroughly before embarking on so radical a change in labor market policy.

Any additional constraint on the freedom of employers to hire and fire should be carefully weighed before being instituted. And it may well be that the costs would not justify the results. But they might. Most of the hard-to-employ have characteristics not too different from many who hold unskilled or semiskilled work. It may be that an assurance that the hard-to-employ have direct access to a job within their present level of competence or their expected level of competence after modest training is the key to solving their problem. The question inevitably arises, what happens to those who currently hold these jobs? It is hoped that under a comprehensive program many could be upgraded.

Individuals who are on the fringes of the labor market because of mental, emotional, physical, or social disabilities need careful assessment and training. While we have begun to move in the direction of establishing effective assessment and rehabilitation centers during the past years, we still have a long way to go. We need more centers that are closely related to real work situations, centers that can, in fact, serve as a way station for the hard-to-employ into regular employment.

One of the important lessons that we still have to learn is that many of those on the fringe of the labor market will probably never be able to hold a competitive job. If they are not to be permanently on the relief rolls, sheltered workshops or some form of permanent subsidized employment are the only alternatives. A rich society has an obligation to enable all who desire to work, even if they cannot meet competitive norms, to do so as long as their output covers the costs of the subsidy—and possibly even if their economic contribution does not. The seriously handicapped are surely entitled to help from more fortunate citizens so that their lives may be a little less bleak.

These are a few of the directions that we might well explore. They have for the most part proved successful abroad. But there remain a few general lessons from the postwar experience of the countries of western Europe that the United States should keep in the foreground as it acts to improve its manpower policies. First and foremost is the necessity to pursue macroeconomic policies that aim at the lowest level of unemployment within the context of tolerable inflationary pressures. Recent experience suggests that an unemployment level of between 3 and 4 percent should be achievable. A higher level would make a mockery of programs aimed specifically at the hard-to-employ.

Second, the United States must move from experiment to institutionalization. We have done a great deal since 1962 to fashion an active manpower policy. But many of the pieces are not yet permanently in place. We have improvised, we have experimented, but we have been slow in making large-scale permanent commitments. That is exactly what must be done and done now. We must construct a permanent structure.

A third task, a difficult one, is to improve the administrative structure and the competence of the personnel who must carry out our several manpower programs. The federal government gets credit for having taken the lead but it needs counterpart strength at state and local levels so that more decisionmaking can be delegated. This has started but current efforts should be intensified. Congress, recognizing the need for more competent administrators, recently specified that 2 percent of all funds appropriated under MDTA must be expended on upgrading of staff.

One final comment is in order: the growing pains which have characterized the development of manpower policy in the United States since 1962 bespeak the lack of knowledge of the policymakers about the nature of manpower and the operations of the labor market. Since new knowledge is the prerequisite for improved policy, Dr. Reubens has made a two-fold contribution. She has added substantially to the storehouse of knowledge about manpower and she has thereby laid the basis for significant advances in manpower programming. Scholars and policymakers alike are in her debt.

Acknowledgments

The debts incurred in a study of this kind are both foreign and domestic. This book could not have been written without drawing on the specialized knowledge of a large number of people in many countries. Their generous cooperation eased my task immeasurably.

Professor Eli Ginzberg, the Director of the Conservation of Human Resources Project at Columbia University, originated and planned this study. He arranged many of my initial contacts in Europe and gave me valuable guidance and support throughout the undertaking. He has read the entire manuscript, which has benefited from his observations.

At the United States Department of Labor, Lewis H. Earl, Chief of the Foreign Manpower Policy Staff, and his associate, Philomena Mullady, extended assistance and encouragement. They obtained documents and information for me and commented in detail on several chapters. The Office of Foreign Labor and Trade of the Bureau of Labor Statistics, through its former chief of research, Kurt Braun, opened its unclassified reports and files to me. Joseph Epstein of the Office of Manpower Research and his assistants discussed my early outlines and made helpful suggestions.

The American labor attachés and their assistants in the nine countries I visited were cooperative and knowledgeable in arranging appointments and briefing me on local conditions. In several countries my program was arranged by an official of the chief manpower agency, and I should like to express my appreciation of their efforts.

I was fortunate in my relationships with the international agencies in western Europe. Through the courtesy of David Morse, Secretary-General of the International Labour Organization, I had office space and contacts in the office in Geneva and the branches in other countries. The Manpower and Social Affairs Division of the OECD in Paris, and in particular Solomon Barkin, Gösta Rehn, and Franz Stendenbach, were a key source of information and ideas during my year's stay in Europe and after my return. On visits to Brussels and Luxembourg I benefited from interviews with a large number of officials of the European Economic Community and the European Coal and Steel Community. The European Free Trade Association in Geneva also provided information.

But my greatest debt is to the numerous experts, in and out of government, whom I saw in the individual countries. It would be invidious to single out particular people because so many were generous with their time and information. Their aid went beyond the period of my visit and I am grateful to those who sent me additional data and publications or reviewed draft manuscript. After distributing credits so widely, it is necessary to concentrate the blame for errors entirely on myself.

At various times Thérèse Beaupain, Carol Burke, and Steven Wycoff served as research assistants.

Ruth S. Ginzberg took time from a busy schedule to read the whole manuscript line by line. She suggested many editorial changes which improved the book's clarity and precision, and the reader as well as the author are indebted to her.

Sylvia Leef coordinated the typing and cheerfully assisted the author in numerous ways. As the editor for the Columbia University Press, Frederick Nicklaus made a valuable contribution in the final stages.

BEATRICE G. REUBENS

January 1970

Contents

Tables

The Hard-to-Employ: European Programs

I | The Problem of the Hard-to-Employ

Why should hard-core unemployment persist under full employment conditions? Few are so optimistic as to expect that high full employment will eliminate all unemployment, but some students assume that only frictional unemployment will remain.[1] The postwar experience of many nations of northwestern Europe, where full or overfull employment prevailed in the first half of the 1960s, suggests that there is considerable residual unemployment beyond frictional joblessness. Nor does this residual consist entirely of the seasonally unemployed, of unemployables, or of those who have in reality retired from the labor market but continue to register as unemployed in order to meet the administrative requirements for certain social benefits.[2]

[1] Arthur M. Ross, ed., *Employment Policy and the Labor Market,* Berkeley, 1965, p. 14; Vladimir Stoikov, "Some Determinants of the Level of Frictional Unemployment: A Comparative Study," *International Labour Review,* May 1966, pp. 530–49; Albert Rees, "The Meaning and Measurement of Full Employment," in Universities—National Bureau of Economic Research, *The Measurement and Behavior of Unemployment,* Princeton, 1957, pp. 13–60.

[2] For example, in West Germany men and women who retire from work when they become eligible for old age pensions register as unemployed and receive unemployment insurance payments for six months. Also, male applicants for early pensions at reduced rates must have registered as unemployed for a year after they reached age 59. In Great Britain, men who have retired before 65 on company pensions continue to sign on as unemployed even after exhausting their unemployment benefits, because the government

The anomalous situation arises where overfull employment coexists with residual unemployment. A full absorption of the manpower supply would be possible only if labor were a fully homogeneous, mobile, and substitutable factor, or if demand were excessive in all industries, occupations, and areas. As it is, under full employment as at other times, both labor supply and aggregate demand are unevenly distributed throughout the economy. A general excess of demand sufficient to absorb all available labor all over the country would create serious inflationary pressures and, in some countries, cumulative balance of payments difficulties. Although countries vary in their tolerance of these undesirable accompaniments of full employment, none has been willing to accept so great an expansion of demand that every kind of residual unemployment could be absorbed. Thus, a high full employment economy does not mean that there is literally full employment everywhere in the country.

However, should not the pull of excess demand in other areas, industries, and occupations dissolve the pockets of unemployment? In fact, an extensive relocation and migration of labor does occur, both autonomous and induced. But some do not or cannot respond to economic opportunity under high full employment. Those who remain attached to the localities, industries, and occupations where demand is slack constitute an important part of the residual unemployed under full employment. In regions of relatively lower demand for labor, the extent of residual unemployment actually tends to be understated in the unemployment statistics because discouraged workers have withdrawn from the search for work and such groups as married women and retired pensioners have lower labor force participation rates than they would have in more prosperous localities.[3]

Another type of residual unemployment is found in all areas in a

---

will then pay the employee's contribution to the state old age pension fund, which must be continued until the retirement age of 65 for full pension; meanwhile they have settled in rural or coastal areas with few job opportunities. (Ministry of Social Security, *Annual Report*, 1966, Cmd. 3338, London: H.M.S.O., 1967, p. 18.)

[3] P. Galambos, "Activity Rates of the Population of Great Britain 1951–1964," *Scottish Journal of Political Economy*, February 1967, pp. 49–54, 61–65; Laurence C. Hunter, "Cyclical Variations in the Labor Suppy: Brit-

full employment economy. In spite of the existence of vacancies, certain workers find it difficult to obtain and hold jobs under existing socioeconomic conditions. The very fact of a labor scarcity encourages those whom employers consider to be of doubtful employability; persons who under less favorable circumstances remain outside the labor market seek work when labor shortages exist. Their numbers are also swelled by the medical, psychiatric, and social advances which return people to society and by a growing belief in the therapeutic effects of work for people with disabilities.

Employers, however, will not accept all of these applicants, even under the greatest scarcity of labor. As an alternative, employers who cannot meet their expanded labor needs through overtime work, contracting-out, labor-saving equipment, or change of location, seek to hire immigrants, married women outside the labor force, retired pensioners, and the employees of other firms. Thus there can be a residual unemployment of the hard-to-employ, even in the face of large numbers of vacancies for unskilled workers.

Some of these residual unemployed may be excluded from suitable vacancies because inflexible or minimum wage rates are too high in relation to the workers' productivity. Others are barred because fixed age, skill, or education requirements are set by law, practice, collective agreement, or trade union regulation. Still others fail to get jobs because employers and supervisors discriminate against capable workers on grounds of background, color, nationality, or religion. A few are excluded because employers fear extra insurance costs or risks with disabled workers. Some jobs remain vacant because em-

---

ish Experience, 1951–60," *Oxford Economic Papers,* July 1963, pp. 140–52; Gösta Rehn, "Manpower Policy and European Unemployment," *OECD Observer,* December 1967, p. 15; Rudolf Meidner, "The Employment Problems of Individuals and Groups," *International Conference on Automation, Full Employment and a Balanced Economy,* (Rome), New York, 1967, pp. 2–3; Gertrude Williams, *Counselling for Special Groups,* OECD: Paris, 1967, pp. 13–15; Geoffrey Gorer, "What's the Matter with Britain?" *New York Times Magazine,* December 31, 1967, pp. 19, 27; Laurence C. Hunter, "Unemployment in a Full Employment Society," *Scottish Journal of Political Economy,* November 1963, pp. 289–304; Trevor Evans and Margaret Stewart, *Pathway to Tomorrow,* London, 1967, p. 27; Adrian Sinfield, *The Long-term Unemployed,* OECD: Paris, 1968.

ployers do not adjust wages and working conditions to current market and social standards.

On the other hand, some of the unemployed do not want to work regularly at the jobs and wage rates open to them. Since society does not permit people to starve in most advanced industrial nations, this may encourage some idleness. Such people can indulge a taste for little or no work if they are willing to live very modestly on relief or by their wits; the latter course may involve illegal activities which are not counted as "employment," although they demand time and skill. However, many who are called work-shy and who outwardly appear to justify the label, have proved, on closer examination, to be willing and able to work after their other problems—personal, social, medical—were uncovered and attacked by sympathetic and skilled professionals.

Most of the residual unemployed under high full employment in northwestern Europe are neither clearly work-shy nor fully qualified workers who are victims of discrimination or restrictive practices. They usually are hard-to-employ in the sense of having physical, mental, and social impediments to easy placement in existing job structures. A lack of confidence in their own ability to work or an unrealistic and overoptimistic appraisal of their abilities or prospects characterizes many of them. An official Dutch statement is enlightening:

It is a well-known fact that at all times—even in days of great prosperity when the level of employment is high—people are to be found who cannot easily obtain employment in the ordinary way on account of their abilities and personality or for reasons due to society . . . the nature of the labour process. In addition to those who are handicapped in some way or other—either mentally or physically—this category is chiefly made up of persons who, because of their advanced age, find it difficult to get employment again after they have lost their jobs for one reason or another. Finally there are the "problem cases" in which the character of the persons concerned plays a part.[4]

4 The Netherlands, Ministry of Social Affairs and Public Health, Social Assistance and Complementary Employment Provisions Section, "Social Employment Provision for Non-Manual Workers," August 1959.

People who would be hard-to-employ under the best circumstances are particularly vulnerable if they happen to live in an area of limited work opportunities or if they are attached to a declining industry. In addition, such a residence or industry attachment may gradually make people hard-to-employ although they might have been employable elsewhere. Thus, immobility is an important ingredient of the hard-to-employ condition.

In the last analysis, however, it is a human being who declares another to be hard-to-employ or hard-to-place. Certain national differences in the attitude toward work as a right and a duty influence the categories into which people are placed, as does the national view of how far government should interfere with, aid, or direct the individual through vocational rehabilitation and other labor market measures. Peoples vary in their receptivity to official programs. Within a country, a degree of arbitrary judgment and response to specific local conditions may be expected from those who assign the labels. For example, in Great Britain, where regional unemployment problems have persisted throughout the postwar period of low overall unemployment, Employment Service officers in regions of higher unemployment, such as Wales and Scotland, have taken a somewhat stricter view of employability than officers in labor shortage areas in the south.

In a broader view, a person who is considered hard-to-employ in one place or at one time might become quite employable in another place or time as a result of changes either in the worker's characteristics or in the number and requirements of available jobs. A complex and changing relationship is suggested by the terms "hard-to-employ" or "hard-to-place." Its current use is a reaction against the harsh experience of the Great Depression, when many who were called unemployable subsequently found work in the war period. The concept of the hard-to-employ or hard-to-place is optimistic and policy-oriented. In particular, it opens the possibility of gainful work for groups who previously have been neglected entirely or aided chiefly through financial assistance.

The countries of western Europe have not found that unskilled migrants from the farms, minority groups, illiterate foreign workers, or youths entering the labor market are hard-to-employ or constitute a hard-core when full employment prevails. A British reviewer of a recent study of American unemployment observed that "a factor unknown in Europe [was] much unemployment due to inadequate training in and after school for modern industrial and service skills." [5] In western Europe, the hard-to-employ are primarily the physically, mentally, or socially handicapped, the long-term unemployed, and displaced older workers. Those with multiple handicaps are particularly apt to remain unemployed when labor shortages prevail. Women with young children who could obtain work easily if they could arrange care for their children are not considered hard-to-employ in the context of this study, although countries like Sweden, which wishes to draw women from the home into the labor market, and the United States, which wishes to limit the numbers on public assistance, may tend to treat these women as hard-to-employ.

PREVENTIVE MEASURES

In considering the reasons why the proportion of the population who are hard-to-employ varies greatly from country to country and over time and from place to place within a country, we take the broadest view of the hard-to-employ. We include those who happen to have jobs and those whose potential for work may be in doubt, as well as the unemployed. Thus, a host of objective and subjective factors influences the situation.

To begin with, the incidence of congenital and environmental disabling conditions is variable among countries and over time. The national distribution of birth defects, war injuries, automobile accidents, industrial diseases and injuries, illness, alcoholism, drug addiction, criminal and antisocial activities, to name the most common factors which cause physical, mental, or social work handicaps, has no regularity. The burden of these and other conditions is directly

[5] *The Times Literary Supplement,* London, July 27, 1967; *OECD Observer,* February 1967, p. 21; Maurice Lengellé, *The Growing Importance of the Service Sector,* OECD: Paris, 1966, p. 43.

affected by the quality and availability of remedial and rehabilitative medical, psychological, and correctional services, the speed with which they are applied, and the attitude of the society toward such persons. Preventive measures such as prenatal care, adequate nutrition in early childhood, vigorous factory and mine inspection, driver education and traffic regulation, also can affect the volume of disablement.

A more fundamental preventive influence can be exerted by the broad character of the society and its success in avoiding alienation, apathy, illiteracy, and extremes in living standards. When countries proclaim as a national aim "a more uniform distribution of income," as the Scandinavian countries and the Netherlands have done, and when they enforce minimum standards, they may have lower proportions of hard-to-employ than the United States, whose boast is the size of its GNP. Furthermore, the hard-to-employ are minimized in countries which do not stop at redistributive taxation and transfer payments, but recognize the importance of maintaining high standards and national uniformity in such public services as basic education, housing, recreation, health and welfare services, and legal and civil rights. Their experience has been that public authorities are best qualified to provide these services.

Certain groups with a high potential for becoming hard-to-employ receive special attention. Children who have special needs or are not adequately supervised are placed in alternative environments more likely to develop their potential. It is recognized that the transition from school to work is difficult and that institutional bridges are required. Anticipatory measures also play a role in the smooth transition from agriculture to industry, from declining to expanding industries or occupations, and from rural to urban settings. Social policies particularly directed toward the acculturation of minorities and immigrants may prevent these groups from having disproportionate numbers of hard-to-employ.

Underlying the European programs is the view that labor is a scarce and valuable resource, that the costs of economic change and growth must not be borne exclusively or disproportionately by the displaced workers, and that assistance should be directed toward productive employment rather than subsidized security in contracting industries or occupations. The European countries are not all equally energetic or effective in their efforts, and it is with a trace of envy of Scandinavia and the Netherlands that an Italian social scientist observed:

The countries in which social and cultural levels in rural and urban areas are substantially equal, if not identical, are at the same time the countries in which, thanks to the development of their social policies and the planning of their social services, the social and cultural infrastructures necessary for adaptation and service to immigrants, at various levels, are the most frequently available. This is one of the sectors in which the inter-relationship between economic and social development —which ultimately determines the progress of a country—is particularly brought to light.[6]

The importance of preventive measures and high standards of social services can hardly be exaggerated as factors in keeping the potentially hard-to-employ in the ranks of the employables. At the same time, the socially-oriented nations are apt to understand more fully and at an earlier date the nature and volume of their hard-to-employ residual. It is not unimportant that these countries are small, homogeneous, and centrally governed, with parliamentary systems. A degree of economic planning and a large role for government are accepted, though many programs are carried out locally. Local government operates through small units which are responsive, efficient, and financed by their own taxation powers and central government grants-in-aid. Finance is not permitted to thwart or distort social objectives, although it sets limits from year to year.

The factors which have been reviewed concern the supply side. To them should be added variations among countries and over time in the age structure of the population, the rate of growth in the labor force, and its mobility.

[6] Magda Talamo, "Internal Migration," in OECD, International Joint Seminar on Adaptation of Rural and Foreign Workers to Industry, *Final Report,* Paris, 1965, p. 38; *Labor Developments Abroad,* January 1969, pp. 6–7.

THE INFLUENCE OF DEMAND CONDITIONS

A whole series of circumstances on the demand side also influences the size and composition of the hard-to-employ population. The ability to maintain unemployment rates under 2 percent for long periods of time has eased the absorption of the hard-to-employ in western European countries and is in considerable contrast to the experience of the United States, where rates under 4 percent cause concern about inflation. Differences in methods of measuring unemployment and levels of frictional unemployment do not explain the variation in residual unemployment rates or the composition of unemployment.

As in the United States, European unskilled, older workers, resident minorities, and, in some countries, young people, tend to have differentially higher unemployment rates, but these higher rates have been of little social concern in western Europe when general unemployment rates have been 2 percent or less. At the very time that unskilled laborers may have had higher than average unemployment rates, shortages of unskilled labor have been officially proclaimed as job vacancies mount and foreign workers are sought. And youths have been in great demand even in countries like Holland which have a high birth rate. More public attention has been given to persistent regional and seasonal differences in unemployment rates under full employment.[7]

When there is a rise in unemployment, as occurred in 1966–68 in western Europe, the impact on the special groups has been somewhat more severe than on the adult male skilled worker. In the case of Swedish youths, including dropouts, who qualify only for unskilled work, the sudden lack of work opportunities brought this

[7] For some details on these points, see Beatrice G. Reubens, "The Hard-to-Employ: European Experience," in Eli Ginzberg and others, *Manpower Strategy for the Metropolis*, New York, 1968, pp. 192–94; Beatrice G. Reubens, "Lessons for the United States from Western European Experience with the Hard-to-Place," in *Proceedings of Industrial Relations Association*, December 1967, pp. 307–308.

group temporarily into the ranks of the hard-to-employ.[8] It is expected that the end of the recession and improved preparation of young persons for the world of work again will give youthful entrants to the labor force a favorable position.

Foreign workers are believed to be particularly prone to unemployment because they tend to be unskilled and may suffer from discrimination. Yet the recent West German experience shows that during a brief recession period the foreign workers came out ahead of Germans in the over-all decline of employment, 1966–67. Moreover, in 1966, when the decline began, Germans lost 196,000 jobs net and foreigners gained 125,000 jobs net. The existence of unexpired work contracts helped the foreign workers in 1966, while over the longer period dismissals followed an industrial pattern and affected both Germans and foreigners. In the recovery period, the demographic factors which are causing a decline in the indigenous German labor force dictate a renewed importation of foreign labor.[9] France did not show a decline in the number of foreign workers entering the country until a year and a half after the recession started.

We can begin to see some of the differences between Europe and the United States. Demographic factors have caused a slower growth of the native labor force in most of the northern European countries than in the United States. Moreover, the expansion of European employment has provided relatively more opportunities for unskilled males in agriculture, manufacturing, and construction than the United States has offered. In 1967 these sectors accounted for 58.6 percent of the West German labor force, 57.2 percent of the French, 51.2 percent of the Swedish, 50.3 percent of the British, but only 38.9 percent of the American labor force. The high productivity of American manufacturing labor is part of the explanation, but account should also be taken of a much lower American output of housing relative to population than in Sweden, for example, and the

[8] Sweden, National Labour Market Board, *AMS Berättelse Angående Verksamheten under 1966–30/6/1967*, Stockholm, 1968, p. 126; *idem, 1967–68*, pp. 121–22; on the United States, see Robert A. Gordon, *The Goal of Full Employment*, New York, 1967, esp. chs. 4, 5, 6, 7.

[9] *OECD Observer*, December 1968, p. 27.

resultant loss of many additional jobs in the U. S. construction industry. These lost jobs for males would have absorbed some unemployed who, for lack of work, became hard-to-employ. Although the relative growth of American employment since 1955 has exceeded that of any western European country, a substantial proportion of the new American jobs have been part-time positions in service occupations which women and students newly drawn into the labor force have filled.[10] Much of the increase in employment, therefore, did not directly reduce unemployment or absorb the hard-to-employ.

Many structural and institutional differences among countries influence the level of unemployment rates, apart from variations in the level of economic development, rates of growth, the industrial structure, dependence on exports, and over-all economic policy. Among the more important are the rapidity of technological and organizational change, the rate of substitutability of capital for labor, the extent of internal labor markets, the degree of labor intensity and specialization, the size of firms, the extent of self-employment, the persistence of family farms, the degree of urbanization, the availability of unskilled jobs and light or repetitive work, the degree of seasonality, the degree of regional disparity, the wage structure and impact of minimum wages, trade union regulations, apprenticeship and training for school-leavers, and employers' attitudes toward retaining their own older or handicapped employees, hiring marginal workers, and adapting jobs to their needs.

A final factor which affects the unemployment rate is the extent of the commitment to full employment. Some American students have stressed that the European maintenance of low unemployment rates is due to the greater political importance of full employment in western European countries and the superior European tolerance for price increases, especially if the result of restraints would be increased unemployment. From the vantage point of 1969, it seems

[10] Edward F. Denison, *Why Growth Rates Differ*, Washington, 1967, pp. 52–53; OECD, *Manpower Statistics 1954–1964*, Paris, 1965, p. 18; OECD, *Labour Force Statistics 1956–1966*, Paris, 1968, p. 20; *OECD Observer*, February 1969, p. 21.

that credit should also be given to the low starting level of European export prices in relation to those of competitors, especially American. Recent balance of payments difficulties have caused setbacks to full employment in several European countries.

Even Sweden, whose devotion to the maintenance of full employment is unsurpassed, has conceded that "price stability has acquired a higher priority in Europe" as American competitiveness has improved. With a slight change of emphasis, the 1968–69 Swedish budget statement declares that "the aim of economic policy is to secure economic competitiveness and growth and to achieve a more uniform distribution of income while maintaining full employment and individual security." [11] Instead of debating the old inflation vs. unemployment issue, Sweden has concentrated on economic and labor market policies to increase employment selectively and to improve the employability of the unemployed.

Criticizing the overly cautious policy of several western European countries during the recession of 1966–68, especially in comparison with earlier actions in 1962–63, Swedish officials declared that their own countermeasures had resulted in considerably lower unemployment than "in other countries that have experienced the same economic development as Sweden." [12] Thus, the general European commitment to full employment has its own internal variations when pressures appear. It remains true, however, that the highest European unemployment rates—those which have produced political protests—have been no higher than the lowest American rates.

[11] Sweden, Ministry of Finance, *The Swedish Economy, 1966–1970*, Stockholm, 1966, pp. 47–51; *idem, The Swedish Budget 1968/69*, Stockholm 1968, p. 16.

[12] Ministry of Finance, *The Swedish Budget 1968/69*, p. 15. See also, Rudolf Meidner, "The Role of an Active Manpower Policy in Contributing to a Solution of the Dilemma between Inflation and Unemployment," at the OECD International Conference on Employment Fluctuations and Manpower Policy, London, February 1969.

SURVEYS OF THE HARD-TO-EMPLOY

Information about the actual size and composition of the hard-to-employ in the northwestern European countries is limited. Only a few countries analyze their unemployment data in terms of the employability of the registrants. In any case, a significant portion of the hard-to-employ may not be registered as unemployed. Some are at work at any given moment; some are in institutions; some are on the fringes of organized labor markets, as is the case for some 300,000 nomads in West Germany; some are long-term unemployed who have ceased to register; some are new entrants to the labor market. These groups are most visible under high full employment, but complete information is rarely available even to the most diligent manpower agencies.

Sweden

One of the rare European attempts to obtain a figure beyond the customary unemployment statistics is Sweden's estimate of the latent or discouraged unemployed.[13] However, this concept is wider than that of the hard-to-employ; it also includes married women and youths who are acceptable to employers but who have themselves placed so many restrictions on the type, conditions, and place of work that they remain out of the labor market in the face of vacancies.

In November 1966, when Sweden had 60,000 unemployed job seekers and 40,000 other persons in training courses, on public works, and in sheltered employment, it was estimated from the

[13] Rudolf Meidner, "The Employment Problems of Individuals and Groups," pp. 2–3; Bertil Olsson, Director of the Swedish National Labor Market Board, estimated in June 1966 that somewhat more than 5 percent of the total Swedish labor force "may not get jobs in the absence of special measures to assist them." (Robert A. Gordon, ed., *Toward a Manpower Policy*, New York, 1967, p. 261.)

labor force survey that another 135,000 outside the labor force would be willing to work if specific kinds of employment were available. Although the Swedish estimate only suggests the size of the concealed segment of the hard-to-employ population, it may be a reasonable guess that the uncounted hidden hard-to-employ are at least as numerous as those who are known. In other countries, the ratio may be still higher.

Since unemployment statistics remain the chief source of information on the hard-to-employ, data from three countries, Belgium, the Netherlands, and Great Britain, will be cited to suggest the dimension and character of that part of the hard-to-employ population.

Belgium

The unemployment data of Belgium are significant for an investigation of the hard-to-employ.[14] For one thing, Belgium pays unemployment benefits virtually without time limit to those who are available for work. The Belgian unemployment statistics therefore show a higher proportion of both older and long-term unemployed than other countries; nowhere else in western Europe are unemployment data presented with separate categories for those who have been unemployed for five to ten years, ten to fifteen, and fifteen years or more! It is not clear whether the Belgian system counts as unemployed those who, in other countries, might be out of the labor market and perhaps receiving social benefits, or whether the Belgians have a much more accurate count of true unemployment than do countries which limit the duration of unemployment benefits. Other variable comparative factors are the age distribution of the labor force, employers' attitudes, and the availability of rehabilitation measures.

[14] Belgium, Ministère de l'Emploi et du Travail, Office National de l'Emploi, (ONEM), *Recensement Annuel des Chômeurs Complets,* 1962–1968; Margaret S. Gordon, *Retraining and Labor Market Adjustment in Western Europe,* Washington, 1965, pp. 81, 93, 96–97; "Improved Statistics on Unemployment: A First Step in Preventing Prolonged Joblessness and Poverty," *OECD Observer,* December 1968, pp. 8–10.

In recent years, Belgium has divided its unemployed into three categories: the fully employable, the partially employable, and those of very reduced employability; the two latter categories are officially called the hard-to-place. The partially employable are those with reduced productivity in their habitual occupation because of one or more factors: stipulated physical or mental disabilities, character difficulties, advanced age, or prolonged unemployment. This group is considered capable of rehabilitation and reintegration into normal employment.

The category "very reduced employability" includes those unemployed registrants who have a 30 to 65 percent physical or mental disability and who can only with the greatest difficulty be rehabilitated or reintegrated into the normal production cycle. Many would be expected to qualify only for sheltered employment. The two groups of hard-to-place are particularly conspicuous when unemployment is at a minimum. In June 1964, when the unemployment rate was extremely low, only 18.5 percent of the 51,387 unemployed in Belgium were judged to be fully employable. Two years later, when total unemployment was up to 61,059, the fully employable share rose to one-third of the total. By 1967 unemployment had increased to 90,000 (about 2 percent of the insured population) and the shift in relative proportions continued. As employable workers lost their jobs, the least employable withdrew from the labor market voluntarily or were removed from the register as not truly available or able to work.

Unemployed Belgian women tend to show higher proportions of fully employables and much lower proportions with very reduced employability than men. Disabled women generally tend to withdraw from the labor market more readily than men, and in Belgium unemployment benefits are curtailed in the case of married women whose ability to participate in the labor market is in doubt. Thus, in June 1964 fully employable women comprised 35.6 percent of all unemployed women, and in June 1966 they constituted 48.9 percent, much higher percentages than men showed.

Perhaps the most remarkable feature of Belgium's unemployment record is the exceptionally long duration of unemployment, even among the fully employables. In June 1966, when the national unemployment rate was low, unfilled vacancies were numerous, and foreign workers were sought, almost one-third of the 12,400 fully employable unemployed males and two-fifths of the 7,897 fully employable unemployed females had been out of work for six months or more. What is more startling, 6.2 percent of the men and 9.9 percent of the women had been unemployed for two years or more, and approximately 2 percent of the fully employable of both sexes had been without work for five to ten years. Furthermore, the males in this group were largely classified as skilled and the females as semi-skilled. It appears that attachment to declining industries and occupations, and residence in slow-growing regions, play a large role in the prolonged unemployment of these groups.

Among the partially employable, still greater proportions had long periods of unemployment. Almost 85 percent of the 18,887 men had been out of work for six months or more. Fully 56.5 percent had had no work for two years or more, and 7.4 percent had been unemployed for ten years or more. The record of the 6,356 partially employable women was not much better than that of the men.

Of course, the worst record was made by those with very reduced employability, a category which had been pruned of 25,000 cases in 1962. In 1966 more than 7 percent of the over 13,000 men had been without jobs for fifteen years or more and another 44.3 percent had been unemployed for five to fifteen years. Only one-tenth had been jobless for under six months. The duration distribution for the 1,889 women with very reduced employability was only slightly more favorable.

Belgium exhibits a marked relation between age, physical or mental disability, and unemployment. The proportion of older disabled Belgians among the unemployed has been consistently high. From 1961 through 1966, men of 50 or older constituted two-thirds to three-fourths of all unemployed men, and even higher proportions of the unemployed with reduced employability. In June 1963 only 9.7 percent of unemployed men aged 50 or over were judged to be fully employable, although 83.6 percent of the under-twenties were in this category. For women, the respective percentages were 27.5 and 55.7. Prolonged unemployment is particularly prevalent among older disabled workers. In 1966 the average length of unemployment among men over 55 who were not fully employable was five years and four months.

The Netherlands

Dutch unemployment statistics are somewhat similar to Belgian in that the hard-to-employ are singled out in the monthly count. Those considered fully employable with regard to the occupation for which they are registered must show sufficient aptitude, training, and experience in that occupation, a rate of speed and proficiency in their work which is normal for workers of their age in that occupation, and an absence of character, moral, or other deficiencies which might be serious obstacles to their placement in that occupation.

The hard-to-employ (*minder geschikten*) consist of those whose productivity is below normal even for quite simple occupations, those who are reluctantly accepted by employers, even in tight labor markets, because of character, moral, or other deficiencies, and those who are difficult to place in the occupation for which they have registered, but, on social grounds, cannot be asked to reduce their status to accept jobs for which they are suitable. Displaced small businessmen and farmers are cited as examples of the last category.

A third group which does not appear in the unemployment statistics are those who are registered for jobs in the competitive labor market but have been judged as "unplaceable" because of severe physical or mental disabilities. Since this classification is regarded as a serious change in the status of the affected worker, it is applied reluctantly after a decision is made by the director of the regional office of the Employment Service in consultation with medical and lay committees, and it is not communicated to the workers concerned.

Two additional subdivisions of the Dutch data throw further light on the hard-to-employ. Among the fully employable, a certain number of males are designated as "suitable for Supplementary Employment"; this is the Dutch form of labor intensive public works to counter regional, seasonal, or cyclical unemployment (see Chapter VIII). This type of job creation under full employment conditions largely benefits older and immobile unemployed men in regions of higher-than-average unemployment. It is, therefore, fair to add to the total of the hard-to-employ the unemployed men who have been declared suitable for Supplementary Employment. Furthermore, the statistics divide the hard-to-employ into the physically or mentally disabled (*minder validen*), on the one hand, and the socially handicapped, on the other; the latter includes such groups as parolees, youth offenders, ex-prisoners, alcoholics, refugees, and those with poor work attitudes. Table I.1 presents these data for November 1964, when a count was made of the unplaceables who ordinarily do not appear in the Dutch unemployment statistics.

TABLE I.1 Labor Reserve and Unemployment of the Hard-to-Employ, the Netherlands, November 1964

Population	12,127,000
Labor Force	4,350,000
Registered Labor Reserve *	*30,396*
Fully Employable	*19,749*
Suitable for Supplementary Employment	(3,064)
Reduced Employability	*10,647*
Disabled	(5,581)
Socially Handicapped	(5,066)
Registered, Declared Unplaceable	*18,630*
Vacancies	124,885

* All unemployed, including males at work on "additional employment projects" (supplementary public works).

Source: Ministry of Social Affairs and Public Health. Population and labor force are the average for 1964.

The Netherlands is one of the few countries whose continuous data permit the establishment of some trends with regard to the hard-to-employ. As total male unemployment rose from 1956 to

1958, the proportion with reduced employability fell from 26.0 percent to 19.6 percent of the total. A steady decline in the total number of male unemployed from 1958 to 1964 was accompanied by a rising proportion of those with reduced employability (from 19.6 to 44.4 percent); the slight declines in the ratios in 1963 and 1964 were attributable to changed methods of counting and increased invalidity pension rates which temporarily reduced unemployment registrations by the hard-to-employ. Female unemployment, which accounts usually for no more than one-tenth of the total, followed much the same movement and has shown just about the same proportions of those with reduced employability in most years.

As in Belgium, the number of recorded hard-to-employ unemployed tends to increase less rapidly than total unemployment in periods of rising unemployment. It appears that at such times employment declines even more than unemployment increases, as was documented in western Europe in 1966–68. This occurs because some displaced workers withdraw from the labor market and do not register as unemployed; the hard-to-employ surely are an important segment of those who withdraw. Over-all unemployment rates thus fail to reflect the true drop in employment. As employment increases, the hard-to-employ tend to be reabsorbed more slowly than the fully employable. Moreover, the number of jobless hard-to-employ is swelled by the renewed search for work by less able workers and the reclassification of some "unplaceables" to the category with reduced employability. As a result, the hard-to-employ unemployed form a rising part of all unemployed in periods of full or overfull employment.

The proportion of the fully employable in Holland has been somewhat higher in recent years than in Belgium, although the Dutch labor market has been tighter, and consequently might have been expected to have a greater share of residually unemployed. However, the two countries may not have identical criteria for the three categories of employability.

As in Belgium, the combination of disability and age is an important factor in Dutch long-term unemployment. Among the 98,851 unemployed males in February 1967, a time of high unemployment,

6 percent had been unemployed for a year or more, but among the subgroup, 15,103 unemployed males with reduced employability, 32 percent had had a year or more of idleness. In the unemployed group as a whole, 22.6 percent were 50 years or older, while 36.8 percent in the reduced employability group were in this age category. Finally, a year or more of unemployment affected only 14.6 percent of all unemployed males who were 50 years or older, but 43.8 percent of such men with reduced employability.[15]

A more intimate view of the Dutch hard-to-employ is provided by materials from the Organization for Economic Cooperation and Development (OECD) Counselling Project which began in March 1965.[16] The cases chosen for the experimental and control groups in Rotterdam and Eindhoven, two average industrial labor markets, had either been unemployed for a longer than average period or had changed employers five times or more in the past two years in industries where this was not normal procedure. So tight were the labor markets in these two cities that one of the OECD selection criteria —at least six months unemployment—was reduced at the outset to four months and later to only one month for unskilled workers, building trade operatives, metal workers, and hotel and restaurant staff. Some legitimate hard-to-employ cases were deliberately omitted either because they already had access to special services (the registered physically and mentally disabled) or because they were considered to have an obvious employment problem (persons over 60).

After studying the characteristics of the 215 selected individuals, the Dutch officials assessed the causes of the poor employment records. Eight categories were established: mentally defective or disturbed (including those under psychiatric care); physically disabled; socially maladjusted (including character defects or unrealistic career ambitions); advanced age; deficient education or training, lack of

[15] Data from the Netherlands Ministry of Social Affairs and Public Health; Gösta Rehn, "Manpower Policy and European Unemployment," *OECD Observer,* December 1967, pp. 15–18, 27–30.

[16] The Netherlands, Ministry of Social Affairs and Public Health, Directorate General of Manpower, *Report on the Findings of the Dutch Study as Part of the OECD Activity 16–17 "Social Adjustment,"* The Hague, August 1966, pp. 21–23, 40–41.

experience, or wrong choice of occupation; structurally or economically displaced; other factors, such as an absence of an economic incentive to work or difficulty in adjusting after repatriation from abroad; and, finally, combinations of chance circumstances.

Recognizing the interrelatedness of the eight causes, the interviewers assigned multiple causes to 58 of the total of 169 persons who were diagnosed. The most frequently selected cause of a poor work record was social or emotional maladjustment, and it was particularly prominent among the frequent job-changers. Physical disabilities were next in importance; together the two factors accounted for 58 percent of the 230 diagnostic selections for the 169 persons. Mental disabilities and advanced age each accounted for 9 percent. In spite of the exclusion of the registered disabled from the investigation, it was found that 79 persons had a physical or mental condition which limited their placement possibilities, although in 10 of these cases other factors were considered even more important.

If the two groups excluded from the sample, the disabled and those over 60, had been included, the factors of disability and age probably would have dominated. Thus, we find that the ordinary Dutch unemployment data which are broken down by age and disability are quite meaningful.

Deficient education or training accounted for only 7 percent of the reasons for poor work records and was applied in combination with other causes only eight times. The structurally or economically displaced accounted for just 3 percent of the total, and the miscellaneous factors for only 1 percent. Under Dutch conditions of overfull employment, personal factors far outweighed the labor market causes of poor work records, and many of the residually unemployed were handicapped by multiple problems.

Great Britain

The British Ministry of Labour (now the Department of Employment and Productivity) twice undertook special surveys of the unemployed—in August 1961 and October 1964. From these surveys one may learn much about the hard-to-employ who register as unemployed. The 1964 survey was superior to that of 1961 because of the inclusion of unemployed registrants who were not claimants for unemployment benefit; some of the long-term unemployed who had exhausted benefits thus were caught. In addition, those disabled unemployed deemed capable of working only under sheltered conditions, and who are usually omitted from the count of the unemployed, were canvassed in the October 1964 survey. The survey also collected separate data for each region. The two categories which were excluded from the survey—unemployed youths under 18 and those on lay-off—are not important sources of the hard-to-employ. Thus, using a sample, the Ministry of Labour presented a detailed picture of residual unemployment in Britain in October 1964 when the general unemployment rate was 1.5 per cent.[17]

One of the basic classifications of the 312,930 registered unemployed workers in October 1964 was according to their prospects for obtaining employment. Over three-fourths were considered likely to have difficulty in securing jobs; thus the hard-to-employ were the overwhelming majority at this time of full employment (Table I.2). The 240,420 British residual unemployed were then classified in terms of the *primary* reason for their poor work prospects. Only one cause was assigned, although it was recognized that many people suffered from multiple handicaps.

Age was the single most important cause of difficulty in obtaining work. It was largely a matter of having lost a job after reaching 55 or 60. According to the Ministry of Labour, a certain number of the registered older unemployed men who are retired on company pensions are not actually seeking work and should not be considered either a social problem or a part of the labor reserve. However, in certain white-collar occupations and in the regions of higher-than-average unemployment, age became a handicap much earlier—around 40. A tiny proportion of unemployed young people, ages 18 to 24, were also classified as handicapped chiefly by age—in this case, insufficient years.

The second most important factor was physical or mental disability. This high rank accords with findings for other countries of western Europe. Other studies in depth have shown that secondary

[17] Unpublished tables made available by the Ministry of Labour.

TABLE I.2. Residual Unemployment, Great Britain, October 1964

		Males as a Percentage of Total in Each Category
Unemployment rate	1.5%	
Total number unemployed	312,930	75.6
Should get work without difficulty	72,510	73.0
Will find difficulty in getting work	240,420	76.3
	Percent Distribution	
Total (240,420)	100.0	
Age	26.3	86.7
Physical or mental condition	25.0	79.9
Lack of local job opportunities	22.4	68.8
Attitude to work	12.2	83.2
Restriction on availability	3.9	12.8
Present qualifications, experience, or skill not acceptable	2.1	64.2
Prison record	1.6	98.9
Lack of financial incentive	1.5	97.8
Color	1.4	66.4
Lack of English	0.4	86.5
Non-members of trade union	0.1	100.0
Other reasons	3.0	55.8

Source: *Ministry of Labour Gazette*, April 1966, p. 157.

handicaps, such as adverse psychological and social reactions to physical illness or hospitalization, may be more important bars to reemployment than the disability itself. The very high incidence of psychological factors among the physically disabled shows how intertwined are handicaps involving ability to work and poor work attitudes.[18]

A lack of local job opportunities was next in importance and it

[18] J. K. Wing, "Social and Psychological Aspects of Rehabilitation of the Disabled in the United Kingdom," *Rehabilitation*, April–June 1965, pp. 13–14, 20–21.

affected some unemployed even in the most prosperous regions. But this factor was relatively most significant in those regions where unemployment rates were above the national average. The bulk of the group lacking local opportunities had been unemployed for less than six months, and women, especially married women, were disproportionately represented, as they also were among those unemployed because of restrictions on availability and miscellaneous reasons. Among the younger unemployed, particularly in the northern regions characterized by higher unemployment, a lack of local opportunities was a prominent cause. It also was a special problem for the white-collar unemployed, but it was relatively insignificant for the unskilled and the colored unemployed.

Those unemployed who lacked local job opportunities showed less willingness to move than many of the other unemployed, and the propensity to move was lower in the sluggish north than in the prosperous south. The scope in Britain for the redistribution of workers and jobs and for a reduction in the number of residual unemployed is still great, according to the results of this survey. Insufficient and costly housing in areas where jobs exist is a major obstacle to successful mobility. Adrian Sinfield's forthcoming study of unemployment in Shields, a depressed town in the northeast, reveals that many of the unemployed had moved to another place earlier in their lives, but had returned home largely as a result of housing problems, while others had been discouraged from moving by tales of housing troubles and costs.

Poor work attitudes were considered to be the chief cause of difficulty in obtaining work for 12.2 percent of the residual unemployed. Native-born, male, unskilled laborers in the prime working ages from the northern regions and the Midlands were disproportionately represented in the group with poor work attitudes. About 60 percent had been unemployed for six months or more and almost 90 percent had had no formal training; a high proportion admitted their disinclination to move. Since the interviewers in areas of higher unemployment, where willingness to work is most difficult to test, are apt to apply more stringent standards to their unemployed than do interviewers in tighter labor markets, some of the reported regional variation with regard to poor work attitudes may be due to preconceptions of the interviewers.

It has also been observed that the unemployed present a different face to overworked officials than they do to outside experts who seek to analyze or aid them. The latter have found relatively few who are truly work-shy among those whose work attitudes were suspect. A psychiatric social worker who consulted experimentally with difficult cases referred by the National Assistance Board found that less than 1 percent of the hard-core unemployed were "on the whole more satisfied with life" when not working. Adrian Sinfield, in his intensive interviews with a sample of unemployed men in Shields, concluded that none were work-shy, although the Employment Service officers believed many to be, to the intense resentment of the men involved.[19]

The October 1964 survey and other studies suggest that there are real differences in the quality of the residual unemployed in the different regions. Objective measures, such as duration of unemployment, amount and type of prior training, occupational status, educational attainment, previous earnings, and disability and illness records, support the view that the hard-to-employ problem is more intense as well as more prevalent in the northern regions.

The 1964 survey also indicated that illiteracy, racial prejudice, and prison records were not important bars to unskilled employment. Racial discrimination was not frequently selected by the investigators as the main cause of unemployment, and it tended to affect colored women workers relatively more often than men. Discrimination in Britain does not take the form so much of high unemployment rates as of limited access to skilled industrial jobs and prestigious or well-paid service occupations, according to the PEP *Report on Racial Discrimination* issued in 1967 and the Institute of Race Relations' mammoth study, *Colour and Citizenship,* published in 1969.

A more intensive survey of hard-to-employ cases was conducted

[19] Eugene Heimler, *Mental Illness and Social Work,* Penguin Books: Harmondsworth, 1967, pp. 111–16; Adrian Sinfield, Unemployment in Shields, unpublished ms.

in Manchester in connection with the OECD Counselling Project. The experimental group was restricted to 200 registered unemployed men aged 21 to 54 who were not Registered Disabled Persons. Three-fourths were long-term unemployed who had been out of work for at least six months. Half of the 154 long-term unemployed had been out of work for over a year and 23 had been jobless for over three years. The 46 job-changers had held five or more jobs in the previous two years (construction and casual workers were excluded from the survey). Three-fourths of the 200 were unskilled workers and 115 were single or lived alone, many in common lodging houses. Their level of education was lower than average.

Manchester was a tight labor market in 1965, and the interviewers concluded that almost 60 percent of the 200 could have filled available jobs if they had not had social or personal problems. Some of the unemployed believed that they could not find or hold a job, while others with such defects as a speech impediment, a slight physique, or an unfortunate appearance were apt to be the last to be hired and the first to be fired. The lack of suitable local jobs affected only 7 percent of the total, as we might expect in a tight labor market; another 28 percent were impeded by a combination of personal or social obstacles and a lack of local jobs. The remaining 5.5 percent were considered virtually unemployable.

The long-term unemployed were classified according to eleven different factors which impaired their ability to work; 120 of the 154 men had more than one handicap, and 20 had four or more. Listed in order of frequency, the factors were: poor work motivation; prison record; color; family trouble or pressure; diagnosed mental abnormality; suspected undiagnosed mental abnormality; uncooperative attitude; common lodging-house dweller; broken marriage; foreign birth; and illiteracy. The fact of being single or living alone, as in the lodging house, emerged as an important condition in many cases of poor work attitudes and mental abnormality. Neither a prison record nor illiteracy was considered a real obstacle to obtaining unskilled employment.

There were 39 colored persons in the survey, an unusually high proportion in light of their share of the labor force and the unemployed as a whole in Manchester. Half of them thought there was prejudice against their color or nationality, but the interviewers observed that "an immigrant who is accepted in his own country as a craftsman cannot always meet the different standards or systems used in this country, and many have to take unskilled work which is not always wholly acceptable." [20] It was noted that the incidence of social and personal handicaps was slightly less among the colored unemployed than among the group as a whole.

In summarizing their impressions of the long-term unemployed, which in this survey excluded the numerically significant categories of older workers (55 and over) and the registered physically or mentally disabled, the interviewers declared:

. . . the overall picture is one of general inadequacy of personality and inability to face the realities of everyday life, aggravated by specific social and personal situations. It is apparent that a common reaction to a personal, social or family problem has been to throw up employment. Very often the behavior pattern is to continue to be unemployed until these personal problems have ceased or diminished by reason of time. But whereas the majority of men recover and return to a normal pattern of employment, these men do not.[21]

TYPES OF HARD-TO-EMPLOY

A summary of the outstanding traits of the hard-to-employ, as revealed by various national unemployment studies, shows considerable uniformity from country to country. Under full employment, the residual unemployed who are difficult to place, in comparison with the labor force as a whole, tend to be disproportionately male, older, physically or mentally disabled, unskilled, untrained, nontrade union members, single or living alone, residents of distressed

[20] Great Britain, Ministry of Labour, *OECD International Counselling Project*, Report on First Experimental Stage, 1st February to 30th April 1965, London, 1965, p. 12.

[21] *Ibid.*, p. 13; Heimler, *Mental Illness and Social Work*, pp. 113–14.

or development areas, and subject to frequent spells of joblessness or long-term unemployed. The employment potential of many is affected by personality difficulties, family troubles, alcoholism, conflicts with the law, unrealistic views of the pay and position to which they are entitled, poor work attitudes, and undetected disabilities. The most difficult cases have several reinforcing handicaps.

We have discussed the extent and character of the hard-to-employ problem in a few European countries. But the full nature of the multiple and interacting work handicaps of the hard-to-employ is best conveyed by individual examples.[22] The cases cited below show the wide range of employability which characterizes the hard-to-employ—from those who, with a little assistance, can be placed in competitive enterprise to those who can function only in a sheltered environment.

Those whose ability to work is below standard. A 42-year-old Swede had worked irregularly at heavy construction jobs. Born with a speech and hearing defect, he had attended a school for mentally retarded children, but had not learned to read or write. He appeared to be bad-tempered and lacking in self-control on the job and at work interviews, and had left jobs frequently.

A British coal miner who had developed chronic bronchitis and emphysema found the dampness and working conditions in mining intolerable and frequently received sickness benefits.

Those who may be rejected by employers, but may have normal productive capacity. A West Indian of 28, unemployed for 11 months in Great Britain, was indifferent to unskilled work because his unemployment benefits were close to unskilled wages. He wanted to be a skilled worker, but had dropped out of an evening training course because employers were reluctant to hire colored men.

[22] Gertrude Williams, *Counselling for Special Groups*, OECD: Paris, 1967; individual country reports for the foregoing; Great Britain, Ministry of Labour, *Steering Group on the Employment Services Experiment in Interviewing in Depth of Long-Term Unemployed*, November 1965; *idem*, Northern Regional Office, *Report on Interesting Cases of Resettlement of Disabled Persons*, March 1966, p. 3; The Netherlands Ministry of Social Affairs and Public Health, *Handicapped Persons Employed in Industry*, The Hague, 1956, p. 26.

A Dutchman of considerable education and ability was rejected for a number of jobs because he was a known homosexual.

A Dutchman of 42 with 11 children was barred by the company doctors from working as a port inspector because of a back disability which was not, in fact, serious.

A Polish national with a good commercial education in Poland and a fairly good command of English could not obtain any work except manual jobs because he lacked the credentials and standard of commercial education in England.

A 44-year-old British woman resident in a postpsychotic hostel registered for work after several years in a mental hospital interspersed with periods of work.

Those who have difficulty in holding jobs. A 34-year-old German constantly changed jobs or left work because of court orders attaching his wages or prison sentences. He drank, had debts, and had been divorced *pro forma* from his wife, who with their four children was on relief; he maintained a shabby room, but actually lived with his family.

A British unskilled worker of 35, with a prison record, had been out of work for a year and a half. He held jobs only for a few weeks to a few months and usually was discharged for poor performance, lateness, or absenteeism.

Those who do not want to work. A retired member of the regular British Army was content to draw his unemployment benefits because with his Army pension his total income was satisfactory.

A British truck driver of 42 who had served one employer for 18 years lost all interest in work when his wife entered a mental hospital.

A well-dressed man did not wish to reveal his finances and rejected all work suggestions. He was assumed to be earning money from unreported work and/or illegal activities.

A man whose wife had deserted him stayed at home to care for his children, living on relief.

Those who are hard to reemploy. A 57-year-old British foreman, forced out by technological change, resisted jobs at lower pay and status.

A 59-year-old London self-employed pictureframe maker was forced to give up his dying business and seek paid employment for the first time.

A British capstan operator of 48 was discharged as redundant after 29 years with a single employer. He worked only two weeks in the next 18 months and lost confidence in his ability to maintain the required speed on production work.

Those who can work only under sheltered conditions. A Dutchman who contracted asthma at an advanced age also was mentally disturbed.

A Swedish housepainter of 59 who was forced to leave his occupation because of a progressive muscular disease, allergic eczema and asthma, resisted references to vocational rehabilitation and sheltered employment, but finally agreed.

Those who need other services before employment can be sought. A 20-year-old German youth, unemployed for three months after frequent job-changing, was considered mentally ill and "unable to cope with the normal exigencies of life in a working community."

A Dutch unskilled laborer of 56 had been in prison 32 times and in an institution for the treatment of alcoholism and depression. At his job interview he appeared highly disturbed and threatened to murder his wife and daughter and commit suicide.

SOCIAL CONCERN ABOUT THE HARD-TO-EMPLOY

If we accept that a considerable variety of hard-to-employ types exists in northwestern Europe, why should there be any particular social concern when the numbers involved are relatively small under full employment? A welfare or humanitarian interest in certain kinds of hard-to-employ has long been shown in western Europe. Those who lost a part or all of their work capacity through war or related circumstances or industrial accidents were long recognized to have a claim on society which at times was met by the provision of employment under preferential terms. Even when rehabilitation measures were added, the efforts were essentially a personal service for a limited group and had no broader social meaning.

New motives for attention to the hard-to-employ appeared after

World War II.[23] The commitment to full employment gave several countries of northwestern Europe an enlarged notion of the right to work and the value of work to the individual. This has been expressed in declarations and recommendations by the International Labour Office, the United Nations, the Western European Union, and other international organizations, as well as the constitutions and policy statements of individual countries. Moreover, the commitment is taken seriously by voters and politicians alike.

Over the years, the standards governing ability and willingness to work have been broadened in some countries. As a Swedish official said:

The achievement of full or very close to full employment for those who are traditionally considered to constitute the labor force, has opened the door to the labour market also for those who were earlier excluded from the practical possibilities of obtaining gainful employment. . . . Over the years our aims in regard to employment have become more ambitious. The concept of full employment now implies a job for everyone able and willing to work, including those who are handicapped in one way or another.[24]

Another Swedish statement declares that the objective of a high employment policy ". . . cannot accept in principle any form of residual unemployment whether in industries or regions affected by structural rationalization, or age groups with limited work capacities or sex groups with the desire to work only part-time. . . ." It therefore becomes necessary to decide "what social efforts to assist groups of elderly, partially disabled, and female labour, are required before a certain rate of growth is felt to be acceptable from a welfare economics standpoint." [25]

[23] *European Seminar on Sheltered Employment*, The Hague, 1959, pp. 9, 12–13, 17, 36.

[24] Ernst Michanek, Secretary of State, Ministry of Social Affairs, Labor and Housing, in OECD, *Age and Employment*, Paris, 1962, p. 12, and *Lesson from Foreign Labor Market Policies*, Committee on Labor and Public Welfare, United States Senate, Subcommittee on Employment and Manpower, 88th Cong., 2nd session, vol. 4, Selected Readings in Employment and Manpower, Washington, 1964, p. 1440.

[25] Meidner, "The Employment Problems of Individuals and Groups," pp. 1, 2.

Dr. Rolf Weber, an official of the West German employers' associations, addressed an OECD international conference in February 1969 and reviewed the ease with which marginal workers find work in an overheated economy. He then outlined the social, economic, and political reasons for continuing their employment under looser labor market conditions:

The loss of employment carries with it not only the loss of a considerable portion of income, thereby reducing the consumption potential of the group, but also an unfavourable effect on the social prestige of those concerned. Long periods of unemployment usually lead to a descent in the social scale, which is a kind of social disease that may wreck a man just as surely as any medical sickness. From the economic point of view, a proportion of the gross national product—often no small proportion—has to be devoted to subsidising unemployed persons so as to afford them at least an acceptable existence. This is an unproductive use of funds which instead might be used to create new jobs.

The political importance of adopting suitable measures consists in the fact that the groups . . . represent a relatively high proportion of the active population. . . . Modern social policy is guided by two principles: the first that prevention is better than cure, and the second that the socially less favored should not *a priori* be helped along charitable lines but rather that they must be made strong again so as to be able to help themselves in future. These two principles must be applied more particularly for the special groups under consideration, in order to help open for them access to the labour market.

The desire to fit the hard-to-employ into productive jobs because they have a right and a need to work has been reinforced in some countries by the philosophy of an "active manpower policy," as formulated by the OECD. Designed to reconcile and integrate the sometimes conflicting objectives of full employment, price stability, and rapid economic growth, active manpower policy stresses a variety of selective manpower measures "to supplement more permanent and general action" in order to "create economic equilibrium while retaining full employment." One of the objectives of an active manpower policy is the augmentation of the labor supply through the deliberate recruitment of those who are able to work but are either outside of the labor force or are unemployed. By filling job vacancies, it is possible to reduce the upward pressures on wages, limit labor pirating, and increase national output.[26] Thus, in its 1964 recommendation on manpower policy as a means for the promotion of economic growth, the OECD Council declared:

Many groups now intermittently or permanently outside the labour force can be helped to participate in useful employment through such aids as rehabilitation, retraining, special job arrangements and efforts to reduce prejudice against their employment. Such measures can be particularly efficient when shortages of labour exist or are impending.

Among the groups singled out in this labor reserve are married women, retired pensioners, foreign workers, and the hard-to-employ, as defined in this study. The Swedish position is that "measures to facilitate the full employment of marginal labour categories form a prerequisite for the realization of present long-term programmes for economic growth." [27] While most countries expect married women and foreign workers to yield greater increments to the labor supply than the hard-to-employ, the latter are particularly sought in a country such as Sweden, which already has a high participation rate among married women and a disinclination to admit

[26] Bertil Olsson, "Employment Policy in Sweden," *International Labour Review,* May 1963, pp. 409–34. See also, Gösta Rehn and Erik Lundberg, "Employment and Welfare: Some Swedish Issues," *Industrial Relations,* February 1963, pp. 1–14; E. Wight Bakke, "An Integrated Positive Manpower Policy," in Arthur M. Ross, ed., *Employment Policy and the Labor Market,* Berkeley, 1965, pp. 358–78; A. D. Smith, "Active Manpower and Redundancy Policies: Their Costs and Benefits," *International Labour Review,* January–February 1967, pp. 49–60; Solomon Barkin, "Dimensions of an Active Manpower Policy," in OECD, Manpower and Social Affairs Directorate, *Scandinavian Regional Seminar on Active Manpower Policy,* Paris, 1967, pp. 5–8; Charles P. Kindleberger, *Europe's Postwar Growth,* Cambridge, 1967, p. 170; Assar Lindbeck, "Theories and Problems in Swedish Economic Policy in the Post-war Period," in Harry G. Johnson, ed., *Surveys of National Economic Policy Issues and Policy Research, American Economic Review,* June 1968, part 2, pp. 15–32, 70–74; International Labour Office, *Manpower Adjustment Programmes: II. Sweden, U.S.S.R., United States,* Labour and Automation, Bull. No. 6, Geneva, 1967, pp. 9–20.

[27] OECD, *Labour Market Policy in Sweden,* Paris, 1963, p. 23.

many foreign workers except from the other Nordic countries. The Netherlands also has a particular reason for looking to the hard-to-employ because relatively few of their married women work.

In many European countries, the older personal welfare approach toward the hard-to-employ has barely been affected by the newer active manpower policy. Even in Sweden, an official committee on labor market policy declared: ". . . the Committee wishes it to be clearly understood that the economic objectives of the labour market policy should be subordinated to social and human considerations." [28]

However, most of the northwestern European countries increasingly regard programs for the hard-to-employ as the concern of manpower agencies. They would be surprised to find the American Rehabilitation Services Administration located in the Department of Health, Education, and Welfare rather than in the Department of Labor, and more puzzled to learn that its officials "object to classification of theirs as a manpower program, arguing that, as a program of integrated services, it might as well be classified as a health or education program or as an antipoverty program since many of its clients are poor." [29] Comparable European programs which are also devoted to improving the employability of vocationally handicapped persons are operated by the central manpower agency. Usually, the work of vocational rehabilitation commences after medical restoration has been terminated by other agencies; the American practice of regarding the removal of a hernia as vocational rehabilitation is not accepted in Europe. Even the admirable Danish rehabilitation program, which offers every type of service and covers the entire population without regard to employment status or age, recognizes that a portion of its clientele and services are related to manpower programs.

[28] National Labour Market Board, *Modern Swedish Labour Market Policy,* Stockholm, 1966, p. 15.

[29] Garth L. Mangum and Lowell M. Glenn, *Vocational Rehabilitation and Federal Manpower Policy,* Policy Papers in Human Resources and Industrial Relations No. 4, Institute of Labor and Industrial Relations of the University of Michigan and Wayne State University, Washington, 1967, pp. 1–2.

The final motive for assisting the hard-to-employ to find work derives from the unwillingness of those who hold jobs and pay taxes to see others idle and living on public funds; those who are too ill or old to work are not targets. Complaints are directed particularly against the hard-to-employ with poor work attitudes, but the strictures are not limited to them, and they reflect religious and moral principles as well as the taxpayers' concern. However, women with young children who do not work are not resented even if they live on public assistance. This is not a large group in European countries and none of the special American conditions exist.

The responses of the western European countries to these varied views, as expressed in legislation and operating programs for the hard-to-employ, are the major concern of the chapters which follow. Wherever possible, actual experience under the legislation will be explored and the effectiveness of the programs in meeting the recognized and latent needs of the individual country will be assessed. The emphasis is heavily on public policies and programs, either initiated by indivdual governments or sponsored by the international organizations of the Common Market. In most of these countries, private enterprise and not-for-profit organizations play a minor independent role in programs for the hard-to-employ, but they are important participants in the execution of government-initiated programs. It is convenient but misleading to refer to northwestern Europe as though the individual countries had identical experience and programs for the hard-to-employ. It attributes a spurious uniformity to a varied situation. Some countries are well ahead of others and they all have much to learn from one another. The experience of the leaders will concern us most.

1534812

The programs considered here are directly concerned with manpower. General economic policies or fiscal and monetary measures which affect the over-all demand for labor and the level of employment are not examined. By the same token, only passing reference will be made to the factors which influence the size, composition, and suitability of the total labor force. While all of these matters are related to the hard-to-employ, they are separate subjects in themselves.

What methods are used to reach, screen, test, rehabilitate, train, and place the hard-to-employ? Are hard-to-employ trainees placed in the same classes as others? If the jobs that are developed for the hard-to-employ are unsatisfactory because of low pay and low prestige, is the investment in training made nevertheless? Are training places geared to local vacancies? How much expense and attention is devoted to training and placing those hard-to-employ who are well below current standards for workers? How are training allowances related to various kinds of welfare payments on the one hand, and to probable wage levels on the other? Are social benefits withdrawn from those who refuse training or jobs? Is institutional training superior to training in the firm? Is the wage structure a factor in the employment of the hard-to-employ?

Among the questions we will consider is the ability of existing enterprise structures to employ the hard-to-employ. How many can be absorbed by private enterprise and the ordinary job markets? Can government agencies at various levels make room for any number of the hard-to-employ? Is self-employment an outlet for more than a handful? What quality of employment is provided for the hard-to-employ?

Various approaches to employers will be weighed. How does legal compulsion on employers to hire the hard-to-employ operate? How much can be accomplished through education and appeals to the social conscience of employers? Have employers hired many hard-to-employ because subsidies are offered?

What is the role of special job creation, outside of the usual channels, for those who cannot be fitted into ordinary employment, either because of their personal characteristics or their residence? A host of issues arises with regard to the amount and type of employment to be created, the financing, the setting of wage payments, marketing of products, facilitation of transfers to regular employment, the selection of candidates, and the dividing line between work and diversionary activity.

In all programs, the division of responsibility between private, public, and voluntary authorities must be defined. Who bears the costs, runs the administration, sets the standards, and establishes program policy? To what extent are the hard-to-employ treated by a single agency in each community, thus obtaining the advantages of consolidated and uniform administration? How do the various levels of government perform in this area? Can one assess all of the private and social costs and benefits—economic, human, and political —attached to such programs?

A major interest is anticipatory and preventive action which might limit the numbers of people who become hard-to-employ. What means are devised to maintain job security for individual workers? Are such attempts made regardless of the contribution to production? What combinations of income maintenance and direction to new jobs are devised for those who might be hard-to-reemploy once they are forced out of familiar fields? What measures aid mobility of the potentially hard-to-employ? How much is done to bring jobs to the workers who are unable or unwilling to move? What is done for older displaced workers who are not ready for the pension but are unlikely to find work again?

Finally, an assessment of the European programs for the hard-to-employ will be made in terms of the aims of an active manpower policy: to achieve a full utilization of marginal human resources and to give an opportunity to individuals to work and participate fully in the society.

Broadly speaking, the European programs analyzed in the following chapters consist of: attempts to rehabilitate and place the hard-to-employ in the competitive labor market; programs to compel or subsidize employers to hire the hard-to-employ; efforts to create special jobs for the hard-to-employ outside of the usual channels; and measures to assist those in jobs who would be hard-to-reemploy if they were displaced.

II | Identifying and Counseling the Hard-to-Employ

Most northwestern European countries foster active placement of the hard-to-employ in the competitive labor market. But there is no unanimity about the groups which should be treated as hard-to-employ, the special services and programs to be offered them, the type of jobs to be sought, the incentives and pressures to be brought on employers, the need for follow-up and supportive services, the provision for those who cannot be placed in competitive employment, the measures to be taken on behalf of the hard-to-employ when general unemployment increases, the administrative structures and controls required to carry out and coordinate the programs, and the degree of integration to be sought with other manpower measures.

In the course of this and the two following chapters, we will examine the successive stages by which the hard-to-employ may be made acceptable in competitive labor markets. The present chapter is concerned with the initial discovery of the hard-to-employ through outreach, intake and screening procedures, and the provision of guidance and counseling services. Next is a discussion of special services to enhance the employability of the hard-to-employ (Chapter III). This is followed by an account of vocational retraining courses for the hard-to-employ and the effort to promote placement in the competitive labor market (Chapter IV). We begin with some general considerations which overlap the chapter divisions.

The European countries with the most advanced programs for the hard-to-employ have done surprisingly little research on the impact and long-range outcome of their efforts. However, they do conduct research on the improvement of rehabilitation or training procedures, and from time to time major reviews of programs are conducted by special commissions which develop original research materials on past experience.

When questions are asked about the effectiveness of individual programs in relation to their costs, the paucity of governmental and academic research becomes apparent. The responsible officials in the northern European nations would be offended if they were asked to conduct a general benefit/cost study of vocational rehabilitation or retraining. They consider that the economic and social validity of such programs is too well established to be subjected to statistical procedures which are difficult to comprehend and deficient in the measurement of the nonmaterial factors. Implicitly, they have already placed such high values on human well-being, maintaining full employment, guaranteeing the right to work, and adding to the national output through the utilization of idle resources, that the benefits of rehabilitation or training, in general, must outweigh the costs.

The same considerations would lead to a rejection of a benefit/cost analysis to determine which individuals should be served first and whether an individual should be given additional rehabilitation services or training for a higher skill. On the basis of such an analysis, those chosen first would show the greatest surplus of benefits over costs, and additional services would be given only when the incremental benefits exceed the incremental costs. But this view is not accepted because it is believed that each individual should be brought to his own highest level of performance, even if others are kept waiting because facilities are scarce. The solution is to increase facilities so that everyone may be served.

Since the expansion of the budget for one program is usually at the expense of a competing program, the need for research on the effectiveness of various programs in meeting their stated objectives and cost comparisons of alternative approaches or programs is coming to be recognized. But thus far such research in western European countries offers little guidance to domestic policymakers or visiting scholars. Sweden has recently instituted the setting of priorities for budget requests by the Labour Market Board and cost-effectiveness procedures are to begin with fiscal year 1970–71.

The progress of actual programs has been noteworthy, however. Under postwar full employment conditions, a somewhat paradoxical situation has existed in several European nations. Awareness and understanding of the nature and extent of the problems of the hard-to-employ have increased, but the tightness of labor markets has made it possible for many of the marginally employable to find work on their own or with a minimum of assistance. The Employment Service understandably seeks to fill its vacancies, and job-seekers usually prefer immediate jobs to preparatory measures and training courses.

As a result, under full employment some countries have shown increased concern for the hard-to-employ without greatly widening or improving their services for them. There are exceptions to this generalization. Moreover, during the recent period of increased general unemployment in 1966–68 many northern European countries turned their attention to measures for the displaced workers, making special provision for the hard-to-employ. The intensified problems of marginal groups lead Swedish policymakers to declare: "In a situation of declining demand for labour, greater efforts to improve the competitiveness of the handicapped may be motivated . . . intensive and highly differentiated labour market policy measures are required." [1]

The most effective programs for the hard-to-employ are likely to be found in countries which accept the permanent existence of such a group. While these countries recognize that a wide variety of conditions contribute to the hard-to-employ situation, they feel that a common designation and treatment may be appropriate. The Netherlands, Sweden, and Belgium, for example, take this unified and comprehensive approach to the hard-to-employ; however, Belgium's acceptance of a general concept of the hard-to-employ in 1961 did

[1] Sweden, National Labour Market Board, *Modern Swedish Labour Market Policy,* Stockholm, 1966, p. 89; National Labour Market Board, *Swedish Employment Policy 1967–68* (Reprinted from Annual Report 1967–68), Stockholm, 1968, p. 1; National Labour Market Board, *Arbetsmarknadspolitiken 1969/70,* Stockholm, 1968, p. 39; Ministry of Finance, *The Swedish Budget 1968/69,* Stockholm, 1968, pp. 33–34.

not lead to the prompt establishment of the necessary range of programs. On the other hand, if a country is slow to develop a general view of the hard-to-employ, as Britain has been, then the excellent measures devised for one segment of the hard-to-employ, in this case the physically and mentally disabled, may only occasionally be used for the benefit of others with equal need. Additional public and private programs are then necessary and problems of duplication, coordination, and adequacy arise.

West Germany, which also gives a privileged position in legislation and practice to its disabled, claims to care well for all of its hard-to-employ through individual counseling, the advice of specialized consultants, and a set of programs for all difficult cases. Even among the Scandinavian countries, there are considerable differences of view and practice concerning marginal workers. A group of experts from these nations agreed that their countries "do not always means the same thing by 'partially able' and there can be wide divergences in the interpretation of 'generosity' and 'modernity' . . ." [2] Few countries are in the happy position of Norway or Denmark, which consider that the physically and mentally disabled are virtually the only kind of hard-to-employ in the nation.

A key role for the Employment Service in executing programs for the hard-to-employ is fairly standard among the western European countries. Where they differ from one another is in the functions assigned to the Employment Service, quality of service, penetration of the labor market, budgetary support, public image, number and type of personnel used to aid the hard-to-employ, the Service's relationships with other agencies in providing for the hard-to-employ, and the place of programs for the hard-to-employ in overall manpower policy. In some countries, the activities of the Employment Service on behalf of the hard-to-employ are supplemented by the work of other government agencies and voluntary organizations.

Private enterprise in western Europe relies on government leader-

[2] Organization for Economic Cooperation and Development (OECD), Scandinavian Regional Seminar on Active Manpower Policy, November 1965, *Final Report,* Paris, 1967, p. 25. Interviews in Denmark, West Germany, Belgium, Great Britain, Sweden, Norway, and the Netherlands.

ship in this area and offers cooperation in government-initiated programs so long as the candidates proposed by the governmental and voluntary agencies have been adequately prepared and subsidized. There is little inclination in western Europe to follow the United States in its recent turning to private enterprise and especially large corporations to render social services and make social investments in the hard-to-employ without government supervision.[3]

SWEDISH APPROACHES

In many ways Sweden possesses the most advanced programs for the hard-to-employ, which are related to a highly developed general manpower policy integrated with economic policy as a whole. The planning and execution of manpower policy is left to the National Labour Market Board. (*Kungl Arbetsmarknadsstyrelsen:* AMS) a semi-independent central government board, which is a form used frequently in Swedish administration. The Labour Market Board is under the general supervision of the Ministry of the Interior, but it is unusually independent financially and has broad policy responsibilities; in 1968–69 the Labour Market Board had a budget of over 1,500,000,000 Sw. kr., about 4 percent of total government expenditure.

The executive governing board of the National Labour Market Board is composed of eleven representatives of employer and labor organizations and the public and an appointed director general and his deputy. Much of the success of Swedish manpower policy has been attributed to the form of organization of the Labour Market Board, its comprehensive functions, and its modest and self-critical approach toward its policies.

In Swedish practice, the hard-to-employ are "persons who, due to

[3] Samuel M. Burt and Herbert E. Striner, *Toward Greater Industry and Government Involvement in Manpower Development,* W. E. Upjohn Institute Staff Paper, Kalamazoo, September 1968; Neil Chamberlain, "Corporate Relations and Public Policy: A New Concentration," *The Hermes Exchange,* October 1968, pp. 13–16.

physical or mental defects or social deficiencies, have, or expect to
have, more difficulties than others to obtain and hold gainful employment." The staff of the Employment Service is trained to look
for the hard-to-employ not only among the physically and mentally
ill and disabled, but also among alcoholics, drug addicts, refugees,
gypsies, older workers, ex-prisoners, school dropouts, youths released from reform schools, and other socially handicapped.[4] This
approach does not lead to identical measures for dissimilar cases. It
is in fact a hallmark of Swedish manpower policy that there is at
hand a wide variety of measures to be applied selectively to individual cases or particular groups with distinct needs.

The advantage of the over-all approach to the hard-to-employ is
realized in Sweden's operation of a Vocational Rehabilitation Service, under the central authority of the Labour Market Board. The
operating bodies are the vocational rehabilitation departments in the
25 County Labour Boards and over 50 local Employment Service
offices. In July 1968, the Vocational Rehabilitation Service had 321
employees. Its officers coordinate national, municipal, and private
rehabilitation work and consult with the municipal Social Boards,
physicians, and social workers on individual cases. Any kind of serious hard-to-employ case can be handled by the Vocational Rehabilitation Service and the larger offices have specialized counselors for
each major disability.

The internal organization of the Stockholm Vocational Rehabilitation office within the Stockholm Employment Service indicates the
comprehensive character of the services. As of June 1966, a staff of
28, and 3 consultants, assisted the director. The staff members, divided into six main groups, are highly specialized. Some deal with a
particular group, such as the blind, epileptics, or gypsies. Others handle individuals who come on their own. Some maintain connections
with the hospitals and institutions in the Stockholm area which develop vocational rehabilitation cases. Those in charge of relations
with municipal and other agencies offer services to test or enhance

[4] OECD, International Seminar on Employment Services, Placement of
the Handicapped, *Report from Sweden,* Paris, 1961, pp. 2, 9; Robert A.
Gordon, ed., *Toward a Manpower Policy,* New York, 1967, p. 9.

employability. Some arrange the placement of vocational rehabilitation clients on certain kinds of created jobs. A more generalized view of Sweden's services for the hard-to-employ is presented in later chapters.

In the Netherlands the concept of the hard-to-employ is similar to Sweden's, but an over-all administrative definition has not been formulated. Therefore, separate groups receive somewhat different treatment within the Employment Service and even among ministries. The Employment Service's selective placement section for the physically or mentally disabled, for example, is not open to refugees or the long-term unemployed.

One measure of the value of the unified concept is the rapid growth in the number of cases handled annually by the Swedish Vocational Rehabilitation Service. At the end of World War II, the Rehabilitation Service treated under 6,000 cases a year. Without much growth of the labor force, the number of cases treated rose to 26,000 by 1959. After 1960 the increase in the caseload was more deliberate. An extensive campaign was launched to search out more clients from medical and social institutions, and the 1963 National Insurance law provided that disability pensions should not be granted until all vocational rehabilitation measures had been attempted. Multihandicapped persons and displaced older workers have been referred in recent years. As a result, the number of cases soared annually until the 1967–68 total reached 86,000. By 1970 it is expected that 100,000 persons will register. This increase, vastly greater than the relative growth of the total population or the labor force, has been attributed to improved services which attract more applicants and result in shortages of personnel, long waiting periods for clients, and demands for further improvements. Expenditures on vocational rehabilitation measures have risen from 6 million Sw. kr. in 1955–56 to an appropriation of 385 million Sw. kr. for 1968–69. For 1969–70, the Labour Market Board requested 546 million Sw. kr.

Other European countries offering comparable services have had a slower rate of increase in their caseloads over recent years. Furthermore, Sweden's Vocational Rehabilitation Service, which specializes in difficult cases, handles a far greater number of cases in relation to the size of the Swedish labor force than do comparable services in other countries. This is true after allowance is made for the fact that the Swedish Vocational Rehabilitation Service is open to every type of hard-to-employ case and that other Swedish governmental or nonprofit agencies are relatively inactive in this area.

For example, in 1965 West Germany's vocational rehabilitation service for the severely disabled accepted 75,000 cases and Sweden took 68,000 cases, although the German labor force is more than seven times the size of Sweden's. The composition of the cases gives a clue to some differences between the two countries. In West Germany, the 54,000 cases overwhelmingly involved the physically disabled; only 4,079 were listed as having mental illnesses, including organic nervous diseases; none was primarily socially handicapped.

Over 42 percent of Sweden's 68,000 cases in 1965 were primarily nonphysically disabled. They included 12,527 mentally ill or defective persons, 6,424 socially handicapped (ex-prisoners, etc.), 6,596 alcoholics, 1,122 older workers, and 2,231 with miscellaneous work handicaps. By 1967–68, these groups constituted 47 percent of the 82,000 cases. Even if other German programs of vocational rehabilitation for the exceptionally hard-to-employ were counted, the penetration rate would not match Sweden's. West Germany has facilities for the vocational rehabilitation of about 12,000 disabled cases a year. Sweden placed the same number of handicapped in vocational training courses in 1965.[5]

Another example of Sweden's comprehensive approach may be drawn from the activities of the National Labour Market Board on behalf of older workers. Although the Scandinavian countries have a relatively good acceptance of older workers, including those beyond pension age, Swedish investigations in the past decade have revealed that some discrimination existed against older workers. In 1961 a

[5] West Germany, Bundesanstalt für Arbeitsvermittlung und Arbeitslosenversicherung, (BAVAV), *Arbeits und Berufsförderung behinderte Personen—Berufliche Rehabilitation—Zusammenstellung der zahlenmässigen Ergebnisse für das Jahr 1965*, Nürnberg, 15 June 1966; data from Swedish Labour Market Board; Sweden, National Labour Market Board, *Labour Market Policy 1969/70*, Stockholm, 1969, pp. 16–17, 28, 43, 48.

program to improve this situation was launched by the Labour Market Board and it is still in effect with the revisions and amendments of 1964 and 1966. Characteristically, it avoids resort to compulsion and relies heavily on the cooperation of employers, trade unions, the public, and the workers concerned.

The lengthy program can be divided into measures directed toward the public, employers, and trade unions; measures for internal execution by the Labour Market Board and its subsidiaries; and measures for the older workers themselves. As regards employers and especially personnel managers, the Labour Market Board tries to discourage the posting of age limits in vacancies advertised through the Board. In 1960 the Swedish Government abolished age limits for the recruitment of personnel in administrative agencies. A campaign against age discrimination is carried to employers' organizations and trade unions. Private employers are informed of research studies on the future age structure of the population and anticipated labor shortages.

The possibilities of trial employment or part-time work are given special attention in sending older people for placement. Physiological and medical research on the work abilities of older workers is sponsored and the results are communicated to employers. The Confederation of Swedish Employers has been asked to request its members to make an inventory of jobs suitable for older workers and to maintain an internal employment service to place older workers. Local Employment Service offices are urged to establish local employment committees, consisting of representatives of the local trade unions, employers, and the municipality. They are devoted to the problems of placing older workers, including taking initiative in individual placements.

The Labour Market Committee—a national organ of cooperation between management and labor—considers the problems of the older worker. A central delegation with tripartite representation was proposed as the authority to carry out the program for older workers and to suggest placement arrangements. Finally, public meetings have been held. A government conference in March 1968 was followed by 23 county conferences, called "Productive 68."

The Labour Market Board set itself the following tasks as regards older workers: to educate its personnel; to make inventories of suitable jobs; to use all of the placement personnel of the employment office instead of specialized officers for older workers; to maintain a continuous inventory of older workers' applications at the employment office; to report and give special attention to those on the register over two months; to appoint senior activation officers in the County Labour Boards to coordinate actions regarding older workers; and to establish a special officer within the National Labour Market Board to coordinate plans and actions in this field.

The older workers themselves are directed toward adult education to prepare them for training and retraining courses. Vocational education and retraining have been stressed in recent years. Mobility allowances, cash assistance, and special job creation (Chapter IX) also have been emphasized recently.[6]

Having examined some programs in an over-all fashion, we may now turn to the more detailed procedures in western European programs for the hard-to-employ.

OUTREACH, INTAKE, AND SCREENING

One of the most difficult and least developed aspects of programs for the hard-to-employ is the identification and location of the individuals who might benefit from special services. A fair proportion of the prospective cases can be expected to register voluntarily with the

[6] *Modern Swedish Labour Market Policy*, pp. 48–49, 51–53, 68, 87–89, 89–90; Sweden, *Arbetsmarknadspolitik*, SOU 1965:9, Stockholm, 1965, pp. 354–59, 378–415; *OECD Observer*, December 1967, p. 34; Robert A. Gordon, ed., *Toward a Manpower Policy*, New York, 1967, pp. 261–63; International Labour Office, (ILO), *Manpower Adjustment Programmes: II. Sweden, U.S.S.R., United States*, Labour and Automation, Bull. no. 6, Geneva, 1967, pp. 41–43; Sweden, National Labour Market Board, *Activity Programmes for Middle-aged and Elderly Workers and for Women Workers*, Circular Notice A 2/61, May 1961; National Labour Market Board, *Swedish Employment Policy 1967–68* (English Summary of the Annual Report 1967–68), Stockholm, 1968, p. 130; *idem, 1966–67*, p. 136.

Employment Service. Some countries rely almost entirely on this procedure. It is especially productive if registration at the Employment Service is encouraged or required of recipients of social benefits other than unemployment insurance payments, as in the Netherlands, or if registration is extensive because unemployment insurance benefits are of indefinite duration, as in Belgium.

But some countries also seek out the potentially hard-to-employ who are on the fringes or outside of the labor market—those who might not voluntarily seek assistance of any kind. Three main categories have been the focus of outreach activities in the most advanced countries: people in institutions, disadvantaged groups, and selected individual cases.

The most widely accepted responsibility is for people in institutions, such as hospitals or sanatariums. Those who may have placement difficulties upon their release from institutions and who might benefit from preliminary services while institutionalized are sought out through a cooperative effort of the institution's officials and specially-trained Employment Service officers. In several countries, the Employment Service has an obligation to offer outreach services to hospital patients who have registered as physically or mentally disabled. In Britain these are called "resettlement clinics" and they involve meetings of a panel of various specialists in addition to the Employment Service representative.

The Swedish Labour Market Board established an outreach policy in 1960 when it called for an active search for cases which could benefit by referral to the Vocational Rehabilitation Service. Stressing the relation between early discovery and effective rehabilitation, the Employment Service seeks organized cooperation with doctors, hospitals, social, alcoholic care, penal and corrective institutions, welfare agencies, organizations of and for the handicapped, and the Social and Sickness Insurance Funds. The latter are asked to report the names of all insured workers who have received sickness benefits for over 90 days. It was decided that disability pensions should not be granted until rehabilitation efforts have been attempted and have failed.

The Employment Service not only calls on the medical and social institutions to send people to the Vocational Rehabilitation offices, but also maintains a network of contact men who work for and are paid by the Employment Service but have no internal functions in the county or local offices. The sole task of the contact men is to bring to the institutions and the patients or inmates the information, programs, services, and point of view of the Employment Service. They participate in the conferences of specialists at the institutions which discuss the future prospects of individuals at various stages of their stay. Some contact men have reported that the institutions try to involve them in internal affairs and that they have to exert care to restrict themselves to their proper functions.

Contact men represent the Employment Service in prisons, reform schools, and other corrective institutions; alcoholic treatment centers; special schools and institutions for the deaf, blind, and other handicapped; hospitals, nursing homes, sanatariums, and mental institutions. Regional contact men coordinate the work of the local men who may be part-time employees. The significant features of the Swedish outreach policy are the formal channels through contact men, the provision of programs and services in institutions, the comprehensive coverage of a network of medical and social institutions, and the growing interest of these institutions in work placement. Some institutions will not release inmates until a job or vocational plan is assured. The relationships are now so well established that Vocational Rehabilitation officers expect cases to be referred by institutions or physicians and not to come on their own initiative.

The benefits of outreach activity have been extended to disadvantaged minority groups.[7] Several European countries have experienced a sudden influx of citizens from a former overseas possession or colony and their needs have prompted unusual efforts by manpower agencies. The Algerians returning to France and the Indone-

[7] OECD, *Manpower and Social Policy in the Netherlands,* Paris, 1967, p. 60; Theodor Scharmann, "Rehabilitation of Disabled Persons in the Federal Republic of Germany," *International Labour Review,* November, 1963, p. 470; Sweden, Kungl Arbetsmarknadstyrelsen, *Berättelse om Verksamheten under 1965,* Stockholm, 1966, pp. 41–42.

sians to the Netherlands are outstanding examples. Refugee groups, such as the Poles and Hungarians in Great Britain, also aroused special efforts by the Employment Service to assist those with particular placement difficulties. A more persistent minority is exemplified by the 300,000 nomads in West Germany and the much smaller number of gypsies in Sweden. These people resist efforts to make them conform to or enter the everyday world of work. Extensive outreach programs have been established to alter their behavior.

Finally, outreach has been offered to individuals who could be in the labor market, but who will not take the initiative to seek employment and might be hard-to-employ if they did. A Dutch case illustrates how outreach has been used in a case of this sort:

The Foundation for Mental Health (a nonprofit organization) enlisted the aid of the local Employment Office on behalf of a boy of 21 who had been lying in bed all day and refused to accept any work. The Foundation proposed to have the boy admitted into a mental home, but all attempts to establish contact with the boy had been thwarted by his mentally unstable mother. His father, who had a job as a cleaner-stoker, was slightly mentally defective.

The placement officer finally gained admission to the house and won the confidence of the mother, who agreed to ask the son whether he would see the visitor. Not awaiting the decision of mother and son, the visitor entered the bedroom and got the boy to promise to accept suitable work. The placement officer approached the local Director of Public Works, who offered work as a painter. The Foundation for Mental Health, the boy's family, the doctor who had been treating the boy for a back condition, and the foreman of the painters agreed that the boy should take the job.

A few days later the placement officer came to take the boy to his appointment with the Director of Public Works, but the boy refused to get out of bed. The officer gave up after a while and agreed to come back in an hour, but the boy still could not be persuaded. A third attempt was made because the Director of Public Works said he would withdraw the work offer if the boy did not come for an interview. The boy was forced to get up, but after he was dressed, he was about to retire upstairs again. An offer of a cigarette made him change his mind. On the way to the interview the boy tried to escape a few times, but he finally had the interview and was taken on. Both he and his supervisor have been satisfied with his work, which had been continuously carried on for over two years at the time of the report; it was planned to find him a job with a competitive enterprise after a further period of adjustment.[8]

This is an extreme case of outreach both because physical contact was necessary and because the action to find a job was initiated without the motive that social benefits were being paid to the boy and could be saved if he worked. The payment of social benefits, particularly unemployment assistance or general relief, has created a demand for outreach activities in several European countries for individuals who do not seek work in any consistent fashion or are work-shy.

As a means of reducing public welfare expenditures, efforts are made to reach and place these hard-to-employ. It is not always the Employment Service which performs this function, although in most countries it plays a part. The British National Assistance Board, later the Supplementary Benefits Commission under the Department of Health and Social Security, gradually developed outreach services in the postwar period for several distinct types of hard-to-employ who either never come before the Employment Service or are not given any special assistance when they register. One group consists of homeless, needy men who use the government's Reception Centers for free shelter and food. Some of these casuals are deemed capable of supporting themselves and every effort is made to induce them to find and keep jobs, even to the extreme of bringing legal proceedings against those who persistently use the free lodgings when they are able to work.

Outreach service is also furnished to the able-bodied, long-term unemployed who receive national assistance, now called supplementary benefits. Finally, particular individuals on the assistance rolls who have not been in the labor market at all or have been out of it for a long time may receive outreach services if they are considered potential candidates for employment. For example, National Assist-

[8] The Netherlands, Ministry of Social Affairs and Public Health, *Handicapped Persons Employed in Industry,* The Hague, 1956, pp. 20–21. (Shortened and edited.)

ance Board officers have induced the reluctant parents of handicapped children of school-leaving age to allow the youngsters to take jobs or training.

Equally as important as the outreach function is the proper identification of the hard-to-employ among those who routinely come to the Employment Service. Intake and screening procedures are crucial. Neither the establishment of a general concept of the hard-to-employ nor the specification of particular characteristics insures that individual cases will be easily recognized among those who register as unemployed.

The circumstances under which the Employment Service conducts initial interviews, even in the most effective agencies, militate against the discovery of many of the hard-to-employ who qualify for and could benefit from specialized services. That this is a key problem was inadvertently revealed in the selection of sample cases for the OECD Counselling Project. The participating countries found that some unemployed were chosen for their experimental groups who should have been excluded because they were eligible for special services for the physically or mentally disabled. But up to that point, no one had identified them or referred them to the available special services. Others in the sample had been listed as ready for direct placement when they should have been designated as hard-to-employ in need of preliminary aid. In both types of case, inadequate screening was revealed.

As a result of the OECD Counselling Project, the Swedish Employment Service concluded that all interviewers needed "more time than at present is possible. . . . Hurried intake-interviews and recommendations with no follow-ups are not sufficient to obtain the accurate and detailed information and to establish contacts necessary to give individualized services to applicants who have difficulties in adapting to working conditions." Since 1967 Sweden has been establishing a more differentiated Employment Service which uses fewer personnel and shorter procedures for easy cases, and thus frees officers for in-depth interviews and amplified services in more complicated cases, estimated at 30 per cent of the total.[9]

[9] Preliminary report by the Stockholm Employment Service, OECD International Counselling Project, October 1965, p. 12; Gertrude Williams, *Coun-*

In some countries, the education and experience of the regular placement interviewers are considered inadequate to the task of separating out the hard-to-employ from the general flow of applicants. The Dutch were so impressed by the value of the initial interview in depth as used in the OECD project that they put into effect on an experimental basis an earlier plan to introduce special counselors. The counselors will help to discover additional hard-to-employ cases which might be overlooked entirely or subjected to a long delay before their needs are recognized. The Dutch system of relying on registrants at the employment office to state whether they have a physical or mental disability is clearly not an adequate way of screening out one of the chief types of hard-to-employ, though the existence of a special register for the disabled is useful in itself.

The provision in several countries that registrants above a stipulated age or those who have been on the register for more than a certain length of time be turned over to a senior official or a specialized person in the Employment Service has been an effective means of identifying a certain number of hard-to-employ. However, there are objections to classifying older workers as hard-to-employ on the basis of age alone. In most western European countries, the tendency is to treat older workers as normal placement prospects until they reveal a need for specialized attention.

The OECD Manpower and Social Affairs Committee agrees with this approach, holding it desirable to minimize "the risk of associating older job seekers indiscriminately in employers' minds with special programmes for difficult categories." [10] Older workers with no other clear disabilities are transferred to the hard-to-employ category only after normal referral and placement services have failed to locate suitable jobs. However, several countries have general programs to aid older workers as a group.

One of the important functions of the screening process at the

selling for Special Groups, OECD: Paris, 1967, pp. 44, 50–51; OECD, Council, *Implementation of Recommendation on Active Manpower Policy,* C (67) 106, Paris, November 1967, pp. 76–77; National Labour Market Board, *Arbetsmarknadspolitiken 1969/70,* Stockholm, 1968, pp. 45–51.

[10] OECD, *Promoting the Placement of Older Workers,* Paris, 1967, pp. 41–45; Irvin Sobel and Richard C. Wilcock, *Placement Techniques,* OECD: Paris, 1966, pp. 20–26.

Employment Service is to discover at an early point those registrants for work whose most urgent need is for medical, psychological, or social services. Some people may require these services rather than employment, while others may need the services before they can be considered for employment. Even countries with comprehensive social and medical services are likely to have such cases, as the OECD Counselling Project revealed. Apart from West Germany, which claimed that its social agencies had already treated all of the relevant cases, the participating countries all agreed that the intensive interviewing in the OECD project turned up a number of persons whose unsuspected need for medical, psychological, or social services had to be met before they could be considered for job placement.

Once the need was disclosed, however, the countries varied in their ability to act on the findings of the screening process. The British Employment Service investigators reported that their social agencies were not adequate to the complex problems of the long-term unemployed, that their clients resisted referral, and that there was no power to send a man for medical, psychological, or social treatment. A British case illustrates these points well:

The 44-year-old man had been unemployed for six years and had had psychiatric treatment for schizophrenia eight years earlier. For the past five years he had lived alone at a variety of inferior rooming houses. At the time of the interview he was shabby and not altogether clean in personal appearance. His response to questions was slow and his answers were not always coherent.

He declined advice to consult his own doctor and refused reference to the Disabled Persons Section of the Employment Exchange. He said he was "fully recovered" but rejected every job suggested by saying "he could not manage that sort of work." He rejected advice to consult a social agency. In his present state he is border line unemployable, and although there is the potential of skilled craftsmanship, until he takes the first essential step of seeking medical and psychiatric treatment there is nothing to be accomplished by employment interviews.[11]

[11] Great Britain, Ministry of Labour, *OECD International Counselling Project,* Report on First Experimental Stage, 1st February to 30th April, 1965, pp. 9, 11, 14, 22.

However, the British National Assistance Board, now the Supplementary Benefits Commission, has had a somewhat better experience with its clients. A voluntary medical examination was introduced experimentally in 1960 for a portion of the recipients of national assistance who were classified as able-bodied and who had been on the rolls for several months. The medical examination was well accepted and by 1964 it became standard for all long-term unemployed. These examinations have repeatedly disclosed that certain applicants for assistance should be reclassified as incapable of work and that others should be recommended for various remedial or rehabilitative measures as a preliminary to placement efforts.[12]

The Dutch investigators on the OECD project found no difficulty in persuading their clients who were not ready for jobs to accept assistance from the medical or social agencies. In turn, the latter offered cooperation with the Employment Service which "left nothing to be desired." The social agencies in fact asked for more intensive future collaboration with the Employment Service as a result of the good contact established. The Netherlands has been praised for its coordination of welfare organizations which "help individuals find their way through the network of social agencies, services, laws, institutions and facilities." [13]

The Swedish investigators also referred cases to social agencies apparently with agreement from the clients and cooperation from the agencies. But it was observed that the OECD project highlighted the "need for more coordinated use of existing resources in the community and closer cooperation between different social agencies." The Danish solution to this widely recognized problem has been to establish Rehabilitation Centers in which all the relevant medical, social, and employment agencies are physically located and the individual may be directed easily from one to another.[14] Other coun-

[12] Great Britain, National Assistance Board, *Annual Reports,* H.M.S.O.: London, 1960–1965.

[13] The Netherlands, Ministry of Social Affairs and Public Health, Directorate General of Manpower, *Report on the Findings of the Dutch Study,* The Hague, August 1966, pp. 50, 54; OECD, *Manpower and Social Policy in the Netherlands,* p. 206.

[14] Williams, *Counselling for Special Groups,* p. 51; OECD, Scandinavian Regional Seminar on Active Manpower Policy, *Final Report,* p. 26.

tries are hampered by an administrative and locational separation between physical and vocational rehabilitation agencies.

The intensive initial interview to identify the hard-to-employ is not as yet adequately developed in any country of northwestern Europe. As a result, some who register at the Employment Service are not recognized as hard-to-employ and may be denied access to existing programs which would enhance their employability. Others are kept on the files as awaiting normal placement when in fact they have medical, psychological, or social problems which should receive attention before they are considered for employment.

Countries which express satisfaction with their current outreach, intake, and screening procedures for the hard-to-employ are likely to have a limited concept of the category or to have many unidentified cases. But poor screening procedures have not resulted in underutilization of existing programs, since waiting lists are common in most countries. The countries which have the most satisfactory initial screening processes to detect hard-to-employ cases also appear to have the most highly developed programs to aid them. A positive relationship seems to exist between the improvement of screening processes and the expansion and improvement of other programs for the hard-to-employ.

GUIDANCE AND COUNSELING

The purpose of identifying the hard-to-employ at the employment office or other agency concerned with job placement is to determine whether they require special services. Some of the hard-to-employ will be immediately ready for placement and they may need nothing more than extra attention in the placement process. A good example is provided from the British experiment in interviewing the long-term unemployed in depth.[15] Among the London cases was a Greek Cypriote of 27 who had been unemployed for more than

[15] Great Britain, Ministry of Labour, Steering Group on the Employment Services, *Experiment in Interviewing in Depth of Long-Term Unemployed,* November 1965.

three months, although he was a qualified truck driver and many vacancies existed. Only after he was included in the experiment and referred to the specialist placing officer did the real cause of his employment problem emerge: he was too fat to fit into an ordinary truck cab or to load and unload in narrow alleyways. Having discovered the problem through the devotion of a little extra time to this case, which may have been complicated by the client's language difficulties, the specialist placing officer began to watch for firms whose trucks had extra-wide cabs and were used for residential or commercial deliveries. A satisfactory job was soon arranged for a man who otherwise might have remained hard-to-employ.

Many cases are more complicated, however, and will first need guidance and counseling. The need for the counselor function has been increasingly evident as countries have extended their services for the hard-to-employ. Not only in the initial screening interview, but also in subsequent interviews which deal with the applicant's personal and social problems, the counselor has a key role, as an OECD statement indicates:

Counselling differs from ordinary employment interviewing in several respects. The counsellor is specially trained to conduct the more intensive type of interview his work requires and to evaluate the information he obtains. He is experienced in handling the range of difficulties likely to beset his client and in the range of services available to help him. Equally important, his specialized function means that he is able to devote the necessary time to interviewing, advising and encouraging his client. . . .

The prime objectives of counselling are:

a) to remotivate the client (particularly the long-term unemployed or underqualified) into a desire for self-improvement, and

b) to restore, strengthen and maintain the client's self-respect.

These are objectives which can be sought and at least to some extent achieved regardless of the client's ultimate success in finding work. Their value may be recognized both in terms of individual and family happiness and also in reduced risk of demands on health and welfare services.[16]

[16] OECD, *Promoting the Placement of Older Workers*, p. 47.

The OECD Counselling Project was designed to discover whether the long-term unemployed and frequent job-changers could benefit from interviews in depth by trained and qualified personnel who would take the time to explore the personal and family factors intertwined with employment difficulties. All of the participating countries found that their case histories were replete with personality and family difficulties, but they differed with regard to the desirability of adding special counselors to their staffs. West Germany maintained that individual counseling already was offered by existing personnel.

Great Britain recognized the value of the experimental findings but did not recommend the addition of counselors, perhaps because its clientele was reluctant to take advice on matters outside of employment possibilities. In the 1960s a counselor service was instituted by the British National Assistance Board (later the Supplementary Benefits Commission) and it has had a fair amount of success with unemployed workers who have disabling personal or social problems. Even more success attended the efforts of an outside consultant, a psychiatric social worker who had won the confidence of the unemployed by seeing them unofficially and away from the assistance office.

Sweden felt that its placement officers, supplemented by the senior officials, were adequate as counselors, but it was noted that the placement officers did not seek the specialized counseling skills of the Vocational Rehabilitation Service on a regular basis. The greatest enthusiasm for the counseling experiment as it related to helping clients with personal problems was expressed by the Dutch, who had already been considering the addition of such personnel. Partially as a result of the OECD project, Holland has begun to train and use counselors to deal with the hard-to-employ.

The Dutch satisfaction with the results of interviews in depth is due to the care taken by their trained interviewers to provide privacy, personal interest, and anonymity; it was reported that "often the most confidential information was proferred." In contrast, the interviewees in the New York OECD project lacked privacy and responded to personal inquiries by "surprise, even shock in some instances." [17] A counseling service is expensive and difficult to maintain; it requires highly qualified, trained, and dedicated personnel. Unless the proper atmosphere and staff are provided for the clients, the counseling service may be a waste of time and funds.

An important function of a counselor, in addition to uncovering the hidden personal factors in unemployment, is to persuade the client that counseling will assist him to find a job. To that end, the counselor may suggest to the placement officer that the client should have the expert services of others who are members of the staff or consultants. In several countries, the Employment Service employs its own doctors, psychologists, psychiatrists, social workers, vocational guidance specialists, technical advisers, and others who may meet in staff conference to discuss difficult cases and to recommend a course of action. The counselor or the placement officer may coordinate these efforts and carry the decisions of the group back to the client. Counselors in large offices may specialize in one disability, such as the blind, or one procedure, such as intake.

In Great Britain, a recent development is the establishment of a link in selected employment exchanges between placement interviewers and the social worker attached to the local Industrial Rehabilitation Unit (see Chapter III). Individuals with personal or social problems were referred to the social worker for preliminary assistance. It was discovered that good results could be achieved not only by social workers but also by experienced placement officers if they were permitted sufficient time for each case. A more general scheme to aid the socially disadvantaged is under consideration by the British Employment Service. In the Netherlands, the Special Plans Officer is a counselor without placement authority who is in charge of developing an occupational and placement plan for each difficult case; the system is satisfactory. However, it has been ob-

[17] Williams, *Counselling for Special Groups,* pp. 37–46, 50–51; Eugene Heimler, *Mental Illness and Social Work,* Penguin Books: Harmondsworth, 1967, pp. 111–18; New York State Department of Labor, Division of Employment, *Personal Problems and Employability,* Albany, January 1966, p. 66; the Netherlands, *Report of the Findings of the Dutch Study. . . ,* p. 43.

served in other countries that the regular placement interviewers with ultimate responsibility often take over the case and disregard the counselors' recommendations. Problems of divided files and incomplete information about job opportunities have also turned some countries against the separate counselor post.[18]

The potential value to the hard-to-employ of a counselor service seems clear. Yet it must be admitted that in the OECD project the experimental groups were not much better at job-finding than the control groups which received no counseling. However, the Dutch officials made the point that the quality of the jobs obtained by the experimental group, which received counseling, may have been superior to those secured by the control group. The British OECD report noted that unemployed men needed to be counseled before they were out of work for six months and became residual long-term unemployed. This was verified by another British counseling project, involving men with only two months unemployment, which had far more successful placement results.

A Swedish experimental study may throw more light on the value of the counseling function. The Stockholm Vocational Rehabilitation Office has sponsored a long-range investigation by an outside consultant who divided a representative sample of vocational rehabilitation clients into three sections: those who were given no counseling, those who were given counseling, and those who were told they were being counseled but in fact were not being given any real assistance. The actual employment position of the three groups was checked at the end of the counseling period and was to be checked again after an interval of time, so that the longer-run effects of counseling might be evaluated.

It is difficult to draw firm conclusions from the OECD Project about the value of special counselors because of the brief period of the study, the exceptionally tight labor markets prevailing at the time, and the absence of detailed follow-up records. Nevertheless, advocates of counseling assert that its benefits should not be mea-

[18] OECD, *Promoting the Placement of Older Workers,* p. 51; Sobel and Wilcock, *Placement Techniques for Older Workers,* pp. 40–45; Williams, *Counselling for Special Groups,* pp. 37–46; Great Britain, interviews.

sured simply by the numbers of unemployed who found jobs.[19] The quality of the employment found through counseling and other factors, including a better social adjustment, should also be considered. Whether to use special counseling personnel or regular placement interviewers who have been given special training and enough time for each case is a matter of choice for each country, but there is growing agreement that the counseling functions are important.

[19] Williams, *Counselling for Special Groups,* chs. VI, VII; Great Britain, Ministry of Labour, Steering Group on the Employment Services, *Experiment in Interviewing in Depth of Long-Term Unemployed.*

III | Special Services to Improve Employability

A certain number of the hard-to-employ need an assessment of their work capacities or services to improve their employability before they can be placed. Such services usually are not offered directly by an Employment Service, even one boasting a large staff of specialists. Instead, in several northern European countries, the Employment Services regularly make referrals to other specialized, permanent institutions.

While the organizational structure and financing of such institutions vary from country to country, there is a basic similarity in the types of services offered: psychotechnical aptitude tests, vocational assessment, work experience and work adjustment programs, and adult vocational training and retraining courses or other education. These services, which also provide information about an individual's vocational abilities and potential, are preliminary to or concurrent with the adoption and execution of a placement plan which is the ultimate purpose of the counseling and special services. This chapter considers all services except vocational retraining, which is left to Chapter IV.

PSYCHOTECHNICAL TESTING AND VOCATIONAL ASSESSMENT

Western Europe lags behind the United States in the development and use of tests of skill, physical capacity, educational attainment, vocational aptitudes, ability to learn, and interests. Aware of the greater American reliance on testing, some European officials have expressed a desire to expand their testing services, but others have voiced a certain scepticism, citing the elaborate and mechanical nature and misleading results of many tests. Simpler alternatives involving subjective evaluation are preferred in some countries.

An OECD manual on the placement of older workers commends tests because they

help to reveal unrecognized abilities, to define sources of difficulty in training or in finding employment, to restore confidence or to establish a realistic basis for self appraisal. They may also indicate likelihood of success in various occupations and provide useful evidence when presenting an applicant's claims to an employer. They can be helpful in diagnosis (discovering an applicant's abilities as compared with others) and in vocational guidance (discovering how those abilities relate to success in different occupations).[1]

The OECD did caution, however, that the tests must be chosen, administered, and interpreted fairly if the hard-to-employ or older workers are not to be discriminated against through a supposedly "objective" instrument.

Some western European countries have developed special facilities which test the physical, psychological, and technical capacities and limitations of selected placement prospects. Other countries rely on the testing facilities within the Employment Service or in non-profit agencies which cater to a specialized clientele. Still others conduct testing along with such activities as assessment of work capacity and industrial rehabilitation.[2]

Belgium established a medico-psychotechnical testing center in Brussels in 1958 on an experimental basis and made it permanent by a Royal Decree in 1963, which also provided for additional regional centers in several of the larger cities. The centers have the task of devising tests for four groups: candidates for vocational

[1] Organization for Economic Cooperation and Development (OECD), *Promoting the Placement of Older Workers,* Paris, 1967, pp. 61–64.

[2] Bertram Black, *Industrial Therapy for the Mentally Ill in Western Europe,* New York, 1965, p. 15.

training classes; workers for firms which are newly established, expanding, or reconverting; young people who have been out of work for a long period or who are having difficulty in finding suitable jobs; and the hard-to-place.[3] The last are a large group in Belgium, even according to the official definition discussed in Chapter I.

Sweden provides psychotechnical tests for some of the hard-to-employ who come to its Vocational Rehabilitation Service; during 1967, about 7 percent of the applicants underwent some kind of test in units in 11 counties. Work assessment is offered in cases where practical work tests under normal conditions will help to establish the handicapped person's interests and aptitudes, physical and mental work capacity, willingness to work, and ability to cooperate with supervisors and coworkers. At the end of 1968 there were about 300 places for vocational assessment in Sweden, including 35 at the Government Clinic, an impressively equipped unit which does research, experimentation, teaching, and assessment of the most difficult cases. The remaining places were established by county councils and county boroughs as departments in work experience centers; each assessment place serves about five people a year. In mid-1969, the Labour Market Board declared an immediate need for a minimum of 1,000 places with an annual capacity of about 5,000. Until 1966 the government subsidies more or less covered actual operating expenses. The formula then gave a subsidy of 75 percent of the operating deficit but not more than 3,000 Sw. kr. per place. As a result the state subsidy covered only 19 percent of costs in 1967–68 and expansion of places was retarded for lack of central financing. Traveling expenses and daily allowances are paid to disabled persons and their attendants if they must make a journey of some distance to the testing or assessment institute. Six months is the maximum time permitted for any case. During that time allowances are paid on the same basis as to vocational retrainees.

The proportion of rehabilitation clients who go to assessment

3 OECD, Manpower and Social Affairs Committee, *Annual Reports,* Belgium, 1964, MO (64) 10, Paris, 1964, p. 32; Margaret S. Gordon, *Retraining and Labor Market Adjustment in Western Europe,* Washington, 1965, p. 62.

clinics has been small; in 1965 less than 1 percent of the 67,819 clients and in 1967, 1.4 per cent of the 85,983 clients were referred to assessment units which had 50 places in 1963 and about 260 in 1967. Of the 1,288 persons handled in 1967, the majority were physically handicapped. The mentally ill and defective made up 35.9 percent of the total, and only a small number of alcoholics and socially maladjusted, chiefly youthful offenders against the law, were represented.[4]

Over 30 percent of the 1,117 cases closed in 1967 were drop-outs, with illness the cause in two-thirds of the cases. Just over 40 percent of the completed cases were sent on to work adjustment centers, discussed in the next section. About 16 percent were given specially created jobs, discussed in Chapter IX. Only 6.1 percent were placed directly in competitive employment, while 8 percent were directed to vocational training courses. In the Swedish view, it is quite acceptable that a large proportion of those given psycho-technical tests should be placed in work adjustment centers or created jobs rather than directly in competitive employment.

An increased attention to testing and assessment was suggested in 1965 by the tripartite labor market policy committee, which found such activities in only 9 of the 25 counties. Declaring that "systematic practical assessment" of work capacity is "in many cases indispensable for an accurate choice of rehabilitation measures," the committee called for the establishment of assessment departments as a complement to work experience centers, preferably in areas with a regional or fully-equipped central hospital. When the *Riksdag* adopted its resolution on labor market policy in 1966, it stressed that the expansion of assessment facilities should occur in such a way that later they could easily be transferred or coordinated with the rehabilitation clinics of hospitals. This statement points to the continuing problem of linking medical and vocational rehabilitation. The Labour Market Board issues advice and directions on assess-

[4] Sweden, National Labour Market Board, *Modern Swedish Labour Market Policy*, p. 49; idem, "Arbetsvårdsnytt, Arbetsvården under år 1967," *Arbetsmarknadsinformation* V, no. 4, 1968, Tables IV, VIII; National Labour Market Board, *Labour Market Policy 1969/70*, Stockhlom, 1969, p. 29.

ment methods procedures and offers extensive programs to train local personnel.

The Labour Market Board, in its 1969-70 budget proposals, called for a doubling over five years in the number of psychotechnical testing and vocational assessment places in order to reduce waiting time and give each county at least one unit. As has been the case thus far, many applicants will be given tests and assessment in institutions which also perform additional functions, such as providing work experience or sheltered employment.[5]

Denmark, which has an advanced rehabilitation system, also maintains a network of psychotechnical and assessment institutes in connection with its twelve rehabilitation centers. Since a very high proportion of Danish rehabilitation candidates are not eligible or interested in work, the testing facilities are used to determine educational capacities as well as vocational interests.

WORK ADJUSTMENT AND EXPERIENCE CENTERS

A few countries have established a network of permanent centers where the hard-to-employ may function and be observed under actual working conditions, become accustomed to normal work habits and pressures, and recover confidence, skills, and speed. Work experience centers are quite distinct from both vocational training courses and sheltered workshops, as they operate in the most advanced northwestern European countries.

Some countries have not established completely separate institutions and functions. For example, both Holland and Belgium have expected their state-financed sheltered workshops to act as work-experience centers as well as sources of created jobs for those unable to compete in ordinary labor markets. However, the Netherlands has moved toward creating rehabilitation sections within the sheltered workshops, because it has become increasingly clear that the workshops overwhelmingly provide terminal employment (see

[5] *Modern Swedish Labour Market Policy*, pp. 48–49, 90–91; *Labour Market Policy, 1969/70*, p. 29.

Chapter IX). Belgium, which has only recently developed public measures for the hard-to-employ, has since April 1966 authorized the placement in sheltered workshops of unemployed workers officially designated as hard-to-place. It is hoped that these below-par workers may be brought up to normal standards through such assignments. While at work, they continue to receive unemployment benefits, which are of unlimited duration in Belgium. At the end of 1967, sheltered workshops included 295 workers on this arrangement. It remains to be seen whether these workers will return to ordinary jobs.

It appears that the countries which maintain separate work-experience institutions have the most highly developed programs and the largest number of rehabilitants. The British and Swedish work experience centers are of greatest interest.

British Industrial Rehabilitation Units

Great Britain pioneered in establishing governmental work adjustment centers as part of a comprehensive set of programs under the Disabled Persons (Employment) Act of 1944. Chapter IV discusses vocational retraining, Chapter V takes up the register of disabled, the quota system, and reserved employment, and Chapter IX considers British sheltered workshops.

The Department of Employment and Productivity, formerly the Ministry of Labour, operates more than 20 industrial rehabilitation units (IRUs), including several recently established in areas affected by large-scale redundancies among coal miners. Thirteen-thousand persons of employable age enter the units each year to take a course designed primarily for those who have completed medical treatment and need help to adapt themselves physically and mentally for a return to work or to find the most suitable job. The course lasts 7 to 8 weeks on the average and 26 weeks at most. A fair proportion of entrants are older workers. In the period July–December 1964 almost two-fifths were over 40 and over 13 percent were 50 to 59 years old. Each IRU unit has a capacity of 100 to 150 persons which is usually 85 percent occupied. Over 200,000 men and women have been admitted to IRUs since the first one opened its doors in December 1943 under the authority of preliminary wartime legislation. Attendance at an IRU is compensated by government at rates which equal or exceed unemployment insurance benfits, but are lower than unskilled wages. Various kinds of allowances for extra expenses are paid to IRU participants.

The IRUs provide an authentic industrial environment. Conditions of factory and office life are simulated, including clocking in and out, checking the quality and quantity of output, meeting the terms of subcontracts from local firms, and other aspects of daily work experience. But unlike a factory or office, an IRU has a large professional staff to observe, instruct, and aid the participants. A team functions under the leadership of a rehabilitation officer in charge of the IRU. The other members are an occupational psychologist, a social worker, a doctor, a technical man in charge of the workshops and workshop supervisors, and a resettlement officer responsible for liaison with the placement officers of the Employment Service. This team controls the IRU with regard to admissions, vocational assessment, work assignments, and placement plans. A nurse and remedial gymnast also may be employed and consultant psychiatric advice is available.

A typical IRU contains five or six workshops. The author visited Waddon IRU in Surrey where separate sections assembled small tools; made metal boxes, jigs, and fixtures; operated machine shops and woodworking; conducted the business records office of a fictional firm; and practiced general clerical and office skills. In other areas, outdoor work such as gardening or concrete pouring is offered. Subcontracts from government departments and local firms govern most of the tasks assigned in the IRUs.

During the first week, IRU clients remain in the Intake Section, where a supervisor observes their dexterity, skills, and attitudes toward work and fellow workers. After a team conference on each case, an assignment to a workshop is made. Further conferences are held and a placement plan is devised. If training for a skilled occupation is recommended, it is given at a government training center or other training establishment.

Among the 12,689 who entered the IRUs in 1967, 83 percent completed the course. Drop-out rates have been highest among those whose disability was classified as psychosis, psychoneurosis, injury or disease of the spine (including paraplegia), or disease of the digestive system. Studies are needed of the dropouts to determine whether they are evenly distributed throughout the units or are concentrated in certain places, perhaps reflecting on the performance of particular personnel. It may be desirable to develop principles of selecting candidates based on the dropout experience. So long as the number of IRU places is limited, the desire to service people with a variety of disabilities should be modified by the principle of optimum utilization of facilities. Difficult social decisions may be necessary.

Over 40 percent (6,369) of the 10,608 persons who completed the course in 1967 were placed in employment within three months of leaving the IRU. The psychotics, psychoneurotics, and mentally subnormal had the best placement record of any disability groups; about 47 percent of those who completed the course were in jobs within three months, against a low of 35.6 percent for those with injuries to head and trunk.

A fair proportion (18.9 percent) of those who completed IRU courses in 1967 were placed in vocational training courses. Such courses were arranged for over one-fourth of four groups: those with amputations, diseases of the digestive system, injuries or diseases of the spine, and injuries to head and trunk. By contrast, only 1.1 percent of the mentally subnormal group were offered vocational training.

If placement in either employment or a vocational training course is the measure of success, those with diseases of the digestive system fared best. Within three months 66.1 percent had been placed. The mentally subnormal and those with other organic nervous diseases had the lowest scores, around 50 percent. Over 63 percent of those listed as having no obvious physical or mental disability, a group which includes the few long-term unemployed who are admitted to IRUs, were placed in either a job or training. This was just above the general average of 60 percent. The over-all results were less satisfactory than they had been in the full employment year, 1965.

A portion of those who complete IRU courses answer a questionnaire on their work status six months after graduation. The results for different time periods from 1964 to 1967 show a consistent pattern. Under one-fifth to about 30 percent had not worked at all since leaving the IRU, and another 13 to 14 percent had worked but were not employed at the time of the inquiry. About 50 to 60 percent regarded themselves as satisfactorily resettled, while 6 to 8 percent were dissatisfied with their jobs. If all who entered the IRUs are considered rather than those who completed the course, then half of the total would have been unemployed, dropouts, or unhappy with their jobs.[6] This is a strikingly high figure, yet it causes no criticism of the IRUs because the difficulty of the cases is recognized.

The IRUs are the chief agency for work assessment and work experience in Britain, but other public and private agencies offer parallel or preliminary work training services for specialized clientele. Nonprofit voluntary organizations have long performed important social services in Britain. Now, financed in part by government subsidies, these organizations assist groups with special needs, such as the blind, spastics, and paraplegics. A recent development in and around mental hospitals, called Industrial Therapy Organizations, has an important place among the agencies which prepare some people for entrance to an IRU or sheltered employment, offer a substitute for the IRU experience, or receive those who are terminated by IRUs. Work training centers conducted by the local authorities, largely for the mentally subnormal, also play this dual role to some extent. On the whole, these agencies assist people who are below the standard of admission to an IRU.

The hard-to-employ who are not physically or mentally disabled are not well served by the IRUs. The 1944 law did not limit admission to the IRUs to persons on the official Register of the Disabled (see Chapter V). In fact, IRUs were specifically authorized to accept the able-bodied long-term unemployed who might benefit from a rehabilitation course. But over the years, no more than 5 to 8 percent of the total intake has been from this group; the prior claim of

6 "Industrial Rehabilitation," *Ministry of Labour Gazette,* November 1966, pp. 723–24; *Employment and Productivity Gazette,* November 1968, pp. 909–10.

the disabled to the limited number of places probably is the chief explanation.

As a result of this neglect of the able-bodied unemployed, it fell to the National Assistance Board, now the Supplementary Benefits Commission, to set up Reestablishment Centers for those long-term unemployed who were receiving government assistance payments and who might be made employable. Reestablishment Centers try to give some men, who on the average have been out of work for three years, a reintroduction to the habits, routines, and demands of a normal working life. The centers are primarily concerned with the men's social and personality problems as factors in long-term unemployment and poor work motivation and they deal to a lesser extent with medical problems.

While most men attend Reestablishment Centers voluntarily, legal means exist to compel attendance. Thirteen of the 969 men took the course on legal order in 1966. Failure to attend may result in the loss of government assistance (supplementary benefits). Originally, the centers were residential, catering mainly to single men; two institutions were operated by voluntary organizations with government subsidies. As more units were planned, the importance was recognized of day centers for married men and men who live temporarily in Reception Centers, the government hostels for recipients of assistance payments, and others in need. Employable women form a small portion of the long-term unemployed and no provision is made for them at Reestablishment Centers.

A further examination of the records of 205 out of 214 men who left the eight centers in the first quarter of 1966 showed that 70 percent had worked at some time and half of these had been on jobs for over six months. However, by the end of the year, 60 of the 148 men who had worked after leaving the Centers were again receiving supplementary benefit allowances. Of the 57 men who remained unemployed throughout the year, all but two were receiving allowances or sickness benefits at the year's end.[7] Thus, the rate of return to

[7] Great Britain, *Report of the Ministry of Social Security for the year 1966*, Cmd. 3338, H.M.S.O.: London, 1967, pp. 63–64; Dr. J. F. Dunn and Dr. W. V. Wadsworth, "The Industrial Unit at Cheadle Royal Hospital," *Rehabilitation*, April–June 1964, pp. 5–15.

full-time, permanent employment was not unlike that of the IRUs.

There may always be a need for reestablishment centers for some long-term unemployed, but it would seem possible and desirable to increase the number who are treated before they become hardened unemployed living on government assistance. The deliberate revision of IRU admissions policies would be the most direct way of assisting the able-bodied hard-to-employ at an earlier stage. Fortunately, internal developments in the IRUs are also pressing in this direction.

In recent years the proportion of mentally disabled in IRUs has risen sharply in response to the rapid advance of industrial therapy units in and near mental hospitals and the willingness of mental hospitals to transport resident patients to IRU courses. It has been found, however, that an IRU functions best when no more than one-third and preferably fewer of the participants are mentally ill or defective; this proportion is consistent with the findings reported to the author in Holland, Sweden, and Denmark. Therefore, the British IRUs have begun a search for additional participants among both the physically disabled and the able-bodied unemployed.

The recommendations in 1965 of an Inter-Departmental Working Party on Industrial Rehabilitation made a special point of the desirability of admitting more able-bodied unemployed to the IRUs. It was also noted that older workers who had been discharged after long service might benefit from IRU courses which were adjusted in length to suit individual needs. Special workshop sections were suggested for those who needed to build up and maintain working speed.

To attract more of the physically disabled to IRUs, better liaison with hospitals and doctors and experiments with combined medical and industrial rehabilitation were recommended. In 1968 such a unit was opened at Garston Manor to serve 400 persons a year, partially on a residential basis. Employers who planned to put their returning injured or sick workers on light jobs should be encouraged to send them to an IRU for toning up, assessment for a new job, or recommendation for a training course. On the basis of limited surveys, it was felt that two employed persons per thousand each year might benefit from full or modified IRU courses. More attention by the IRUs to the needs of physically and mentally handicapped school-leavers was also urged.

To obtain better geographical coverage and to benefit the smaller towns, the Inter-Departmental Working Party suggested that the IRUs be housed jointly and share facilities with government training centers, Reestablishment Centers, and other suitable agencies. It also recommended that a few quality residential IRU centers be built, providing arrangements for home visits and appropriate financial inducements to prospective residents. New IRUs should be built on a somewhat smaller scale, but with at least 60 places.[8]

There is every indication that the British IRUs will continue to expand their coverage of cases and areas, since a large untapped market for IRU services exists in Britain. The units are well accepted and relatively inexpensive; they are simply housed and equipped and earn part of their expenses through subcontracting with business enterprises. Their effectiveness will be enhanced by reductions in the number of IRU participants who drop out, remain unemployed, or obtain unsatisfactory jobs.

The Swedish IRU

The British innovation of the IRU to provide toning-up and work experience was copied by Sweden, which has gone beyond the originator in some respects. Instead of setting up a chain of government-operated IRUs, as in Britain, the Swedish National Labour

[8] "Developments in Industrial Rehabilitation," *Ministry of Labour Gazette,* May 1966, pp. 202–205; "Industrial Rehabilitation," *Ministry of Labour Gazette,* November 1966, pp. 723–24; "Industrial Rehabilitation and the Employed Worker," *Ministry of Labour Gazette,* February 1967, p. 121; Ministry of Health, Ministry of Labour, "Industrial Rehabilitation of the Mentally Disabled," November 1965; J. K. Wing, "Social and Psychological Aspects of Rehabilitation of the Disabled in the United Kingdom," *Rehabilitation,* April–June 1965, no. 53, pp. 14–20; Bertram J. Black, *Industrial Therapy for the Meutally Ill in Western Europe,* pp. 13–17; Interviews in Great Britain.

Market Board subsidizes and supervises the counties, which open and operate IRUs in accordance with the high standards set by the Labour Market Board. An experimental IRU for the mentally retarded was established by a nonprofit organization with a state subsidy.

The grants-in-aid are made separately for building and machinery costs, on the one hand, and for operating expenses, such as rent, materials, supervisory salaries and allowances paid to the clientele, on the other. The amount of the individual allowance varies with individual circumstances, but ordinarily the allowance is not less than the vocational training allowance. In its 1965 report, the tripartite committee which reviewed labor market policy recommended that the central government's share of the subsistence allowances paid to those attending IRU courses be increased from 50 to 100 percent. While this proposal was not accepted by Parliament, it was agreed that the government would subsidize the allowances to selected individuals beyond the previous limit of six months.

The grants for construction of buildings are set at a maximum number of Swedish crowns per square meter of floorspace, with a stated amount of space for each workplace. Grants may also be made for the acquisition of existing work centers. If new construction is undertaken, the Labour Market Board exercises control over the actual building, supervises the insurance of the premises, etc. Purchases of machinery may be subsidized, usually to one-half of the cost but as much as two-thirds in exceptional cases. Because of rising prices, the central government's share of costs dropped from 37 percent in 1964 to 28 percent in 1967.

A distinctive feature of some of the Swedish IRUs is their physical integration with sheltered workshops as a means of obtaining broader geographic coverage. Grants-in-aid are given for the construction or purchase of premises which offer both work training and sheltered work but as separate functions. Although the two activities are conducted side by side, they are supposed to have a different clientele, character, and duration. The process of separation of functions is still going on in some units which may make clear distinctions among their clientele only in their annual statistical reports. Such overlapping was shown in the 1965 report for Stockholm, for example.

The number of work experience places increased from 1,190 in 1963 to 1,450 in 1967, but the total number entering doubled in the four-year period. In July 1966, when the Swedish IRUs had a total of 1,419 places, 532 were in the central region and 382 were in the south, which includes the large Stockholm metropolitan region; each of the 25 counties had at least one IRU. Although some units are small and costly to operate, Sweden's geographic coverage is superior to Britain's. The Swedish IRUs have a variety of workshops, but metal and woodwork shops are most numerous. Training kitchens or apartments are maintained in some IRUs for disabled homemakers who form part of the Vocational Rehabilitation Service's caseload. The maximum time for each case in the IRU generally is six months.[9]

The Swedish device of joint housing for two or more types of vocational rehabilitation facilities has begun to find favor in other countries where the high overhead costs of separate facilities have been an obstacle to wide geographic coverage outside of major cities.

In Sweden over 4,000 persons entered work experience centers in 1967. This total is one-third of Britain's intake although the Swedish labor force is less than one-seventh the size of Great Britain's. Yet, Sweden does not select relatively more able-bodied, hard-to-employ cases for the IRUs than Britain. Although as many as one-fourth of the persons registered with Sweden's Vocational Rehabilitation Service are socially maladjusted, alcoholics, superannuated workers, and other able-bodied hard-to-employ, people with these disabilities formed only 6.5 percent of the total passing through Swedish IRUs from 1965 through 1967. This was about the same proportion of nondisabled as in British IRUs, which have been heavily predis-

[9] National Labour Market Board, *Modern Swedish Labour Market Policy,* pp. 49, 91; Sweden, Royal Ordinance no. 394, of June 5, 1963; no. 493 of June 4, 1964; no. 107 of May 7, 1965; *Labour Market Policy 1969/70,* p. 29; Karl Montan, *Rehabilitation in Sweden,* The Swedish Institute: Stockholm, 1967, pp. 12–14.

posed toward selecting only the physically and mentally disabled.[10]

It is clear that the Swedish IRUs, to which only 5.1 percent of all Vocational Rehabilitation cases were referred in 1967, do not treat a proportionate share of the nondisabled. Along with general recommendations for the expansion of work centers, specific support has been given to the greater use of such facilities for alcoholics, released prisoners, and other nondisabled hard-to-employ, especially those coming from institutions.

The tripartite committee on labor market policy, basing its findings on operations through 1964, saw an urgent need for "a qualitative improvement of the treatment provided by the training workshops." The committee's recommendation that the Labour Market Board be more active in drawing up training programs and giving instruction on the conduct and activity of the work experience centers has been carried out. In 1967–68, Sweden reported improved performance by the enlarged IRUs.

The drop-out rate from Swedish IRUs has been considerably higher than in Britain. This may be due to the Swedish selection of more severely disabled cases; the British generally do not admit persons to IRUs who are judged unlikely to be placed in competitive employment. Dropouts cause underutilization of facilities and a waste of funds, but Sweden has not considered any limitations on the entrants in order to reduce the dropout rate.

Of the 1,812 who completed courses at Swedish IRUs in 1967, over 57 percent entered competitive employment or vocational training; the group was almost evenly divided between jobs and training. The comparable British figure was 70 percent in jobs or training courses within three months of completing the IRU course, with jobs accounting for over 50 percent of the total. Whereas the remaining British graduates of IRUs were apt to be unemployed, the Swedish residual group tended to be placed in created jobs. This outcome of an IRU course is acceptable in Sweden, since the IRU course may make it possible for a previously substandard worker to

[10] Great Britain, *Ministry of Labour Gazette,* November 1966, p. 723; Sweden, "Arbetsvårdsnytt, Arbetsvården under år 1965," *Arbetsmarknadsinformation,* V, no. 2, 1966, Table IX; *idem,* 1966; *idem,* 1967.

be accepted for a created job. However, it may be questioned whether some who occupied IRU places could not just as well have been sent directly to created jobs.

Reporting that the expansion of work experience places in IRUs had not kept pace with the demand, the Labour Market Board in its budget proposals for 1969–70 called for a doubling of places over the following five years.[11]

Denmark appears to make relatively heavy use of work-experience centers in relation to the small number of persons being prepared for jobs; housewives, retired persons, and juveniles also are in the rehabilitation program. In terms of personnel and expenditures, Denmark ranks very high in vocational rehabilitation. Two kinds of centers are used: government-operated and government-subsidized. Due to the Danish system of placing all medical and vocational rehabilitation facilities in physical proximity to one another, Denmark has fewer problems of coordination than other countries.[12]

The provision of permanent government-controlled or financed centers for work testing, assessment, and experience is well accepted in a few northwestern European countries, and these centers increasingly are becoming accessible to the nondisabled hard-to-employ. Although only a small proportion of all hard-to-employ cases are now directed to IRUs, this type of service has proven its value and seems marked for considerable expansion as trained personnel and facilities become available.

A national network under central initiative, planning, and direction is more likely than undirected local government or voluntary efforts to establish wide geographic coverage, a standard quality of services, a varied clientele, well-trained personnel, and intimate relations with placement authorities. Countries which rely on nonprofit efforts may have superior individual centers, but their over-all performance in this area is usually less satisfactory than that described for Britain and Sweden.

[11] *Labour Market Policy 1969/70*, p. 29.

[12] Denmark, Statistik oversigt over de ved revalideringscentrene og de offentlige arbejdsanvishingskontorer i finansåret 1963/64 behandlede sager vedrørende erhvervshænmede, Tables XI, XII.

However, the degree of local government initiative and the opportunities for participation by nonprofit organizations and private enterprise should not be underestimated in the Swedish system. The high quality of municipal government is an important asset; the Stockholm City Vocational Rehabilitation Bureau, for example, carries on a full-scale program, except that the regional office of the national government's Vocational Rehabilitation Service chooses the candidates for vocational training courses (Chapter IV) or created jobs on outdoor public works (Chapter IX).

The Stockholm Bureau then offers a variety of medical, social, and employment services to its clients. It sends them to its own nationally subsidized testing, work-experience, and sheltered work centers. In addition, Stockholm has several assessment and experience centers, as well as sheltered workshops, operated by nonprofit organizations with contracts from private enterprise. Some private companies even offer places within the firm for assessment and work experience. Yet, the entire system depends on a close participation by representatives of the central government in the every-day decisions of the local bodies which accept national standards and leadership. In the same way, private enterprise, which has a high sense of social responsibility in Sweden, expects government to conduct almost all of this kind of activity and offers its facilities only when no competitive disadvantage or excess cost is involved.

IV | Vocational Retraining and Placement

In many western European countries there has been a marked growth in government sponsored and supported adult training and retraining programs. The desire to aid and utilize various hard-to-employ groups has played a part in the expansion of programs in several countries. Sweden, which has committed itself to a substantial public retraining program, stated the case explicitly in the 1965 report of its tripartite committee on labor market policy:

Effective training measures are in the first place needed for solving the *employment problems of certain categories* of jobseekers: unemployed or underemployed workers, particularly in labour surplus areas, disabled persons, jobseekers who are difficult to place because of their age, female applicants re-entering the labour market, and seasonally or temporarily unemployed workers. However, an effective labour market policy must also make it possible to cope with acute *shortages of trained manpower.* . . . The Committee maintains that one of the most serious obstacles to a better balance between the supply and demand for labour is that the unemployed lack the skills in demand. The anticipated rapid technological and structural changes will make it necessary for an increasing number of workers to change their occupations. Moreover, the population development, with a shrinking recruitment base among the younger age groups, means that the need for trained labour will in the future largely have to be satisfied by increased training for people already in the labour force.[1]

[1] Sweden, National Labour Market Board, *Modern Swedish Labour Market Policy,* Stockholm, 1966, pp. 23–24.

A British statement makes some of the same points, but specifies somewhat different problem groups:

The Vocational Training Scheme has a dual purpose. First, economic: to help meet persistent shortages of skilled labour, particularly in the engineering and construction industries where there is an important contribution to be made to national economic growth. Second, social: to help in the resettlement of the disabled, of regular ex-servicemen and of unemployed people with special resettlement problems. It is to be noted that the carrying out of the social purposes of the Scheme can assist also in the achievement of its economic purposes.[2]

The prevailing policy of offering adult training primarily to the unemployed or those about to lose their jobs has been undermined by the emphasis on meeting labor shortages through retraining. In the Scandinavian countries a strong case has been made by the trade unions that retraining opportunities must be opened to employed unskilled workers so that they may improve their economic position. It is maintained that this movement toward higher productivity and better earnings would also stimulate economic growth and restrain inflationary wage pressures.

The assertion of a general right to adult training, as stated in the 1964 OECD Recommendation on Manpower Policy, has been resisted by Swedish employers, but they have conceded the need to relax the unemployment criterion for admission to adult training. If government retraining should be offered to sizeable numbers of employed low-wage workers, it might become a means of forestalling the development of some hard-to-employ cases.

PARTICIPATION OF THE HARD-TO-EMPLOY

Since countries usually do not provide public adult vocational training or retraining solely for the hard-to-employ, it is important to examine the size of the total program, the degree of participation of the hard-to-employ, and the factors influencing participation.

[2] Great Britain, House of Commons, Reports and Papers, 548, 1966–67, Estimates Committee, *Manpower Training for Industry*, H.M.S.O.: London, 1697, p 3.

However, training programs in only a few countries are so comprehensive and centralized that all sources of adult vocational training for the hard-to-employ can be surveyed easily.

Some countries rely heavily on separate public or nonprofit training facilities for various disability groups, such as the blind, the deaf, or spastics. In such countries, not only are the relevant statistics difficult to find, but there also may be adverse implications regarding the size and quality of the vocational training programs available to the hard-to-employ. Greater attention is therefore given here to the countries with centrally-controlled, inclusive public programs.

The Swedish emphasis on adult retraining, now a decade old, has shown a significant trend: the hard-to-employ have more than kept pace with other trainees as the public program has expanded rapidly. In mid-1957 there were only 634 trainees in public facilities in Sweden, enrolled in 55 courses covering 14 occupations. During 1967–68, 1,050 courses were available through the Board of Education and 78,650 Swedish workers received adult retraining from all sources. Over 2 percent of the labor force will be in retraining as the total number goes to 100,000 a year. About one-third of all trainees were handicapped persons referred by the Vocational Rehabilitation Service. In addition, other hard-to-employ cases, particularly older, redundant workers, are sent directly to vocational training by placement officers. Perhaps half or more of all adult retrainees in Sweden are in some way handicapped in the labor market.[3] Bearing in mind the relatively large number of adult trainees in Sweden, we must rate the substantial share of the hard-to-employ as another evidence of Sweden's penetration into fringes of the labor market that other countries have barely explored or serviced.[4]

[3] *Modern Swedish Labour Market Policy*, p. 22; Anna Wiman, *Vocational Training for Adults in Sweden*, Stockholm, 1967, p. 10; Trevor Evans and Margaret Stewart, *Pathway to Tomorrow*, London, 1967, p. 51; OECD, Scandinavian Regional Seminar on Active Manpower Policy, *Final Report*, Paris, 1967, p. 24; E. Michael Salzer, "Putting Him Where He Counts," *Sweden Today*, September 1967, pp. 44, 46.

[4] OECD, Scandinavian Regional Seminar. . . , *Final Report*, pp. 22, 26; Margaret S. Gordon, *Retraining and Labor Market Adjustment in Western Europe*, Washington, 1965, pp. 38–39, 198–99.

Great Britain also has a centrally-organized, comprehensive public training program for adults, but its history is quite different. Over most of the postwar period Britain devoted the great majority of adult training places to the hard-to-employ, although the legal framework existed for a much broader coverage. Britain had expanded government vocational training at a rapid pace just after World War II, but as early as 1947 a sharp retrenchment was forced by trade union opposition to large-scale training of construction workers at a time when heavy unemployment plagued the industry.

Shortages of materials prevented the expansion of training in other trades, and the transfer of the training of coal miners to the National Coal Board sharply reduced the trainees in government centers; from 25,700 at the end of 1946, the number fell to 4,200 by the end of 1947. Therefore, the number of government trainees remained small and training was largely confined to the disabled, ex-servicemen, and able-bodied unemployed who were difficult to place; the training of these groups was approved by the trade unions.

Since about 1963 the trade unions have accepted the need for increased adult training of all workers. An expansion of training places has occurred and more are planned, including a heavy concentration in the northern areas of high unemployment. By the end of 1970 there should be 55 government training centers with a capacity to turn out about 23,000 trained men a year.[5] This is still a small total compared with current Swedish performance and that country's plan for 100,000 trainees a year by 1970, especially when account is taken of the fact that the British labor force is six times larger than the Swedish.

Moreover, as the number of British trainees has risen, the proportion of the hard-to-employ in training institutions has not increased. Even their absolute number continues to be low in comparison with other countries. At the end of March 1967, the British Ministry of

[5] Gordon, *Retraining. . .* , pp. 30, 33–34, 43–46, 136–38; Great Britain, "Government Vocational Training of Adults," *Ministry of Labour Gazette,* May 1964, pp. 196–97; "Expansion of Government Training Facilities," *Ministry of Labour Gazette,* February 1968, pp. 104–105.

Labour was providing or paying for vocational training for a total of 7,218 workers; this included 1,668 disabled persons and about 1,200 ex-servicemen and other hard-to-employ. A small additional number of disabled were being trained at the initiative and expense of local government or voluntary agencies. While British industry may undertake more retraining within the firm than Sweden or other countries, the hard-to-employ in all countries rely largely on government for vocational training and retraining.

It is difficult to determine what share of total adult vocational training facilities is allocated to the hard-to-employ in other European countries, either because the sources of training are diffuse or the statistics are inadequate. The evidence suggests that no western European country has reached the Swedish standard, but several are ahead of Britain both in the proportion of the hard-to-employ offered training and in their share of total training places.

In 1965 West Germany, whose labor force is slightly larger than Britain's, completed the vocational rehabilitation of 54,204 severely handicapped persons. Some 11,223 of these people were sent for vocational training courses, including 2,810 who were placed in apprenticeship or similar training posts; an additional 1,177 were enrolled in trade schools, high schools, or technical institutes. While no over-all data are available on West Germany's training of other types of hard-to-employ, the German Employment Service is known to finance ordinary and special training courses for various kinds of hard-to-employ cases.[6]

Denmark, Norway, and the Netherlands also stand high in the use of vocational training for the disabled. In January 1967 the Netherlands, in response to increased unemployment, introduced a plan for reimbursing the fees for training or study courses for jobseekers, especially older workers, the handicapped, repatriates, persons made redundant by technical progress, and married women reentering the labor market. The European Social Fund of the European Economic Community extended the scope of its Regulation in 1963 to

[6] West Germany, Bundesanstalt für Arbeitsvermittlung und Arbeitslosenversicherung, *Arbeits und Berufsförderung behinderter Personen-Berufliche Rehabilitation-Zusammenstellung der zahlenmässigen Ergebnisse für das Jahr 1965,* Nürnberg, 15 June, 1966, Gordon, *Retraining. . .* , pp. 66, 93–96, 149.

permit the retraining of handicapped workers. Twelve per cent of the 38,890 retrained adults were classified as handicapped by 1967, and 42 percent of total training expenditures went for these cases.[7]

In most of western Europe, a general expansion of adult vocational training courses has been impeded by the ease of obtaining employment and the relatively low training allowances, especially for married men. As a result, some training programs have at times catered largely to the disabled.

Older Workers' Share

One measure of the participation of the hard-to-employ in adult vocational training programs is the proportion of trainees who are 45 years old or older. Higher unemployment rates and reemployment difficulties plague older workers as established occupations, industries, and regions decline in a dynamic economy. The older displaced worker, in comparison with the average, tends to have a lower level of education, greater immobility, more physical limitations, a heavier representation in the unskilled or semi-skilled occupations, and more inflexible job-seeking attitudes.

These factors, together with employers' fixed age limits, discriminatory job listings, and the institutional barriers to new hirings erected by collective bargaining contracts, pension plans, tenure and seniority practices, and status and salary traditions, operate against the older worker. As automated processes spread, the older worker's seasoned experience and reliability become less important assets because a greater premimum is placed on speed, attentiveness, and the ability to make decisions rapidly.[8]

[7] European Coal and Steel Community, European Economic Community, European Atomic Energy Commission, *Premier rapport général sur l'activité des Communautés en 1967,* Brussels-Luxembourg, 1968, p. 265; OECD, Council, *Implementation of Recommendations on Active Manpower Policy,* c(67) 106, Paris, November 1967, p. 64.

[8] Irvin Sobel and Richard C. Wilcock, *Placement Techniques for Older Workers,* OECD: Paris, 1966, pp. 17–29; Rudolf Meidner, "The Employment

These handicaps have led authorities to urge that a large proportion of displaced older workers be offered retraining courses to make them more competitive in the labor market; in turn, this policy calls for the elimination of age criteria in choosing trainees. But there are obstacles to the retraining of older workers, and particularly to giving them a share of training places commensurate with their burden of unemployment. Employers, the training officials, and the older workers themselves all resist. For example, a survey in Great Britain indicated that men over 40, and especially over 50, were underrepresented in the government training courses. But the cause was found to be the small number of applications from older men rather than the policies of the centers. It was suggested that Employment Service officials probably were not recommending retraining to adequate numbers of older men and were not working hard enough to overcome the workers' own doubts.

Against this background, it is not surprising that many western European countries enroll only a small percentage of their adult trainees from the ranks of older workers and that countries which consciously strive to increase the proportion have had only minor success. The Scandinavian countries and West Germany have the best record, but none has reached 20 percent as yet. The European Coal and Steel Community's support of programs in member countries aids older workers, but retraining has not been as important as other types of programs. It is too early to judge whether Britain's drive to recruit more older trainees will change the age structure of these programs. Belgium, the Netherlands, France, and Italy generally favor younger workers in retraining courses, although special programs for particular groups of older workers may be found.[9]

Problems of Individuals and Groups," *International Conference on Automation, Full Employment, and a Balanced Economy* (Rome), New York, 1967; OECD, *Promoting the Placement of Older Workers,* Paris, 1967, pp. 16–21; G. Marbach, *Job Redesign for Older Workers,* OECD: Paris, 1968.

[9] R. M. Belbin, *Training Methods for Older Workers,* OECD: Paris, 1965; Sobel and Wilcock, *Placement Techniques. . . ,* pp. 46–48; OECD, *Promoting the Placement. . . ,* pp. 73–76; Gordon, *Retraining. . . ,* pp. 34–36, 93–97; OECD, Regional Seminar on the Employment of Older Workers, *Final Report,* Paris, 1966, pp. 22–27; OECD, International Management

By the test of concern for the retraining of older hard-to-employ workers, Sweden again is outstanding. It should be noted that Sweden does not conduct separate courses for older workers, relying instead on adjustment of curricula and training methods, individualized and flexible dates of entrance, and variable periods for completion of a fixed curriculum. This serves to minimize comparisons of performance among students and eases the placement of graduates. Other countries feel that separate classes are the best way to train older workers. This appears to be an issue to be resolved through experience in each country.

The hard-to-employ, just as other workers, are influenced by the size of training allowances. Their desire to participate in courses is greater in countries whose training allowances are superior to unemployment or other social benefits. A few countries withdraw unemployment benefits from those who refuse training, while others offer a small bonus to those in training. For some of the hard-to-employ, the treatment of invalidity or disability pensions is a key issue. A reluctance to undertake training or subsequent employment has been observed among disability pensioners in The Netherlands and Great Britain and it undoubtedly is a factor in other countries too.

The access of the hard-to-employ to adult vocational retraining is a combination of the size of the over-all program and the concern for special groups. France, which has maintained a large general public program, has more or less excluded the hard-to-employ and has been slow even to develop special public training for them. If a country has a small training program, it will not service a high proportion of the hard-to-employ, even if they dominate the program. This has been the British case. In training the hard-to-employ, the tendency is to select the most trainable individuals; there is no attempt to choose the most disadvantaged, as in the United States, although a desire to include the various types of handicap does interfere with a strict selection by trainability.

Seminar on Job Redesign and Occupational Training for Older Workers, *Supplement to the Final Report,* Paris, 1965, pp. 127–28; International Labour Office (ILO), *Manpower Adjustment Programmes: I. France, Federal Republic of Germany, United Kingdom,* Labour and Automation, Bull. no. 4, Geneva, 1967, pp. 57–58, 203–204.

TYPES OF TRAINING

The number of hard-to-employ exposed to adult retraining in various countries is important, but attention must be given also to the amount and quality of the training and the type of employment which follows.

The case of West Germany indicates the wide range in quality of training available when various federal agencies, each state (*Land*), and a host of nonprofit and private agencies are active. A 1964 survey showed 122 different institutions capable of giving vocational training to some 10,000 disabled at one time. Many of them continue to teach handicrafts, producing "an excess of training facilities for such traditional craftsmen as basket and broom makers and blacksmiths. . . ." [10]

At the other extreme, West Germany boasts one of the finest vocational retraining centers in the world in the impressive *Berufsförderungswerk* at Heidelberg. Catering to the physically disabled, the center has 1,200 students, drawn from all over the country. They live away from their families for one or two years while they acquire a modern skilled occupation based not only on their physical limitations but also on the discovery of their highest aptitudes. They are also offered general intellectual and cultural enrichment and an opportunity to change their life styles. Here is a model institution whose graduates are sought eagerly by employers and whose methods and equipment could easily be used for nondisabled trainees. Because the Heidelberg center is expensive per trainee, it is unlikely to be duplicated throughout the country. Yet, it is not merely an experimental or teaching institution.

This wide range in quality of vocational retraining for the hard-to-employ is much less common in Sweden, Denmark, Norway, Holland, and Britain, where government direction is more general. But this is not to say that only one type of standardized government training center is available in these countries. In Sweden at least

[10] ILO, *Manpower Adjustment Programmes: I. . .* , pp. 113–14; Interviews and visits in West Germany.

four sources of training and retraining for adults are recognized: the courses organized and operated by the Board of Education for the Labour Market Board; the ordinary vocational educational schools, special courses offered by such institutions as the Institute for Industrial Engineering Training and the National Board of Private Forestry; and training within industry.

More than half of all Swedish trainees usually are in the Board of Education courses, and this proportion holds also for the trainees sent by the Vocational Rehabilitation Service. Four main types of courses are offered: beginners (*nyobörjarkurser*), retraining (*omskolningskurser*), further training (*fortbildningskurser*), and refresher (*reactiveringskurser*). As an experiment, a readjustment course (*omställningskurs*) was established on a small scale to give information, vocational orientation, aptitude tests, etc. to those who are uncertain about the type of training they should enter. This course is potentially very useful for the hard-to-employ.

In general, every effort is made to train handicapped persons alongside the nonhandicapped. Some severely handicapped persons may be given a preliminary course to adjust them psychologically and technically to their disabilities before vocational training is attempted. Special vocational schools, often residential, are provided for such disability groups as the deaf, the blind, the mentally retarded, the socially maladjusted, delinquents and alcoholics. The government pays for training fees, board and lodging, and travel. Courses are set up in areas where the need is great and no center exists. Over 3,000 workers taking training courses away from home were housed by the Labour Market Board in June 1968. Mention should also be made of the extensive opportunities for vocational training in prisons and correctional institutions.

Britain's hard-to-employ are given training in government centers, but an equal or larger number receive their vocational training in technical and commercial colleges, residential centers run by non-profit agencies and in industry. Different kinds of training can be provided under government supervision in this way, geared to the needs of the particular case. In September 1968, 1,624 disabled persons were in training; of these, 776 were in government training centers, 504 were at residential training centers, 310 at technical and commercial colleges, and only 34 in business firms.[11]

Sometimes the flexibility required of a government agency is slow in coming, as this interesting case from Britain suggests:

An uneducated and aggressive man with a large family of young children left his employment of his own accord. . . . Twelve months' continuous efforts by a National Assistance board officer to persuade the man to return to work met with no success, the main obstacle being that the wages offered to him locally as an unskilled labourer were little different from the unemployment benefit he was receiving.

During this period of unemployment the family's problems accumulated . . . most of the local welfare agencies . . . were involved, and a case conference was called to discuss ways and means of assisting the family. The conference concluded that the man's manner suggested he was mentally ill and that as a first step a medical and psychiatric report should be obtained. . . .

The man, however, refused to undergo a medical or psychiatric examination, and resented the inference that he might be in need of psychiatric help. He also refused to consider attending a Ministry of Labour training course (which would have involved a medical examination) unless he could be given tuition in driving; *he maintained that if he could obtain a driving licence he would never again need to apply for assistance.* (ed. ital.) Although told that the Ministry of Labour were unable to provide driving tuition he continued to insist that the solution to all his employment problems lay in his obtaining a driving licence. In the end, driving lessons were arranged by the Board's officer, and the man justified all the efforts made on his behalf by passing the . . . driving test at his first attempt. Shortly after he obtained employment as a driver.

He has made only one application for help since obtaining his driving licence, and it seems that the problems which arose from and during his

[11] Salzer, "Putting Him Where He Counts," *Sweden Today,* p. 44; Sweden, National Labour Market Board, *Swedish Employment Policy* (English summary from Annual Report, 1965), Stockholm, 1966, p. 13; *idem,* 1967–68, pp. 15–16; Great Britain, *Ministry of Labour Gazette,* annual data on training; House of Commons, Estimates Committee, *Manpower Training for Industry,* pp. 36–37; Gordon, *Retraining. . . ,* pp. 82–88; *Employment and Productivity Gazette,* November 1968, p. 921.

period of unemployment, including his anti-social behaviour, have been solved by his return to work.[12]

Training within Industry

The western European countries have used direct training by employers to varying degrees for workers in general. Although the Scandinavian countries have long been prejudiced against on-the-job training because it tends to be narrowly specialized, they have begun to follow Sweden's lead in accepting training in industry provided that it is given "in accordance with a programme adopted by the employers' and employees' organizations concerned either as special courses or on the job, in which case the training element must be clearly defined, and that the trainees are paid wages established by the collective wage agreements." [13]

Labor market authorities are attracted to this type of training for the hard-to-employ by its lower cost per trainee, the possibility that the training firm will later employ the worker, and the potential for a rapid expansion of training places without the construction of new facilities or recruitment of staff. A special use of on-the-job training occurs in several countries in connection with programs for development areas. New, converted, or expanded enterprises in certified development areas can obtain training subsidies from Government for newly hired unemployed workers. It is not specified that the trainees must be hard-to-employ, but some are likely to be, especially in Sweden's northern counties. The companies are not required to keep the workers after the training period, but they are usually subsidized only for the number of workers needed to meet the enterprise's production goals. From 1964 to mid-1968, in Sweden, 17,833 training places in 565 firms were subsidized; almost two-thirds were in the seven northern counties.

Subsidized on-the-job training specifically for the hard-to-employ

[12] Great Britain, Ministry of Social Security, *Annual Report 1966,* Cmd. 3338, H.M.S.O.: London, 1967, p. 110

[13] *Modern Swedish Labour Market Policy,* pp. 25–26, 50, 52; OECD, Scandinavian Regional Seminar, *Final Report,* pp. 24, 36.

also exists. In Sweden firms can qualify for a training subsidy for three months in the case of older workers or for six months for seriously handicapped persons recommended by the Employment Service. In May 1966, one-third of the 3,634 persons who were being trained in industry were handicapped clients of the Vocational Rehabilitation Service. But on-the-job trainees as a whole accounted for only 15 percent of all trainees in 1967-68.

The Swedish subsidies are intended to lead to employment after training, but other countries have been satisfied to subsidize employers merely for the training, asking no commitment on subsequent employment. A West German program which reimburses up to 70 percent of wages for the first four weeks and no more than 50 percent for the remaining nine to twenty-two weeks aims to encourage on-the-job training of unemployed workers who are not fully qualified for the job. Employers are said to have responded indifferently to the subsidy, preferring to hire young foreigners without subsidies.[14]

Great Britain hopes that in the long run its Industry Training Boards, which currently are concerned with establishing standards and programs for young entrants, will provide for the retraining of older workers within firms.

Although one must wait to see how training within industry for the hard-to-employ will fare, it can be said that only limited numbers have been trained in this way and that some problems of the quality of the training have arisen. As will be shown below, the subsequent employment of handicapped on-the-job trainees in Sweden was not with the firms which had trained them.

Preparation for Vocational Training Courses

Some hard-to-employ persons who could benefit from vocational training courses are excluded because their educational background is inadequate. In the northwestern European countries illiteracy is

---

[14] ILO, *Manpower Adjustment Programmes: I. . .* , p. 107; ILO, *Vocational Guidance in France,* Studies and Reports, New Series no. 39, Geneva, 1954, p. 52; Gordon, *Retraining. . .* , pp. 100–101.

rare among the native-born who have the mental capacity to learn to read and write. Occasionally, French farmers who attended inadequate rural schools are unable to take vocational training courses of a fairly simple type until they have improved their literacy.

By and large, the literacy obstacle has plagued foreign workers seeking to learn new skills. Special primary courses have been organized for them outside of the vocational training centers and there are also special vocational training sections which integrate the basic reading and writing lessons into the training course. The latter procedure is particularly favored "to avoid the implication that the trainees, who may be experienced workers, are lacking in the necessary educational groundwork." [15]

Sweden's effort on behalf of its small gypsy population is noteworthy for the variety of approaches. In 1966 a special school was established by the National Labour Market Board to provide basic schooling for gypsies. A residential school was also set up. For those who can not leave their homes, individual instruction is offered at home.[16]

Inadequate or rusty basic arithmetic is more general and affects older native-born workers as well as foreigners. The Scandinavian countries which particularly favor the retraining of older, redundant workers have noted that many potential trainees are at a disadvantage because they had fewer years of education than younger people and have been away from school for so long. Introductory and orientation courses are offered. A Scandinavian regional seminar on an active manpower policy in 1965 "emphasized that adult training, although primarily directed towards an occupational objective, should also include elements of general education (mathematics, languages, civics, etc.) . . ."

In Germany and France, rural and foreign workers have been given basic arithmetic courses either separately or incorporated in vocational training courses in construction and metal work.[17] Re-

15 ILO, *Manpower Adjustment Programmes: I.* . . , pp. 56–57.

16 Sweden, National Labour Market Board (AMS), *Berättelse om verksamheten under 1965*, Stockholm, 1966, p. 41; *idem, 1966–30/6/1967*, p. 57; *idem, 1967–1968*, p. 59.

17 OECD, Scandinavian Regional Seminar. . . , *Final Report*, p. 36; Anna

cently Britain has made efforts to recruit a larger number of older workers for courses at government training centers. It was suggested that older applicants whose education appears rusty or below standard should be accepted if they are otherwise eligible. Remedial education can be provided either by an educational instructor at the center or by adult education facilities in the locality.

Preparatory education at still higher levels is offered in several countries to special groups, such as the disabled, hospital patients, and handicapped young people. The British Council for Rehabilitation of the Disabled, a nonprofit organization, maintains a Preparatory Training Bureau which helps candidates for government training courses make up educational deficiencies. Various governmental bodies use this nonprofit organization as their agent for this activity.[18]

GENERAL FEATURES OF TRAINING

One of the issues in vocational training and retraining of the hard-to-employ in the United States has been the offering to some trainees of low-wage jobs which may yield less income than training allowances plus dependents' allowances. In fact, the trainees may find that their new jobs pay less than welfare, if they have large families. This problem seems rare in western Europe. Women on welfare with young children are not often given training courses. Furthermore, family allowances are common for those in employment, and the amounts are frequently larger than for dependents under training allowances. General welfare payments are set nationally, with regional cost-of-living differences, and they are usually held below training allowances or unskilled wages. Usually it is arranged, as in Sweden, that the training allowance should not exceed the average wage in the area for the given occupation, bearing in mind that training allowances are not subject to income tax in Sweden. Finally, if the low-level service jobs which older workers take

Wiman, *Vocational Training for Adults in Sweden*, pp. 7–8; OECD, *Promoting the Placement of Older Workers*, pp. 79–80.

[18] *Rehabilitation*, April–June 1965, no. 53, p. 48.

after brief training in Sweden or West Germany should pay the same or little more than the training allowance, the placement officers make a strong appeal to the moral value of work. Social benefits might be withheld from a trainee who rejected a suitable job after training.

Certain features of the adult training programs of various western European countries are particularly favorable to the hard-to-employ.[19] Local labor needs, as determined by employers and the Employment Service, are used to select some of the training courses, especially in Sweden and West Germany. Local employers thus become involved in the placement of the trainees. When, in addition to the established training centers, courses can be established in places where the potential trainees are clustered, the travel and living problems of the handicapped who live away from the urban centers are eased. The provision of hostels and canteen meals aids those using centers. Individual entry dates and completion schedules give the hard-to-employ confidence and permit mixed classes. Informal admission procedures also assist the hard-to-employ.

In summary, it appears that the access of the hard-to-employ to adult training and retraining and its quality are favorably affected when such programs are under public auspices, are part of a general adult program, and are directed by an agency of central government which encourages local initiative.

RESULTS OF TRAINING

Few European countries conduct studies in depth of their vocational retraining programs and fewer conduct specific inquiries concerning the hard-to-employ trainees. As for more sophisticated analyses which raise questions of the alternative use of funds for training or other programs, the establishment of principles by which scarce funds for training shall be allocated among various candidates, the choice of one training program over another for individuals, and the weighing of the costs of training against its benefits—

[19] Gordon, *Retraining. . .*, pp. 146–54.

very little has been done along these lines either in or outside of western European governments. In the absence of a large body of research, the few Swedish studies of vocational retraining for older and handicapped workers assume considerable importance.

Older Trainees

The performance of 1,674 older persons who had finished retraining courses was explored initially in a survey in March 1964.[20] The group included 267 workers who were 45 or older; of these, 201 were men and 66 women. Just over half of the older workers were 50 years or more, mostly 50 to 54. As might be expected of an older group, they had relatively less education and prior vocational training than the labor force as a whole; 93 percent had completed only compulsory schooling (eight years or less, according to the period of school-attendance). However, the younger workers in the retraining courses had had no more education.

The older workers took somewhat shorter retraining courses than the younger workers; fewer older workers trained for structural metal work. Older women trained for office and sales jobs relatively more frequently than younger women. The drop-out rate was lower for older than younger retrainees, in spite of a higher incidence of illness among the older workers. Over 80 percent of the older retrainees either finished the full course or obtained training-related jobs before the course ended.

The jobs held by the retrainees immediately after the end of the course were surveyed. With only 2.2 percent of the group unaccounted for, 85.8 percent of the older workers were found to be employed and 52.4 percent were in jobs for which they had been trained. The record of those under 45 was not superior. The employment picture as of the end of March 1964 was then reviewed.

[20] Sweden, National Labour Market Board, "Undersökning rörande äldre personer (45 år och däröver) som under Mars och April 1963 slutade utbildning vid köy:s omskolningskurser för arbetslösa M Fl," *Arbetsmarknadsstatistik,* no. 16, 1967.

Most of the older trainees were in the jobs they had obtained immediately after the course ended. Some 28 percent were not at work (unemployed, ill, taking care of households, on emergency public works, or in another retraining course). The younger retrainees had somewhat less unemployment.

A further follow-up in December 1966 produced replies from 83.2 percent of the members of the original survey group, an unusually high response rate.[21] This survey investigated only a few subjects by age groups. Older workers (35 to 64) to a greater extent than younger workers were in the same type of work in December 1966 that they held in March 1964. In the same way, the older workers tended to remain in the type of work for which they had been trained to a greater extent than younger workers.

Unemployment was measured for the entire group and for those who were 45 or older. The results showed only a slight differential between the two age groups, indicating that older retrainees have less unemployment than do older workers as a whole. Over-all the older trainees demonstrated that the retraining investment in them yielded results comparable to those for younger workers. If the outcome in other countries is as favorable, some of the prejudice against retraining older workers should be undermined.

Handicapped Trainees

Another group which has been investigated are the retrainees with physical, mental, or social handicaps. Early in 1964, the Swedish Vocational Rehabilitation Service began a continuing study of over 4,000 handicapped persons who were scheduled to complete vocational retraining courses between April 1964 and the end of that year. The survey covered about 40 percent of the handicapped who received vocational retraining in 1964 and they were considered representative.[22]

21 Sweden, National Labour Market Board, "Uppföljningsundersökning av personer som slutade köy:s omskolningskurser under Mars och April 1963," *Arbetmarknadsstatistik*, no. 1B, 1968.

22 Sweden, National Labour Market Board, "Undersökning Rörande Ar-

The report begins with a delineation of the relevant characteristics of the 3,086 men and 936 women in the sample. The disabilities of the 4,049 retrainees corresponded fairly closely to those of the 61,000 persons who sought vocational rehabilitation in 1964. Among the retrainees, the orthopedically handicapped were somewhat overrepresented (40.3 percent vs. 33.6 percent), while the alcoholics, socially maladjusted, mentally disabled, and the superannuated were underrepresented. This outcome resulted from selecting those individuals most likely to benefit from vocational retraining. As will be shown, the underrepresented groups proved less responsive to retraining opportunities than the physically handicapped.

Of the 4,049 retrainees, 161 were judged to have a serious secondary handicap; mental disability and alcoholism were cited most frequently. There was a high representation of cases from the northern forestry counties where outdoor work and bad weather lead to rheumatism and back trouble. Almost one-third of the male retrainees had previously worked in factories, while 18.4 percent had been in farm or forestry work. The women retrainees came overwhelmingly from service occupations.

Some 23 percent of the men and 16.4 percent of the women were 45 or older, a higher proportion than prevailed among the total group of retrainees. Young people under 21 accounted for 24 percent of the women but only 15.2 percent of the males. The age and sex distributions were quite varied for the individual handicapped groups. For example, the socially maladjusted, who were overwhelmingly males with criminal records, tended to be quite young; of the 279 males in this category, 46.6 percent were under 21. By contrast, those with orthopedic handicaps had the highest proportion in the over 45 age group.

The handicapped trainees utilized special schools and the adult retraining courses of the Board of Education to a greater extent than all trainees, but the pattern for men and women differed considerably. Over two-thirds of the handicapped males but only 46 percent of the women were assigned to the adult retraining courses. The women used the ordinary vocational education schools and special schools heavily. Training in industry was given to 16 percent of each sex, about the same proportion as among all trainees.

On-the-job training was briefest; its trainees had an average of 24.7 weeks against 53.8 weeks for those in the special schools, 45.2 weeks in the vocational education courses, and 38.9 weeks in the adult training courses. Women's courses were shorter than men's on the average. Among males, the drop-out rate was highest (32.2 percent) for those attending the adult retraining courses; this group also had the highest rate of premature completion of courses due to obtaining employment in the occupation for which they had trained. Women tended to complete the full course more frequently than men, especially when attending the vocational education schools or adult training courses. The completion rate for handicapped women was 81 percent against 85 percent for all female retrainees. Handicapped males had a completion rate of 61 percent compared with 67 percent for all male trainees in the earlier study. The differential is small enough to afford satisfaction with the handicapped retrainees, especially when account is taken of their high rate of termination of training due to illness.

The location of training courses and their duration are influenced by the type of training chosen, and this in turn is related to the sex of the trainees and the nature of their handicaps. Thus, more than half the men took mechanics' courses which, in the Nordic occupational classification, are called workshops and structural metal work. They learned to be welders, riveters, borers, grinders as well as repair men for tractors and other machinery. More than half the women were trained in office and business skills, with textiles and related manufacturing skills a poor second.

The alcoholics and socially maladjusted, largely male, accounted for relatively few entrants to the technical or skilled courses; they were heavily concentrated (70 percent) in the workshops and structural metals courses. They had high drop-out rates (around 60 percent) and they often left or were discharged because of violation of the rules, lack of interest, or conflicts with students and instructors. Their subsequent unemployment rates were disporportionately high, and those who obtained employment took longer than other retrainees to get settled. Their record was far worse than that of the male retrainees classified as mentally ill and defective, whose drop-out rate of 34.7 percent reflected a high incidence of illness. Among the women, the mentally ill and defective showed the poorest record, since there were too few alcoholics and socially maladjusted among the female retrainees to make separate statistical groupings.

A particularly interesting part of the survey concerns the agency through which the 3,151 handicapped retrainees who were employed as of March 1965 found their first jobs after completing retraining. Just over three-fourths of the retrainees were placed by the Employment Service and another 2.3 percent obtained their jobs through officials of the training institutions. Over 10 percent used newspaper ads or called at factory gates while 5 percent relied on personal contacts. Former employers rehired 3.1 percent of the retrainees, and 1.8 percent started their own business. It should be noted that only 1.2 percent obtained positions with the firms which had provided on-the-job training, although 16 percent had taken this type of training. The hope that on-the-job trainees would be kept on as employees was not fulfilled.

One measure of the success of the vocational retraining courses was the high proportion (94 percent) of placements in open, competitive jobs, as of March 1965. The 6.3 percent who were placed in various types of created employment were a lower proportion than were assigned to such posts from the work assessment and work training institutions, described earlier.

Over one fifth of the retrainees were without jobs in March 1965; the rates were slightly lower for men than women. The northern forestry counties, which provided 30 percent of the retrainees, had only 23.5 percent of the unemployed, an indication of success in the policy of retraining northern unemployed in southern areas as a means of achieving mobility. A high correlation existed between failure to complete the retraining course and not having a job. In addition to the unemployed, a certain number of the retrainees were ill, caring for a household, or in other ways not in the labor market. Some of the unemployment arose because retraining had been in a field, such as textile manufacture, which in 1965 began undergoing rationalization and curtailment of employment. Thus, 37.2 percent of the retrainees in this and related industries were without jobs, against an average of 16 to 24 percent in the other industry groups.

Some calculations of the length of time between the end of retraining and the start of the first job showed that two thirds of the retrainees obtained work within 11 weeks after leaving their course. Men obtained work slightly more rapidly than women, workers in industry more rapidly than office or professional employees, and the orthopedically handicapped more rapidly than other groups, especially the alcoholics and socially maladjusted.

A comparison of the first job obtained with the retraining course showed that women (62.3 percent) were more likely to remain in the occupation for which they were retrained than men (54.9 percent). Almost three-fourths of the women remained with office work, but only half of the men stayed with workshop or structural metal jobs. Those retrained for the textile industry were particularly unlikely to find their first jobs in that field; women retrainees were severely affected.

A further follow-up of these rehabilitees as of March 1967 produced data on 2,063 persons in contrast to 4,049 in the original study. The new survey indicated that those who took and remained in jobs which were related to their vocational training changed jobs less frequently and were better paid than those who turned to other occupations, either initially or after trying a job for which they were trained. The lowest turnover rates occurred among those who were trained for technical and professional work and who were in such jobs. Male rehabilitees from the depressed northern forest counties showed the greatest tendency to seek work in another area. Among the 2,063 persons in the survey, 526 were on some kind of social benefit as a supplement to their wages or as a replacement if they were unemployed. At the time of the survey in March 1967, 597 of the retrainees were without work, most frequently because of illness.

General surveys of retrainees, whether handicapped or not, have shown a high proportion in the occupation for which they had trained, substantial numbers earning more than they had before training, almost half moving to another town or city after retraining, and lower unemployment rates among those in trades for which they were trained than among those who took other work in order to remain in their home area. The cost of retraining was about $3,200 to $3,400 per worker. The increased mobility of manpower and the improved situation of those in the areas from which the trainees moved were cited as benefits to the whole society.[23]

Studies such as these show weak points in the retraining courses, methods of selecting trainees, and follow-up procedures. The Swedish manpower authorities react quickly and effectively on the national and local level; improvement and expansion follow, not curtailment. Given the persistent labor shortages, the Swedish belief in employment rather than maintenance, and considering the high cost and problems of providing created employment (Chapters VIII, IX), the Swedish emphasis on retraining, especially in periods of increased unemployment, is understandable. Other countries have different values and conditions, but there is a general trend toward enlarged vocational training for the hard-to-employ in western Europe.

PLACEMENT

From the time they are identified, the hard-to-employ are potential candidates for employment in the competitive labor market. To a considerable extent, the authorities measure their success by the number of placements in the open market. The vast majority of the hard-to-employ at present are not given the special services de-

[23] Salzer, "Putting Him Where He Counts," *Sweden Today*, p. 44. For a discussion of the problems of computing costs of training, see Pierre Drouet, "Vocational Training Costs: Results of a Pilot Study and an Essay in Methodology," *International Labour Review*, February 1968, pp. 115–33. Svenska Handelsbanken, *Economic Review*, Index no. 10, 1968; National Labour Market Board, *Swedish Employment Policy 1967–68* (Summary in English of Annual Report), Stockholm, 1968, p. 130; Sweden, National Labour Market Board, "Sysselsättningsförhallanden M M Fram Till Mars 1967 För Arbetsvardssökande Med Arbetsmarknadsutbildning Avslutad Under April–December 1964," *Arbetsmarknadsstatistik*, no. 5b, 1969; Reports from U.S. Embassy, Stockholm.

scribed in the previous chapter—work testing and assessment, work experience in an IRU, and vocational training. Nor do most of the hard-to-employ ever see the counselors and other specialists described in Chapter II. They are usually interviewed and placed by ordinary placement officers, unassisted by the senior officials or other special personnel designated to assist with placement plans for difficult cases.

Certain exceptions should be noted. Some hard-to-employ are given job-placement services by the municipal welfare or social organizations which originally have charge of their cases. Usually, the local employment service is called in to assist or take responsibility for the actual placement. In the Netherlands, a local contact committee is established, consisting of representatives of the municipality, the Employment Service, and the central government. Other countries have similar arrangements for formal or *ad hoc* committees.

Great Britain has introduced an interesting type of placement officer in connection with its efforts to limit the number of unemployed on its welfare rolls. (The unemployed eligible for welfare are those who either have exhausted their unemployment insurance benefits or did not qualify for unemployment insurance.) In areas of labor shortage, the unemployed on welfare are referred to unemployment review officers of the Supplementary Benefits Commission, whose main function is to assist placement, but who may serve as counselors as well. An intensive experiment in the Brixton area of London, where unemployment has been relatively high and a sizeable concentration of immigrants exists, showed that a well-trained special placement officer could drastically reduce the number of claimants for benefit by finding them jobs. The 60 officers operating on a regional basis should be increased to 400, with one in every local office, according to the Civil and Public Services Association, an organization representing the clerical officers who examine claims for benefit.

Belgium, which has an official designation of difficult-to-place unemployed and an unusually large proportion of workers in this category, recently established special sections in the 29 regional Employment Services offices (ONEM) to deal with the hard-to-employ exclusively.[24] In countries where the physically and mentally handicapped are registered or are covered by special legislation, specialized placement officers of the Employment Service, usually called Disablement Resettlement Officers (DRO), have prime responsibility for the progress of a disabled individual from the hospital or home to ultimate job placement; conference of experts often assist the DRO.

Sweden is exceptional in that its Vocational Rehabilitation officers usually rely on the ordinary placement officers of the Employment Service. But Swedish clientele are not drawn from a register set up by law, as in Great Britain, West Germany, France, Holland, Belguim, Luxembourg, and Italy. In these countries, following the British lead, there may be a Disablement Resettlement Officer (DRO) in every large employment office. Britain also has specialized placing officers for the blind. Some countries rotate their personnel in the DRO function, while others select some for permanent duty.

Denmark's vocational rehabilitation system employs labor market specialists who perform part of the placement function. The Danish situation is special in that the Ministry of Labour has not been directly in charge of vocational rehabilitation, and trade unions have traditionally carried on much of the employment service function. Recently, legislation has been enacted to concentrate placement activity in the Ministry of Labour.

In addition to the disabled, other types of hard-to-employ are handled by specially trained or designated placement interviewers. Discharged prisoners or hard-to-place older workers may be directed to particular placement officers. In principle many countries reject the specialized approach because it might brand the hard-to-employ job-seekers as inferior labor.

Sweden has conducted a survey of successful placements in the competitive labor market during the first quarter of 1967 among applicants for work at the Vocational Rehabilitation Service offices in order to learn how the placements were made and whether personal

[24] Belgium, Ministère de l'Emploi et du Travail, Office National de l'Emploi, *Rapport Annuel, 1966,* Brussels, 1967, p. 29.

introductions to employers were used. Of the 40,000 applicants at the Vocational Rehabilitation Service offices during the first quarter of 1967, it was found that 6,194 were considered suitable for placement in the open market and that 2,793 were actually placed; of this number, slightly more than two-thirds were men. Among those placed, 30 percent had chiefly social handicaps and 11 percent had more than one handicap. Over 30 percent of the males and 42 percent of the females placed were under 25 years old.

The placement officers of the Employment Service made over two-thirds of all placements. About one-fifth of the jobs were located by staff members of the Vocational Rehabilitation Service which also made the placements, and the remaining 12 percent were made by the Vocational Rehabilitation Service following suggestions of suitable jobs by Employment Service officials. The relative importance of the several placement sources varied considerably according to the rehabilitants' disability, age, sex, and county. The general results appeared to justify leaving the primary responsibility for placement with the Employment Service, provided that the supplementary placement activities of the Vocational Rehabilitation Service were encouraged.

Only a small proportion, 16 percent of all placed and 18.6 percent of women placed, were personally introduced to their new employers. Much higher rates of personal introductions were found for certain categories: the multihandicapped, older workers, socially maladjusted women, and persons in the Stockholm area and in some northern counties. Three-fourths of the introductions were made by officials of the Employment Service or Vocational Rehabilitation Service, with the remainder through such people as vocational instructors or company officials. Sweden has been revamping its Employment Service in order to offer more assistance to the hard-to-employ.[25]

25 Sweden, Arbetsvårdsnytt, "Undersökning rörande arbetsvårdssökandes placering i arbete på öppna marknaden under första kvartalet 1967," *Arbetsmarknadsinformation,* V, 1, 1968, Stockholm, 1968; OECD, International Management Seminar on the Public Employment Services and Management, *Supplement to the Final Report,* Paris, 1966, p. 211. Sweden, *Arbetsmarknadspolitiken 1969/70,* Stockholm, 1968, pp. 46–51.

It is difficult to determine whether the Swedish placement officer who handles both regular and hard-to-employ cases is less effective than, for example, the British DRO who is specialized. Many other factors influence the number and type of placements of the hard-to-employ, and comparisons from country to country are misleading. However, in individual countries a specialized service such as the DRO may perform better than the whole of its Employment Service, especially if the Service has a low penetration rate or a poor image.

Great attention is given to the selection, education, preliminary training, and in-service training of the personnel involved in placement work and all other programs for the hard-to-employ in most western European countries. Expansion of a program is not undertaken until the staffing and capacity to deliver the services are provided. The allocation of money is not considered the prime requisite or an assurance that other factors will be forthcoming. The Netherlands, for example, meets shortages in some of these fields by employing promising but unqualified candidates and giving them paid leave to complete their degrees. Pay scales and other benefits for personnel are competitive with other occupations, and considerable numbers of men are attracted to such work.

The efficient functioning of permanent programs to aid the hard-to-employ in the northern European countries appears to be related to some general characteristics of these countries. We can point to the small size of the countries, their parliamentary systems, the power of central governments, the high quality of local government officials, the homogeneity of the population, good interagency cooperation, a comprehensive approach toward the hard-to-employ, and the high value set on social welfare and participation in work. Not least, there is a willingness and ability on the part of government agencies and their personnel to take a paternalistic attitude toward the hard-to-employ and an acceptance by the latter of a degree of direction and interference which might be resisted in other countries.

Placement Techniques

The techniques used to promote the placement and retention of the hard-to-employ are fairly similar from country to country. A key aspect is the continuous education of the Employment Service staff with regard to employment and occupational trends, local job opportunities and personnel practices, and the needs and views of individual firms in the locality. It has been observed in Sweden that job opportunities for the hard-to-employ have been adversely effected by the decline in the relative number of unskilled and light jobs, the trend toward larger industrial units, and the decrease in self-employment. A Swedish management representative emphasized that specific employment forecasts are necessary in order to direct hard-to-employ labor "into sectors of the labour market where there is less risk of their losing their jobs through over-severe competition." A survey conducted in 1966 by the National Labour Market Board among all industrial firms with 500 or more employees indicated that enterprises which were undergoing technical or organizational changes and were expanding employment were most likely to hire the hard-to-place, especially those whose handicaps were not severe.[26]

The flow of information and research is also important in conducting a general educational campaign to convince employers and the community that the hard-to-employ should be hired. Employers are supplied with information on the availability, capacities, and trainability of the hard-to-employ, as well as on subsidies for training and employing them and ways of minimizing extra pension, insurance, and other costs of hiring them.

[26] OECD, International Management Seminar on the Public Employment Services and Management, *Supplement to the Final Report*, p. 211; *Modern Swedish Labour Market Policy*, p. 51; Sweden, National Labour Market Board, "Anpassningsåtgärder för svårplacerad arbetskraft inom större industriföretag. Resultatet av en undersökning 1966 utförd inom AMS," *Arbetsmarknadsinformation*, M, 1, 1967, pp. 19–20.

Job development along general lines takes several forms. Employers are encouraged to undertake systematic job analyses so that excessive hiring standards are not formulated; to devise methods to evaluate job candidates fairly; to consider job redesign or modification of machinery and workplaces to accommodate handicapped or older workers; to find places for sheltered employment within the plant; and to undertake job reallocation to help existing workers as well as make room for others.

Good relations between employers and placement officers, frequent visits by the latter to factories and offices, participation of employers in the policymaking and practical operations of the Employment Service, and some interchange of personnel between business and the Employment Service are most conducive to effective job development. Sweden and West Germany are particularly effective in this area.

Job orders can be secured by personal visits to employers. For example, the Belgian specialized placement section for the hard-to-employ began to canvass employers in the last quarter of 1966. They visited 1,498 employers and produced 1,056 jobs orders, of which 415 were for the hard-to-employ. At the end of December, 358 hard-to-employ had been placed, including several older workers who had been unemployed for as long as 8 to 15 years.[27]

Job development for specific hard-to-employ individuals is time-consuming, costly, and tends to be especially undertaken by DROs on behalf of the registered disabled. Jobs are developed through visits, phone calls, letters, and responses to employers' newspaper advertisements. Welfare agencies often are active in job placement for their clients, usually with the aid of the Employment Service. The British National Assistance Board, now the Supplementary Benefits Commission, has used the participation of local employers in its committee work as a means of developing jobs for welfare clients. Holland forms local contact committees with representatives of several levels of government for the same purpose.

Sweden calls on employers to report suitable vacancies for the

[27] Belgium, Office National l'Emploi, *Rapport Annuel, 1966*, p. 29; OECD, *Promoting the Placement of Older Workers*, pp. 85–93.

hard-to-employ to the municipal offices, which are asked to inform the local employment service of residual openings. If employers are induced to offer employment on a probationary basis, some hard-to-employ may gain permanent jobs. Local tripartite employment committees have consultative functions and help in finding jobs for the hard-to-employ cases.

The construction of hostels near work centers by government or nonprofit organizations has proved a valuable means of opening job opportunities for various types of disabled persons who otherwise remained virtually unemployable. Interarea or national clearance of job openings, housing priorities for the unemployed, and the existence of mobility and commuter allowances offer other opportunities to develop jobs for the hard-to-employ. However, this tends to be a relatively immobile group. The Netherlands has made little use of its special mobility allowances for disabled workers.

Finally, personal efforts on behalf of hard-to-employ individuals, especially approaches to potential employers, are an important part of the placement officer's work. An unpublished Dutch description of the personal and direct approach to the employer is typical:

Special care is devoted to the introduction of the applicant to the potential employer. Preferably in a personal talk with the employer or personnel officer the essence of the background and data of the person concerned—with his knowledge and consent—is thoroughly discussed. This personal type of approach has more chance of success when it relates to the placement of workers who, for instance because of their age and the accompanying phenomena, do not fully meet the standards of the firm in question.

Some hard-to-employ clients are accompanied by a placement officer in the first interview. Studies are needed to compare the experience of workers given special placement services with similar workers routinely handled. The number placed, the type of jobs secured, the new wages in comparison with prior earnings, and general job satisfaction should be measured.

The Dutch procedures regarding persons who have come into conflict with the law or have been in prison are noteworthy. Since the end of World War II, the Netherlands has made a concerted effort to minimize the number sentenced to prison. Instead, the Dutch place most offenders on probation and use probation officers and psychiatrists to rehabilitate them for society. Thus the stigma of having served a prison sentence is avoided by many types of people who must bear it in other countries. With a rising population, Holland has had a declining prison population year after year. During 1966 no more than 7,500 persons spent time in prisons and, because of the very short sentences, only about 1,800 were imprisoned at any one time. Sweden, whose population is one-third smaller, has prison accommodations for over 6,000 persons.

In Holland probationers and ex-prisoners are aided in their search for employment by the five chief private probation societies whose 500 officers are paid by the Ministry of Justice. The probation officers may send their clients directly to jobs, but they are more likely to direct them to the local employment office where one placement officer is designated to handle such cases.

A distinctive feature of Dutch procedures is the deliberate concealment from the prospective employer of the prison or probation record in most cases. The protection of the worker is the foremost consideration. It is difficult for ex-prisoners or probationers who were teachers, civil servants, or in other professions to return to their former occupations, but officials agree that unskilled and skilled manual workers, the bulk of the cases, are easily placed.[28]

In addition to their extra efforts to find jobs for hard-to-employ clients, placement officers also make follow-up calls to check that the job adjustment has been satisfactory.

There are, of course, some individuals who do not respond to the efforts to place them. British authorities identified a type of hard-to-employ who resist all placement attempts. They tend to be unattached men living in hostels operated by the local authorities or voluntary agencies such as the Salvation Army. These unemployed men seem content with their aimless lives and poor standard of living on public assistance. They show no interest in the higher income available through work, even on part-time jobs.

The British study for the OECD Counselling Project also took

[28] OECD, *Manpower and Social Policy in the Netherlands,* Paris, 1967, p. 60; Interviews in the Netherlands, Ministry of Justice, Employment Service, and Probation Societies.

note of the fact that 34 of the 200 long-term unemployed men in the sample received a weekly social benefit of £9 or more, chiefly because they had many dependents. Since this sum was the same as the basic weekly rate of pay for day-shift unskilled work, excluding overtime and bonuses, a few unemployed men may have resisted jobs at the lowest level, especially if they had been concealing occasional earnings or illegal income while on social benefits. However, it has been found in Britain and other western European countries that unemployed family men welcome opportunities to upgrade skills and earnings, although they seem to be work-shy with regard to unskilled jobs which pay no more than social benefits.

"It is interesting to conjecture," the Ministry of Labour officials wrote, "what would happen if National Assistance allowance, which ensures the minimum subsistence standard, was not so readily available or was gradually reduced to the point of discontinuance." [29]

Partial moves in this direction have actually been made in Great Britain. In areas where jobs are plentiful, a rule was instituted that welfare allowances of the Supplementary Benefits Commission (the successor to the National Assistance Board) should be limited to four weeks for unemployed people under 45, who then face a review by a special officer to discover why they are unemployed. The initial restriction was placed on those without dependents, but it was extended to all undisabled unemployed under 45 when it appeared that most of them obtained jobs, with or without official help, when they knew their cases were to be reviewed. The unemployed who cannot be placed after interviews continue to receive supplementary benefits, but further review of their cases may be undertaken. The number of work-shy and fraudulent claims is expected to be reduced through these procedures.

Other countries have also reported that single men, the solitary drifters, are the hard-core of the work-shy. In the United States, many of these men are not even regarded as prospects for employment because they have not been given the prerequisite social serv-

[29] Great Britain, Ministry of Labour, *O.E.C.D. International Counselling Project,* Report on First Experimental Stage, pp. 11, 12, 14, 15, 17.

ices and because so many others are ahead of them in the hard-to-employ queue.

A more difficult group are the industrial injury pensioners whose income is fairly adequate and whose pensions would be reduced if they took up work. British studies have observed that equally incapacitated victims of automobile accidents are more receptive to efforts to rehabilitate them for work because their incomes are less adequate.[30] Again, attention may be called to the Scandinavian practice of granting only temporary benefits until it is established whether rehabilitation is possible. The withholding of disability pensions is a deterrent to the formation of "pension psychology."

In some countries, the fact that wages are very close to social benefits, particularly disability benefits, would not be accepted as a reason for refusing work. An attempt is made to maintain a significant differential between social benefits and wages, but in individual cases an overlap may occur. When this factor appears to cause persons to remain hard-to-employ, the authorities in, for example, West Germany, Sweden, and Holland, take a twin approach: pressure to the point of denying social benefits if suitable work is refused and personal investigations to ascertain that other causes are not responsible for a disinclination to work.

Public attitudes toward programs to aid the hard-to-employ and toward the hard-core unemployed themselves are very important in shaping the response of the work-shy and the success of the programs. General acceptance of social responsibility, which blends interfering kindness with stern supervision, is stronger in Scandinavia, the Netherlands, and West Germany than it is in Great Britain, France, Italy, Switzerland, Belgium, or the United States.[31] The existence of paternalistic forces in a country appears to result in a lower proportion of work-shy cases than occurs in countries where individual responsibility is highly valued.

[30] *Rehabilitation,* July–September 1961, p. 32; Great Britain, Department of Health and Social Security, *Annual Report 1968,* Cmd. 4100, HMSO: London, 1969, p. 251 ff.; *The Guardian* (London), September 17, 1969.

[31] Adrian Sinfield, *The Long-Term Unemployed,* OECD: Paris, 1968, pp. 58–62.

Another factor which is emphasized in Sweden's approach to the work-shy is the maintenance of full employment. It is claimed that the argument that unemployment is caused by people not wanting to work

will exist as long as the job opportunities are lacking, either owing to shortage of demand in the economy or owing to lack of labor market adjustments or owing to both conditions simultaneously. The only sure way to find out about this matter is the empirical approach. The Swedish experiences prove that the unemployed prefer jobs instead of taking benefits if jobs are available and the employment service never stops offering them the openings. In serious cases, when the offered jobs are clearly suitable, the benefits have to be withdrawn. However, sometimes the best solution is training and retraining to increase the power of initiative and self-confidence of the unemployed. It seems obvious that unemployment in the most cases represses the personality of the individual and gradually makes more difficult his adaptation to a new work.[32]

It should be noted that the European countries do not regard women with young children who live on public assistance as employable. If the women desire to work, they are given information and services, just as would be given to any woman not on social benefits. Some countries maintain or finance child care facilities to aid women who seek to work, but no special campaign is directed toward women on relief. It is also true that this type of recipient is relatively less important on western European public assistance rolls than in the United States.

Type of Placements

All of the authorities concerned with the placement of the hard-to-employ concede that full or overfull employment is more responsible for the absorption of the hard-to-employ than the exertions of placement officers. Labor shortages make workers acceptable who

[32] Nils Kellgren "An Active Labor Market Policy," in *Lessons from Foreign Labor Market Policies,* Subcommittee on Employment and Manpower of Committee on Labour and Public Welfare, U.S. Senate, 88th Congress, 2nd session, vol. 4, Selected Readings in Employment and Manpower, p. 1502.

are rejected in looser markets. Adrian Sinfield, in his study of unemployment in Shields in northeast England, comments that local employers turned down ex-prisoners and those with a history of mental illness because unemployment was relatively high in the area, but London firms, finding that their advertisements in a tight labor market were answered only by such persons, accepted them. The high degree of success in Holland in placing many mentally retarded in jobs directly from their special schools has been attributed to full employment, the excellent special schools, and the comprehensive Social-pedagogic Service which gives full assistance and aftercare in every aspect of living to the mentally retarded, beginning before they leave school and supporting them throughout their lives.

A study of the mentally retarded in England found that "under conditions of full employment, at least 20 percent of the adult defectives formerly classified as imbeciles may be capable of securing and holding employment in the open job market." [33] Moreover, their accident rate and rate of rejection of finished articles is often lower than that of other employees; their output is sometimes so great that the union and the other workers become uneasy. Yet, the prejudice against employing them persists and is set aside only when other workers are not available.

In West Germany, the head of the chief society to aid prisoners told the writer in the summer of 1966 when unemployment was minimal that employers were eager to hire released criminals who had taken vocational training courses and passed their examinations in prison because they preferred German workers to foreigners. At an interview later that year in The Hague, the assertion of a Dutch Probation Society official that no employment problem existed for ex-criminals was eloquently confirmed by a telephone call from an employer asking him to recommend a bookkeeper. The probation official said, regretfully, that he knew of no one who was out of work!

[33] Wallace W. Taylor and Isabelle W. Taylor, "Employment for the Mentally Retarded in England," *Employment Service Review*, September, 1966, p. 46; United States, Department of Health, Education, and Welfare, Public Health Service, Report of the Mission to the Netherlands by the President's Panel on Mental Retardation, Washington, 1962, pp. 57, 59, ch. VI.

The spirit of full employment was also vividly conveyed to the author in Stockholm when she went to an appointment at the regional Labor Market Board and was mistakenly directed to an eager placement officer. Before the error was cleared up, the officer gave assurances that a job would be found for the American despite her lack of Swedish.

It is not only the general state of labor demand that influences the rate of absorption of the hard-to-employ. The structure of the economy, particularly if it includes a relatively high proportion of jobs in smaller firms and a continuing high demand for unskilled workers in manufacturing and construction, increases the number of suitable places for the hard-to-employ. In most of the northern European countries persistent shortages of unskilled and manual workers have been reported.[34]

Citing the diversity of unskilled jobs available for the mentally retarded in Great Britain, some have claimed that the routine processes in industrial jobs make possible an increased scope of employment for the less able. But others, looking ahead, are fearful that technological advances will greatly limit the opportunities for those with less than average intelligence.[35]

Some questions have been raised about the quality of the jobs that are provided for the hard-to-employ in western Europe. The report on a recent Scandinavian conference noted that

[34] Beatrice G. Reubens, *The Hard-to-Employ: European Experience,* in Eli Ginzberg and others, *Manpower Strategy for the Metropolis,* New York, 1968, pp. 192–94; Detlev Zöllner, *Social Legislation in the Federal Republic of Germany,* Bad Godesberg, 1964, p. 12; OECD *Manpower and Social Policy in the Netherlands,* pp. 181, 182. Great Britain, Ministry of Labour, OECD International Counselling Project, *Report on First Experimental Stage,* p. 11; ILO, *International Differences in Factors Affecting Labour Mobility.* AUT/DOC/7, Geneva, 1966, p. 134; the Netherlands, Ministry of Social Affairs and Public Health, Directorate General of Manpower, *Report on the Findings of the Dutch Study as part of the OECD activity 16–17 "Social Adjustment",* The Hague, August 1966, p. 9.

[35] Wallace W. Taylor and Isabelle W. Taylor, "Employment for the Mentally Retarded in England," *Employment Service Review,* September 1966, pp. 44–47; ILO, *Manpower Programmes: I. . . . ,* p. 181.

one common feature in these countries is that vocational rehabilitation is predominantly directed towards manual occupations and often to one specific group of manual occupations. This, and other disadvantages . . . would appear to justify the view that labour welfare measures in the Nordic countries need to be broadened and developed.[36]

Specific complaints about the type of jobs available to them were voiced by men with prison or court records. Adrian Sinfield noted that such men in northeast England were able to get only heavy, dangerous jobs of short duration in nonunion enterprises. It was a source of bitterness that those who successfully concealed their prison records were able to obtain more satisfactory and permanent jobs. A probation officer in Holland said that some of the ex-prisoners and probationers believed that unattractive jobs were purposely reserved for them.

While much more information is needed on the type of job secured and the level of wages, it is clear that even the most advanced European countries are not yet as concerned about avoiding dead-end, low wage jobs for the hard-to-employ as are recent manpower programs and public policy statements in the United States.

Placement Results

Statistical information on placements of the hard-to-employ is limited. Perhaps the most useful data are those for the Swedish Vocational Rehabilitation Service. Table IV-I presents results for 1960 and 1965, a year of high full employment, and shows the changes which occurred between the two dates. Only the most difficult cases are referred to the Rehabilitation Service and it is likely that an equal or larger number of hard-to-employ are handled directly by placement officers, probably with a higher rate of placements in competitive labor markets.

If placement in competitive employments is the prime goal of vo-

[36] OECD, Scandinavian Regional Seminar on an Active Manpower Policy, *Final Report*, p. 26.

TABLE IV.1. Results of Vocational Rehabilitation, Sweden,
1960 and 1965

	1965	1960	Percentage Change 1960–1965
Total number applicants	67,819	31,359	116.3
Considered for placement in competitive employment	(16,904)	(11,898)	42.0
Placed in competitive employment	15,446	10,622	45.4
of which:			
Females	(3,500)	(2,406)	45.5
Orthopedically handicapped	(4,657)	(3,253)	43.2
Psychologically ill or defective	(2,946)	(2,153)	36.8
Socially Maladjusted	(2,219)	(892)	148.8
Alcoholics	(1,164)	(464)	153.0
Obtained work on their own	4,359	2,122	105.4
Aided to self-employment	1,849	1,800	2.7
Entered military service	15	40	−62.5
Given services to increase employability	15,265	6,571	132.3
Placed in created jobs	14,797	3,599	311.1
Rejected for vocational rehabilitation:			
because of limited work capacity	8,673	2,800	209.8
for other reasons	11,740	5,509	113.1

Source: Sweden, National Labour Market Board, Vocational Rehabilitation Division. Subtotals may not add to totals because individuals may have had more than one service in a given year or repeats of a single service.

cational rehabilitation activity, the Swedish performance leaves much to be desired. Placements in competitive employment rose comparatively little from 1960 to 1965 and actually declined from 1966 through 1968. Similarly, the number aided to self-employment hardly rose, despite augmented financial encouragement. However, those who found jobs on their own showed a large relative increase from 1960 to 1965 and constituted a substantial portion of the total. A significant growth occurred from 1960 to 1965 in placements in competitive jobs of alcoholics and the socially maladjusted, two groups which have received increased attention in recent years from the Vocational Rehabilitation Service. Data is needed on the character of the placements and their relation to the workers' previous employment and income.

The substantial increase in applicants from 1960 to 1965 and in succeeding years was more than matched by the rise in the number who were rejected for vocational rehabilitation. To be rejected for vocational rehabilitation is not a permanent judgment in Sweden; it reflects a current scarcity of facilities for improving employability or providing created employment. These rejections provide the basis for forecasts of how many additional places are required in the various services for those who cannot immediately or ever be placed in competitive labor markets.

It is anticipated that the constant increase in the number of applicants for vocational rehabilitation will continue because medical and social agencies are more aware of the possibilities of vocational rehabilitation and because a growing number of multihandicapped applicants, persons for whom adjustment to working life was previously considered impossible, now can be helped to participate in production. In addition, rapid technological and structural changes in the economy since 1965 have resulted in closures, cut-backs, or alterations of production which have released older and handicapped workers. As a result, it is estimated that, at a minimum, 15 to 20 percent of those who lose their jobs through closures or other changes in production must be referred for vocational rehabilitation services.[37]

From 1960 to 1965, placements in created jobs, described in Chapter IX, increased more than any other rehabilitation measure. This lead was maintained through 1968. It is regarded as more satisfactory to place workers on created jobs than to have them unem-

[37] Sweden, National Labour Market Board, *Swedish Employment Policy 1967–68,* (Reprinted from Annual Report, 1967–68), Stockholm, 1968, pp. 11–12.

ployed, out of the labor force, or in institutions under care. A very significant increase also occurred from 1960 to 1965 in the proportion offered work assessment, work experience, and vocational retraining, and this trend has continued in subsequent years. It would be particularly interesting to follow up such persons' subsequent work history to see whether they had better records than comparable workers who had not been given services.

The Netherlands, with a labor force about one-fifth larger than Sweden's in 1965, had a total of 13,330 registered disabled persons who were classified as placeable in competitive employment. During the year, 4,951 of these were placed by the DROs. Socially handicapped unemployed males (*minder geschikten*) averaged about 5,000 in 1966. A total of 3,358 placements was made during 1966.[38] Belguim had 7,772 placements of the hard-to-employ of all types in 1966, but at the end of 1966 there still were 42,079 unemployed who were classified as having partial or very reduced employability.[39]

In 1965 the West German rehabilitation service for the severely disabled processed 54,204 cases, of whom 15,029 were placed in work and 4,769 found jobs or on-the-job training positions for themselves. These numbers are similar to the Swedish totals, which relate to a much smaller labor force. Over 12,000 German applicants were rejected as incapable of being rehabilitated or having poor attitudes, 411 were referred to other social institutions, and more than 7,000 cases were closed because of withdrawal by the applicants.

The Swedish vocational rehabilitation record suggests that as a country discovers and utilizes more of its residual labor supply, the single-minded objective of placement in competitive employment cannot be maintained, even under full employment conditions and a highly developed labor market policy. We will consider next some modifications of free placement which certain countries have adopted.

[38] Unpublished data from the Netherlands, Ministry of Social Affairs and Public Health.
[39] Belgium, Office National de l'Emploi, *Rapport Annuel, 1966*, pp. 28, 29.

V | Quota and Reserved Employment: Great Britain

Several western European countries do not rely entirely upon the placement techniques described in the previous chapters to provide jobs in the competitive labor market for their hard-to-employ. Legal compulsion is also used selectively to encourage or insure the hiring of specific categories of workers.

By far the most important method, in terms of numbers of workers affected, is the legal requirement that employers hire a given percentage of their total staff from a designated group of hard-to-employ workers. Called the quota system, this method of providing jobs is supplemented by other legal forms which either reserve specific jobs or give preference to hard-to-employ workers for particular posts. In several countries, these legal obligations are imposed on government agencies and public enterprises as well as private employers.

The belief that certain individuals should be guaranteed employment on a compulsory or preferential basis is an outgrowth of war and has existed in some western European countries at least since the end of World War I.[1] As an expression of public sympathy and moral obligation to those whose earning capacity had been impaired by war service, legislation was passed to set aside a certain proportion of private and public jobs for disabled veterans. In addition, certain occupations were reserved entirely or partially for disabled

[1] "The Legal Obligation to Employ the Disabled," *International Labour Review*, March 1957, pp. 246–64.

veterans, and entry to some kinds of public employment was facilitated by reductions in the physical or mental qualifying standards or by other preferential treatment.

A parallel development in some countries stipulated that workers who suffered industrial injuries should be reemployed by the responsible employer and that such employment might be counted toward the employer's quota of disabled veterans under certain circumstances. While the primary emphasis was on aid to those whose working capacity had been directly affected by war service, some countries also considered war widows and orphans as suitable candidates for quota or preferential employment.

The desire to reintegrate the disabled into the world of work was an important motive for other interwar legislation, but by comparison with the current period, earlier efforts must be considered weak and partial. Measures establishing quota or preferential employment were in part a compensation for the inadequacy of social benefit programs—unemployment compensation, disability and sickness benefits and pensions, and welfare assistance. One example, not involving the war disabled, is a French law, enacted in 1940 as an outgrowth of the depressed 1930s; it provided that heads of households with dependents should be given priority in employment. However, it has not been necessary to implement this protective legislation.

Since the end of World War II, much additional legislation has been enacted which extends, supplements, or replaces the older laws on obligatory quota employment, or, in some countries, introduces it for the first time. However, the principle of quota employment is resolutely opposed in parts of western Europe, notably Switzerland and the Scandinavian countries. The Netherlands, which enacted a quota law in 1947, has not felt that public opinion or employment conditions warranted the enforcement of its act.

In the larger countries of western Europe the heightened interest in quota employment for specific categories of the hard-to-employ, namely, the physically and mentally handicapped, has not led to an extension of the quota system to other types of hard-to-employ, such as older workers. Belgium is exceptional in that serious consideration has been given to a quota system for the older unemployed who constitute a particularly large proportion of the jobless; they are entitled to almost unlimited unemployment benefits under the Belgian system. West Germany considered but has not adopted a proposal to require employers to hire one salaried employee over 55 for every ten salaried employees under that age. The Swedish construction industry has had a quota of 25 percent for older workers, but this is not official or statutory and the idea is not widely approved in Sweden, which has no quota system as such.

The French Commission which issued the Laroque Report on older people opposed quotas. In Britain the National Advisory Committee on the Employment of Older Men and Women opposed the imposition of legislative restraints or even voluntary commitments by employers to hire a specific percentage of older people because such measures would suggest that there was something special and by inference possibly uneconomic about hiring older workers, the majority of whom require no special preference. In Sweden it was feared that a quota might become a maximum standard, even if additional jobs were available for older people. Many countries have tended to reject any singling out of older unemployed workers on the ground of age alone, even in voluntary placement activities.[2]

Although the postwar legislation on quota employment has not

[2] Interviews in Sweden, Denmark, the Netherlands, Belgium, France, Italy, West Germany, Great Britain. Irvin Sobel and Richard C. Wilcock, *Placement Techniques for Older Workers,* OECD: Paris, 1966, pp. 58, 61–62, 64; Organization for Economic Cooperation and Development, (OECD), *Age and Employment,* Paris, 1962, p. 16; International Labour Office, (ILO), *Report of the Director-General, Part 1: Older People,* Geneva, 1962, pp. 38–39, 44; OECD, International Labour Seminar on an Active Manpower Policy, *Supplement to the Final Report,* Paris, 1964, pp. 17–18; OECD, Regional Seminar, *The Employment of Older Workers,* Paris, 1966, p. 7; France, Haut comité consultatif de la population et de la famille, *Politique de la vieillesse,* Rapport de la commission d'étude des problèmes de la vieillesse, la Documentation Française, Paris, 1962; ILO, *Manpower Adjustment Programmes: I. France, Federal Republic of Germany, United Kingdom,* Labour and Automation, Bull. no. 4, Geneva, 1967, p. 113; Sweden, National Labour Market Board, *Medelålders och äldre arbetskraft,* Report by a Working Party, Stockholm, 1960.

encompassed additional types of hard-to-employ workers, it has shown an enlarged concern for those it does protect. The most conspicuous trend of the new legislation has been to broaden the eligibility for quota employment to include all who are physically or mentally handicapped, without seeking a war-related cause. Moreover, the mentally ill and retarded have received increasing attention. Another marked characteristic of the recent legislation and practice has been the emphasis on vocational rehabilitation and training of the disabled which will develop their highest capacities and qualify them for skilled, well-paid jobs under the quota schemes.

Finally, the most advanced programs rely upon persuading employers rather than forcing them to accept the handicapped. Well-planned rehabilitation programs, careful matching of jobs and workers, and assistance in the adaptation of workplaces enable the most successful quota employment schemes to obtain employers' cooperation in accepting referrals of the disabled.

The legal obligation to provide employment for certain categories of the physically and mentally disabled seems to be the chief method of assisting the hard-to-employ in several western European countries, judged by the number of beneficiaries. Close to two-million persons hold their jobs under quota employment schemes in five western European countries alone—Great Britain, West Germany, Luxembourg, France, and Italy.[3] Of course, many of those on quota jobs would be employed at the same level or in slightly inferior positions even if the quota laws did not exist. There is no evidence that the quota system provides worse jobs for some than they could obtain on their own. Those disabled who feel they can do better for themselves outside of the quota system need not register as disabled.

Though the principles of the quota system are much the same wherever it is used, the individual systems which are examined in this and the next chapter vary considerably in the burden imposed on employers, the degree of compulsion, and the extent of employer compliance.

[3] Belgium is in the process of setting quotas through agreements of industry-trade union committees in about 80 industry branches.

Great Britain has one of the least complicated quota systems. Before World War II, apart from voluntary agencies, the British had relied upon two official but noncompulsory schemes to help ex-servicemen obtain work—the King's National Roll and grants to enterprises which employed severely disabled men. The King's Roll, originated in 1919, was a list of firms, maintained by the Ministry of Labour, which voluntarily employed a certain percentage of disabled World War I veterans. The government also was involved in schemes for the employment of the blind, a group long favored in Britain; aid was given without regard to the cause of blindness.[4]

Unburdened by extensive prewar government programs for particular groups of disabled or by a quota scheme for World War I disabled servicemen, Great Britain initiated its quota system in 1944. The Disabled Persons (Employment) Act of 1944 made no mention of war disabilities; any cause of disability made one eligible. The Act imposed on all private employers of twenty or more the obligation to employ a certain proportion of registered disabled workers. To qualify for registration as a disabled person (RDP) in Britain, a worker must be substantially handicapped in obtaining or keeping employment or self-employment, he must have a disablement likely to last at least a year after registration (before 1958, six months), he must be seeking paid employment or self-employment with a reasonable prospect of obtaining and keeping it, he must normally be resident in Great Britain, and he cannot be a full-time patient in a hospital or similar institution, an inmate of a prison, or a person of habitual bad character. Medical evidence is almost always required both for registration and placement. Registration is entirely voluntary.

Applications for the disabled register are passed on by the Disablement Resettlement Officer (DRO) in the local Employment Service office, and doubtful cases are referred to a panel of the local Disablement Advisory Committee whose recommendation is forwarded to the Secretary of State for Employment and Productivity (for-

[4] British Information Services, *Rehabilitation and Care of the Disabled in Britain,* London, May 1965, p. 3; *International Labour Review,* November 1922, pp. 825–27; March 1957, p. 253.

merly the Minister of Labour) for final decision. The Advisory Committee is a local body consisting of an independent chairman, representatives of employers and workers, and other citizens with experience and interest in the problems of the disabled. Although they lack the power of final decision, the three-hundred local committees are influential in shaping final opinions.

Registration lasts for one year to ten years, depending on the nature of the disability and other individual circumstances, and reregistration is granted if the eligibility conditions are still met. A worker who remains with the same employer continues to count toward the employer's quota, even if the worker's registration has expired and is not renewed. Since 1958 it has been possible for a person to ask to be removed from the register before the expiration of his registration period. Pensioners of World War I have been accepted on the register easily; they have permanent registration until their pensions cease or they ask to have their names removed and, along with other ex-service men and women, they have priority in placement over other equally qualified disabled workers.

The Disabled Persons Register is divided into two sections. The first part, comprising 88 to 90 percent of the total register, consists of those deemed suitable for ordinary employment. The second part includes those classified as so disabled that they are unlikely to obtain employment except under sheltered conditions. The British decision to exclude the severely disabled from the quota system and provide permanent substitute employment for them is an important factor in the cooperative attitude of employers.

The employment quota for registered disabled workers has been set at 3 percent of total staff for all liable firms except ships' crews, which have the understandably low quota of 0.1 percent. Public and government employment is excluded from the quota system. A reduction in the quota may be sought by an employer who can demonstrate that the circumstances of his business require a lower percentage. After consideration by the Disablement Advisory Committee and a decision by the Secretary of State for Employment and Productivity, approval of a reduction may be granted for a period of twelve months.

Most disabled workers in the quota system are employed at

normal wage rates, but an employer covered by the Wages Councils Act of 1959 or the Agricultural Wages Acts may request a permit to pay less than the statutory minimum rate to a disabled worker whose productivity is demonstrably lower than average. (About one-sixth of all employees are covered by the Wages Councils and Boards which evolved from an Act of 1909 designed to eradicate sweated labor and which presently provide minimum wage rates in low-wage industries with weak trade unions.) During 1968, Wages Councils issued 37 new permits and renewed 88 permits for the employment of individual handicapped workers at rates below the statutory minima. The permits for 61 workers were cancelled.

An employer who does not meet his quota is not in violation of the law, but he may not hire any worker who is not registered as disabled without a permit issued by the Department of Employment and Productivity. If the permit is refused, the employer can appeal to the Disablement Advisory Committee. An employer is forbidden to discharge a registered disabled person without reasonable cause if the firm is below quota or would fall below after the discharge. The law provides fines or imprisonment for violations, but these penalties have rarely been threatened or used.

When the quota was first enforced in 1946, employers turned to their existing employees to discover how many could be registered as disabled. In those early years, employers often were the chief sponsors of registration, and the bulk of a firm's quota tended to be filled from those already in jobs. Since then, the DRO's responsibility as regards the quota has been to fill vacancies for employers, serve new or expanding firms, accept registrations from young disabled people reaching school-leaving age and adults who become disabled, re-register those with expiring registrations, and obtain satisfactory quota employment for the unemployed registered disabled.

THE COMPOSITION OF THE REGISTER

A growing population might be expected to result in an increasing registration of disabled persons over the years. Instead, after reaching a peak registration of 936,196 in 1950, the British register showed a marked decline thereafter, settling around 650,000 in re-cent years. The decrease occurred chiefly among men, particularly the surviving pensioners of World War I who are now mostly re-tired from work. Failure to re-register by those who felt con-fident of holding their jobs without aid was another cause of the drop in the register.

Older ex-servicemen have dominated the register. In April 1968, slightly less than half of the 560,277 adult males on the register were ex-servicemen, although only 97,377 were classified as having service-connected disabilities. The remaining 94,511 on the register consisted of 90,542 women (953 with service-connected disabili-ties), 2,159 boys, and 1,810 girls. In April 1965, males over 50 years old constituted 60 percent of all male registrants, who in turn were a very high percentage of the total register of 658,925. Al-though the registers of other countries are not fully comparable, they seem to have a greater representation of younger people and in some countries of women also.

From the outset, the disabled persons register has consisted pri-marily of those with physical disabilities. Not until December 1959 were "certain mentally disordered persons" permitted to register at all. In April 1968, only 12 percent of the registered were listed as having a nervous or mental disorder as the primary cause of disable-ment at the time of registration. It should be recognized, however, that the cause of disablement at the time of registration may not be the chief handicap to employment or the main or only current cause of disablement. The proportion of mentally disabled on the register in Britain has not grown as much as might have been expected in view of medical advances, public acceptance, and employment op-portunities, particularly in comparison with the experience of such countries as Holland, Sweden, and Denmark. A higher proportion of younger and female registrants also results when special efforts are made to cover the mentally retarded and ill.

Occasionally charges are made that persons who seek to register as disabled are refused by the DRO at the local office of the Em-ployment Service. Even if some refusals have actually occurred, it still is not clear whether the rejections involved too great or too slight a disability to meet the legal requirements. Presumably, the complaints chiefly concern those with slight disabilities, since the reports often conclude by stating that the rejected individuals obtained employment subsequently without the aid of the DRO.

It is far more likely that qualified disabled unemployed will be overlooked. When the National Assistance Board began an experimental program in 1960 to give medical examinations to able-bodied recipients of assistance who had been out of work for six months or more, it found that over 10 percent of the group were eligible for registration as disabled. As the medical tests became general over the years, smaller proportions were turned over to the register, but every year some eligible cases were discovered which the interviewing officers at the Employment Service had missed. Similarly, the OECD Counselling Study in Britain turned up several cases which should have been on the disabled register. Sinfield has also cited several recent British studies which assert that people who need to be on the register are unregistered through choice, sometimes due to their doctors' ignorance or doubts about the value of registration.[5]

How many unregistered but eligible disabled unemployed are there who could benefit from quota employment? Such persons would be found both among the registered unemployed and among those on the fringes of the labor market who have ceased to register as unemployed or who have never registered. For the peripheral group there is little information, but much can be learned about the unregistered disabled unemployed from the special survey on October 1964 by the Ministry of Labour, which has permitted its unpublished data to be presented here.

[5] Adrian Sinfield, *The Long-Term Unemployed*, MS/S/67. 125, OECD: Paris, 1967, pp. 21, 65; Great Britain, *Ministry of Labour Gazette*, June 1965, p. 279; July 1964, pp. 280–81; March 1967, p. 227; April 1967, p. 306; July 1966, p. 393; data from the British Ministry of Labour (now the Department of Employment and Productivity); Great Britain, Ministry of Labour, *OECD International Counselling Project*, Report on First Experimental Stage, 1st February to 30th April, 1965, London, 1965, p. 10; Great Britain, National Assistance Board, *Annual Reports*, 1960–66; *Employment and Productivity Gazette*, July 1968, p. 559.

Of a total of 312,930 unemployed in October 1964, 43,400 were section 1 Registered Disabled Persons (RDP) and 6,260 were section 2 RDPs. Some 13,360 other unemployed were classified as disabled within the meaning of the law but were not on the register. The unregistered disabled persons had disproportionate numbers of women, especially married women. Their disinclination to make a formal admission of disability has been recognized. Regionally, the unregistered disabled were more highly concentrated in several areas of labor shortage than were the section 1 RDPs, which suggests that a scarcity of jobs was not the primary cause of the failure to register as disabled. In addition, 16,870 other unemployed not eligible for the disabled register were considered likely to have difficulty in obtaining employment primarily because of a physical or mental handicap. Thus, for 50,000 unemployed who were on the disabled register, there were 30,000 others who probably could have benefited from registration.

Another way of examining the adequacy of the coverage of the register is to consider the unemployed whose primary cause of unemployment in October 1964 was a physical or mental handicap. Of 60,400 so classified, only 37,560 or 62.5 percent, were RDPs. Some who were not RDPs may have had physical or mental problems which could have been eliminated through medical treatment and they therefore did not qualify for registration.

On the other hand, some registered disabled persons, although fulfilling the basic requirements of registration, have relatively minor physical or mental handicaps; a fair part of the quota is filled with such cases, and they are also found among the unemployed RDPs. In October 1964 the primary obstacle to reemployment for about one-fourth of the unemployed RDPs was something other than their physical or mental condition. Age, lack of local work opportunities, and poor work attitudes were the chief alternative reasons given. These unemployed undoubtedly had multiple handicaps and were classic hard-to-employ cases.

Voluntary registration as a disabled person in Great Britain opens the door to intensive services by the DRO, special programs to improve employability, and quota placement. Most of these services are not available without registration. How adequate is the register in terms of its own mandate and in terms of the needs of the hard-to-employ? We have seen that considerable numbers of disabled persons—registered unemployed, other jobseekers on the fringes of the labor market, as well as some in jobs—fail to take advantage of their right to register as disabled. To the extent that they or their medical advisers are not sufficiently informed of the eligibility regulations and the benefits, a general educational and outreach campaign and specific instructions to regular Employment Service interviewers might be helpful. But if there is some feeling among nonregistrants that the DROs are not helpful or that training will not be given or jobs found, an investigation of individual cases or perhaps certain local areas might clear the air and increase voluntary registrations.

Another group whose unemployment is attributed primarily to physical or mental handicaps appears not to qualify currently for registration as disabled. Studies in depth by the OECD Counselling Project and the National Assistance Board suggest that many could benefit from being handled by the DRO instead of the regular interviewer. It would seem that a broadened administrative interpretation of the law rather than amended legislation would be needed to include this group. Even if they are not eligible for quota employment but simply have access to the DRO and all his special services, they would benefit.

Finally, some of the hard-to-employ unemployed whose multiple problems may include minor physical or mental handicaps could be helped by being referred to the disabled register and the DRO. This broadened eligibility might require legislation, but it is interesting to note that many employed persons have been accepted on the disabled register on the basis of a very slight physical or mental disability. The unemployed who are hard-to-employ for reasons which do not primarily involve disability need not be made eligible for quota employment. However, their inclusion on the disabled register, which might be given a broader name, would afford them access to the DRO and his special services. It could be argued that a new and somewhat parallel structure should be established for those hard-to-employ who do not qualify for the disabled register as presently constituted, and that the register should be left unmodified. However, the institutions to which the register is related, such as the Industrial Rehabilitation Units, are already moving toward a broader concept of the hard-to-employ. Moreover, the DRO service probably is the best base on which to build the necessary expansion of personnel. A final argument for expanding the coverage of the register is the wealth of evidence already cited that multiple handicaps and personality inadequacy must be treated along with clearly definable physical and mental disabilities.

UNEMPLOYMENT EXPERIENCE OF THE DISABLED

Unemployment is in every way more serious for the disabled than for other jobless workers. In the first half of the 1960s unemployment among those on the disabled persons register who are classified as suitable for ordinary employment (section 1) ranged between 35,000 to 40,000 in the summer months and 50,000 to 60,000 in winter. The number rose to near 70,000 in the recession years, 1966–68, and there was less seasonal variation. The over-all unemployment rate of the registered disabled is four to five times higher than that of the labor force as a whole. Thus, in August 1966 when the general unemployment rate was 1.3 percent, the rate for the registered disabled was 6.6 percent. In April 1967, the higher general rate of 2.4 percent was matched by 8.9 percent for the disabled.[6] These rates might be higher if all eligibles were registered as disabled.

Not only the amount of unemployment but also its duration is more burdensome to the disabled unemployed than to the unemployed in general. According to the survey in October 1964, more than half of the RDPs had been out of work for one year or more, in contrast to under one-third of the total unemployed. Almost 70

[6] Data from the Disabled Persons Branch, Ministry of Labour, Great Britain. The unemployment rates cover both sections 1 and 2 RDPs; Section 2 RDP unemployed usually are excluded from unemployment statistics.

percent of the RDPs had been out of work for six months or more and three-fourths of these had had no jobs at all during the previous year; the respective percentages for the whole group were 46.3 and 60. RDPs also had more unemployment over the preceding three years than the entire group and a good deal more illness.

Other characteristics of the registered disabled unemployed are also adverse to reemployment. In October 1964, a higher proportion (43.2 percent) were laborers than among the unemployed as a whole (32.4 percent) and relatively fewer of the RDPs were clerical, administrative, technical, or professional workers, the stable occupations. The RDPs were older on the average than the total unemployed and considerably less willing to move to work opportunities beyond daily traveling distance. They had had less rehabilitation and training during the preceding year; a higher proportion had never had any formal training; they were considered less able to benefit from training for semiskilled work; and they were deemed less suitable for government vocational training than the total unemployed. With all of these unfavorable circumstances, it is to be expected that fewer of the RDP unemployed than of the whole group would be judged likely to obtain work without difficulty; only 4.4 percent of the RDPs (section 1) had favorable prospects, against 23.2 percent of the total unemployed.

Placements by the Employment Service of registered disabled have numbered around 70,000 a year, including repeats. The Disablement Resettlement Officer (DRO) is the key person in the placement of unemployed registered disabled persons in quota jobs. The DRO does not call an employer and say: "Look here, you are below quota. You must take this man." Rather, the DRO carefully surveys all of his openings and his candidates for employment and tries to match them as well as possible. He uses an employer's under-quota status primarily as a means of approach. The implied element of compulsion is rarely present, yet one cannot say that the placement process is identical to that for hard-to-employ persons not covered by a quota law.

Not all placement of the registered disabled is through the quota system. Perhaps as many as one-third of the 600,000 registered disabled work for employers who are not subject to the quota system, either because they have fewer than twenty employees or because they are public or quasi-public agencies.

Central government departments have been a good source of jobs for the registered disabled, and usually have employed more than the 3 percent of staff required of eligible private employers. The difficulty in recent years has been that while the number of nonindustrial central government employees increased year by year, from 627,127 in October 1960 to 745,630 in October 1966, the number of available unemployed registered disabled was stable or declining. As a result, the number of disabled employed in government nonindustrial posts dropped steadily from 26,554 to 21,619, from 4.2 percent to 2.8 percent of the total, over the six years 1960–66. Government industrial employment has not risen as much, but the number of disabled employees declined from 14,768 in 1960 to 11,322 in 1966, or from 4.2 percent to 3.2 percent of the total. By October 1967 there was a small increase in the total number of disabled employees in industrial and nonindustrial establishments of central government, and they constituted 3 percent of the total. When employment opportunities for the disabled are favorable, few choose government jobs, and government departments do not voluntarily hire the most disabled who remain unemployed even under severe labor shortages.

COMPLIANCE WITH QUOTAS

Private employers who are legally subject to the quota law have also found that full employment creates over-all and local shortages of suitable unemployed registered disabled. In July 1965 liable employers throughout Britain maintained a 2.7 percent quota instead of 3 percent, and only slightly more than half of all liable firms employed 3 percent or more of quota workers (Table V.1). At the two extremes of compliance, some 9 percent of the firms overfulfilled their quotas by employing 5 percent of more RDPs, while 10.6 percent of the eligible firms had not satisfied the 3 percent quota at any time in the past five years. Even if every unemployed registered disabled person had been placed, a considerable number of firms would have remained below quota. There is therefore scope for increasing the number on the register by an active campaign to enlist those already eligible as well as by a broadened interpretation of eligibility.

TABLE V.1. Employment of Registered Disabled Persons by Liable Firms, by Region, Great Britain, July 1965

	Average Percentage of Employment Counting Toward Quota Among Liable Firms	Percentage of Firms Satisfying Quota	Percentage of Liable Firms with 5% or More of Registered Disabled Persons	Percentage of Firms not Meeting Quota at any Time During Preceding Five Years
Great Britain	2.7	53.2	9.0	10.6
London and Southeast	2.6	46.6	7.7	14.1
Eastern and Southern	2.6	49.7	8.4	12.2
South Western	3.0	57.1	12.0	7.9
Midlands	2.7	51.5	8.3	11.8
Yorkshire and Humberside	3.0	58.2	8.8	5.8
North Western	2.8	62.2	10.4	5.9
Northern	2.7	58.4	9.7	9.1
Scotland	2.7	53.5	9.0	12.0
Wales	3.4	68.4	13.8	4.0

Source: Disabled Persons Branch, Ministry of Labour, Great Britain.

The regional record of compliance by firms and data on the distribution of quota employment and unemployment raise some questions about the desirability of a uniform national quota. Employers in areas of relatively high unemployment seem to be more willing or able to hire the disabled than those in areas of labor stringency. Table V.1 shows a consistently better compliance record for employers in Wales and the Northern and North Western regions than in labor-short London, the Midlands, and the Eastern and Southern regions. But this is an incomplete picture. We must also examine other regional information on the distribution of the labor force, the registered disabled, quota employment, and unemployment.

Table V.2 suggests that the registered disabled are not distributed regionally as is the labor force and that three of the four northern regions of higher than average unemployment carry a disproportionate burden of disabled; Scotland is the exception here. Not unexpectedly, areas which have a good deal of coal mining and other heavy industry tend to have disproportionate numbers of registered disabled, while those with diversified industry and services start out with a relatively smaller demand for quota places.

The second conclusion is that the regional distribution of quota employment is even more out of line with the distribution of the total labor force than is the total disabled register. (No information is available on the regional distribution of the employment of the registered disabled in enterprises which have no legal quota obligation: public and government enterprises and agencies, and private employers with fewer than twenty workers).

The RDPs eligible for quota jobs were best off in the London area, which provided 36.3 percent of the nation's 404,833 quota jobs, although the region had only 19.2 percent of the registered disabled, 25.1 percent of the total labor force, and the poorest quota performance in the country. This paradox arises because the London region has a high proportion of firms and a large volume of employment subject to the quota regulations. If they ever are to be able to fill their quotas, London employers either must draw from a larger pool of disabled or must be given lower quotas.

A final conclusion is that the northern regions which have a disproportionate share of the registered disabled tend to have a still more disproportionate share of the country's unemployed disabled. Furthermore, in these regions the disabled unemployed constitute a larger share of all unemployed than they do in the more prosperous regions.

In Wales employers comply with the quota more fully than any

TABLE V.2. Employment and Unemployment, All Workers and Registered Disabled, Great Britain, 1965

	Total Labor Force (employee status)[a] June 1964	Registered Disabled Persons Sec. 1 and Sec. 2[b] April 1965	Quota Employment of RDP Sec. 1 July 1965	Unemployment among All Workers June 1965	Unemployment of RDP Sec. 1[a] July 1965	Ratio to All Unemployed of RDP Sec. 1 Unemployed[a] June 1965	Unemployment Rate RDP	
							Total Sec. 1, 2 June 1965	RDP June 1965
Great Britain	23,120,000	658,925	404,833	276,142	36,699			
Percentage Distribution								
All Regions	100.0	100.0	100.0	100.0	100.0	13.7	1.2	6.7
London and Southeast	25.1	19.2	36.3	15.7	11.7	10.2	0.7	4.1
Eastern and Southern	11.4	10.3	8.8	7.6	7.9	13.5	0.8	4.8
South Western	5.7	6.0	4.3	5.9	4.4	11.3	1.2	6.8
Midlands	15.7	16.1	15.3	9.7	11.0	19.3	0.7	4.8
Yorkshire and Humberside	9.6	10.5	8.2	7.1	11.5	15.4	1.0	6.9
North Western	13.1	15.1	12.3	15.6	18.0	14.7	1.4	7.1
Northern	5.7	6.8	4.0	10.2	11.4	15.8	2.2	11.3
Scotland	9.5	9.7	7.5	20.3	14.5	10.6	2.6	10.4
Wales	4.3	6.2	3.3	7.8	9.6	16.1	2.2	10.4

Source: Data from the Disabled Persons Branch, Ministry of Labour, Great Britain; Ministry of Labour Gazette, June 1965, p. 253; July 1965, p. 312; July 1966, p. 146. Totals may not add up to 100.0 percent because of rounding.

[a] Data refer to regional boundaries in effect prior to April 1965. Since the boundaries of four regions were changed in April 1965, comparability with some of the other columns is slightly affected for London, Eastern and Southern, Midlands, and Yorkshire and Humberside.

[b] Data do not indicate whether regional boundaries are those in effect prior to or after April 1965.

135

others, but the net result is still unfavorable to the disabled. Because Wales has a greater initial burden of disability as well as a lower proportion of firms and total employment subject to the quota, Welsh employers provided only 3.3 percent of all quota jobs in the country, although Wales had 6.2 percent of the nation's registered disabled and 4.3 percent of its labor force. Furthermore, the Welsh RDP section 1 unemployed constituted 9.6 percent of Britain's disabled unemployed, a higher proportion than Wales's share of total unemployment, which was disproportionately high at 7.8 percent. Finally, the ratio of the Welsh RDP unemployed to the total unemployed in Wales was one of the highest of the regional ratios (Table V.2).

REGIONAL DIFFERENCES AMONG THE DISABLED UNEMPLOYED

Just as it was shown earlier that the characteristics of all unemployed RDPs compare unfavorably with those of the unemployed as a whole, so do the characteristics of the unemployed RDPs who live in the northern areas of higher general unemployment compare unfavorably with the unemployed RDPs from the more prosperous south. To sharpen and simplify the contrast, data on section 1 RDPs will be presented for the two regional extremes—Wales and London.

In the October 1964 survey, Wales had a larger share of the RDP unemployed than of the total unemployed. In contrast, the London area had 11.8 percent of the RDP unemployed, but 15.4 percent of the total unemployed. However, a slight offset was provided by the 13,360 disabled unemployed who were unregistered but qualified as RDPs, since London had 18.9 percent of the group and Wales only 8.8 percent.

The RDP unemployed in Wales were far more subject to long-term unemployment than were the London RDPs. Less than one-third of the latter were out of work for a year or more, but three-fifths of the unemployed Welsh RDPs were in this category (62.7 percent in the Northern region). Conversely, a third of London's RDPs but only 16.1 percent of the Welsh RDPs had been out of work for two months or less. Not only was the duration of unemployment more severe among the Welsh RDPs, but the proportion who had had no job in the previous years was higher (62.1 percent) in Wales than in London (36.7 percent). The Welsh unemployed RDPs were more handicapped by illness than the London RDPs. This was true whether measured by the number of weeks of illness in the previous year or by the proportion of each group whose unsuitability for government vocational training was due to poor health.

The lack of local employment opportunities was more marked in Wales than in London. Furthermore, the Welsh RDPs were less qualified for work than the London RDPs, as indicated by their previous level of employment and type of training. Although laborers were the single most important occupational category among the unemployed RDPs in both London and Wales, they were almost half of the total in Wales, but a little over one-third in London. Similarly, London's clerical workers constituted 9.6 percent of the total RDP unemployed, against Wales's 5.1 percent. The data for other occupations showed the same bias toward a more qualified group of disabled unemployed in London than in Wales.

While the vast majority of RDP unemployed had had no formal training, the Welsh RDPs had the worst record in the country, with 90.4 percent untrained; London had the best record with 75.9 percent. The Londoners showed 9.4 percent with apprenticeship training against Wales's 3.4 percent; 1 percent of the London group had had professional-technical training, but this was true of only 0.2 percent of the Welsh. Even government vocational training was more generously provided in London; it had reached 3.7 percent of the RDPs in the London area compared with only 1.9 percent in Wales. Other formal training favored the Londoners in a ratio of about three to one. In general, the training profile of the London unemployed RDPs was comparable to that of the unemployed in the country as a whole, although it was less satisfactory than for all unemployed in the London area. The Welsh RDPs had less training than RDPs in all other areas and also less than the other unemployed in Wales.

In addition to their superior earlier training, the unemployed

RDPs in the London area also had had, on the average, more weeks of training and rehabilitation during the year preceding the survey than the Welsh unemployed RDPs. The Londoners were also judged relatively more able to obtain employment without governmental vocational training than the Welsh. Similarly, the Welsh were considered more in need of training for semi-skilled work than the Londoners.

POLICY IMPLICATIONS

The foregoing has shown the quantitative and qualitative disadvantages of the disabled unemployed in the regions where general unemployment is higher than average. One of the obvious suggestions is to increase the types and coverage of manpower programs in these regions and to improve the employability of the disabled unemployed along with others. In fact, the three new Industrial Rehabilitation Units opened in 1967 are located in these regions. The difficulty with providing additional rehabilitation and training opportunities on a large scale in areas like Wales, either for the disabled or for other residual unemployed, is the lack of local job opportunities and the low propensity of these groups to move to other areas. Subsidized mobility schemes for the disabled might well run into all the obstacles experienced with regard to other workers, except that jobs could be guaranteed in advance through the quota. It would then pay to train the disabled unemployed in the northern areas and move them to other regions. If the disabled are trained but not relocated, it is doubtful whether they would be chosen for such jobs as open up locally. As has been indicated, employers in the development areas already comply with the quota to a greater extent than in other areas.

However, the Department of Employment and Productivity has shown no dissatisfaction with the present ratio of disabled to all unemployed and is committed to a very restrained use of the compulsory aspects of the quota. As Adrian Sinfield's study in depth of the unemployed in North Shields shows quite forcefully, to remain unemployed while the rest of the nation prospers is a bitter experience, especially if earlier periods of work have been intermittent and poorly paid. The disabled, Sinfield found, were particularly vulnerable in the less prosperous areas. No doubt, detailed studies of the prosperous areas would show similar cases of hardship in and out of employment among the disabled. Britain's lack of a program to create jobs for the regionally unemployed intensifies the competitive disadvantage of the disabled.

West Germany has managed to keep its RDP unemployment much lower than Britain's; the total number of German disabled unemployed often is no higher than the British unemployment among section 2 disabled alone. The chief factors seem to be lower over-all unemployment, narrower regional disparities in unemployment rates, and a greater pressure on employers to hire the disabled. If Britain does not wish to train and relocate its disabled in order to permit greater compliance with the quota law, it has the alternative of increasing created jobs for the handicapped (Chapter IX). That would involve a reclassification to section 2 of section 1 RDPs who are unlikely to obtain work in certain localities. The establishment of variable local standards for designating section 2 RDPs and their placement in sheltered work would enable areas of higher-than-average unemployment to reduce the number of unemployed disabled competing for scarce jobs in the competitive labor market.

The British quota system has been challenged at times because of the quality of the jobs workers hold. Voluntary organizations and individuals have stated that the best abilities of the deaf, spastics, or epileptics, to name a few of the disabled, have not been realized through the jobs provided by the quota system. Some surveys in the early years showed that dissatisfaction was greater among the disabled who were placed in new work than among those remaining with their old firms after a disablement.[7]

[7] *Rehabilitation*, No. 38, July–September 1961, p. 31; Thomas Ferguson, M.D., D. Sc., and Angus N. MacPhail, M.D., "A Scottish Study of Persons Registered as Disabled under the Disabled Persons (Employment) Act, 1944," *Glasgow Medical Journal*, August 1953, pp. 344–47; V. V. Brown and others, "A Limited Survey of 768 Registered Disabled Persons," *Trans-*

The shorter work life of handicapped workers with certain ailments is considered an obstacle to satisfactory placement. Incentives to work are still another issue, since handicapped workers who receive invalidity or disability pensions or sickness insurance payments may have little inclination to take low-paid work. Such evidence as is available shows that a high proportion of placements are in unskilled work, but it is not clear whether the work is inconsistent with the qualifications of the disabled.

Some recent cases of placements of persons on the disabled register, not necessarily in quota jobs, may give a clearer picture of the process than generalized remarks. The examples cited are drawn from a 1966 report of the northern region, an area of heavier-than-average unemployment and third-ranking in employer compliance.[8]

A construction firm which was below quota had recently moved into a local office area. On contact from the local DRO, the head of the firm declared that he could not use disabled workers in his type of work and he was given a permit to hire up to six nondisabled workers. Subsequently the employer had more vacancies and was induced to hire a one-armed bricklayer as a handyman; this man left after one day because he expected to be paid bricklayer's wage rates. Another man, a bronchitic ex-miner who had left a vocational training course because of family problems, took the handyman job and remained with it.

A firm which was installing radio service to its trucks was persuaded to hire disabled persons to man the control office. Four disabled persons, including a wheel-chair case, were hired.

A one-armed housewife, with no substantial job experience in twenty years, registered for work. Responding to a newspaper advertisement for

actions of the Association of Industrial Medical Officers, (London), January 1955, p. 114; OECD, International Management Seminar on an Active Manpower Policy, *Supplement to the Final Report,* Paris, 1965, p. 105; Interviews and data from the Ministry of Labour, Great Britain; *The Ministry of Labour Gazette,* February 1967, p. 121.

[8] Great Britain, Ministry of Labour, Regional Controller, Northern Regional Office, *Report of Interesting Cases of Resettlement of Disabled Persons,* (no. 16), 1966.

semi-clericals, the DRO arranged a job for the woman, who was above-average in intelligence and eager to work.

Since leaving school, a badly crippled boy of 19 had worked as a brush-maker for a sympathetic employer. He left this work to become a re-placement guitarist with a professional group. His physical appearance distressed audiences and he was dropped from the band. His old job had been filled and special approaches to prospective employers failed. He was unemployed for four months before a firm printing Bingo cards, which recently had come under the quota regulations because of an ex-pansion of staff, agreed to give the boy a month's trial. After eight months, he was still employed assisting compositors and doing store-keeping.

A hemophiliac man of 29 had been on sickness benefit for four years after previous self-employment as a clock and watch repairman. An em-ployer with a vacancy for a moulding machine operator took him on at £ 18 a week, quite good pay.

With minor exceptions, the operation of the quota system is gen-erally approved in Britain. It is deemed creditable that the compul-sory aspects of the law are barely visible, although some would pre-fer more enforcement in order to reduce the rate of unemployment. A key factor in the system's acceptability is the care taken by the DRO to send suitable disabled workers to employers and the respect for employers' labor requirements in granting exceptions. Good re-habilitation and training services, adaptation of jobs and work-places, construction of new buildings with ramps and other devices to aid the handicapped, and cooperative employers and trade unions reinforce the British quota system. Voluntary organizations are ac-tive in educating the public and bringing pressure on behalf of par-ticular disabled groups or individuals. A full employment economy at most times has been a major factor in the ease of administering the quota system.

It may be asked whether the placement of the disabled in Britain would not proceed just as effectively without a quota system as long as the over-all demand for labor continues at a high level. Some of-ficials with experience in this area believe that the record-keeping and formalities of the system have been a greater burden than the benefits they have brought. In disagreement, others point to the educational value of the quota law when they are dealing with employers. They cite the entree they obtain to below-quota firms which otherwise might not be receptive to the DRO.

The quota system also encourages firms to reemploy their own industrially injured. A steel company investigated in 1951 indicated that over one-fourth of its registered disabled workers were men who had been injured while employed by the company. A report on the employment of paraplegics in 1961 noted that some workers had returned to their old employers but were working at different jobs because neither suitable work nor premises were available for paralyzed workers. However, these employers had fulfilled and often exceeded their quotas. It is possible that a quota system may expand the total volume of employment in the nation if employers make room for the disabled by creating jobs that would not otherwise exist. The net contribution to productivity may be small or zero.

The most compelling reason for endorsing the quota system under full employment conditions is the uncertainty that such conditions will continue indefinitely. Most authorities agree that if Britain were to experience a period of greater unemployment than has existed since 1946, the employed disabled would suffer disproportionately unless they are protected by a quota system. Officials are hopeful that such a test will not be faced, but few are willing to risk the suspension or abolition of the quota law.

RESERVED EMPLOYMENT

Reserved jobs are both less important and less successful for the British disabled than the quota system. The Disabled Persons Act of 1944 authorized the Minister of Labour, after consultation with organizations of employers and workers, to reserve certain jobs for disabled persons, and in September 1946 the first and only order to date was issued. Two jobs were designated to be exclusively held by registered disabled persons, except by special permit: starters or operators of electric passenger elevators and attendants on open parking lots; closed garages were not included. Permits were not required for nondisabled employees who held these jobs before September 1946, former employees entitled to reinstatement, or employees who spent less than half of their working time in designated employment.

Disabled persons referred to designated jobs must be suitable for such work and willing to undertake it. The disabled in designated employment may not be counted toward the general quota imposed on employers of twenty or more, but the disabled in designated employment are counted as part of the total staff in order to determine whether an employer falls under the quota system.

The total number of jobs created for the disabled by the two designated types of employment has not been significant in private firms or in government. In June 1968, of all passenger elevator attendants in government employment, 330 or 94 percent were disabled. The most telling argument against adding any other occupations as designated employment is the tendency of the chosen jobs to be menial or secondary in character, giving the impression, as a PEP pamphlet stated, "that such jobs are the only ones the disabled can do whereas the intention is that the jobs should only be done by the disabled."

Through the quota system and other measures, the attitude of the British public toward the disabled has altered:

The idea has now been generally accepted that it is the normal thing for a disabled person to work alongside the able-bodied in factories, rather than to sell papers, or sing in the streets. The disabled are at all points being accepted into the life of the community.[9]

[9] Political and Economic Planning (PEP), "The Disabled Worker," *Planning,* vol. XX, no. 368, July 23, 1954, pp. 176, 184, 188; information from Disabled Persons Branch, Ministry of Labour, Great Britain; OECD, International Seminar on Employment Services, Placement of the Handicapped, *Final Report,* Paris, December 1961, p. 8; *Ministry of Labour Gazette,* April 1967, p. 306; *Employment and Productivity Gazette,* January 1969, p. 51.

VI | Quota and Reserved Employment: West Germany, Italy, France

Unlike Great Britain, the other countries in western Europe which have quota systems are bound by traditions and legal authority which date back to post-World War I days. Some of the effects are visible in the current West German, Italian, and French quota and reserved employment systems. West Germany has the most advanced program and is most nearly comparable to Great Britain.

WEST GERMANY

The German system of quota employment originated in a 1919 ordinance which was superseded by a 1920 law and then replaced by a 1923 basic law; the latter, with minor amendments, remained in effect until World War II. Seriously disabled ex-servicemen and industrial accident or disease pensioners were the original beneficiaries, but the 1923 law broadened the coverage by giving equivalent status to blind persons, disabled individuals whose earning capacity was reduced by at least 50 percent regardless of cause, and less severely disabled servicemen. Germany thus was an early leader in providing quota employment for the handicapped whether or not the disability was war induced.

In the first years after World War II, no federal authority existed in West Germany to renew the earlier quota legislation and it was left to the individual states (*Länder*) to make regulations. Not until

June 1953 was a uniform federal law passed which consolidated earlier legislation. Subsequent orders, administrative regulations, and directives were incorporated in an amending law of 1961. West Berlin retained a few special provisions of its own.

The definition of disability in the German legislation is less general than the British and tends to stress physical, war-connected injuries. In addition to direct victims of the two World Wars, the German law on the disabled includes persons whose injury or ill health is due to acts of violence under the National Socialist regime or detention in the Soviet Occupation zone or East Berlin. The law also includes foreign nationals or stateless persons residing in Germany who have sustained injuries from similar causes. Victims of industrial accidents or disease and blind persons of German nationality also are eligible.

To qualify as severely disabled, a claimant must have a 50 percent disability or an incapacity adding up to 50 percent if there is more than one cause; in some cases receipt of a government pension is required in order to establish eligibility. Equivalent status is granted to those with at least 50 percent incapacity due to nonenumerated causes (*Schwererwerbsbeschränkte*) and to those with 30 to 50 percent incapacity due to the enumerated causes (*Minderbeschädigte*).[1]

Qualification as a severely disabled person may help a German to obtain quota employment even when his primary job problem is not related to his disability.[2] An interesting example is that of a prewar law student who had lost one eye in the war. He resumed his legal

[1] Interviews and data from the West German Ministry of Labour and the Social Structure, Bonn, and the Federal Institute for Labor Placement and Unemployment Insurance (BAVAV), Nürnberg; H. J. Becker, *The Employment of Seriously Disabled Persons,* Social Policy in Germany, Monograph 4, Federal Ministry of Labour and the Social Structure, Essen, 1965; P. Leve, "Two Years Experience of the Disabled Persons Act," *Bundesarbeitsblatt,* October 1955; *International Labour Review,* March 1957, pp. 247–48, 262–63; *idem,* March 1962, pp. 284–91; *idem,* November 1963, pp. 458–75.

[2] West Germany, BAVAV, *Results of the Pilot-Study on Methods of Job Counselling and Placement for Special Groups,* Nürnberg, August 1965, pp. 14, 17, 18–19.

studies after the war, passed the second professional examination in 1951, and therafter became a solicitor and legal consultant. He was subsequently disbarred on a charge of embezzling his clients' funds. Soon he began to drink heavily and his domestic life became stormy. Since he was "naturally unwilling to descend in the social scale," as an official of the Employment Service put it, it was decided to give him the status of a severely disabled worker, for which he qualified by his loss of an eye. He was placed under the quota system in a salaried position requiring mental work but without great responsibility; in preparation he was to undertake a subsidized training or adjustment course.

Classification as a seriously disabled person may be sought or it may be given by an Employment Service official. Apparently, some eligible unemployed escape the notice of the ordinary Employment Service interviewers. The OECD Counselling Study in West Germany found that 22 out of 186 experimental cases should have been classified earlier as severely disabled. However, some of these cases may resemble that of the solicitor above whose chief job handicap was something other than his physical disability.

The German quotas are variable and flexible among industries, regions, and employers. Distinctions are made according to the ability of the industry to employ disabled persons and the local need for quota jobs. Thus, quotas range by law from 2 percent to 24 percent and are subject to adjustment by the local employment offices. Every effort is made to set identical quotas for employers whose type of business and location are similar. The highest quotas are borne by the public authorities which, unlike their British counterparts, are subject to the statutory quota obligation.

All employers who have a staff of more than nine persons are obliged to provide quota jobs, in contrast to the British stipulation of twenty or more in staff. In counting units toward the quota, various flexible arrangements are made in West Germany. A miner with a pension certificate is counted even if he is not seriously disabled as defined by law. A disabled employer may count himself toward his quota. He may also count as half a unit a woman worker who is the wife or widow of a victim of war or industrial injuries, if the woman would otherwise be hard-to-place; in spite of the allowance, this group of women workers has not proved attractive to employers.

Permission may be sought to count as two units such seriously disabled persons as those with brain injuries, tuberculosis, blindness, and those with a loss of earning capacity of at least 80 percent. Workers capable of part-time work of at least 24 hours a week may be counted as one unit. These inducements to employers to take on the most seriously disabled workers are reinforced by the requirement that each employer under the quota must hire a reasonable number of such workers.

An employer's quota may be partially satisfied in other ways. The Chief Welfare Authority may permit an employer to count toward his quota a seriously disabled person to whom a cash payment has been made, a home provided, or other material assistance granted. Such persons presumably are not able to work. The *Land* employment office can also certify that an employer has complied with his quota obligation in part or in whole if he has made it possible for another employer to employ an excess number of seriously disabled persons. One example is that of an employer who gives a subcontract to a recognized business run and staffed largely by seriously disabled persons.

Employers in West Germany are directed by law to adapt workplaces and provide technical aids to make possible the permanent employment of "as many seriously disabled persons as practicable" in jobs such "that they can utilize and develop their special skills to the greatest possible extent." Employers may not reduce wages below the normal level provided by a collective agreement merely because the disabled worker receives a pension, but if the worker's output is subnormal, a lower wage may be provided in the collective agreement. An employer must also grant disabled workers a minimum of six days a year of paid vacation over and above the normal vacation period. The legal protection against dismissal for those under quota employment is stronger in West Germany than in Britain.

In West Germany, liable employers must fill a stipulated number of jobs in each enterprise as quota places for disabled persons or pay a fine for each unfilled place. Since a much larger number of quota places than eligible candidates has regularly been established, many willing employers have been consistently below quota. However, some quota places remain unfilled because the work is too arduous for the unemployed disabled or the location of the place of work is inconvenient.

The number of quota jobs set aside in accordance with the law rose from a low of 700,750 in 1955 to a high of 807,992 in 1959, while the filled quota jobs rose from a low of 424,093 in 1953 to a high of 494,113 in 1957. An adjustment in 1961 reduced employers' obligations somewhat, so that the gap between designated and filled places has been narrowed. Further reductions in quotas are under consideration in order to ease the administrative burden and make a more realistic adjustment to the reduced need for quota employment for the severely disabled, as defined by current law. No action to widen the eligibility for quota jobs is contemplated.

Although the law specifies 6 percent of total employment as the normal quota for private and public businesses, 70 percent of the liable enterprises actually had lower quotas in 1965. The average quota in industry was 3.67 percent, while in such fields as public administration, banking and insurance, it was 6.7 percent. In 1963 half of the total quota places were in manufacturing industries, particularly in the iron, steel, and metals manufacturing branches. Public administration and similar services accounted for 29 percent of the total quota places.

In terms of the proportion of quota places actually filled, mining was first with 95.3 percent. At the other extreme was hairdressing shops with only 24.3 percent. Among regions the best record was compiled by West Berlin, which met 72.0 percent of its quota obligations, while South Bavaria, an agricultural area, was lowest with only 55.8 percent of its assigned posts filled. The industrial North Rhine-Westphalia region, which met 59.1 percent of its quota, accounted for over one-fourth of all quota employment.

Perhaps the most striking difference between West Germany and Britain with regard to employers' obligations is the German requirement that every employer with unfilled places in his quota must pay 50 DM ($12.50) per month per unfilled place into a Compensation Fund. About 3 million DM ($750,000) has been collected since 1953; this is a very small amount against the number of unfilled places listed each year, and it suggests that provisions for excusing these payments are liberally administered. Originally the purposes of the compensation levy were to induce employers to hire the disabled unemployed and to equalize the burdens among employers.

An even stronger compulsory feature is incorporated in the German law. A recalcitrant employer can be forced to enter into a contract of employment with a disabled person, but this procedure has rarely been used. Officials doubt that it could be effective "because experience shows that it is impossible to create good working conditions and an atmosphere of confidence on the basis of compulsion, and it is particularly in the employment of a disabled person that such conditions are indispensable." [3]

Compliance by employers is attributed to a sound law and supporting institutions, reinforced by the active social conscience of German employers, who responded well to their quotas in the mid-1950s when general unemployment was still high, the ranks of the eligible disabled were swelled by refugees, new categories were added by law, and problems were created by the internal migration of the disabled. Some German employers hire the disabled in excess of their quotas; in November 1963, 33,380 disabled were employed in above-quota firms. Very small firms which are not liable also provide some jobs, but fewer than uncovered enterprises in Britain.

The degree of intervention and assistance by various government agencies appears to be greater in West Germany than in Britain. Financial and engineering aid is given to employers who are willing to adapt workplaces and use technical auxiliary devices. A technical advisory service is attached to the employment office of each *Land* and supplements the work of the special placement officer for dis-

[3] H. J. Becker, *The Employment of Seriously Disabled Persons,* p. 14; Organization for Economic Cooperation and Development, (OECD), International Seminar on Employment Services, Placement of the Handicapped, *Report from Germany,* Paris, 1961, pp. 1–9.

abled persons, and, nationally, the German Employment Service maintains an office of technical advice in its rehabilitation subsection. Branch offices have staff physicians, psychologists, counselors, and technical advisors to assist the placement officer.

The provision of housing has been an important aspect of matching disabled workers and quota jobs in West Germany. Especially in the early years, when there was much voluntary and involuntary internal movement, some subsidized housing was built specially for the disabled and priority to occupy other housing was granted. Just as the interregional clearance of vacancies is an important part of general German labor market policy, so it is used in the placement of the disabled.

The Compensation Fund is used to finance part of the government's outlays on housing and jobs for the disabled. One of the most interesting devices developed in West Germany is an Equalization Fund, which siphons off 20 percent of the Compensation Fund's receipts. The Equalization Fund compensates those *Länder* which through migration and immigration have acquired a disproportionate number of disabled. This Fund also finances the construction of housing for the disabled who would benefit by living closer to their place of work. It also makes grants to training and retraining institutes which serve more than one *Land*.

Placement officers of the German Employment Service follow the progress of the disabled in quota employment and also consult with employers about changing job assignments within the enterprise. Their purpose is to move the least disabled into the most difficult quota jobs and thus make room for more severely disabled in the easier work.

Any firm or office which employs at least five seriously disabled persons must hold an election among its disabled employees to choose one special representative and at least one deputy. The special representative, who is allowed time-off without loss of wages for his activities, protects and guides the disabled on the job, negotiates with the employer, and generally speaks for the disabled in work matters. Furthermore, the Works Councils in each enterprise, established by law in Germany, have among their duties the protection of the interests of seriously disabled employees, the persuasion of employers to comply with their quotas, and the encouragement of business development which makes possible a greater employment of the disabled. It is not clear how much attention Works Councils actually pay to these matters.

It is difficult to compare the efficacy of the German and British quota systems even in quantitative terms, and the important qualitative aspects are still more elusive. Although the population and labor force are roughly the same size in the two countries, West Germany may have a larger number of seriously disabled workers as a result of its direct and indirect war experiences. In addition, tuberculosis, whose incidence has diminished markedly in Britain, still is an important cause of work disablement in West Germany, where foreign workers from southern Europe may have introduced new strains of the disease.

Compared with the British definition of disability as any physical or mental handicap which substantially decreases the chances of obtaining employment, the German definition of 50 percent loss of earning capacity is much stricter. Nor has Germany the section 2 classification for those who cannot be placed easily in ordinary employment. As a result, the Germans in quota employment probably include more severly disabled cases than the British. On the other hand, the Germans use the quota jobs for relatively fewer mentally disabled.

The quality of the jobs provided by the two systems cannot be compared, as little is known for each country separately. British efforts to place the blind in competitive employment appear to be further advanced than Germany's. Great stress is placed in Germany on maintaining the disabled worker's occupational and social standing. Both countries take pride in their rehabilitation, training, and placement programs for the disabled, and it would require a detailed investigation to determine whether the results in one country are superior.

However, there is no doubt that West Germany has a better record than Great Britain as regards the numbers and proportions of disabled out of work. The German achievement is the more significant because their quota employment appears to cover a more severely physically disabled group. Much tighter labor markets than Britain has experienced and greater government pressure on employers probably are the main factors in Germany's performance. In 1964 only 6,167 severely disabled were unemployed, against Britain's low of around 30,000.

Preferential or reserved employment has been used chiefly in government jobs in West Germany, especially to assist older clerical workers who were displaced by the shift of the capital from West Berlin to Bonn.

ITALY

The Italian system reflects the unfavorable consequences of a loose labor market. Employers have their choice of so many fully employable workers that they have little interest in the less competitive groups. They are further antagonized by the exceptionally heavy cumulative quotas for various groups of hard-to-employ, the inadequate rehabilitation and training services for the disabled, and the complex legal and administrative provisions. Public agencies and enterprises appear to accept their quotas more willingly than private employers.

The complexity of the present Italian quota system can be suggested by a brief account of the quota laws. After World War I, Italy imposed a quota on all private employers of more than ten men, obligating them to hire at least one war-disabled serviceman for every twenty men. The fines collected as penalties for nonobservance of the law were used to provide prosthesis and rehabilitation for the disabled servicemen. Anyone who posed as a disabled serviceman in order to obtain employment was subject to six months' imprisonment. Here we see both the pressures of unemployment on workers and the inclination of employers to fill their quotas with able-bodied or slightly disabled workers who were presented to the authorities as having major disabilities. The latter means of evading the law is still in use today, as officials of the Ministry of

Labour confirm, and it is an indication of employer resistance to the quota system.

A rash of legislation extending the quota appeared after World War II and involved three different government agencies: the National Institute for War Disabled (ONIG), the Ministry of Labour and, in one special case, the National Institute for Social Welfare (INPS). Recognition that government pensions and other social assistance payments available to the handicapped unemployed were inadequate led to the transfer of a portion of the burden to private employers via an enlarged quota system. Support for such an approach was provided by articles 4 and 38 of the new Italian Constitution, which stipulated, respectively, "the principle of the right to work" and the "right of the unfit or handicapped to receive vocational training or instruction."

Employers with more than ten employees are required to set aside 8.5 percent of their posts for those whose working capacity was reduced substantially or lost through war-caused injuries or infirmities, whether or not they served in the armed forces. Of the 8.5 percent quota, 6 percent is to be composed of war-disabled veterans and 2.5 percent of war-injured civilians. Since 1965, war widows and orphans and veterans' children under 25 must form 1 percent of the 8.5 percent quota. At the end of 1964, 246,000 war-disabled workers and 7,700 war orphans were employed under this quota, and 70,000 registered war-disabled workers and 4,700 qualified orphans were on the waiting list.

Firms employing over 100 workers must reserve one out of every three posts earmarked for the civilian war-disabled (one-third of 2.5 percent) for those suffering disabilities as a result of military or government service, not directly war-connected. The orphans and children of such persons may be substituted when no candidates from the primary group are available. At the end of 1964, 12,619 disabled persons and 630 orphans and children were employed under this quota, while an additional 5,796 eligible disabled and 538 children and orphans were waiting to be placed.

These quota provisions are administered by the ONIG, the National Institute for War Disabled. Another set of laws is administered by the Ministry of Labour. The earliest and most important provides for those disabled by industrial accidents or diseases. Every firm employing more than fifty persons must choose 2 percent of its work force from those men under 60 and women under 55 who have had a reduction in work capacity of at least 40 percent as a result of an industrial disability. At the end of 1964, 35,230 were employed in this quota and 6,645 were waiting for jobs.

A new provision for the civilian disabled who were not covered by previous legislation was enacted in 1962. Those whose disability was due to such causes as automobile accidents, congenital defects, and diseases other than industrial ailments were drawn into quota protection, provided they were under 55 and had lost at least one-third of their work capacity, but not so much as to compromise the safety of other workers. Firms employing more than fifty workers are required to have 2 percent of their staff consist of civilian disabled. The blind and deaf-and-dumb were excluded because they have other protection under the Ministry of Labour.

Employers get some relief because the civilian war-disabled employed under the ONIG program are counted toward this new quota even if they are over 55 or have recovered their work capacity. When the Employment Service submits quota candidates to employers, it takes account of family responsibilities, date of registration, financial resources and property (including earnings of other family members), and other factors giving evidence of need. At the end of 1964, 10,723 civilian disabled were employed under this quota and 17,796 were waiting for jobs.

Refugees of various types also have been entitled to quota placement. Firms employing over 500 workers were required to reserve 10 percent of their positions for refugees from territories ceded to Yugoslavia, while firms working on government contracts and local government bodies were to hire 5 percent of their staff from refugees from Libya, Eritrea, Ethiopia, and Somalia. No data are available on the numbers employed under these quotas, which have been allowed to lapse as the candidates were absorbed.

Enterprises with more than 300 workers must employ deaf mutes in the ratio of 3 percent among their wage earners and 1 percent among the auxiliary personnel, such as messengers or watchmen. At the end of 1964, there were 1,559 deaf mutes in jobs and 1,061 on the waiting list. Blind persons trained as telephone operators have protected employment; each office which needs one or more operators must give preference to a blind operator for the first post. At the end of 1964, 170 blind operators were employed and 440 were registered as available and capable of such work. Another such provision has been made also for blind masseurs and physiotherapists, but the number so employed is not available.

A special quota arrangement concerns those who have been clinically cured of tuberculosis and are able to work in the sanatariums and convalescent homes for tubercular patients. Ten percent of the total personnel of such institutions, whether public or private, must consist of cured patients.

A number of the foregoing quota arrangements apply to public as well as private employers and some of the employment figures cited above cover both types of enterprises. In addition, public agencies of various kinds, including nationalized industries, are obliged to reserve certain jobs or to relax standards and give preference in appointments to disabled persons as well as to other categories of the hard-to-employ.

To fulfill the conditions of all the quota laws, a large firm would have to assign upwards of 10 percent of its posts to special categories. The actual numbers employed under the various quotas appear to be small, even when account is taken of Italy's large agricultural population and the small scale of industrial and commercial enterprises. Many exceptions to the quota laws are made for individual firms, and few skilled posts are filled through the quota. It is difficult to see how employers can understand all of their obligations, much less how inspectors can police so elaborate a structure. Given the relatively large supply of underemployed labor in Italy, employers' reluctance to take on disabled workers, and the rarity of rehabilitative or skill training, it is hard to credit the Ministry of Labour's view that the quotas are well enforced. There are unofficial reports of large numbers of menial jobs, make-work tasks, excessive exemptions, substitutions of able or slightly handicapped workers for the registered disabled, and even of employers who hire and pay the required number of quota workers but urge them to stay away from the factory.[4]

FRANCE

The French reservation and quota system also has its origins in post-World War I legislation for disabled veterans, but in its recent evolution it has been less complex than the Italian scheme. However, both share a tendency to offer jobs to the needy who are poorly provided for by pensions and welfare payments, but are not necessarily hard-to-place in the labor market.

The initial French measure in 1923 did not establish quotas, but simply reserved certain posts in central and local government service, the colonies, public enterprises, and private firms holding government contracts. These posts were filled by disabled ex-servicemen who received pensions, war widows (including those not legally married) with dependent children, and eligible orphans and children. Five categories of employment, including 374 occupations, were established according to the degree of training required. From 1953 to 1962, the number of war disabled in such jobs in central government offices varied between a low of 1,478 and a high of 3,112, and averaged about 2,500; an unknown number were in other agencies. This appears to be a rather elaborate program of reserved employment for so small a number of beneficiaries.

The quota system was introduced in 1924 and remained unchanged until 1955. A quota of 10 percent of total staff was set for employers who had ten or more wage earners above 18 years of age; in agriculture and forestry, employers became eligible when they had fifteen or more wage earners. The quota was to be filled by servicemen receiving permanent or temporary pensions. A disabled employer counted himself as one unit, while the severely disabled,

[4] Interviews in Rome; data from the Italian Ministry of Labour; OECD, Manpower and Social Affairs Committee, *Annual Reports, Italy, 1963,* Paris, 1963, MO(63)17/12 pp. 8–9; *International Labour Review,* March 1957, pp. 250–51, 258–60; July 1963, pp. 78–81.

with 80 percent or more reduction in capacity, counted as two units. Firms employing thirty or more persons were required to fill at least one-third of their quota posts with war pensioners who had severe reductions of work capacity. Workers receiving pensions as a result of industrial accidents could be counted toward the quota if they were employed by the enterprise in which the accident occurred.

In 1955 the eligible list was enlarged to include war orphans (especially boys), wives of disabled veterans in mental institutions, and unmarried mothers who had lost one or more children in the war. As before, victims of industrial accidents counted toward the quota, and new incentives were offered to employers who had hired other types of civilian disabled. Still, France had not moved much beyond providing quota employment for highly selected groups, some of whom—the industrially injured, for example—might have been retained by the firm in any case.

Employers were not quite meeting the 10 percent quota at the end of 1955, when 335,162 quota positions were filled in 67,593 reporting enterprises with 4,369,414 employees. More than half of the quota posts were held by industrially injured who had remained in their firms. Moreover, the type of jobs held, the rehabilitative services available, and the general level of absorption of the disabled in an economy facing severe labor shortages were not impressive. Many of the jobs held by the disabled were as guards or doorkeepers in public institutions such as museums and historical monuments.

The decreasing numbers of war disabled, a heightened social conscience regarding all handicapped persons, and a hope of relieving labor shortages combined to cause the enactment in November 1957 of a basic law on the resettlement of physically and mentally handicapped workers. This statute was all-inclusive with regard to the cause of disablement and the range of treatment, and provided for a screening and guidance board, reserved jobs, quota employment, subsidized self-employment, and sheltered workshops. The quota provisions were not actually put into effect until 1964 and 1965 when a series of decrees, laws, and orders modified, clarified, and specified the details of the 1957 law and reconciled it with the 1924 quota law.

The result has been that firms still covered by the quota law of

1924 have continued with a 10 percent over-all quota, but they are now permitted to fill part of their quota with the handicapped as defined under the 1957 law. Private firms brought into the quota system in 1964 had only to fill 3 percent of their jobs with handicapped persons.

The 1957 law defines the establishments liable to employ the handicapped in exceptionally broad terms. It covers not only industrial, commercial, and agricultural entrepreneurs, but also cooperative organizations, whether lay or religious, including educational and charitable agencies. Also included are industrial and other associations whose financial resources come from compulsory contributions. In addition to the usual list for the public sector, the law covers semipublic establishments, companies under partial state control, and private undertakings responsible for a public service. The definition of "handicapped worker" in the 1957 law also is broad, and includes anyone "who is substantially handicapped in obtaining or keeping employment as a result of a deficiency in or a diminution of his physical or mental powers."

An unusual feature of the 1957 law is the provision that the local manpower offices should carry out a census of part-time jobs and "light" jobs suitable for handicapped workers who cannot be employed at jobs which demand full-time or a normal rate of production. Firms are required to allow such workers a probationary period before they are discharged. When the output of handicapped workers is lower than average, their wages can be reduced by 10 or 20 percent, but not below the guaranteed minimum wage (SMIG). For purposes of calculating fulfillment of the quota, each handicapped worker is classified as one-half unit, one unit, or two units, according to the severity of his handicap. Such a system appears to be a useful way of encouraging employers to accept the more severely handicapped.

Enterprises whose quota obligations originate under the 1924 statute have not widened their selection of workers, although the 1957 law gave them new sources of disabled. Of a total of 525,336 in quota employment in 1963 (on a base employment of 6,729,926), all but 62,554 were selected from the two formerly designated categories—the war disabled and the industrially injured in the original enterprise. As might be expected, the numbers of war disabled had steadily declined over the years, while the number of industrial accident victims rose; the latter increased from 174,726 in 1955 to 326,378 in 1963.

The 62,544 remaining quota workers consisted of 46,108 disabled by industrial accidents which occurred *outside* of the employing enterprise and 16,446 other physically handicapped. Perhaps employers were willing to hire more of these workers but had not been provided with their names by the slow-moving official review boards established by the 1957 law.

It is too early to judge the effectiveness of the general quota for handicapped workers under the 1957 law because of the long delay in its implementation. The object is not to impose less productive workers on employers but to put pressure on employers to accept handicapped workers who have been rehabilitated and trained. Toward this end, the quota is to be a supplementary measure in a full program of improving the employability of the handicapped and placing them suitably.[5] Thus far, French employers have not been receptive to attempts to place the handicapped, protesting that their premises are physically unsuited to the handicapped and that such workers are difficult to absorb in the work force.

From the foregoing review of quota and reserved employment in four western European countries it is clear that considerable variation exists in the size of quotas, the extent of rehabilitation and training efforts, the degree of compulsion, and the groups offered protection. Employers are apt to resist and resent systems which impose high quotas, include a large number of job categories, fail to rehabilitate and train the disabled, mismatch candidates and vacan-

[5] Interviews and information provided by the French Ministry of Social Affairs and others; *International Labour Review,* March 1957, pp. 251–52, 263; March 1960, pp. 160–64; April 1963, pp. 369–70; ILO, *Industry and Labour,* October 1961, pp. 259–60; OECD, International Management Seminar on an Active Manpower Policy, *Supplement to the Final Report,* Paris, 1965, p. 42.

cies, or lack supplementary programs to provide sheltered employment for the most disabled. If the labor market is loose, as in Italy, an added obstacle to acceptance of the disabled is present. It is difficult to judge the efficacy of a quota system when full employment prevails or to evaluate the results of voluntary placement in some countries against the quota system in others.

While it might seem that a full-employment economy hardly needs quota or reserved employment if it has good rehabilitation, training, and placement services, the fear that full employment may not always persist and a sense of permanent obligation to the disabled prevents serious consideration of repeal of the quota system in countries which have had years of experience with it. The tendency is rather to make compliance voluntary by close cooperation with employers, as in Great Britain and West Germany.

Theoretically, an effective quota system should influence the distribution of existing jobs in favor of groups which would otherwise not hold so many jobs in total or so many of the more desirable positions. To the extent that the quota system secures places for those who are excluded by discrimination from work they can perform satisfactorily, the quota imposes no economic burden on employers and brings considerable benefit to society and the individuals concerned. This is a very creditable and useful application of the quota.

To the extent that the quota system leads to the creation of extra, nonessential positions or the placement of workers of lower-than-average productivity at standard wages, employers are being asked to absorb some of the costs that would otherwise be borne by public programs or the workers themselves. If the quota is moderate and there is a reasonable matching of workers and jobs, little or no visible effect on an employer's competitive position or on domestic or export prices may be anticipated. It is, in any case, difficult to isolate this cause of increased costs from other factors.

From the viewpoint of the workers who are given employment through the quota and would otherwise be idle or employed on created jobs outside of the usual channels, the quota system affords a better sense of participation in society and as good an income as any existing alternative.

From the point of view of government manpower policy, the quota is an inexpensive and rapid method of dealing with discriminatory employment practices which are not based on ability to perform. The quota can be used much more broadly than it has been in western Europe, where direct physical and mental disability or, to a lesser extent, family need due to a wage earner's disability or death have been the conditions of eligibility. Job discrimination due to age, color, national origin, or other factors can be attacked through quota laws.

When government uses the quota as a substitute for rehabilitation, training, and the adaptation of workplaces, the results are likely to be unfavorable to all concerned. But, in any case, quota employment should not be expected to absorb all of the residual hard-to-employ, nor is it a suitable method of job creation to offset regional, structural, seasonal, or cyclical unemployment (see Chapter VIII).

VII | Subsidized Employment and Self-Employment

Another form of intervention in order to place the hard-to-employ in competitive labor markets is financial. Subsidies, loans, grants, tax credits, and exemptions are offered to induce employers to hire hard-to-employ workers. These measures may be alternative or supplementary to the quota system, or they may be used to help workers considered unsuitable for quota jobs. The incentive to employers to hire the hard-to-employ also may take the form of a subsidy for the adaptation of the workplace or machinery so that disabled or older workers may perform satisfactorily. In addition, as Chapter XII describes, some countries pay wage subsidies directly to certain workers who transfer from declining industries to lower-paid jobs elsewhere. Still another type of subsidy makes self-employment possible for those hard-to-employ who cannot be fitted into employee status or who might perform better as independent businessmen or craftsmen.

SUBSIDIZED JOBS FOR THE HARD-TO-EMPLOY

The idea of stimulating the acceptance of the hard-to employ through offers of subsidies to prospective employers has been explored in several western European countries. It is assumed that some hard-to-employ workers need additional time on a job in order to bring their output up to the average, and that employers will be encouraged to hire such workers at the normal pay for the job if the difference between their output and the average is compensated by a subsidy. Although a distinction is made between subsidized training and subsidies-to-wages, in practice the two often overlap.

Belgium has experimented over a number of years with subsidized employment of the hard-to-place. Since Belgium has virtually no limit on the duration of unemployment benefits, manpower officials could consider wage subsidies a valuable and perhaps cheaper alternative than unemployment insurance benefits. In other countries, wage subsidies may replace other social benefits, such as unemployment assistance, disability pensions, or welfare, or they may represent net additional government outlays.

By a Royal Decree of February 25, 1961, Belgium established a subsidy to wages on behalf of certain hard-to-place workers. The subsidy was payable to employers for a minimum of one month and a maximum of twelve months on a descending scale: 20 percent of the normal wage plus social charges for the first six months; 15 percent for the next three months; 10 percent for the remaining three months. Two groups of hard-to-place workers were eligible: registered unemployed persons who had drawn unemployment benefits in twelve of the preceding eighteen months and who had reached the age of 55 (manual workers) or 40 (white-collar workers); registered unemployed persons who had drawn unemployment benefits in six of the preceding nine months and whose working capacity had been reduced by at least 30 percent as a result of physical impairment or 20 percent as a result of mental impairment.

Unsubsidized placements of hard-to-place workers also are a special activity undertaken by the Belgian Employment Service and have been far more important than subsidized placements, as Table VII.1 indicates. The decline in such placements after 1963 led the ONEM to establish special regional centers and to hire and train additional specialized personnel to aid the hard-to-employ.[1]

The number of unsubsidized placements is not entirely compara-

[1] Belgium, Ministère de l'Emploi et du Travail, Office National de l'Emploi (ONEM), *Rapport Annuel, 1966,* Brussels, 1967, pp. 28–29; idem, *Rapport Annuel, 1967,* pp. 19–20.

ble with that of subsidized placements; the former includes repeat placements of the same person, while the subsidized placements involve separate individuals only. Nevertheless, the discrepancy between the two categories was sufficiently great to provoke an inquiry by the Employment Service in 1962. The employers who had accepted the 13,180 unsubsidized hard-to-employ were queried about their reasons for not requesting a subsidy. In 10,280 cases, the

TABLE VII.1. Placements of Hard-to-Employ Unemployed, Belgium 1961–1967

Year	Total Placements of Hard-to-Employ	Subsidized Placements		Unsubsidized Placements
		Handicapped	Older Workers	
1961 [a]	3,733	272	285	3,176
1962	13,764	324	260	13,180
1963	12,350	225	81	12,044
1964	9,300	240	101	8,959
1965	7,706	210		7,496
1966	7,772	173		7,599
1967	7,062	235		6,827

[a] Last seven months only.

Source: Belgium, Ministère de l'Emploi et du Travail, *La Politique de l'Emploi,* Brussels, 1965, p. 25; Belgium, Office National de l'Emploi (ONEM), *Rapport Annuel 1966,* Brussels, 1967, p. 29; *idem, Rapport Annuel 1967,* p. 19.

handicapped or older workers had not been unemployed long enough to qualify for the subsidy. But in the remaining 2,900 cases, the employers accepted subsidizable workers but did not apply for the subsidy.

The reasons for employers' indifference to the subsidy and their reluctance to hire the hard-to-place in general were explored by the Belgian Employment Service. Employers object to the administrative formalities which attend the application for the subsidy payment, particularly where the worker leaves or is dismissed after a brief period on the job. Since the alternative is open to hire young foreign workers, many Belgian employers decline to bear the expenses of training and the possible higher absenteeism rates of Belgian hard-to-employ workers. Employers fear the bad work history, lack of skills, and personality difficulties of the hard-to-place, who often are embittered by successive job failures along with long periods of inactivity. Employers also feel that the highest priority should go to providing jobs for workers who become disabled in their own service. However, most of these arguments against the hard-to-place are irrelevant in the case of the employers who accepted 2,900 hard-to-place workers but declined to apply for the subsidy.

Speculation that the subsidies were paid for too short a time and that the declining percentage payment was discouraging to employers led to a revised plan at the end of 1963. A rising scale of subsidies replaced the earlier descending scale, but no change was made in the qualifying period of unemployment or the age and disability requirements. The new subsidies paid 20 percent of the wages and social charges for hard-to-place workers retained for up to six months, 25 percent of the wages for those employed up to one year, and 30 percent for workers employed for a year or more. Subsidies could be paid for no less than one month or more than one year.

If a hard-to-place worker was above the specified age and also physically or mentally handicapped, the subsidy percentage for each time period rose by 5 percent. Another 5 percent for each period was added if the worker was over-age, physically or mentally handicapped, and had been unemployed for more than three years. Thus, a maximum of 40 percent of the wages could be subsidized.

In 1963 another group was added to the eligibles. The Belgian government decreed that repatriates to Belgium from the Congo, Rwanda, or Burundi were to be regarded as hard-to-place unemployed and were eligible for wage subsidies if they were registered as applicants for employment with the Employment Service for at least a month, were not in paid employment or self-employment, and were over 55, if manual workers, or over 40, if office workers.

In May 1966 a special scheme was introduced to subsidize the employment of hired older or handicapped miners affected by collective dismissals; the European Coal and Steel Community shares the costs. Usually 20 to 35 percent of the wage and social security taxes are subsidized, but a maximum of 60 percent of wages plus social charges can be obtained by an employer who retains a hard-to-place miner for two years. During 1966, five miners were subsidized, and in 1967 only four subsidized placements of miners were made. The other ECSC-supported measures on behalf of displaced miners were considered more favorable and were used more frequently.

During 1965 the National Fund for the Handicapped (*Fonds National de Reclassement Social des Handicapés*) began to provide services for the handicapped and to offer the same type of subsidy as previously was granted by the National Employment Fund. A slight change in the rules permits the registered handicapped who have been in sheltered work or training to count these months as qualifying unemployment. During 1965, 203 employers requested a wage subsidy for handicapped workers, but the requests of only thirteen employers were approved, each for one handicapped worker. Some were rejected because their requests were made on behalf of handicapped workers who already had been in the employ of the firm for a year or more.

The Fund for the Handicapped also initiated subsidies to employers who undertake to adapt a workplace for a handicapped worker. The employer must agree to retain the worker for a minimum of six months, or for a longer period of time if his subsidy is large. By mid-1966, only one request for such a subsidy had been received. A final form of job aid to handicapped workers is the provision of tools and workclothes when employers are not obliged to provide them.

Table VII.1 shows that neither the changed terms of the subsidy in 1963 nor the addition of another agency to aid the handicapped had increased the absolute or relative number of subsidized placements through 1966. Disappointment with these results led in 1967 to another revision in the terms of the subsidy. In order to make more workers eligible for the subsidy, days of compensated illness or disability were to be counted toward the qualifying period of unemployment. Furthermore, hard-to-place workers who are laid off due to the closing down of a firm may be exempted by the director of the regional ONEM office from the required period of prior compensated unemployment.

The amount of the subsidy was recast as an absolute hourly figure for blue-collar workers and a monthly amount for white-collar workers, and both were related to the index of retail prices. After six months on the subsidized job, and again after ten months, the amount of the subsidy was to be reduced. Thus, once more, the original principle of a declining subsidy was reintroduced. Subsidized placements rose in 1967, at a time of a general increase in unemployment and a decline in unsubsidized placements (Table VII.1). Whether the initial success was attributable to the alteration in the conditions of the subsidy or to assiduous efforts by the specialized personnel is not clear. In any case, the balance between the unsubsidized and subsidized placements has hardly changed, and the former remains a more important measure.[2]

Despite the small number of Belgian hard-to-place benefiting from the wage subsidy, it has been valuable both to those who otherwise might have remained unemployed and to the unemployment insurance fund. The situation as of the end of 1964 was described by Raymond Etienne, then Director-General of the ONEM:

Expenditure under these agreements has totaled about 8 million francs ($200,000), but this expenditure has made it possible to save about 30 million francs in the form of unemployment benefit. Furthermore, the unemployed who were found jobs worked for more than 206,000 days during the same period which, assuming an average wage of 30 francs an hour, earned them more than 55 million francs in wages and led to

[2] Interviews in Belgium with officials of l'Office National de l'Emploi (ONEM) and Fonds National de Reclassement Social des Handicapés; Ministère de l'Emploi et du Travail, *La Politique de l'Emploi,* pp. 24–25; Fonds National de Reclassement Social des Handicapés, *Rapport Général, 1965,* Brussels, 1966, pp. 14–16; ONEM, *Rapport Annuel, 1962,* Brussels, 1963, pp. 34–35; *idem. . . , 1965,* Brussels, 1966, pp. 17–18; *idem, 1966,* pp. 28–30, Brussels, 1967; *idem. . . , 1967,* Brussels, 1968, pp. 19–20; Margaret S. Gordon, *Retraining and Labor Market Adjustment in Western Europe,* Washington, 1965, pp. 99–100.

the payment of more than 17 million francs in the form of social security contributions.[3]

The other western European countries which have offered a wage subsidy to encourage the employment of hard-to-place workers have not yet met any marked enthusiasm among employers. Sweden and Denmark have fostered semisheltered workshops, divisions of regular plants where workers with reduced physical or mental abilities can be employed under a state subsidy. The early program faltered in Sweden because the hourly allowance per worker was considered too small; the allowance was increased in 1962 and again in 1964. Some increase in the number of enterprises which maintain separate semisheltered departments occurred, although the total number of semisheltered workers never exceeded 150.

Sweden enlarged its support of this type of labor market measure by emphasizing the absorption of individual workers. The tripartite committee on labor market policy, in its long and impressive report in 1965, declared: "In order to facilitate placement on the open market, it is proposed that part of the wages be paid from government funds for certain difficult-to-place applicants during a limited probationary period." Picking up this suggestion, the Swedish government, at the parliamentary meetings in the spring of 1966, endorsed probationary subsidized employment not only for handicapped workers but also for older workers and those whose skills are rusty. As in other countries, the line in Sweden between subsidized employment and subsidized training is not always clear, but probationary employment which involves training is favored.

A dramatic increase in semisheltered employment was projected in 1967 under the stress of increased unemployment. Sweden planned that private firms should absorb some 5,000 handicapped workers under semisheltered conditions by the middle of 1968; a revised program on an experimental basis was begun in 1967 for two years and was continued in 1969. Special departments in large workplaces and individual posts in smaller factories and offices (private and nonprofit as well as municipal and county council) were to be

[3] International Labour Office (ILO), *Redundancy Procedures in Selected Western European Countries,* Geneva, 1966, pp. 146–47.

designated as semisheltered, with the approval of the relevant trade unions. These posts, subsidized at 2,500 Sw. kr. per six-month period, were to be filled by the Employment Service from its waiting list of unemployed persons with reduced work capacity. Employed handicapped persons might also be transferred to these jobs, if the Disablement Resettlement Officer and the trade unions approved. During the recession of 1967–68, employers turned to the new measure as an alternative to dismissal of their own disabled workers and showed little interest in taking in outsiders. This use of the semiseltered job program has been approved, provided that the firm sets aside an equal number of semisheltered jobs to be filled by the Employment Service. The wages and fringe benefits on semisheltered jobs must be identical to those of current collective bargaining agreements.

Employers planning semisheltered workplaces also could apply for two other forms of aid: a nonrecurring grant of half the cost, up to a maximum of 12,000 Sw. kr., to adapt a workplace for a handicapped person and a subsidy to hire a permanent attendant to assist a severely handicapped employee who otherwise might not be able to continue working. The employer cannot obtain the subsidy for the attendant if he receives the grant for the handicapped worker himself. By July 1969, 43 firms had applied for grants toward work attendants on behalf of 47 handicapped workers; the subsidies are at the rate of a maximum of 2,500 Sw. kr. for each six-month period.

The semisheltered program faltered in its first years, and by July 1969 only 1,300 workplaces had been designated as semisheltered with 790 workers actually placed. The original goal of 5,000 semisheltered jobs has been restated in the 1969–70 plans of the Labour Market Board, which usually has a better record of meeting its goals for manpower programs.[4]

[4] Sweden, *Arbetsmarknadspolitik,* SOU 1965: 9, Stockholm, 1965, pp. 345–47; interviews in Denmark and Sweden; The National Labour Market Board, *Modern Swedish Labour Market Policy,* Stockholm, 1966, pp. 50, 88, 112. National Labour Market Board, *AMS Berättelse Angående Verksamheten under Budgetåret 1967–1968,* Stockholm, 1968, p. 57, *Arbetsmarknadspolitiken 1969–70,* Stockholm, 1968, p. 30; data from the Vocational Rehabilitation Division.

It should be noted that Sweden has several other methods of creating jobs for the handicapped which provide considerably more employment than semisheltered work, even at the planned maximum of 5,000 jobs.

In West Germany, an effort was made as early as 1951 to subsidize job creation for the hard-to-place who had lost their jobs through war or expulsion. When the program ended in 1956, it was estimated that 80,000 new jobs had been created and that older workers filled more than half of the new posts.

In 1958 the Employment Service (BAVAV) instituted a new subsidy program for some types of hard-to-place unemployed. A West German official explained the rationale of the subsidy:

Firms offering employment cannot, however, be expected to bear the whole burden of the difficulties which arise with workers, who after a long spell of unemployment have lost the habit of working, or who have to get used to a strange form of employment, or whose inadequate knowledge or total lack of knowledge and ability in their new occupations, etc., lead initially to reduced performance.[5]

The subsidy is an integration or settling-in grant or loan to encourage employers to hire the long-term unemployed or handicapped for permanent positions at full wages. From 1958 to 1960 a long-term unemployed worker was defined as one registered with an employment exchange for over two years. But, as the unemployment rate dropped, the required period was reduced to one year, and to only six months for those over 45. Over the years the subsidy rate has been increased from 50 to 60 percent of the gross wage, and the maximum period was lengthened from six months to two years. The wage subsidy may not exceed one-and-a-half times the amount of the unemployment allowance which the worker might receive.

It has been reported that West German employers have rarely sought the subsidy. Employers are said to be willing to pay for the training or the retraining of desirable manpower and to be uninter-

[5] H. J. Becker, *Labour Placing,* Monograph 4, Social Policy in Germany, Essen, 1963, pp. 15–16; ILO, *Redundancy Procedures. . . ,* pp. 144–45.

ested in the residual unemployed who are eligible for the subsidy.[6]

France has used a tax exemption rather than a subsidy to encourage the employment of disabled workers. In 1952 craftsmen who employed one handicapped worker became eligible for a tax exemption; it was estimated that 100,000 craftsmen could take advantage of this provision.[7]

Britain has not generally favored subsidies to employers on behalf of individual employees or types of workers. However, the Board of Trade has built factories, chiefly in South Wales, in order to provide employment for disabled miners. Employers may lease these factories at reduced rentals if they agree to employ a certain proportion of registered disabled; more favorable rentals are granted to those who employ higher proportions of disabled. Such factories are operated as commercial firms without any further government subsidy.[8]

The question arises as to why European employers have not responded more actively to the various subsidy programs for the hard-to-employ. Assuming that poor publicity is not the cause, one must look to the way in which employers calculate the costs of taking on hard-to-place workers. The employer may reckon the costs on quite a different basis than the Employment Service. The latter considers only the probable difference in productivity between an average worker and the hard to-place. But the employer may count additional costs due to his reduced freedom to choose his work

[6] ILO, *Manpower Adjustment Programmes: I. France, Federal Republic of Germany, United Kingdom,* Labour and Automation, Bull. No. 4, Geneva, 1967, p. 108; Hans Klabunde and Karl Josef Meyer, *The Labour Market in the Federal Republic of Germany,* Monograph No. 2, Social Policy in Germany, Ministry of Labour and the Social Structure, Essen, 1965, pp. 24–25; Gordon, *Retraining. . . ,* pp. 100–101; interviews in West Germany; BAVAV, *Geschaftsbericht fur das Rechnungsjahr,* 1964, p. 29; Information from U.S. Embassy, Bonn, February 1967; Organization for Economic Cooperation and Development, (OECD), Manpower Committee, *Annual Report on the Manpower Situation in 1960, Germany,* MO (61) 6/17, Paris, 1961, p. 25.

[7] ILO, *Vocational Guidance in France,* Studies and Reports, New Series, No. 39, Geneva, 1954, pp. 49–56.

[8] Political and Economic Planning, (PEP), "The Disabled Worker", vol. xx, No. 368, July 23, 1954, p. 181.

force and the expenditure of time on filling in application forms, filing reports, making claims for subsidy, undergoing investigations, etc. Finally, the employer must be concerned about the attitude of his other workers toward the hard-to-place. Under these circumstances, it may be that a small increase in the subsidy will have little effect on the employers' response, as appers to have been the case in Belgium and Sweden.

Two alternative methods of placing the hard-to-employ in competitive private enterprise have been considered in this and the preceding chapter—compulsion and financial incentives. The more effective of the two methods appears to be compulsion—the quota system and other procedures which impose legal restrictions on employers' freedom to choose their workers. When marginal workers are offered to employers for voluntary acceptance, employers tend to respond feebly, even with financial incentives. Employers are more amenable to unsubsidized voluntary placements of hard-to-employ workers of a better quality, especially when they are well prepared and chosen for the specific job.

Of course, the statutory obligation to hire a certain proportion of the hard-to-employ or to give them preference or exclusive rights to particular jobs cannot be read as net new job creation, since many might have held the same or equivalent jobs in any case, particularly under full employment conditions. But even when allowance is made for this factor, the compulsory method appears to provide more permanent jobs for the hard-to-employ at lower cost to the government than wage subsidies. By the same token, the quota is apt to be more costly to employers than the subsidy.

If the subsidy were more effective than it seems to have been in western Europe, its voluntary aspect might outweigh its cost to the government, especially in countries which could not for political reasons consider compulsory measures. The subsidy permits more flexibility in regard to the types of hard-to-employ persons who can be aided, since quota employment in practice has been limited to the physically and mentally disabled. Further experimentation with subsidy programs, along Swedish and Belgian lines, may be needed in western Europe before it can be concluded that subsidized employment will make a negligible contribution to the problem of the hard-to-employ.

SUBSIDIZED SELF-EMPLOYMENT

For some of the hard-to-employ, the most satisfactory solution is a business or workshop of their own. In some European countries the individual shopkeeper or craftsman is still so common that programs to place some of the hard-to-employ in this way are valid aspects of general labor market policy. Despite the trend toward declining percentages of self-employed in the nonagricultural labor force in virtually every western European country, all save Britain still have a higher proportion in this category than the United States.[9]

In practice, self-employment has most frequently been suggested for the physically handicapped, especially those whose former occupation is no longer feasible for them, who were previously self-employed, or who have never worked. In Sweden nonhandicapped single women and older workers are also eligible if they cannot find work in the open market. Several types of aid are offered: loans or grants to establish a business or workshop; preferential or monopolistic access to certain licenses; reservation of the right to conduct given businesses; auxiliary aides such as motor vehicles, work clothes and tools, and adaptation of the home to permit work on the premises.

The French legislation of 1957 on the vocational rehabilitation of the handicapped made provision for loans to the disabled who were judged capable of conducting a business or craft at their residence. A decree of September 1964 set the maximum amount of the loan at 20,000 F. (about $4,000) for twenty years at 2 percent interest. Other countries have similar programs for assisted self-employment.

Sweden regards this activity, called *Näringshjälp,* as labor market

[9] Gordon, *Retraining. . .* , pp. 23–24; :Edward F. Denison, *Why Growth Rates Differ: Postwar Experience in Nine Western Countries,* Washington, 1967, ch. 16.

policy worthy of inclusion in an over-all strategy. Five kinds of assistance are provided: to open a productive enterprise; to establish a kiosk for the sale of newspapers, cigarettes, candy, etc.; to purchase minor working equipment; to purchase a car or motor-driven invalid vehicle if needed for work or vocational training; and to employers who make special arrangements to enable disabled persons to perform their work. Initial grants, extra assistance, and interest-free loans are made by the central government through the Labour Market Board. Funds are also provided by the provincial enterprise associations and local government sources. Those eligible to apply for grants or loans to start, take over, or continue a business must submit evidence on the economic prospects of the venture which the county trade association or other experts analyze and approve or disapprove.

As a result of the findings of the tripartite committee on labor market policy, the Ordinance of 1966 provided increased amounts of grants and loans, introduced the possibility of additional aid to established businesses of disabled persons which might otherwise flounder, and transferred the authority over grants and loans for motorcars to the Labour Market Board. Despite the added assistance offered in 1966, the number of persons benefiting has actually declined in some categories. In 1964–65, 743 people were enabled to start their own business or open a kiosk. But in 1967–68 the total was only 655; among them were three gypsies, who were assisted to conduct scrap iron collections. The cost to the National Labour Market Board for the smaller number of grants in 1967–68 was more than twice that for 1964–65. The rising costs of establishing a viable business had in fact become an obstacle to offering such opportunities to all the people who could benefit from self-employment. In 1967–68 the average subsidy per business was over 9,000 Sw. kr. and the average cost of opening a kiosk was over 12,500 Sw. kr. because of regulations requiring higher standards of hygiene.

Those who were helped to purchase a motor vehicle increased from 880 in 1964–65 to 1,150 in 1967–68, but the rising costs of vehicles and the upper limits on income for applicants have restricted grants in 1968–69. Only a small number of workers have benefited from the provision that employers may get a grant of up to 12,000 Sw. kr. ($2,400) for adapting a workplace to fit a disabled person. This was attributed to the high costs to employers of such changes over and above the subsidy; for the eight workers whose employers did receive such a subsidy, the average subsidy was a little over 2,000 Sw. kr. The number of persons receiving grants to purchase minor working equipment has remained under 200 for some years and their average grant in 1967–68 was about 1,250 Sw. kr. The Labour Market Board has proposed changes in the regulations to enable more people to qualify, but so long as prices continue to rise steadily, the present system of fixed subsidies will constantly become outdated.

A special analysis was conducted of grants made to 330 handicapped individuals between July 1962 and September 1963 in five Swedish counties. The majority, 280, were assisted to purchase, replace, or repair an automobile which they used in their business. Next in importance was aid to establish or improve a business, followed by aid in the purchase of tools and work clothing. Good cooperation existed among the responsible local, county, and central government agencies. Some 3,113,104 Sw. kr. ($591,490) was spent in over a year on behalf of the 330 clients, an average expenditure of $1,792. Close to 45 percent of the total cost was borne by the national government.

In the follow-up study made in September 1964, the results of the assistance were investigated. Some 108 enterprises had been established or improved as a consequence of the earlier aid. More than half of the 108 enterprises provided full support for their owners, 26 yielded a substantial portion of the owners' income, 13 offered no more than a minor contribution, and only 12 had ceased to operate. Businesses were found to be far more successful than workshops or crafts activities in the home.[10]

The circumstances in individual countries must be considered in

[10] Sweden, *Arbetsmarknadspolitik*, pp. 347–54, 369–75; Information provided by the National Labour Market Board; National Labour Market Board, *Modern Swedish Labour Market Policy*, pp. 50–51, 91–92, 112–14; *Information om Rehabilitiering*, No. 1, January 1967; National Labour Market Board, *AMS Berättelse . . . 1966–67*, p. 131; idem, *AMS Berättelse . . . 1967–68*, pp. 53–54, 59; *Arbetsmarknadspolitiken 1969–70*, Stockholm, 1968, p. 32.

determining whether self-employment is a reasonable economic solution for many of the hard-to-place. If they have a high rate of business failures or many individuals have inadequate income from self-employment, and if the cost of business subsidies greatly exceeds the cost of direct support, it might be wise to limit the subsidization of self-employment in competitive fields. Less competitive activities, such as the operation of newsstands, probably yield more certain income and require little subsidization.

SUBSIDIZED JOB CREATION IN DEVELOPMENT AREAS

A more general encouragement to the expansion of employment by private enterprise has been given in many countries through subsidies to firms in development areas where unemployment is higher than average and the hard-to-employ are a particular problem. The countries which have been most active in subsidizing job creation in development areas—Great Britain, Holland, Belgium, Sweden, and France—have not usually specified the type of worker to be hired. Therefore, the hard-to-employ have no special claim to jobs and often are passed over in favor of women who have not been in the labor force, pirated workers from other firms, and employed workers from other areas.[11] The benefits to the hard-to-employ from such job creation may come chiefly in the form of tighter labor markets, induced by the introduction of new employment opportunities in areas of traditionally higher unemployment rates.

Subsidies based on the number of employees in total or the number of new employees are rare. Great Britain, which has experimented over the longest period of time and has tried the greatest va-

[11] J. F. B. Goodman and P. J. Samuel ("The Motor Industry in a Development District: A Case Study of the Labour Factor," *British Journal of Industrial Relations,* November 1966, pp. 336–65) provide interesting evidence that the unemployed obtained relatively few of the jobs when a British automobile company opened a new plant in a development district; OECD, *Manpower and Social Policy in the Netherlands,* Paris, 1967, pp. 173–75.

riety of inducements to new or expanding enterprises in the problem areas, has adopted this method in addition to other assistance to firms, such as general-purpose loans or grants, grants for buildings or extensions, and the provision of government-built factories for sale or rent at advantageous terms. The new approach was taken in 1967 as the Department of Economic Affairs determined that it was "impossible to foresee with confidence more than a limited reduction in the disparity in unemployment levels between the Development Areas and the rest of Britain, or a growth in employment fast enough to cut down migration, from the Development Areas to a great extent." [12] Therefore, the proposal for a Regional Employment Premium to manufacturing industries in the development areas was designed to reduce the disparity in unemployment rates "without adding effectively to inflationary pressures or leading to any worsening in the balance of payments." By granting subsidies to existing as well as new manufacturing industries according to the number employed, the Regional Employment Premium has wider scope than earlier development measures. The emphasis on manufacturing industries is related to the British desire to increase exports and was previously expressed in the Selective Employment Tax.

During the discussions of the proposed Regional Employment Premium a good deal of criticism was offered, chiefly by representatives of management. The most fundamental criticism was that the manufacturing industries in the development areas would not greatly increase their share of the national output or their contribution to exports, but would absorb the premium in increased wages or profits. Despite considerable opposition, the measure was put into effect in September 1967 for seven years. A payment was to be made of 30s. per week for every full-time male employed in manufacturing, 15s. for each woman and boy, and 9s.6d. for each girl. Part-time employees working eight to twenty-one hours a week would command half the full-time premium. Eligibility under the Selective Employment Tax, which at that time provided a premium to manufacturers

[12] Great Britain, Department of Economic Affairs, *The Development Areas: A Proposal for a Regional Employment Premium,* London, 1967, p. 9.

throughout the nation, was a prerequisite to qualification for the Regional Employment Premium.[13]

In April 1968 manufacturing employment in the development areas was given a further differential advantage. The Selective Employment bonus which previously was paid throughout the nation was withdrawn from all manufacturing firms except those in the development areas. The refund of the Selective Employment Tax was made to all qualified manufacturers, but firms in the development areas continued to receive their refunds plus 7s.6d. per week for each adult male, 3s.6d. for each woman and boy, and 2s.6d. for each girl. These sums are paid in addition to the Regional Employment Premium and together cover 8–9 percent of the wage costs in manufacturing in the Development Areas.

It was estimated that in 1968–69 £100 million will be distributed in Regional Employment Premiums, with 40 percent going to Scotland. Some years must pass before an evaluation can be made of this latest effort to reduce higher than average unemployment rates in the northern regions and an opinion can be formed of its effects on the hard-to-employ in those areas.

In assessing the general role of wage subsidies in the employment of the hard-to-employ, we observe that in theory subsidies are well accepted in several western European countries. But in practice subsidies have not yielded the anticipated results, largely because of employers' reluctance to limit their freedom of hiring and dislike of reporting on each worker to the government agency. However, subsidies to employers are only one of many manpower tools used to assist the hard-to-employ on an individual basis in western European countries and, as we shall now see, direct action by government to create jobs has far more importance than subsidized private employment in the most advanced countries.

[13] The Development Areas (Cmd. 3310), H.M.S.O.: London, 1967; Financial Times, November 10, 1967.

VIII | Special Job Creation for Regionally and Seasonally Unemployed

Despite the attention and resources devoted to placement of the hard-to-employ in regular private and public jobs, described in the preceding chapters, many western European countries have recognized a need for deliberate job creation for the residual unemployed who temporarily or permanently find no place in regular employment, even under full or overfull employment conditions.

The situations which call for job creation have been identified in an official Swedish statement:

Regardless of the long-term trends, we must, in fact, assume that there will continue to be such unemployment as can only be combatted by the creation of additional opportunities for work. The need for such special employment-creating measures can arise from a lack of effective demand, from temporary or local disturbances in employment which cannot suitably be remedied by other methods, or from difficulties in placing unemployed persons owing to their personal circumstances.[1]

The special job creation under discussion must be distinguished from other job-creating economic and labor market measures, such as regional industrial development. Special job creation usually occurs outside of established enterprise structures, stresses labor intensive activities, and fosters socially useful activities which might not be undertaken at all or might be done in a different way or at a later date. By general agreement, special job creation should be

---

[1] OECD, *Labour Market Policy in Sweden,* Paris, 1963, p. 22.

a last resort—to be offered in individual cases only when all other measures to combat unemployment have been tried or found inappropriate.

Commitment to special job creation varies in intensity among the European countries. It is perhaps strongest in the Netherlands and Sweden, whose declarations are matched by their actions. The Dutch labor market authorities explain that "full employment is interpreted quite rigorously; only a very low level of unemployment is permissible . . . [an] important reason for giving high-priority to full employment is the unforgotten experience of the mass-unemployment of prewar depression days. It left deep scars and made public opinion allergic to any degree of unemployment." [2] The Dutch deplore the human and social wastes of unemployment. They respect the right to work, even the right of those who cannot produce enough to justify the going wage rate or who require a sheltered environment.

In Sweden the Labour Party has declared: "We do not accept any percent of unemployment." It has been a cornerstone of manpower policy that the provision of employment is in general superior to unproductive financial maintenance of the unemployed. Furthermore, social and humanitarian considerations make it "urgent to provide employment even for very low-productive manpower." [3] In both countries, full employment and the high level of social benefits have strengthened the support for job creation for the small minority left behind.

Yet, neither the Swedes nor the Dutch feel an obligation to guarantee employment for all the unemployed and certainly not for the underemployed or those whose full-time wages are low or substandard, as has been discussed in the United States.[4] Employed per-

[2] OECD, *Manpower and Social Policy in the Netherlands,* Paris, 1967, pp. 63, 67, 74, 205.

[3] Sweden, National Labour Market Board, *Modern Swedish Labour Market Policy,* Stockholm, 1966, pp. 50, 99; David Jenkins, "Brains Before Beauty," *Sweden Now,* December 1968, p. 32.

[4] Garth L. Mangum, *Practical Consequences of Guaranteeing Employment,* unpublished paper for the U.S. Chamber of Commerce, pp. 35–37, 41–42.

sons are not eligible for created jobs in western European countries, nor would many seek them. Those European workers whose earnings are low because they work part-time usually have chosen such a schedule voluntarily and do not wish a full-time week which might raise their earnings. A few in low-paid full-time work might be better off in some types of created jobs.

In the United States, however, perhaps ten-million workers have lower hourly earnings than they would receive at the federal minimum wage. In addition, millions of American workers who involuntarily work part-time might prefer full-time guaranteed jobs. The unemployed are thus only one of the claimants for created jobs in the United States.

Not only have the European countries no demand by the employed for their limited supply of created jobs, but they also have excluded many of the unemployed from such jobs by legislative principle, administrative procedures, choice of projects, and budgetary limitations. In no sense can they be said to provide guaranteed employment.

AN OVERVIEW

Special job creation has been undertaken for two main groups in western European countries. The first group is hard-to-employ because of structural, regional or seasonal factors which may be intensified during recession periods. Further impediments to placement may be lack of skill, age, or attachment to a particular industry, occupation, or area. The worker is theoretically fully employable, but he needs created employment to bridge periods of unemployment between his regular jobs.

The second group is severely handicapped or unplaceable in existing labor markets for personal reasons, quite apart from questions of skill, age, location, or industry, although these factors may complicate the situation. These workers' low productivity and other characteristics limit their possibilities of entering or reentering competitive employment under present socioeconomic conditions.

TABLE VIII.1. Special Job Creation in Four Western European Countries, 1965

	The Netherlands	Sweden	Great Britain	West Germany
Civilian labor force [a]	4,374,000	3,749,000	25,109,000	26,699,000
Average monthly unemployment [b]	34,000	45,300	329,000	140,000
Employed under quota system	0	0	404,833 [c]	478,992 [d]
Employed on special public works	2,202 [e]	4,630 [f]	0	see [g]
Employed on created jobs for handicapped:				
sheltered workshops	20,137 [h]	5,032 [i]	11,941 [c]	2,200 [j]
homework	200 [h]	971 [i]	1,150 [c]	n.a.
outdoor projects	6,493 [h]	3,778 [f]	see [c]	3,000 [g]
white-collar workers	1,798 [h]	2,525 [f]	0	4,200 [k]

[a] *OECD Observer*, February 1967.

[b] OECD, *Economic Outlook*, July 1967, Paris, 1967, p. 38; Sweden, Ministry of Finance, *The Swedish Budget 1969/70*, Stockholm, 1969, p. 54. The Netherlands figure is for the labor reserve; unemployment is about 32,000. The figure for Great Britain is adjusted from the total for the United Kingdom.

[c] Great Britain, Department of Employment and Productivity. Sheltered workshops include 133 trainees. Some sheltered work is on outdoors projects.

[d] Total is for 1963. H. J. Becker, *The Employment of Seriously Disabled Persons*, Federal Ministry of Labour and the Social Structure, Essen, 1965.

[e] The Netherlands, Ministerie van Sociale Zaken en Volksgezondheid, Directoraat-Generaal Voor de Arbeidsvorziening, *Jaarverslag*, 1965, p. 105. Includes about 80 handicapped unemployed. Excludes employees of contractors.

[f] Sweden, AMS, *Berätelse om Verksamheten under 1965*, pp. 41, 55, 63; National Institute of Economic Research, *The Swedish Economy*. Special Public Works excludes skilled workers. White-collar workers include musicians.

[g] West Germany, Federal Institute for Labor Placement and Unemployment Insurance, (BAVAV). A small number of workers, not handicapped, should be allocated to Special Public Works.

[h] The Netherlands, Ministerie van Sociale Zaken en Volksgezondheid, *Algemene interne documentatie*, no. 390, 4 May 1966, p. 3; no. 369, 26 November 1965, p. 1. Annual average.

[i] Sweden, National Labour Market Board, Vocational Rehabilitation Division. Number of places available at end of year in sheltered workshops and homework.

[j] Bent Andersen, *Work or Support*, OECD: Paris, 1966, p. 66.

[k] Total is for 1964. OECD: Manpower and Social Affairs Committee, *Annual Reports*, Germany, 1964, MO (64) 10/01, p. 16.

The jobs created for the first group are here called "Special Public Works" to distinguish them from job creation for the severely handicapped, which take a more varied form: outdoor projects, sheltered workshops, homework, and jobs for white-collar workers. Table VIII.1 shows the extent of job creation in Sweden and the Netherlands, the two leading countries, and, for contrast, in Great Britain and West Germany. Although it is not a form of special job creation, employment under the quota system has been shown because some officials maintain that the existence of the quota reduces the need for special job creation (see Chapters V, VI).

The number of registered unemployed is a rough guide to the need for job creation. But it should be noted that some groups for whom jobs are specially created are not canvassed for the unemployment statistics. Their created jobs therefore do not reduce the count of the unemployed. Most of the unemployed who are placed on Special Public Works are subsequently excluded from the unemployment count, although they continue to be listed as available for work at the Employment Service offices. To discover how much unemployment there would be without job creation and other programs is a complex matter, since each country has its own rules of exclusion and inclusion.

Both Sweden and the Netherlands have permanent, nationwide programs to create jobs in each of the five categories which have been distinguished in Table VIII.1, while Britain has sheltered workshops, home workers, and a small number on outdoors projects. West Germany maintains every type of job creation but the numbers employed under each are small and jobs for white-collar workers are created chiefly for older people in West Berlin. Several other northwest European countries support one or another type of job creation for the hard-to-employ, quite apart from traditional public works of the anticyclical or compensatory variety.[5]

The Netherlands has created more special employment in relation to the size of its labor force and its level of unemployment than other countries, although Sweden has been catching up in the

[5] E. Jay Howenstine, *Compensatory Employment Programs,* OECD: Paris, 1968.

last few years. To convey the extent and character of Dutch special job creation and the particular hard-to-employ groups which benefit, a statement is given in Table VIII.2 of the situation in November 1964, when unemployment was extremely low. It is deliberate policy that relatively few fully employable jobless males should be provided with created jobs, especially when over-all unemployment is low. Because of the nature of the created jobs, described below, fully employable unemployed women have been excluded from the program.

TABLE VIII.2. Special Job Creation, the Netherlands, November 1964 [a]

	Male	Female
Unemployed: fully employable,	16,442	3,307
on Special Public Works	(1,419)	(0)
Unemployed: reduced employability,	9,328	1,319
on Special Public Works	(79)	(0)
on created jobs for handicapped	(6,356)	(835)
Registered but not counted as unemployed		
because classified as unplaceable,	16,094	2,536
on created jobs for handicapped	(14,595)	(2,206)

[a] The number of created jobs for the handicapped in November 1964, according to data from the responsible agency, the Complementary Social Provisions Division of the Ministry of Social Affairs, was 27,615. Table VIII.2 lists only 23,992, using the breakdowns and figures of another directorate of the Ministry.

Source: The Netherlands, Ministry of Social Affairs and Public Health.

The unemployed of reduced employability need created jobs, and two-thirds had them. Even in a tight labor market they are difficult to place in competitive jobs. Over 90 percent of the group which was registered for work but had been classified as unplaceable in the competitive labor market was in created jobs. From this record it can be seen that the Dutch provision of specially created jobs for the hard-to-employ is highly developed. By mid-1968 Holland had over 45,000 in created jobs, still exceeding Sweden's record job creation in 1968.

A more detailed appraisal of job creation for the hard-to-employ in western Europe follows in this and in the next chapter, with separate discussions of the distinct types of programs listed in Table VIII.1. The present chapter is concerned with job creation for the cyclically, structurally, regionally, and seasonally unemployed.[6]

SPECIAL PUBLIC WORKS

Each country has its own name and organizational structure for its job creation program for the unemployed who are not physically, mentally, or socially handicapped, but who are hard-to-employ, usually because they are unskilled workers in areas of higher than average unemployment or in seasonal or declining occupations and industries. In Holland where the program is called Supplementary Employment (*Aanvullende Werkgelegenheid*), it is entirely distinct both from ordinary Public Works and from outdoor projects for the handicapped. However, a few handicapped workers in isolated districts are permitted on Supplementary Employment projects, as Table VIII.2 indicates. Sweden also has an Emergency Public Works program (*Allmänna Beredskapsarbeten*), but the line of demarcation between this program and outdoor created jobs for older, immobile workers, who are listed with the handicapped (Chapter IX), is not sharp and raises statistical problems for recent years.

In the programs of other countries, such as West Germany's Productive Work Relief (*Wertschaffende Arbeitslosenhilfe*) and Belgium's system of centrally subsidized employment provided by the local authorities (*Pouvoirs Publics*), the whole range of hard-to-employ types may be found under one administrative unit. Separate programs for distinctive groups emerge when central governments play a leading role and when the total program is relatively large.

[6] The sections which follow rely heavily on interviews, unpublished internal reports and statistics from the various western European countries, as well as the published data.

186 | *Special Job Creation*

Selection of Workers

The method of selecting candidates for Special Public Works varies from country to country. In Belgium selection is left entirely to the local authorities, who also choose and execute the projects; the central government, through the manpower agency, merely allocates the subsidy funds according to the amount of unemployment and the size of the request from each area. West Germany also relies on local initiative and administration, but there is more central decision about where subsidy funds are most needed.[7]

The Netherlands uses a particularly formal and complex method of selecting men for its centrally administered Special Public Works program. All registered unemployed males between 21 and 65 who have been classified as fully employable (see Chapter I) are screened by the local Employment Service and a certain number are declared "suitable for placement in Supplementary Employment." Because of the nature of the projects, selections are almost entirely limited to unskilled manual workers and preference is given to older workers.

As a result of the decline in the proportion of the unskilled in the labor force, smaller percentages of the male labor reserve (unemployed plus those on Supplementary Employment) have been classified as suitable for Supplementary Employment over the years; in 1958, 1959, and 1960, one-fourth or more were found suitable, but in 1963 the ratio fell to less than 12 percent and it has remained at that level or lower since then.[8]

All who are found suitable for Dutch projects are not actually placed because of budgetary limitations and the location and labor needs of individual projects. Placement is carried out by the local

[7] ILO, *Manpower Adjustment Programmes: I. France, Federal Republic of Germany, United Kingdom,* Labour and Automation Bull. no. 4, Geneva, 1967, p. 110.

[8] The Netherlands, Ministry of Social Affairs and Public Health, *Arbeidsmarktbeschrijving,* annual.

Employment Service offices in accordance with directives indicating the order of placement. The directives are formulated by the central Directorate for Supplementary Employment Policy in consultation with the Advisory Committee for Supplementary Employment, which is a subcommittee of the Central Advisory Committee for Manpower and includes representatives of labor, management, and other groups, such as the Netherlands Union of Municipal Authorities.[9] On the average, 70 to 75 percent of all suitable and available workers are assigned each year, but in 1963 it was as low as 49 percent.

Sweden requires that unemployed candidates for Special Public Works (*allmänna beredskapsarbeten*) meet certain tests of citizenship, age, and willingness to work, and that they be classified as unlikely to obtain work soon in the open market. They also may be given a means test and a waiting period before being referred to a project by the local Employment Service office. Advanced age, lack of suitability for competitive jobs, heavy family responsibilities, need for income, firm local ties, and an expectation of lengthy unemployment are the criteria by which the limited supply of jobs is rationed.[10] However, a good potential for reentering the competitive market should be present, in order to distinguish these workers from the older, immobile workers placed in projects for the handicapped.

Those who actually have been chosen for Special Public Works in Sweden and Holland have been predominantly male and older. In Sweden about three-fourths of the men were over 45 and 20 to 25 percent were over 60 in the early 1960's. The Dutch, who discharge men from Special Public Works when they reach 65, consider 50 and over as the upper age group; in most years this group constitutes from half to three-fourths of all men on Special Public Works. Holland does not quite match Sweden in providing created employment for older unemployed men. In both countries, the proportion of older men is higher on Special Public Works than it is in the male labor force or among unemployed males.

[9] OECD, *Manpower and Social Policy in the Netherlands,* pp. 103–104.
[10] Sweden, *Arbetsmarknadspolitik,* SOU 1965: 9, Stockholm, 1965, pp. 204, 208, 239, 241; *Modern Swedish Labour Market Policy,* pp. 40, 97–98.

Workers on the projects in both countries have come over-whelmingly from agriculture (or forestry in Sweden), construction, and miscellaneous unskilled occupations. It is likely that these characteristics also predominate among the nonhandicapped on Special Public Works projects in Norway, Denmark, West Germany, and Belgium.

One concomitant of job creation through Special Public Works is the need to employ a considerable number of supervisory and skilled workers on projects, even though their skills may be in short supply in the rest of the economy. If a country uses private contractors to carry out its Special Public Works, as the Netherlands does, these skilled workers are not considered part of the program although their wages figure in cost calculations. But if, as in Sweden, all contractors' employees are counted and the projects' skilled workers (*särskild yrkeskunning arbetskraft*) are referred by the Employment Service, they are counted in the total employment provided by the program. The present study excludes the skilled workers wherever the data permit.

Regional Emphasis

Several European countries use Special Public Works to supplement and reinforce an array of regional development, seasonal stabilization, and geographical mobility programs which, along with other labor market measures and full employment conditions, have greatly reduced unemployment rates in the regions of traditionally high unemployment.[11] However, these areas continue to have proportionately more idle workers than other areas and, in fact, the relative gap between the highest and lowest regional unemployment rates may increase as the over-all rate declines.

As a result, the centrally planned job creation programs in Sweden and Holland, for example, have a persistent bias in favor of their

11 Beatrice G. Reubens, "Lessons for the United States from Western European Experience with the Hard-to-Place," in *Proceedings of the Twentieth Annual Winter Meeting*, Industrial Relations Research Association, December 1967, pp. 307–308.

northern areas, which have a higher incidence of structural and seasonal unemployment. In December 1965, 92 percent of the men on Swedish Special Public Works projects resided in the seven northern forestry counties; 43 percent were from one of these counties, Norbotten, where over 50 percent of unemployed males were placed on project employment. While the balance may have shifted somewhat since 1965, the northern counties still play a major role in terms of expenditures and man-days worked. Their share of the created jobs remains larger than their proportion of Sweden's population, labor force, or registered unemployment.

In Holland about 90 percent of the unemployed who are deemed suitable for and actually are on Special Public Works are found in the four northern provinces of Groningen, Friesland, Drenthe, and Overijssel. In these provinces, there also has been a downward trend in the proportion of the male labor reserve declared suitable for supplementary employment but it still is considerably higher than the national proportion.

Such a heavy representation of men from these areas is due partly to higher unemployment rates and partly to the tendency of the projects to accept a larger proportion of the suitable unemployed from these regions than from the rest of the country. The dominance of these regions in the program is little affected by fluctuations in unemployment from month to month or over the years.

The high concentration of eligible project workers in a few areas has created policy and planning problems for the Special Public Works programs. Although the principle is accepted that workers should live within easy traveling distance of their jobs, it is not always possible or desirable to conduct so many projects in the underdeveloped areas. As of June 1968, the Swedish Labour Market Board provided barracks for 2,943 workers on Special Public Works and outdoor projects for the handicapped; about 10 percent of the workers on all types of created jobs thus were housed by the government. In the past, when Holland had larger numbers on projects than it has had in the 1960s, barracks were used by those who had to work away from home; recently, foreign workers have occupied the buildings.

Swedish employers maintained that the location of a large proportion of the projects in the northern areas was fostered by local political interests who feared depopulation and the erosion of their communities' tax base. They welcomed roads and other improvements which promised to enhance their competitive position. As a result, it was charged, less urgent roads were built in the stagnant north as Special Public Works at the very time that the bustling areas of the south and center needed more new roads.[12]

To counteract the heavy regional imbalance, a few unemployed from the seven northern forest counties have been placed on projects in the central and southern areas in the hope that these men might thus effect a permanent transfer to another area and competitive employment. The transferred men have constituted 6 to 8 percent of the total number on the program and numbered 500 in 1967–68.

The newer approach has been to use Special Public Works projects and outdoor projects for older, immobile workers to build up the infrastructure and facilities of selected economic development areas in the north, instead of spreading the effort thinly throughout the region. In 1967–68, the increased general unemployment in Sweden had especially adverse effects on the north. The usual road work, forestry and water, and sewerage projects were not sufficient for those needing created jobs. As a supplement, larger projects were established in the populated coastal areas of the north where unemployment had become a problem. Some unemployed from the isolated inland communities were placed on these projects, using daily bus transportation or camps provided by the Labor Market Board.

As part of the Special Public Works program, municipalities have built factories for rental to private enterprise. Vocational training centers to prepare workers for the new enterprises have been erected as Special Public Works. Prefabricated houses have been assembled and buildings have been repaired. These measures not only provide employment immediately but they also give promise of making additional future employment possible. However, the

[12] OECD, International Management Seminar on Active Manpower Policy, *Supplement to the Final Report,* Paris, 1965, pp. 115–16.

construction of buildings involves high costs per man-day and such projects have been increasingly rejected for Special Public Works.

The Netherlands, which has used the same approach in its northern provinces, has attacked the high cost problem by establishing, jointly with the Ministry of Economic Affairs, special subsidy rules for expensive projects in development areas. The recession of 1966–68 reinforced the Dutch interest in using Special Public Works for regional development purposes and also led to a greatly increased regular public works program in these areas.

The dominance of the northern areas in the Swedish program persists in spite of a desire "to sever the selection of projects from the present dependence on the domicile of the unemployed," as the government and the tripartite committee on labor market policy recommended in 1965–66. A countervailing pressure is exerted by the need to provide jobs for displaced older small landowners and forestry workers in sparsely populated regions and other "older workers or persons tied to their domicile for other reasons." [13] The solution of transferring many of these people to the outdoor projects for the handicapped has been tried in Sweden, but it has been called as an administrative and budgetary device rather than a substantive change. The number of unemployed on Special Public Works would be considerably higher if a proper count were kept, some Swedish officials maintain. A study by the Statistics Section of the Labour Market Board in mid-1969 contrasted the totals of the Technical Division, which has been responsible for defining the categories and issuing the statistics, with the records kept by the Employment Service. The latter tends to count men as on Special Public Works unless they have distinct physical, mental or social handicaps. In January 1969, for example, when the Technical Division counted only 4,346 unemployed on Special Public Works, the Employment Service enumerated 8,040. If a new statistical series is issued, it may cause some revision of the data and trends in this and the next chapter.

The tripartite committee in 1965 questioned whether created jobs, which should be of brief duration and lead to regular jobs, were a

[13] *Modern Swedish Labour Market Policy*, pp. 39, 40, 97, 98.

remedy for the long-term unemployment which affects many of these older and immobile workers. Swedish surveys showed that workers had been on created jobs for long periods. A third in 1961 and 22 percent in 1963 had been at work on projects for over a year, while 47 percent in 1961 and 35 percent in 1963 had been employed for over nine months. The proportions were even higher in the northern counties. A 1969 survey of all on outdoor projects showed no marked change.

Clearly, some conflicts exist between the needs of the unemployed in the north and the other pressures on and functions of the Special Public Works program. The greater the regional disparities in unemployment rates, the greater is the need for created employment in the distressed or underdeveloped areas and the more difficult it is to find urgent and economical projects in those regions.

Seasonal and Cyclical Variations

Administrators of the Special Public Works programs attempt to respond to seasonal and cyclical variations in unemployment. Lagging behind the seasonal movement of unemployment by one to two months, the Dutch program reaches peak employment in February or March and its minimum level in September or October; the Swedish program has the same high months but tends to reach its lowest levels in July or August. The gap in total project employment of skilled and unskilled between the highest and the lowest months can be substantial. For example, Sweden reached a high of 11,067 at work during February 1967, following a build-up from a low of 1,880 in July 1966, with an average of 3,660 men in the calendar year 1967. For the sake of the workers, the program tries to provide jobs soon after unemployment occurs. Thus, a Swedish survey in October 1959 showed that 36 percent of those referred to projects had been employed for under one month and only 21 percent had been out of work for over four months.

These countries also desire to curtail specially created employment as private enterprise shows a seasonal or cyclical expansion.

If potential employees are tied up on created jobs, the Special Public Works program will be in conflict with basic labor market policy. However, Swedish authorities have observed that the seasonal cutback of project employment in the spring frequently makes little contribution to the labor supply, since many of the released workers become unemployed or underemployed until the next expansion of project employment.

The attempt to coordinate the number of men on Special Public Works projects with seasonal and cyclical fluctuations in unemployment imposes several kinds of tasks on the administrators of the program. Good unemployment statistics and forecasts of unemployment are required. In the Netherlands monthly unemployment statistics are subdivided into categories which aid the policymakers. The Employment Service, through its regional and local office, estimates the numbers likely to be suitable for supplementary employment six months in advance. In Sweden the Labour Market Board office in each county forecasts in May or June the expected need for Special Public Works employment in the following budget year (July through June); this is subject to later modification. In 1963 the adequacy of Swedish unemployment data for such forecasts was questioned by the OECD examiners of Swedish labor market policy. Some new and improved data have subsequently been collected, based on household surveys.

Additional elements in the achievement of proper seasonal and cyclical timing are the stockpiling of projects long in advance, a wise choice of new projects from the stock or pipeline to absorb the increase in unemployed, and a prompt distribution of the unemployed among existing and new projects on a week-to-week basis.

In Holland the functions are initiated at the regional level under Provincial Employment Committees consisting of representatives of the provincial authorities, the regional representatives of the Public Works Directorate, the Land Improvement Service, the district offices of the Supplementary Employment Service, and labor and management organizations. Since the reclamation and drainage of land and building of dikes are important as special public projects in Holland, the relevant agencies are represented.

The Working Committee of the aforementioned groups draws up regional plans twice a year from its varied stockpile and regulates the initiation, acceleration, deceleration, and termination of projects. Central assessment and supervision of the regional plans and co-ordination of supplementary employment policy with government policies on economic growth, tourism, and recreation are exercised by the Supplementary Employment Service and an interdepartmental Public Works Coordination Board.[14] Many projects are devoted to increasing and improving recreational facilities for citizens and tourists.

The Swedish system is centralized in the Labour Market Board, which has a technical division to devise, finance, and supervise Special Public Works based on estimates of job needs from each county. The Board also conducts many projects itself and has its own construction organization, machinery, and stores, thus supplementing the projects planned and executed by the municipalities, and some dozen and a half central government agencies; special provision is made for the Lapps in the extreme north. All levels of government draw up five-year programs from which projects for Special Public Works are selected. Planning subsidies are made by the Labour Market Board to other government agencies as well as nonprofit or private groups, which may hire private architectural and engineering firms to aid them in planning a stockpile of suitable projects.

Private contractors execute many of the projects. In addition, some of the large lumber companies and individual farmers are approved to have projects on their private lands. An estimate of the extent of nongovernmental organization and execution of Special Public Works may be made from the 1967–68 official report, which in some categories includes projects for the handicapped, discussed separately in Chapter IX. One-third of the Labour Market Board's total expenditure of 212,500,000 Sw. kr. on its own projects for both employables and handicapped was under the direction of entrepreneurs or nonprofit institutions; these nongovernmental agen-

14 OECD, *Manpower and Social Policy in the Netherlands*, pp. 104–106, 210–11.

cies accounted for 28 per cent of the total man-days attributed to the Labour Market Board. Private sources also created jobs for employables and handicapped on private lands and property and they supervised the expenditure of 16,700,000 Sw. kr., of which the government contributed 62.5 per cent. These jobs entailed 62,600 man-days of work, of which 44,600 man-days were for Special Public Works. In all, Special Public Works provided 1,754,700 man-days of work in 1967–68.

Budgetary provisions is made each year by the central government for its subsidy to Special Public Works; discretionary amounts may be spent through the Labour Market Board without further legislative authorization if circumstances warrant. The municipalities generally are subsidized to one-third of their total costs, but larger grants are permitted to districts with high and persistent unemployment. The municipalities accounted for about one-fifth of the man-days in 1967–68. Central government subsidies plus outlays by individual agencies at the national level have accounted for over 85 percent of the total expenditures on Special Public Works in recent years.

The Dutch have been generally satisfied with their timing performance, but Sweden has found difficulties in reducing project employment quickly. These problems have been attributed to the large role of road construction and other heavy building activities which, if left unfinished, involve substantial losses. The tripartite committee on labor market policy indicated that timing difficulties were in part due to the fact that Special Public Works were not included in the ordinary activities of the various government departments. As a means of closing this gap, the committee suggested that some unemployed persons be placed on an experimental basis on regular public works and road construction jobs.[15] The *Riksdag* did not act on this point, however.

One type of build-up in project employment was specifically disapproved by the tripartite committee. This is the employment of men who year after year alternate between regular seasonal jobs and Special Public Works projects in the off-season. The oppor-

[15] *Arbetsmarknadspolitik*, pp. 248–52.

TABLE VIII.3. Employment on Special Public Works, Selected Countries, 1954–1968

Year	The Netherlands [a]		Sweden [b]		Belgium [c]	West Germany [d]	
	Average Number of Unemployed on Special Public Works	As percentage of male Unemployed plus those on Special Public Works	Average Number of Unemployed on Special Public Works	As percentage of male Unemployed plus those on Special Public Works	Average Number of Unemployed on Special Public Works	Average Number of Unemployed on Special Public Works	
						Excluding West Berlin	Including West Berlin
		percentage		percentage			
1954	14,100	20.6				56,000	
1955	11,900	24.1					
1956	10,067	27.0		7.0	9,790	23,000	
1957	10,559	22.0	1,788 [f]	6.7	5,343		
1958	16,174	17.7	3,219 [f]	8.5	10,464	15,000	
1959	13,760	19.3	8,469 [f]	22.3	17,279	12,000	20,000
1960	7,603	17.1	5,006	19.8	9,833	6,400	13,000
1961	4,123	13.1	2,265	11.3	7,114		9,000
1962	2,850	10.0	3,853	17.6	6,661		6,000
1963	1,786	6.2	8,356	28.0	6,057		4,000
1964	2,004	7.8	5,658	20.0	6,266		4,000
1965	2,202	7.3	4,630	22.2	6,062		3,000
1966	1,800	4.5	3,416	13.9	5,669		2,000
1967	2,400	3.5	3,660	11.4	5,706		2,450
1968	2,100 [e]	2.8 [e]	4,898 [g]	11.6 [g]	5,719 [h]		3,000

tunity to eke out a full year's work in this fashion might keep some younger and middle-aged workers attached to occupations and localities which offered no full-time future. However, more workers are actually immobile than the theorists expect. Provision of created jobs for some of them may be the only recourse, but most are referred to other programs first.

The recession of 1966–68 in western Europe revealed that less reliance is now placed on Special Public Works jobs to counter cyclical unemployment than in earlier years or than might have been expected. Table VIII.3 indicates only slight upward movements in the numbers employed on projects in the four countries studied and significant secular declines in the proportion of unemployed males on these created jobs in the two countries for which such calculations were made. The explanation lies chiefly in the increasing resort to other labor market measures such as retraining, the expansion of regular public works, added investment in development areas, and other countercyclical economic and financial measures which absorbed some of the potential and actual unemployed.

NOTES TO TABLE VIII.3

a The Netherlands, Ministry of Social Affairs and Public Health, *Arbeidsmarktbeschrijving;* Central Bureau of Statistics, *Maandschrift,* April 1967, pp. 342–43; October 1968; letter from Dr. A. H. Heering, December 19, 1968. Excludes employees of contractors.

b 1956–1963, *Arbetsmarknadspolitik,* SOU, 1965:9, Stockholm, 1965, pp. 210–11; 1964–1968, *Arbetsmarknadsstatistik,* monthly; National Institute of Economic Research, *The Swedish Economy.* Percentages after 1963 not strictly comparable with earlier years. Excludes skilled workers.

c Belgium, Institut National de Statistique, *Bulletin de Statistique,* monthly. Includes handicapped also.

d West Germany, Federal Institute for Placement and Unemployment Insurance. Includes handicapped also.

e Estimated number. Percentage based on average unemployment for first eight months.

f Includes a small number of handicapped who in later years are separated out.

g Average of first nine months, excluding estimated number of skilled workers.

h Average of first seven months.

Sweden, whose 1966–68 recession lasted longer than that in other countries and was intensified by structural changes in the economy designed to meet international competition, has shown how a variety of measures permitted the Special Public Works program to increase very modestly at a time when substantial numbers were losing their jobs. The first effort involved private enterprise; in February–March 1968, when seasonal factors intensified the recession, some 23,350 persons were kept from unemployment by various actions which maintained or increased the number of private jobs, while about 20,000 others indirectly gained jobs through the release of company investment reserve funds, advance orders to industry from government, and authorization of government and private construction ahead of schedule; these measures are described in Chapter XI.

Another 34,900 were taken off the labor market temporarily by their enrollment in vocational retraining courses. An additional number of unemployed youths were kept on in schools in extended training courses. Finally, special job creation for those who are handicapped in the labor market provided for 28,360 persons. The large increase in this category was in part the result of a redefinition of the groups considered to be handicapped in the labor market and the inclusion of older, immobile men who formerly would have been eligible for Special Public Works. In addition, recently discharged older industrial workers who might have qualified for Special Public Works were placed instead in a new type of workshop organized by the Labour Market Board.

In all, some 111,600 workers were saved from possible unemployment in February–March 1968 by labor market and economic measures, leaving the Special Public Works program to care for no more than 12,000 through created jobs, including the skilled workers on projects. There were still 51,933 persons registered as unemployed in March 1968, and not on any of the aforementioned programs. This was a higher total than normal frictional and seasonal factors would produce, but it could have been as high as 175,000, had Sweden not offered such varied alternatives to idleness.[16] And the Special Public Works program might have been called upon to play a much larger role.

The fact that the Swedish Special Public Works program did not expand greatly in the recession did not mean that it could continue in its accustomed fashion. Pressures developed from several groups of unemployed who previously held few or no created jobs on Special Public Works projects. Certain prosperous areas of Sweden which had little need for projects in the earlier period of full employment now had to devise useful and suitable work for displaced local workers. Local governments played a more active role in creating jobs involving municipal functions, such as water supply, sewage disposal, and road maintenance, thus supplementing regular activities. The type of projects which had long been familiar in the northern communities were introduced in some middle and southern municipalities (*kommunal regi*). Nevertheless, projects initiated by the municipalities and private authorities accounted for only 22 percent of the man-days on Special Public Works in 1967–68. Workers still relied primarily on central government projects which tailored their geographic distribution to local job needs.

Another change was the inclusion of a number of youths under 25 in Special Public Works. Since the recession had a considerable impact on young school leavers and older youths, in October 1967 the Labour Market Board adopted an activity program to combat unemployment among youths. Its five leading points consisted of a rapid expansion of training facilities within the vocational education system; increased utilization by youths of adult retraining courses; the creation of temporary housing for youths accepting employment outside their home areas; increased job creation for handicapped and maladjusted youths; and improved employment services and information.

The Labour Market Board budget for 1969–70 called particular

[16] Sweden, National Labour Market Board, *Arbetsmarknadspolitiken, 1969/70*, pp. 26–27; National Labour Market Board, *AMS Berättelse Angående Verksamheten under Budgetåret 1967–68*, Stockholm, 1968, pp. 71–77.

attention to the need for an increase in Special Public Works for young workers up to 25. Conceding that vocational training is the best solution for youths facing unemployment, the Board noted that other expedients have to be tried because many youths feel that their compulsory schooling has been long enough and they want jobs immediately. Others lack interest in or aptitude for training. Therefore, created jobs are needed in periods of unemployment. In fact, the situation improved markedly and the special projects which employed a few hundred youths at the maximum have now been closed.

The innovation which may have the greatest long-run significance is the extension of Swedish Special Public Works to unemployed technical and professional workers for whom other programs were inappropriate or lacking. New types of projects had to be devised to fit the skills of these groups. Women, usually excluded, now could be assigned to created jobs, although their numbers on Special Public Works are likely to remain small. The projects gave created jobs to about 140 unemployed engineers, technicians, and student trainees. The tasks to which they were assigned may be characterized as supplementary public service projects which support existing governmental functions. Some made surveys of buildings for the revision of tax assessments while others located and mapped water and sewerage systems in ten municipalities. Toward the end of 1968 some technical workers were assigned to the Industrial Medicine Institute where their task was to chart all of the mines, tunnels, and factories where workers run a considerable risk of silicosis. The Technical Division of the National Labour Market Board assists in finding projects for traditional and innovative Special Public Works.

In the first year, 1967–68, the new groups accounted for only 1 percent of the total man-days on Special Public Works. But the National Labour Market Board recognizes a need to increase job creation for unemployed white-collar and service workers on projects which permit workers to exercise existing skills and facilitate transfer to jobs in the competitive labor market.

COSTS AND CONTENT OF PROJECTS

It appears that the failure of the Special Public Works programs to expand during the recent recession is partially attributable to persistent problems as regards costs and choice of projects. Even if there were no difficulties in timing and in matching project employment to the needs and location of workers, the Special Public Works programs, much more than other manpower programs, would be plagued by conflicting objectives involving the costs and content of created jobs.

An overriding issue is the cost of created jobs versus the cost of other labor market measures to aid the unemployed. Sweden, which earlier found up to two-thirds of its generous manpower budget devoted to the creation of jobs year after year, has repeatedly stressed that retraining courses and mobility allowances cost much less per capita and have more enduring effects. The rising costs and other features of created jobs have led some Swedish authorities to press for less emphasis on created jobs and more on maintenance of income for those who can be reabsorbed quickly by the competitive market as well as for those displaced workers who are unlikely to work again before retirement. The Dutch authorities noted that rising costs per man-week were one of the chief factors in the pending changes in Supplementary Employment policy.

Since the need for created jobs is not completely eliminated by a great expansion of other types of measures, efforts are made in the European countries to understand and control the rising costs of Special Public Works. Several bases are used for the analysis. Sweden has been comparing the costs of Special Public Works projects with the costs when the same work is done under the ordinary government departments.

Analyzing road construction, which accounted for about 50 percent of man-days of work and almost 60 percent of total costs of

Special Public Works in 1965, the Swedish tripartite committee on labor market policy found several inevitable reasons for lower output and higher costs on the Special Public Works. The latter were carried out mostly in the winter, the most expensive time for construction. When they were forced to curtail operations in the spring or when cyclical forces increased demand in the rest of the economy, the result was either expensive completion operations or wasteful unfinished work. Because the purpose of the projects basically was to provide employment, many unskilled and perhaps unsuitable workers were used, reducing average productivity. Finally, restrictions on the use of machinery had been adopted to make construction projects more labor intensive. While the costs per man-day were thus reduced, the total costs of the Special Public Works projects were higher than on comparable work done by labor-saving methods.

Restrictions on the use of machinery were never entirely effective. On roads, labor costs fell to one-fifth of total costs and the over-all need for labor declined markedly. But the proportion of skilled workers required to operate the machinery rose, further reducing the places for the unskilled unemployed. Moreover, the skilled workers were not candidates for Special Public Works for the most part, and most of them could have found alternative employment.

Mechanization at once reduces the number of openings for unskilled workers and raises the costs per man-day of hiring them. Nevertheless, the tripartite committee recommended that all restrictions on mechanization and the use of skilled workers should be lifted and that the test of low man-day costs be supplemented by a comparison with the costs of doing the work by prevailing advanced methods. The committee acknowledged that certain projects would become entirely uneconomic. The choice of projects is complex, as the Swedish *Riksdag* indicated in laying down the guiding principles of future labor market policy in May 1966:

The selection of projects for relief work is, generally speaking, no easy task. The projects should be of such importance that they would in any case be carried out within the next few years. They must also be of such type that they can mainly be carried out during the winter and be interrupted at short notice. Finally, they should preferably also provide employment for workers without previous experience of similar work. In a situation when the general employment level is high but certain unemployment pockets exist, which call for relief work, it is necessary to take care not to select projects with significant secondary effects on the economy. In such cases labour must account for a great share of total costs. If all the above requirements cannot be satisfied, the requirement that the project should be of definite importance must always be fulfilled.[17]

A significant difference exists between the Dutch and Swedish programs on the issues of the urgency of the project. While the Swedish practice is to take parts of the regular five-year public works plans for the Special Public Works projects, the Dutch specifically seek useful projects which otherwise would not be done at all as normal work or would be done much later. Yet, both countries have been facing much the same type of problem with regard to the costs and content of Special Public Works.

In 1965, as Table VIII.4 shows, roads and building construction projects accounted for the bulk of the worktime on Swedish Special Public Works projects and both had high man-day costs. The Labour Market Board has urged reductions in the expensive projects and a search for labor-intensive work such as light forestry work, which needs little supervision, few skilled workers, and almost no machinery. The Board appears to have made some progress, according to the report for the fiscal year 1967–68, which does not separate the projects for the employables from those for the handicapped and therefore is not fully comparable with Table VIII.4. However, the mechanized, high-cost projects are still prominent— roads, water supply and sewerage projects, and building construction, including barracks for project workers assigned away from their homes.[18] The cost problem has not yet been solved on the Swedish Special Public Works program.

[17] *Modern Swedish Labour Market Policy*, p. 97; *Labour Market Policy 1969/70*, pp. 25–26.

[18] Sweden, National Labour Market Board, *AMS Berättelse Angående Verksamheten under Budgetåret 1967–68*, pp. 72–77.

TABLE VIII.4. Special Public Works, Employment and Costs,
by Type of Work, Sweden, 1965

	Number of Man-years Worked	Man-day Costs (Sw. kr.)
Total	5701.9	422
Roads	2895.1	367
Public road construction	(1714.5)	459
Road repair and maintenance	(567.7)	237
Forest roads	(566.3)	213
Other roads	(46.6)	394
Building Construction	1531.2	637
Factories	(843.9)	650
Other	(687.3)	621
Harbor, lighthouse, docks, bridges, channels —repairs and improvements	71.9	582
Waterworks and sewerage—repairs and improvements	545.1	364
State railways—work on tracks and right of way	50.3	252
Timber floatways—repairs and improvements	2.0	288
Armed forces—fortification repairs and other	66.2	339
Reforestation and allied projects	396.6	108
Other	143.5	347

Source: National Labour Market Board, Technical Division.

The Netherlands also concluded that their Supplementary Employment program should be altered, largely because of the rising costs per man-week due to increased mechanization. However, Holland has had a smaller proportion of worktime than Sweden on roads and buildings. The difficulty noted by the Dutch is a scarcity of low-cost projects, such as soil improvement, and a disturbing rise in the cost of supervisory personnel on these projects. Both Holland and Sweden conduct and subsidize projects on privately owned lands, provided the owner pays a stated portion of the costs, but private lands thus far have not been an important source of projects.

A need for changes in the program was also foreseen by the Dutch authorities because the number of suitable unskilled unemployed will continue to decrease. And at the same time a change in the nature of the projects and the selection principles for workers will be required because "the system as it stands offers no remedy for the growing groups of unemployed, such as skilled workers and administrative personnel." [19] As we have seen, Sweden has begun to remedy this deficiency through special projects, although the primary reliance is on further education and retraining. Sweden has also used job creation in a new fashion for youths leaving school, a group heretofore rarely included. The Labour Market Board's forecast of policy for 1969–70 called for job creation suitable as a transitional measure for manpower laid off due to closures and for agricultural and forestry workers displaced by structural change.

The adaptation of Special Public Works to the characteristics of the unemployed is a persistent and difficult issue. However, the western European countries do not have the additional burden of avoiding projects which conflict with the vested interests of trade unions and professional groups. Nor do they have to set aside socially desirable projects for fear that potential workers might consider the activities personally degrading.

It is worth noting that these countries have not been troubled, as other countries might be, by high costs due to inefficiency, corruption, leakage of funds, competitive and overlapping activities of agencies, and the choice of inappropriate or private-benefit projects. Characteristically, also, neither country has voiced any dissatisfaction over its method of executing Special Public Works projects. The Dutch use of private contractors with their own basic labor force on a fixed price or a wages-plus-costs basis suits their pluralistic approach. Sweden controls the hiring of the skilled workers and uses public bodies to carry out a substantial number of projects. Such cost problems as have been discussed are inherent in this form of job creation and are not administratively remediable.

[19] OECD, *Manpower and Social Policy in the Netherlands*, pp. 106–107.

POSITION OF WORKERS ON SPECIAL PUBLIC WORKS

Support for Special Public Works by workers arises from its superiority to income maintenance programs, such as unemployment insurance. Wages on Special Public Works are at the prevailing rates for similar work in the competitive labor market and project wages and fringe benefits often are negotiated according to trade union agreements. Therefore, many project workers suffer no loss of income and some may earn more through assignment to a higher-paid occupation. They also maintain continuity of eligibility for all social benefits. Project work has respectability and acceptability; no stigma attaches to it. At the same time, the hours of work, discipline, pace, and other conditions resemble normal work so closely that project jobs are not viewed as loafing, and pride is taken in the completion of schedules. European officials complain neither of recruitment problems nor of reluctance of project workers to transfer to the open market. Indeed, since a limited supply of project jobs is rotated among eligible unemployed men, there is a sense of achievement in obtaining project work.

What does project work do to maintain and improve skills? The nature of the projects definitely restricts the possibilities. Some on project jobs obtain an introduction to construction work as their basic attachment to forestry and agriculture is being eroded by a lack of year-round work. The projects may also serve as a bridge to regular construction work, which in many European countries is open to unskilled recruits and is the chief way of introducing agricultural people to industrial life. There is little formal training on any of the projects. Sweden is exceptional in that it uses construction projects involving repairs and conversions of buildings in order to maintain the construction skills of older unemployed workers. But in general, Special Public Works are not a good source of training or a means of stimulating personal development and upward mobility. Nevertheless, project jobs maintain work habits in a normal work setting. This is regarded as an important function in Europe, where upward mobility is not promised so freely as it is in the United States.

Another goal of project work is the transfer of large numbers of workers directly to jobs in the competitive labor market. The record here has been disappointing. The Netherlands reported that only 795 of the 7,759 men who held project jobs during 1964 left Special Public Works because they had found work in the open market; in 1965 the ratio was slightly higher, 946 out of 7,420. The usual pattern is that a project worker who is dropped when the budget contracts remains unemployed for some time and eventually finds work or returns to a project.

In Sweden the tripartite committee on labor market policy was dissatisfied both with the rate of transfers to competitive work and the machinery available for effecting transfers. The government agreed in 1966 that a placement officer from the Employment Service should be added to the staff of certain major projects. It will take several years to determine whether direct placement services are a sufficient remedy or whether there is a need to give a greater emphasis to training and upward mobility in project work itself. Above all, tighter labor markets are required.

It may be asked why the European countries are so devoted to job creation through Special Public Works in the light of the relatively limited benefits project workers seem to obtain and the various administrative, financial, and operational difficulties which accompany even the best organized program. Yet, Sweden regards Special Public Works as "the most important means at the disposal of the labour market policy to achieve a rapid short-term increase in employment." The Netherlands calls the program "one of the major potential instruments of labour market policy." [20] Implicitly, these nations regard the benefits, broadly conceived, as greater than the costs.

The features of the Special Public Works which are valued are the speed of implementation, the ability to vary the magnitude of the impact, the capacity to exercise a selective geographic and oc-

[20] *Modern Swedish Labour Market Policy,* p. 96; OECD, *Manpower and Social Policy in the Netherlands,* p. 49.

cupational effect, the potential for limiting or encouraging secondary effects on the economy as required, and the utilization of idle labor for projects which contribute to the general welfare. The relative importance of Special Public Works may decline if full employment is maintained more consistently and other types of economic, fiscal, and labor market measures are used more effectively, but it may be assumed that this sort of job creation, perhaps in revised form, will remain an important feature of labor market policy in many western European countries.

Countries which have not yet established this type of job creation on a permanent basis might be well advised to begin with a more varied set of projects, which provide many public service jobs for others apart from unskilled males, following the new Swedish trend. It also is desirable to establish job creation programs with built-in training features and procedures for transferring to the competitive labor market. The European use of contractors and projects on privately-owned lands must be evaluated in terms of the conditions in each country.

Nations which are contemplating such programs must also assess their basic institutions to determine whether the administrative complexities of Special Public Works programs will be as well handled as they are, for example, in the Netherlands and Sweden. These countries and others in western Europe are dedicated to long-range, over-all planning for economic growth and have an established public works planning organization with a tradition of five-year plans. Their government departments work well together at all levels and the quality of local officials is high. Financial commitments are made centrally for a reasonably long period of time and political differences do not threaten such programs. The general agreement on the importance of work in the life of the individual and the progress of the nation adds substantial nonmaterial private and social benefits. The high valuation of work lends support to job creation, sustaining its image and fostering its accomplishments. Without these characteristics, a country's Special Public Works program might fail to win public approval and might seem excessively inefficient and expensive.

IX | Special Job Creation for the Severely Handicapped

Even countries which have made strenuous efforts to place the hard-to-employ in competitive labor markets have not been successful with the tail end of the group—those whose age and financial circumstances indicate that they should be employed, but whose productivity in relation to accepted wage levels or whose behavior and work attitudes are currently unacceptable to employers, despite labor shortages. Many might be vocationally rehabilitated for the competitive market, given sufficient time and expense. But present methods are too costly in view of the expected returns and the alternative claims on the limited supply of rehabilitation facilities. Improvements in vocational rehabilitation techniques may aid future cases, but not these current unplaceables.[1]

Many might also become employable if management undertook a wide-ranging redesign of production methods; this is not likely in the foreseeable future. Similarly, economic and technical change in years to come may open new job opportunities for groups which are excluded from present job structures. But currently these potential workers are a residual problem.

Most modern societies have accepted two simultaneous and overlapping methods of providing for those who are severely handicapped or unplaceable in the labor market. One method has been to make cash payments which provide a limited command over

[1] Sweden, *Arbetsmarknadspolitik,* SOU 9: 1965, p. 233; Bent Andersen, *Work or Support,* OECD: Paris, 1966, pp. 15–17.

goods and services to unplaceables with no other source of income. The other approach, often through private philanthropic efforts, has stressed deliberate job creation. Historically, voluntary agencies have tended to favor selected disability groups, have covered the country unevenly, and have provided a low standard of living for their beneficiaries.

Dissatisfaction with these approaches has led several western European countries to undertake the creation of special jobs outside of ordinary enterprise structures in order to implement "the right to work" and to offset the inability of unplaceables to compete for normal employment opportunities. The Netherlands, Sweden, and Great Britain have the most important public programs to create "productive, remunerative employment . . . under conditions specially designed to meet the temporary or permanent employment needs of handicapped people," in the words of the International Seminar on Sheltered Employment at The Hague in 1959, reaffirmed at the Stockholm Seminar in 1964.

EVOLUTION OF PROGRAMS

The Netherlands not only has the largest job-creation program in relation to the size of its labor force, but it also has had a sizeable program for a longer period than other countries. Holland initiated its Municipal Social Employment program for manual workers (G.S.W.) in 1950 and for nonmanual workers (S.W.H.) in 1953 because large numbers of persons with severe physical, mental, or social handicaps were unable to obtain regular employment or to qualify for Supplementary Employment, described in Chapter VIII. The Dutch definition of eligibility for created jobs has been broad from the outset and includes pioneering efforts to employ the mentally retarded. Older workers, young people in trouble, former prisoners, alcoholics, and even "querulous persons, cross-grained fellows, intriguers" are also sought out. Those who never have worked before are accepted and "this has been a great blessing for thousands of persons who have been handicapped from their birth or childhood. . . ." [2]

The Dutch emphasis on the provision of work

corresponds with the appreciation of labour as a condition for social prestige and human happiness as these are seen in our western civilization. A man who cannot earn his living, is a devaluated man in the eyes of the community, of his family, his wife, his children. . . . Without social prestige it nowadays is hardly possible for any human being to maintain moral standards and therefore society being such as we have shaped it into—it is our duty to take care for social prestige that it may come within anybody's reach, also of the disabled.

The objective of the Social Employment program is said to be the creation of remunerative, productive jobs in special enterprises in order to increase, maintain, or restore social independence and capacity for normal employment. A spirited case is made for such programs:

The work performed . . . protects against the mental and moral dangers inherent in forced idleness. The performance of *productive* labour gives the worker the gratifying idea of being engaged in and of being of importance to the production process . . . The wages they earn with their work free them from the state of dependence . . . reference should also be made to the psychological aspects, the value of which is difficult to assess, but which is none the less real, because in most cases those working under the scheme will feel they are gradually becoming useful members of society again. . . .

Production, either directly for the benefit of the community, or for the commodities market or for certain industries which have commissioned work, is only one aspect of the social scheme for providing employment . . . Another aspect which should be borne in mind is that the persons concerned would for the rest of their lives be dependent on Government

[2] This and following quotations and references are from official releases in English by the Ministry of Social Affairs and Public Health, Complementary Social Provisions Division, issued in the 1950s and 1960s. Much of the information in this chapter was provided by officials of the various countries through interviews, letters, and unpublished studies and data.

assistance . . . They would either have been granted a benefit under some government regulation or have become charges on the municipality.[3]

This statement, in which various elements of a benefit/cost analysis are roughly assembled, goes on to recognize that government must subsidize the wages of those on created jobs. Since these subsidies offset the savings to government from reduced claims on other government benefits, it is further argued that the wage subsidy is justified because many of the workers on created jobs are rehabilitated and eventually enter or re-enter the competitive labor market. They then cease to draw subsidized wages and can become taxpayers, whereas pensioners or relief recipients are a permanent drain.

Furthermore, the wage subsidy is needed because social workshops, some of which might be self-supporting if they accepted the most favorable subcontracts, must choose those subcontracts and jobs which contribute most to the rehabilitation of their workers. Finally, the guiding principle of Social Employment, whether on outdoor public works or in workshops, is that a close resemblance to normal industry must be maintained in all regards. This implies that capital must be invested in up-to-date machinery and modernized buidings. It also offers another justification for government subsidies.

Much of the implicit evaluation of the program in Holland is based on the assumption that a high proportion of the workers on created jobs will move on to competitive jobs. This is also an important part of the Swedish rationale for public expenditures. Yet, in all countries the vast majority of people on created jobs for the severely handicapped do not succeed in obtaining regular jobs. Even in the early days of the programs when more employable workers were taken in, only a minority transferred to competitive employment. As the programs expanded and accepted workers of lower productivity, the rate of transfers tended to level off or drop. In fact, most holders of created jobs for the handicapped are in "sub-

[3] European Seminar on Sheltered Employment, The Hague, 1959, pp. 31, 9.

stitute permanent employment," the term coined in an OECD study.[4]

The contradictions inherent in a program devoted to rehabilitating everyone for competitive employment which in fact succeeds with only a tiny proportion has led Dutch officials to defend created jobs for those who must work indefinitely under sheltered and subsidized conditions:

For these persons the work they perform within the framework of the Social Employment scheme is the most they can attain; yet even these workers—though under sheltered conditions—are also doing productive work. . . . These activities do not in any way bear the mark of just keeping the man busy. Through adapted work the man is given the opportunity to earn his living through a real job.

There is another defense of sheltered work as long-term or terminal employment which is of some importance in Holland. It is the use of created jobs as a substitute for or supplement to institutional or home care, especially of the mentally retarded or ill. The social and personal gains are considerable because fewer personnel are needed in the work situation than in custodial or home care, thus freeing professionals and family members for other work. Furthermore, many who would otherwise be institutionalized are able to live in hostels, boarding houses, selected private homes, or with their own families. Finally, under full employment conditions, the output from created jobs constitutes a net addition to the economy and does not deprive other workers of jobs, although the cost of production may exceed ordinary costs. But at the root of all Dutch calculations is the consideration that modern society tends to guarantee a minimum standard of living to all whether they work or not and that participation in the world of work is intrinsically valuable.

Sweden's expansion of public job creation for the handicapped began in the 1960s as a part of its active manpower policy. The Swedish view is that "even during a high level of business activity, the need for sheltered employment for disabled persons will remain

[4] Bent Andersen, *Work or Support,* pp. 18–19.

unsatisfied." They see "a general trend on the labour market . . . towards increased need for employment-creating measures for the handicapped," namely, those who "cannot immediately or in the long run find work on the open market." [5] As broad a definition of the handicapped as was noted in Holland has been adopted by Sweden, and every type and combination of physical, mental, or social disability is included.

Apart from the long-run need for a steady increase in created jobs, Sweden is also concerned about expansion in the shorter recession periods. An official statement in the 1968–69 Budget proposal to the *Riksdag* declares:

Development in recent years has shown that [handicapped persons] face special difficulties in times of rapid economic change. Their difficulties are further increased when the demand for labour slackens. Since full employment includes everyone, society must make special efforts in the form of relief work as well as sheltered and semi-sheltered employment.[6]

In an earlier statement, Swedish authorities described the varieties of created jobs in terms which cover the main forms in use in other countries as well:

Sheltered workshops—a working environment without competition from other labour—offer a form of employment that in strain and tempo is adapted to the handicapped persons' capabilities. Municipalities, in particular, and voluntary organizations have arranged such workshops. . . . Employment for the handicapped is also provided in special outdoors jobs with low general demands. Institutions and authorities have so-called archives work available as a form of training and sheltered employment for white-collar workers and educated refugees. Some persons who, for medical or social reasons, cannot be placed in open employment, can be given work to be done at home.[7]

[5] Sweden, National Labour Market Board, *Modern Swedish Labour Market Policy*, Stockholm, 1966, pp. 49–50; OECD, *Labour Market Policy in Sweden*, Paris, 1963, pp. 21, 34; National Labour Market Board, *Arbetsmarknadspolitiken 1969–70*, Stockholm, 1968, p. 39.

[6] The Swedish Budget 1968/69, a summary published by the Ministry of Finance, Stockholm, 1968, p. 27.

[7] *Labour Market Policy in Sweden*, p. 21.

A major innovation in Sweden during the recession in 1966 was the creation by the Labour Market Board of industrial workshops for groups of displaced older factory workers. Previously, individual unemployed older men had been placed on created jobs of various kinds, but the new workshops try to give groups of redundant older workers familiar work assignments. The present form was devised as it became clear that a substantial number of older factory workers, including women, were being discharged because of rationalization and reorganization of firms as well as the international recession. Formerly such workers had been helped to retain their jobs by advance orders from government to private firms (Chapter XI) and occasionally by government purchase of firms about to close down, but such action is regarded as unsuitable where long run rationalization is involved.

The new industrial workshops resemble sheltered workshops, but the administration and clientele are distinct. The authorities hope that workers will stay in these workshops only until the Employment Service can work out a plan to return them to competitive jobs. These workshops are important because they are started by the Labor Market Board rather than by the municipalities, they place groups of redundant workers in familiar occupations, and they satisfy the need for work with low man-day costs. Relying on subcontracts obtained by the Labor Market Board from industry and government, the shops started in 1966 with 169 workers and by April 1969 had 650 workers in over 20 workshops. The 20,000 man-days worked in the workshops in 1966–67 rose to 94,700 in 1967–68. This approach to redundancy among older workers is only one of several used in Sweden, but it marks an interesting enlargement of job creation programs.[8]

The Swedish authorities maintain that a created job permits an idle person to train "for a new occupation and at the same time make a productive contribution under specially arranged conditions." It is emphasized that, to the greatest possible extent, cre-

[8] Sweden, National Labour Market Board, *Berättelse Angående Verksamheten under Budgetåret 1967–1968*, Stockholm, 1968, p. 56; *Arbetsmarknadspolitiken, 1969–70*, Stockholm, 1968, p. 32.

ated jobs should "serve as preparation for employment on the open market," but no stigma attaches to those who remain behind. Swedish estimates in 1959 indicated that about 0.4 percent of the population of 7.5 million, or 30,000 handicapped people, needed special job creation.[9] Now that this aim is within sight, additional needs have been discovered and higher goals have been set.

Great Britain pioneered by bringing the national government directly into the creation of sheltered jobs. In 1945 the government set up Remploy, Ltd., a nonprofit public corporation entirely financed by the central government and whose Board of Directors is appointed by the Secretary of State for Employment and Productivity (formerly the Minister of Labour). From its head office in London, Remploy supervises some ninety factories throughout Great Britain which offer sheltered employment to 7,500 severely disabled persons. Britain's remaining created jobs are in traditional workshops, homework, and a few outdoor projects. The emphasis is on creating jobs for manual workers, and there are no separate white-collar projects.

In comparison with Sweden and Holland, Britain has fewer created jobs, both in absolute and relative terms. One of the chief reasons is that Britain establishes created jobs only for those who are severely disabled physically or mentally. Britain does not provide sheltered employment for the socially maladjusted or handicapped or the less severely disabled who may be hard-to-employ. The incidence of these conditions appears to be no lighter in Britain than in Sweden or Holland. It has been suggested that the British services of rehabilitation, training, job counseling, and placement, described in earlier chapters, open up many jobs in competitive industry, and that the need for sheltered work is consequently reduced. However, there is no evidence that Britain provides more or better services than, say, Sweden, or that Britain achieves a higher rate of acceptance of marginal workers in open employment. Therefore, we may conclude that Britain has a smaller number of created jobs, even for the physically and mentally disabled,

[9] OECD, *Labour Market Policy in Sweden*, p. 21; *Modern Swedish Labour Market Policy*, p. 40; "En Ny Giv inom Arbetsvården," *Arbetsmarknaden*, November 1959, pp. 195–99.

not because of a lesser need, but rather because of philosophical, administrative, and financial limits on the program. Created jobs are regarded as an economic burden on the British government and have not been made a part of labor market policy or the commitment to full employment. Yet, Britain is ahead of France and West Germany in this field and its considerable accomplishments should not be slighted.

The British exclusion from sheltered work of all who are not seriously disabled has been challenged by officials of the Department of Employment and Productivity, formerly the Ministry of Labour. After conducting intensive interviews with able-bodied, long-term unemployed men, the officials reported that personality difficulties and an unfortunate appearance constituted important ingredients in border-line employability and called for solutions not presently available:

These men are not eligible for sheltered employment . . . under the present arrangements . . . and they therefore experience great difficulty in securing normal employment. There is an apparent need for facilities which would provide openings for the below average man who is nevertheless anxious to work and such opportunities might also remove from the less willing the excuse that they cannot find any suitable vacancies.[10]

A distinctive feature of British sheltered workshops is their acceptance that their workers may not move to competitive employment. The Personnel Director of Remploy has said:

The true sheltered workshop is one which is designed primarily to provide long-term employment for those who cannot expect to benefit from a planned rehabilitation programme—at least to the extent of being able in the foreseeable future to enter into competitive employment.

And the Executive Director of Remploy told the 1959 Hague Seminar on Sheltered Employment:

I see no reason why severely handicapped people for whom no other suitable work is available should not be proud to work in a sheltered

[10] Great Britain, Ministry of Labour, OECD International Counselling Project, *Report of Follow-up Action, 3rd August to 17 September 1965*, p. 6.

factory or workshop, and, above all, there should be no stigma attached to such employment.

British officials, challenging the view that rehabilitation always implies a return to competitive employment, declare that the opportunity to advance within a sheltered workshop may be superior to a transfer to less skilled work outside:

. . . rehabilitation can take place within a sheltered workshop, especially if the sheltered workshop is run on businesslike lines and has an industrial rather than an institutional atmosphere. Rehabilitation lies in a person's satisfaction in knowing that he is doing a useful job and making the best use of his abilities—not necessarily in the place where he works.[11]

As we shall see, the difference in viewpoint between Britain and the leading Continental nations on the issue of the return to competitive work has some day-to-day impact on the organization and conduct of created jobs. At a minimum, the belief that created jobs can be a bridge to normal employment has stimulated the growth of the Swedish and Dutch programs.

GROWTH OF PROGRAMS

At the outset in 1950, created jobs in Holland were to be "of an additional character, interfering as little as possible with the existing employment situation." This stipulation was not surprising in view of high general unemployment, the use of subsidized emigration to relieve pressures on the job market, and the rapidly growing population. As a result, in the first years open-air projects of a public works character furnished almost all of the created social employment for manual workers. In 1953 a decision was taken to favor workshops because open-air projects did not offer a sufficient variety of jobs or training opportunities for the program's declared

[11] D. R. Molloy, "Management and Staff Requirements," International Seminar on Sheltered Employment, Stockholm, September 1964; Air Commodore G. O. Venn, "Labour Conditions and Relations," European Seminar on Sheltered Employment, The Hague, 1959, p. 129.

purpose of rehabilitating workers for normal employment. Furthermore, outdoor jobs were unsatisfactory for women, mentally retarded youths, and persons with certain other disabilities.

Table IX.1 shows that employment in Dutch sheltered workshops increased faster than jobs on open-air projects in the second half of the 1950s, and that the number employed on outdoor work actually declined 1959–1965 while sheltered work rose rapidly. Thereafter, both increased substantially, in response to the recession of 1966 and long-range objectives.

The Dutch absorption of several thousand new entrants in sheltered workshops between mid-1966 and mid-1968 was a considerable accomplishment. It was not done by organizing new workshops, which is time-consuming, but rather by expanding the capacity of existing workshops. Because a number of workshops completed their long planned replacement of old buildings in this period, they were able to expand employment easily. It has been characteristic of job creation programs in most countries that a certain amount of underutilization of places exists at all times due to high rates of turnover, particularly among those leaving because of illness. At the same time, waiting lists and unmet needs are also common, because of geographic factors, time lags in filling places, and administrative regulations.

The shifting emphasis in Holland in the early years toward sheltered workshops permitted the increased participation of women in the Municipal Social Employment Scheme for blue-collar workers (*Gemeentelijke Sociale Werkvoorzieningsregeling voor Handarbeiders: G.S.W.*). In 1959 only 1,238 out of 22,404 G.S.W. workers were women; by 1965 the women numbered 5,398 out of a total of 33,274. This ratio is close to the proportion of Dutch women among both the registered disabled and the unemployed with reduced employability.

The expansion of the Dutch workshops also facilitated the absorption of handicapped young people, especially among the mentally retarded and ill. For example, in 1961 it was estimated that of the 6,000 mentally defective persons working under sheltered conditions, three-fourth were in workshops and one-fourth were on outdoor projects. The proportion of workers in workshops whose handicap was primarily mental rose from 19 to 39 percent from 1959 to 1965. In the same period the social workshops showed a marked increase in the proportion of workers under 35; they rose from 21.3 percent of the total to 34.3 percent. By contrast, the age composition of those in open-air projects showed no discernible trend in this period.

In 1965, when all created jobs in Holland for the handicapped under the G.S.W. employed almost 27,000 workers, two-fifths were primarily physically handicapped, 36 percent were primarily mentally handicapped, 8 percent had a combination of physical and mental handicaps, and the remaining 16 percent had social or character maladjustments. More than half of the workers on created jobs were chosen from those whom the Employment Service had declared "unplaceable," while the remainder were classified as having "reduced employability" (*minder geschikten*).

Table IX.1 indicates that Sweden, later to start its public programs and slower to increase them in the first years than Holland, has recently had a rapid expansion, especially in outdoor projects. However, comparability may be affected by the inclusion in Swedish statistics recently of older, immobile workers with slight hope of finding new jobs. The Technical Division which issues the statistics tends to allocate more workers to outdoor projects and fewer to Special Public Works than the Employment Service. For example, in January 1969 the Technical Division counted 12,293 unemployed on outdoor projects for the handicapped, while the Employment Service listed 7,688.

The over-all increase in Swedish job creation resulted from the guidelines laid down by the tripartite committee on labor market policy in 1965, and the parliamentary resolution and Royal Ordinance of 1966, and was stimulated by the recession of 1966–68. As in Holland, Swedish outdoor projects are not used extensively for women, the mentally retarded or mentally ill, but they do serve the socially maladjusted as well as older workers who are tied to rural areas or declining industries and who formerly were placed on Special Public Works projects.

TABLE IX.1. Job Creation for the Severely Handicapped, the Netherlands * and Sweden,† 1954–1968

Year	Outdoor Projects		Sheltered Workshops		Home Workers	Projects for Nonmanual Workers	
	The Netherlands a	Sweden b	The Netherlands a	Sweden c	Sweden c	The Netherlands d	Sweden b
1954	7,556		1,817	436	90		
1956	6,980		5,779	614	500		832
1958	9,119	32	10,475	1,020	709	1,598	878
1959	9,765	150	12,639	1,246	741	1,925	1,152
1960	9,275	556	14,989	1,577	783	1,876	1,360
1961	8,304	825	16,606	1,878	789	1,716	1,523
1962	7,491	1,387	17,254	2,164	773	1,604	1,635
1963	6,894	2,105	17,851	3,273	759	1,631	1,903
1964	6,793	2,580	18,995	4,268	767	1,639	2,194
1965	6,493	3,778	20,337	5,032	971	1,798	2,525
1966	6,848	4,525	21,935	6,257	941	2,072	2,848
1967	8,332	8,279	24,812	7,466	1,108	2,476	3,301
1968	10,032	13,474	28,743	9,175	1,031	3,264	4,146

a Ministry of Social Affairs and Public Health. Number at work at the end of June. Sheltered workshops include a few hundred home workers.

b National Labour Market Board. Annual average of mid-monthly totals on outdoor projects. Monthly averages of non-manual workers are presented for budget year (July–June).

c National Labour Market Board, Vocational Rehabilitation Division. Number of workplaces available at the end of December.

d Ministry of Social Affairs, Social Assistance and Complementary Employment Provisions Section. Number at work at the end of June. Excludes artists receiving grants; about 600 a year recently.

* The total population of the Netherlands was 10,615,000 in 1954 and 12,455,000 in 1966.

† The total population of Sweden was 7,213,000 in 1954 and 7,808,000 in 1966.

221

Sweden, with a smaller population and labor force, already has surpassed the Netherlands in the numbers on two types of created jobs for the severely handicapped, outdoor projects and white-collar jobs, but is behind in sheltered workshops. By 1973 Sweden expects to have over 17,000 places in sheltered workshops, which the Labour Market Board considers far fewer than the actual need. The numerical leadership may remain with Holland, especially since Great Britain has no aspirations to overtake. In addition to about 7,500 sheltered workers in the Remploy system, the British Department of Employment and Productivity's subsidies and direction have led to the revitalization of 60 workshops for the blind. They are organized by local authorities under legal compulsion, were serving 3,700 persons as of October 1966, and have recently devoted about 10 percent of their places to severely disabled sighted persons. Some 825 blind homeworkers are also supported through central government subsidies. Finally, workshops for the sighted disabled which are organized by local authorities or voluntary agencies are subsidized on the same terms as workshops for the blind. In October 1966, 1,732 persons were employed in 57 workshops of this type; in 1959 there had been 40 workshops with about 800 workers.

The statistical comparisons among the countries are confined to the officially recognized and subsidized programs of specific government agencies. We cannot count precisely the additional numbers of created jobs attributable to the activities and subsidies of other government agencies or the unsubsidized sheltered workshops maintained by voluntary agencies and business firms. Some examples of government programs which are not counted in the statistics are the sheltered jobs in prisons and youth schools which increasingly resemble ordinary industrial activities. Sweden has introduced an experimental program to pay prisoners going wage rates for normal work. In turn, the prisoners pay full income tax, room and board to the prison at market rates, and family support. Another type of government participation is the subsidization by the British Department of Health and Social Security of occupational work centers, mental hospitals, and other institutions which create jobs, usually for those whose capacities are below the sheltered workshop standard.

Some of the voluntary institutions which create jobs with or without subsidy establish long-term residential centers or villages for paraplegics, the tubercular, or other handicap groups which require segregation or special living conditions. The provision of work opportunities is part of a total program. Voluntary agencies also organize and finance sheltered workshops which are wholly or partially unsubsidized by government. Central government subsidies are declined or forfeited because of the desire to cater to groups which are excluded by the public programs, such as people beyond pensionable age or below a specified work capacity. Some shops therefore may receive state subsidies only for a portion of their workers and overhead, but may obtain county and local funds. Certain voluntary agencies forego subsidies due to a reluctance to submit to government supervision or a desire to depart from the regulations. For example, a Dutch workshop which pays its workers higher wage rates than are stipulated by the government regulations and therefore is unsubsidized, manages very well through private contributions and profitable business operations.

A few business firms also maintain unsubsidized sheltered workshops or positions for their own disabled employees. In Sweden where provision by employers for their own workers tends to be generous, a survey in 1966 among the largest private and public industrial enterprises in the country (500 employees or more) showed that only 15 out of 245 had true sheltered divisions or workshops on their premises and 16 others had some sheltered workers.[12] A sheltered workshop within the firm is likely to be far more satisfactory to the workers concerned than assignment to light tasks such as those of sweeper or doorkeeper. There is, however, a certain amount of job creation within industry when disabled or older workers are retained, even if they are not in a separate workshop.

While the total number of persons in miscellaneous and unsubsidized created jobs is not known, it is believed to be small in

[12] Sweden, National Labour Market Board, "Anpassingsåtgärder för svårplacerad arbetskraft inom större industriföretag," *Arbetsmarknadsinformation*, M, 1/1967, pp. 18–19, 21, 23; Bertram J. Black, *Industrial Therapy for the Mentally Ill in Western Europe*, New York, 1965, p. 39.

Sweden, the Netherlands, and Great Britain. In some instances, the work provided is closer to occupational therapy or diversionary activity than regular employment. We therefore concentrate on the public, subsidized programs.

ORGANIZATION AND FINANCE

The Netherlands has a highly unified organization, since all types of job creation for the severely handicapped are administered by the Complementary Social Provisions Division of the General Directorate for Social Provisions and Labour Relations of the Ministry of Social Affairs and Public Health; this Ministry has jurisdiction over all labor and manpower issues. The division maintains a close working relation with same Ministry's General Directorate for Manpower, especially the Employment Service. The Complementary Provisions Division through its general supervision of outdoor projects, social workshops, projects for nonmanual workers, and grants to artists is able to obtain good coverage, uniformity of conditions, and a balanced distribution of people among programs.

The actual decision to initiate job creation and the choice of programs rests with the 960 municipal authorities. The municipality is considered the best agency for determining the local need for created jobs because it administers unemployment assistance and public welfare payments as well as various social services. In 1960, 530 municipalities participated, and at present only a small number are not represented. A municipality may act alone or jointly with other municipalities or it may delegate the execution of the program to a "foundation," a legal creation which has job creation as one of its main objectives and which has municipal representatives and other government officials as members of the executive board. The municipalities receive and distribute the state subsidies, which are given after a representative of the central government's Complementary Social Provisions Division is satisfied that all requirements have been met and that the costs are properly compensable.

Central government subsidies (formerly 75–90 percent, but now flexible) cover wages, bonuses, vacation pay, charges for social insurance programs, and travel expenses of workers. Subsidies are also available to help pay the salaries, social charges, and other expenses of management, work supervisors, and industrial medical officers. Various transportation costs of the business are also subsidized. The annual financial reports of each social workshop and project are sent to the Complementary Provisions Division and the subsidy percentage for the next year is varied accordingly. Open-air projects generally receive the highest permissible wage subsidy of 90 percent; the residual costs are paid by municipal, provincial and private sources. Capital costs are usually met by the municipalities and private philanthropic agencies, but provincial governments may make loans or grants toward the establishment and equipping of workshops which otherwise might not obtain sufficient financing.

Social employment committees must be established in each municipality to pass on admissions to programs, the application of the national wage system, hours of work, the choice of activities, and similar matters. These committees are composed of at least three representatives of official agencies (the municipality, the Complementary Social Provisions Division, and the Employment Service) and three representatives of the leading workers' organizations (Protestant National Federation of Trade Unions, Roman Catholic Workers' Union, and National Federation of Trade Unions). On issues of more than local importance, the municipalities require the consent of the Minister of Social Affairs, who is advised by a committee on which the trade unions, employers' associations, municipalities, and Ministry are represented.

The Swedish organization is more complex. Because outdoor projects for the handicapped evolved as an offshoot of Special Public Works for fully employable men, these programs at the national level have been in one administrative division of the National Labour Market Board, while sheltered workshops and "archive works," created jobs for nonmanual workers and musicians, have been in another. Thus, outdoor projects, jobs for nonmanual workers, sheltered workshops, and homework have been somewhat separated in planning, financing, and the choice of workers. Locally, coordination occurs through the active role of the County Labour Boards and the reservation of all placements to the Employment Service which cooperates with the municipal authorities (*kommuner*) in the selection of workers. The Employment Service must check that placement in the competitive labor market is not possible before making an assignment to sheltered work.

One advantage of the Labour Market Board's direct control over outdoor projects and white-collar employment is its ability to start projects through central government offices, in government-subsidized enterprises, and at offices of public utilities, instead of relying entirely on the municipal authorities or voluntary organizations. Sweden is thus able to expand the number of jobs of this type very rapidly (Table IX.1).

Swedish government subsidies for outdoor projects, white-collar jobs, and sheltered workshops each are on a different basis. The state, through appropriations by individual Boards and Departments and general subsidies, pays the full cost of outdoor or white-collar projects initiated by branches of the central government. For projects instituted by the municipalities, one-third of the costs are subsidized, with higher percentages permitted in extraordinary cases, such as jobs arranged in "areas with high and persistent unemployment and a diminishing number of inhabitants."

Sheltered workshops are organized by County Councils, local governments, associations, and foundations. They have separate scales of state grants and loans for overhead costs and operating costs. Grants-in-aid for construction are based on an allowance for floor space of 15 square meters per worker in most cases. The ordinary allowance can be increased for the construction of workshops in designated development areas where sheltered workshops are especially needed. The Labour Market Board offers planning assistance in construction and supervises the safety, health, insurance, and related features of each building. Rented premises also command a subsidy based on square meters of floor space. Most of the costs of machinery may be subsidized if the procurement plan is approved. In 1967–68, three-quarters of each workshop's operating deficits, excluding rent and other costs which are compensated by grants-in-aid, were subsidized with a maximum of 2,000 Sw. kr. per year per workplace. It is estimated that this subsidy covered 26 percent of operating costs in 1967, exclusive of workshops for the mentally retarded. In 1965 the subsidy had covered 33 percent, and in 1963, 27 percent of costs.

While new workshops have been created and expansions have occurred, the number of places is considered insufficient. In its budget presentation for 1969–70, the Labour Market Board proposed new and better conditions regarding subsidies for the establishment and operation of workshops. The Board also undertook some technical coordination of production with a view to guaranteeing steady employment in the workshops and holding down costs. In 1967 the Labour Market Board obtained first-time business orders for the workshops worth 2.6 million Sw. kr., compared with 1.6 million Sw. kr. in the previous year.[13]

British subsidies concern sheltered workshops, since the few open-air projects are under workshop jurisdiction. As has been noted, Remploy is financed entirely by central government funds. In order to qualify for a subsidy, a local authority or voluntary organization providing sheltered work must obtain approval of the workshop and the individual workers from the Department of Employment and Productivity. Approval normally is given only if the following conditions are met:

i.) the Workshop must provide adequate facilities for the employment, under special sheltered conditions, of severely disabled persons on work on which they can maintain a reasonable level of output;

ii.) the employees must be under contract of service (paying Class I National Insurance contributions) and receive satisfactory

[13] Sweden, National Labour Market Board, *Modern Swedish Labour Market Policy*, Stockholm, 1966, p. 91; National Labour Market Board, *Berättelse Angående Verksamheten under Budgetåret 1967–68*, Stockholm, 1968, pp. 56–57; National Labour Market Board, *Arbetsmarknadspolitiken 1969–70*, Stockholm, 1968, p. 30.

wages without supplementation from the Department of Health and Social Security; and the other conditions of employment must be satisfactory;

iii.) a normal week (of about 40 hours) must ordinarily be worked;

iv.) the articles produced, or services rendered, must be of sufficient economic value to contribute substantially to the costs of the undertaking;

v.) proper arrangements must exist for the efficient conduct of the workshop;

vi.) the constitution of the undertaking must provide that the income and profits (if any) shall be applied solely to the promotion of its objects, and it must not allow any payment of dividend or distribution of profits;

vii.) the undertaking must have sufficient resources to meet that part of any expenditure for which assistance cannot be given from public funds; and

viii.) the Minister must be satisfied that financial assistance is justified.

Usually, approval of subsidization is given only for severely disabled workers who have been judged unlikely to obtain normal work and have been placed in Section 2 of the Register of the Disabled.

The financial help available consists of an annual capitation grant for each approved worker to the local authorities or a deficiency grant of 75 percent of net losses to voluntary agencies, with a fixed maximum per approved worker in each case. In addition, capital grants not in excess of 75 percent of approved expenditure may be made; both the local authorities and voluntary agencies are expected to make substantial capital investments themselves. Finally, training allowances to workers and training fees are provided for those who require a period in the workshops before they can be offered regular wages.

Table IX.2 brings together Dutch, Swedish, and British data on full or partial expenditures for job creation, including the programs for Special Public Works for employables, described in Chapter VIII. Comparability is limited even within a country, permitting only the most limited observations on relative costs. The Dutch central government subsidies for sheltered workshops, outdoor projects, and nonmanual workers cover only a portion of the costs; it is not known how much additional financing is contributed by local governments and private sources. Using the measure of central government outlays alone, expenditures on sheltered workshops and outdoor projects almost quadrupled from 1960 to 1967, while the number of workers rose by just over one-third. Similarly, created jobs for white-collar workers have increased less rapidly than the rise in subsidy costs. In 1967 the average subsidy per nonmanual worker was larger than for each worker in a sheltered workshop or outdoor project.

The total expenditures on Special Public Works declined from 1959 to 1963 but at a slower rate than the decrease in the average number of workers (Table VIII.3). Owing mainly to the rise in wages and prices, the total costs were approximately the same in 1958–59 as they were in 1967–68, although the number of workers served by the program was sharply reduced. In 1965 the average cost per worker was 14,532 guilders ($4,067).

Swedish data require more standardization before any conclusions should be drawn over a period of time for a single program. Even more caution should be exercised in comparing costs among the programs. Many elements of costs and receipts are not covered in the data in Table IX.2.

British data relate only to two kinds of sheltered workshops. Since Remploy workshops obtain all their financing from the Department of Employment and Productivity, some of it in the form of interest-free loans, the cost per worker should not be compared with the second type of British workshop or with costs in other countries. It is estimated that the central government bears half the total cost of the non-Remploy workshops, described earlier. The average cost per worker appears to be low (Tables IX.2 and IX.3).

The author's attempts to ascertain the total direct and indirect

TABLE IX.2. Expenditures on Job Creation, the Netherlands, Sweden, and Great Britain, 1956–1969

| | The Netherlands (1 fl. = $ .28) | | | Sweden (1 kr. = $ .19) | | | | Great Britain (1 £ = $2.40) | |
| | Total Cost | Subsidies by Central Government | | Total Cost | Subsidies by Central Government | | Total Cost | Department of Employment and Productivity Expenditures f | |
Year	Special Public Works a florins (000)	Sheltered Workshops and Outdoor Projects b florins (000)	Nonmanual Job Creation b florins (000)	Special Public Works c kronor (000)	Outdoor Work for Handicapped c kronor (000)	Nonmanual Job Creation d kronor (000)	Sheltered Workshops e kronor (000)	Reemploy, Ltd, Loans and Grants pounds (000)	Other Workshops g pounds (000)
1956	64,700	31,600	n.a.	n.a.	n.a.	n.a.	5,327	2,737	670
1957	59,700	45,400	n.a.	88,005	1,522	n.a.	7,275	2,820	778
1958	84,200	57,100	n.a.	210,526	2,077	6,987	8,263	2,955	859
1959	91,700	59,000	7,600	373,576	10,000	9,179	9,251	2,972	935
1960	61,000	56,500	7,500	332,973	23,500	10,606	11,116	3,044	908
1961	36,200	69,170	7,600	195,884	25,577	12,480	13,307	3,188	1,245
1962	26,700	68,300	7,085	186,427	31,442	17,029	15,476	3,302	1,307
1963	20,400	81,661	7,150	403,460	47,791	19,122	16,817	3,513	1,417
1964	27,600	90,110	7,410	453,848	60,837	21,469	27,387	3,614	1,549
1965	32,000	111,270	8,567	436,972	85,334	25,466	39,167	3,767	1,578
1966	32,500	173,066	15,891	362,928	124,451	33,323	56,092	3,902	1,695
1967	80,000	207,326	20,053	382,291	274,462	46,157	71,902	4,144 h	1,780 h
1968	98,000	n.a.	n.a.	434,161	n.a.	n.a.	97,540	4,477 h	2,184 h
1969	n.a.	n.a.	n.a.	n.a.	n.a.	n.a.	n.a.	4,370 h	2,232 h

costs of the various job creation programs revealed that administrators and policymakers have been slow to collect data beyond
their own immediate needs. If benefit/cost approaches become more
common in evaluating these programs, it will first be necessary to
improve over-all data.

GENERAL ISSUES IN JOB CREATION

The creation of employment opportunities for those who cannot
be placed in the competitive labor market immediately or in the
long run results in a new region between the ordinary work world
and a more shadowy area where people of working age engage in
diversionary activities, industrial or occupational therapy, or are
idle. The issues which arise thus are different from those in the
job creation program for the fully employable, which operates in
tandem with normal employment (see Chapter VIII).

NOTES TO TABLE IX.2

a 1956–64: OECD, *Manpower and Social Policy in the Netherlands*, Paris,
1967, p. 106; 1965–1968: Ministry of Social Affairs and Public Health.

b Ministry of Social Affairs and Public Health, Hoofafdeling Complemen-
taire Sociale Voorzieningen, *Algemene interne documentatie*, no. 390, 4 May
1966, p. 10; Communications from Dr. Anton Heering.

c 1960–65: Sweden, National Labour Market Board, Employment Service
Division, *AMS Statistik till Husbehov*, February 1966, p. 6; 1966–68: *Arbetsmarknadspolitiken 1969–1970*, Stockholm, 1968, p. 42; *AMS Berättelse Angående Verksamheten under 1967–1968*, p. 108. 1967 and 1968 are budget
years (July–June) for Special Public Works. 1957, 1958 and 1967 are budget years for Outdoor Work for Handicapped.

d 1958–63 budget years and total expenditures: *Arbetsmarknadspolitik*,
SOU 1965: 9, Stockholm, 1965, p. 222; 1964 and 1965 are calendar years.
1966 and 1967 are budget years and cover only Labour Market Board net expenditures. National Labour Market Board, *AMS Berättelse Angående Verksamheten*, 1966–67, 1967–68.

e Total costs including capital costs. 1956–1963 includes also work training,
semisheltered employment and homework. 1964–68 includes workshops for
mentally retarded.

f Data provided by Department of Employment and Productivity.

g It is estimated that grants cover about one-half or total costs, including
training allowances.

h Estimated.

Standards of Eligibility

After it is decided which types of handicaps and age groups are to be accepted on created jobs, standards must be established to exclude those who are considered eligible for competitive employment as well as those who are not qualified for created jobs because of limited work capacity or personal characteristics. To begin with, not all of the hard-to-employ unemployed require a sheltered environment. Among those who are more suitably placed in the competitive labor market or in job creation programs for employables are workers who are hard-to-employ because of lack of education or training or because of prejudice or discrimination.

British efforts on behalf of blind and partially sighted persons illustrate how the public and employers can accept an increasing proportion of an entire disability group in competitive employment. Because of their success in training and placing blind persons in ordinary jobs, the number in workshops has leveled off or decreased in recent years. In mid-1966, eight blind persons were placed in open employment for every one sent to a sheltered workshop, and more than twice as many blind people were working in open employment as in sheltered workshops. In 1946 only slightly more than half of all blind persons at work were in open employment.[14]

An example of movement in the reverse direction comes from the files of the British National Assistance Board. An epileptic man of 22 with a speech impediment who had been employed in competitive industry could not get along with his fellow-workers and had been discharged from several jobs because he took offense at derogatory remarks. After the young man remained unemployed for some time, the Assistance Board officer asked the Ministry of Labour to place the youth in a Remploy factory where he could learn bookbinding. He was later reported to be happy

[14] Interviews with the Disabled Persons Branch, Ministry of Labour; *The New Beacon, passim.*

working in a sheltered environment where his disabilities were not discussed.[15] His productive capacity was adequate for competitive employment, but his psychological adjustment to his physical condition was not.

Britain's classification of the disabled who register for employment assistance into sections 1 and 2 creates certain difficulties. Because job opportunities for the disabled vary greatly from region to region, the classification as section 1 may exclude some men from consideration for sheltered work although they are in fact not placeable in competitive jobs. Nor has Britain a Special Public Works program. Thus, it has been found that a substantial proportion of section 1 registered disabled unemployed (those deemed capable of obtaining and holding jobs in competitive industry) suffer from prolonged unemployment in regions where general unemployment rates are higher than average and the main economic activities offer few suitable posts for disabled workers.

In individual cases, a reclassification to section 2 is possible, but it is desirable only if a place is or will be available in a sheltered workshop. In general, officials hesitate to reclassify workers from section 1 to section 2 because of possible psychological damage. But the psychological harm from prolonged unemployment may be equally great. A case was cited of two section 1 unemployed men living on unemployment benefits in northwest Wales, an area of limited employment opportunities for the disabled. They asked the Manton Work Centre to give them created jobs based on subcontracts from local employers. Although the Centre was not up to sheltered workshop standards and could not offer the amount of work or pay of a full sheltered workshop, the two men reportedly were happy to find some paid activity. They had to leave the Centre when the unemployment insurance authorities ruled that they would lose their unemployment benefits and credits if they continued.[16] Had such men been eligible directly for sheltered

[15] Great Britain, National Assistance Board, *Annual Report for 1949*, Cmd. 8030, H.M.S.O.: London, 1950, p. 49.

[16] E. J. Miller, "The Work Centre," *Rehabilitation*, January–March 1964, p. 19.

work, and had places been available for them, their desire to work and income needs would have been met more adequately and the government would have saved on unemployment benefits.

If more sheltered workplaces were established in the regions of Britain where unemployment among section 1 disabled is high and persistent, a group could be served which may be capable of open market placement in another area but tends to remain idle in the present location. Having visited and admired Remploy workshops for section 2 disabled in regions of high unemployment, the author is keenly aware of the social and psychological advantages of this type of activity over the loneliness and discouragement of long-term unemployment. While the need for additional workshop places for section 1 disabled is greatest in the northern regions, a good case could be made for reviewing the records of all section 1 disabled who have been unemployed for, say, six months, with a view to recommending sheltered work. The chief obstacles to an expansion of created jobs for the less severely disabled may be financial and administrative. However, a recommendation to establish such jobs for the socially handicapped in Britain who have serious employment problems might face an additional hurdle: a lack of public sympathy and acceptance. Still, as Great Britain becomes increasingly concerned with its disadvantaged groups, the need for additional job creation is likely to be recognized.

The Dutch procedures to establish eligibility for created jobs are more responsive to changes in the employment situation, regional variations, and individual differences. Each hard-to-employ case is judged separately at the time it arises. Admission to or retention on a created job is specifically forbidden if a worker could be assigned to a vocational training course or Special Public Works (Supplementary Employment), or if he is suitable for available competitive employment. When there is a doubt about whether a worker should be classified as unplaceable, he is often assigned to a social (sheltered) workshop for testing before the decision is made.

The Dutch method is not foolproof against the admission of overqualified persons. In the OECD Counselling Study, the Dutch authorities cited the case of an unemployed 42-year-old man, "stupid and dull-witted in appearance, sleepy eyed, indolent and self-centered." During the course of the interviewer's attempts to rouse him to find a regular job, he somehow had been accepted for sheltered employment and had worked for one week. The interviewer discovered this while visiting the man's wife, who complained that she could not manage on the sheltered wage. The man was induced to visit the interviewer again:

By means of emotional arguments regarding his loss of status by working in sheltered employment, B. was motivated to apply for a job. B. admitted that he did not belong in sheltered employment and promised to find other work at once. He paid a third visit to the interviewer of his own volition to say that he had gotten a good job as a storeman in a large department store. He appeared satisfied and cheerful. Follow-up seems desirable, though a social worker will not be accepted.

This case has been cited primarily to illustrate that people who can easily obtain ordinary jobs may be accepted for created jobs because their personalities are borderline. But it does show two other things incidentally. Even in a well-ordered administrative system, two agencies can work at cross purposes and be out of touch. And apparently some feeling exists, even among officials, that sheltered work is second class.

Exclusions from created jobs also occur because some people are too disabled to perform at the minimum standard currently in force. Each program has some provision for those who are somewhat below standard but show promise of improving their performance. Great Britain pays training allowances to a selected number of such persons. They enter sheltered workshops on a provisional basis and, if their training period is successful, become full-fledged sheltered workers. In Sweden, as we saw in Chapter IV, some below-standard workers become capable of entering created jobs after assignment to a work experience center (IRU) or through training in a workshop or a vocational training course.

The Netherlands admits people to created jobs if they are mentally as well as physically able to do productive work, are able to work regularly under circumstances which are adapted to their physical and mental condition, and can achieve at least one third of a reasonable minimum production in the same kind of work in normal industry. In 1963 category B was added, consisting of those who could not meet this one-third level of productivity but who might be brought up to the minimum or above through training and regular work experience on a created job. The numbers and proportions of "B" workers have increased. As of the middle of 1965, 8.3 percent of the 26,821 G.S.W. workers were in category B, but in 1967 the percentage rose to 10.4 of 33,274 workers. Only 100 "B" workers were on outdoor projects; almost all were in the sheltered workshops.

Every program in every country has its success stories involving individuals or groups who appeared to be hopelessly below standard, but were given a chance and proved themselves. One of the initial surprises occurred in the Dutch program. In 1953 the Social Employment Scheme began to place some of its unemployed in the municipal sheltered workshops which had been established earlier for physically handicapped persons receiving assistance under the Poor Law. It was soon observed that the relief recipients who had been excluded from the Social Employment program produced at the same or better levels than the unemployed in the program. Therefore, the relief clients were elevated and given the full benefits of the government subsidy and the higher wages of the Social Employment program. Over the years, many other groups have shown an unexpected capacity to produce.

A more difficult category consists of persons whose working capacity is adequate for sheltered conditions but whose personalities threaten disruption of the workshop. The establishment of separate projects or workplaces for those with specific handicaps, particularly the socially maladjusted, is one preventive measure. Another approach is to control and limit the mixture of various disabilities through physical or organizational separation. For example, the ratio of the mentally ill and retarded to all other workers in a shop or a room usually is restricted.

Despite a growing tendency to ignore the nature of physical disabilities in placement on created jobs, complete integration of those with mental or social disabilities is deliberately avoided in the interests of minimizing disruptive influences. The ideal continues to be the position taken at The Hague and Stockholm Seminars on Sheltered Employment: that a maximum degree of integration is desirable in order to overcome prejudices of different handicap groups against one another, to save capital and operating expense, and to facilitate the recruitment of sufficient and competent staff. But the ideal must be modified by the needs of individuals and by medical, psychological, social, and practical considerations.

The mere fact of providing created jobs for the socially maladjusted, as Sweden and Holland have done, introduces an increased incidence of absenteeism involving many disciplinary cases, dismissals, and transfers, as well as voluntary leaving without cause. The records of special outdoor projects for ex-criminals in Sweden from 1962 through 1965 show that a high proportion was discharged for drunkenness or other cause or left the projects without finding other work. Much the same was true of the alcoholics on projects reserved to them. In the three-month period from April 16 to July 15, 1965, 558 of the 767 alcoholics on Swedish outdoor projects who left work were separated because of drunkenness, breaking of rules, dissatisfaction, or related causes. A report for 1967–68 notes that an increased use of drugs by Swedish youth, especially those coming from institutions for delinquents, has resulted in frequent interruptions of sheltered work because of a return to drugs.

Yet, the Swedish National Labour Board's directives have stressed that placement of the socially maladjusted on created jobs should not be limited to those who appear certain to adjust well. Chances should be taken with more doubtful candidates, but they should be given full information in advance about the kind of work, the location of the work site, the nature of routines, and disciplinary rules. Difficult cases should be given special attention at the work site but they should be separated if they fail to fit in after a reasonable period.

The willingness to experiment with sheltered work for questionable personalities seems strongest in countries which accept the need for sheltered work for a wide variety of disabled persons, including the socially maladjusted. In addition, if a job creation program has many openings in relation to the needy population, if many types of jobs are available, if outdoor projects as well as sheltered workshops are in use, and if possibilities exist for separate sections or projects for specific disability groups, then a country is more likely to accept dubious individuals. It remains a high-risk undertaking. Higher turnover rates and more supervisory and disciplinary problems may be expected, but many individuals are reclaimed for society through repeated efforts to establish regular work habits on created jobs.

Conditions of Work

As job creation programs grow larger and more uniform standards are achieved throughout a country, there is a tendency for work conditions on created jobs increasingly to resemble ordinary work. In the broad sense, this is reflected in the tone and conduct of management and workers, but specifically it refers to hours of work, rest periods, paid holidays, sick leave, coverage for social benefits, labor contracts, industrial health and safety, and the role of trade unions. Wages and incomes are discussed in the next section.

The attempt to duplicate ordinary industrial conditions has two themes: to refrain from overprotecting the sheltered workers (for example, by setting a shorter workday than is customary) and to offer workers on created jobs the types of social benefits and contractual protection afforded other workers. While practices in the European countries vary considerably, changes are tending to reduce the differences between ordinary and sheltered workers.

One Danish workshop which deliberately maintains a shortened workday has an interesting economic rationale. It runs two shifts of workers for six hours each, thus utilizing its machinery 50 percent more than shops with one full day shift and reducing the unit cost of its output. The shorter hours also suit the workers because all are disability pensioners who stand to lose part of their pension payments if their earnings exceed a certain level.

The maintenance of a normal workday and week is not inconsistent with a slower pace of work and more frequent rest periods than ordinary workers have. In the same way, paid holidays and sick leave tend to equal or exceed those in normal industry.

Workers in created jobs are usually covered by all social insurance schemes. In Holland they are excluded from the unemployment insurance program but have an unemployment provision of their own. Many workshops carry workers on full wages during periods when work is not available. Often the workers' contribution to the insurance fund is borne by the state as part of its subsidy of wages.

The Netherlands, which did not offer workers on created jobs an employment contract, introduced the protection of a special sort of legal contract in 1969. The aim was to replace the workers' one-sided legal obligation by a two-sided relation in which the local authorities were bound to recognize certain rights and legal obligations toward workers on created jobs.

Industrial health and safety are quite naturally of extra concern on created jobs, since the particular problems of the disabled have usually led to higher than normal safety standards to begin with. Policing and subsidies have been beneficial in individual cases where a lack of funds may have led to unsafe conditions.

In general, sheltered workers are not unionized to the same extent as ordinary workers, although worker representatives may be chosen in some workshops and projects, even if a union does not function. Remploy, the British sheltered workshop network, actually has functioning trade unions, and some strikes have been called. A description shows how similar to ordinary British industrial relations are the arrangements at Remploy:

Employees have a completely free hand regarding membership of trade unions, and in practice almost all of them have joined a trade union appropriate to their particular occupation. Works Managers are encouraged to extend to officials of these trade unions the usual facilities for consultation, and there are shop stewards in each factory. Joint consultative committees consisting of representatives of management and of employees also exist for the discussion of such matters as production, factory conditions and welfare; in accordance with general British practices, wages, hours of work and similar matters are outside the scope of these committees and are reserved for negotiation between the management and trade union representatives.[17]

Wages and Earnings

The most complex issue is the compensation to be paid to workers on created jobs for the handicapped. As sheltered work first evolved under the sponsorship of philanthropic agencies, tasks such as basket weaving and broom making predominated. The workers' earnings from their output was minimal, often pocket money, and they depended on supplementary private or public charity. With the entry of governments into the job creation field, the quality of the jobs was upgraded and in many cases could be compared directly with work performed in competitive industry.

There were thus two pressures to adopt another system of payments. The trade unions wanted to be sure that sheltered workers would not be exploited and thus undercut the established wage rates. And government wanted to pay a weekly wage which would give the workers in created jobs pride in their activity and a decent standard of living, so that they would need little or no supplementation by public assistance authorities.

Yet, the authorities also recognize that, in general, earnings in created jobs must not be too high. They should reflect the lower productivity of these workers and provide an economic incentive for them to move on to competitive jobs at higher earnings. Exceptions to this view have been taken by workshops which pay their workers at a higher rate than normal workers because the handicapped have extra expenses. But, by and large, voluntary organizations also accept the formula of lower earnings for those on created jobs.

Where piece rates can be applied, the solution is fairly easy and

[17] J. L. Edwards, "Remploy: An Experiment in Sheltered Employment for the Severely Disabled in Great Britain," *International Labour Review,* February 1958, p. 154.

needs only to be backed by a guaranteed minimum hourly or weekly earnings provision. This additional subsidy is usually given as wages rather than welfare. However, when the tasks on outdoor and white-collar projects and the workshops cannot be rated by units of output, hourly and weekly wage rates are substituted, with some stipulation of a percentage reduction of normal rates. The reduction is usually less than the actual difference in output.

Trade unions play an active role in the determination of the applicable wage rates for created jobs, and union participation in the planning and administration of the programs at every level has been a vital precondition for the effective operation of European job creation programs for the handicapped. One difficulty in setting wage rates through negotiations with the concerned trade unions is that a large number of trade unions may be involved in the diverse work of each shop and thus discrepancies in earnings among sheltered workers in the same shop may appear. An extreme case was that of Remploy, which at first dealt separately with a large number of trade unions and provided a wide scale of wages, usually 70 to 80 percent of the going rate in each trade union agreement. This was later changed to a uniform Remploy wage, regardless of the occupation.

Sweden is trying to standardize the wage rates which have been jointly set by sheltered workshops and trade unions. Swedish workers on outdoor projects receive a percentage of the full rates paid to workers on Special Public Works projects. White-collar workers on "archive" projects and unemployed musicians have been on a low wage scale, originally based on municipal cash assistance rates. Their earnings have been increased in recent years and further raises have been proposed, but their wage system is still not related to that of the other types of created jobs.

The Dutch wage system on created jobs for manual and non-manual workers is the most uniform, formal, and complex. A general rule is that the hourly wage on a created job should be set at less than 95 percent of the hourly wage for the same or similar work done by normal workers in the same town. In the same way, the official minimum wage for adult males in normal industry is

5 percent higher than the minimum income on created jobs which is guaranteed to male workers over 23 who have had a reasonable work performance in a 45-hour work week, have one-third working capacity, and are in the "A" category. In February 1969, Dutch women between 24 and 65 became eligible for the first time for coverage under the revised minimum wage law. Presumably, the new law makes it possible to provide a minimum wage for selected female workers on created jobs, similar to that enjoyed by males.

In those countries of western Europe where legal minimum wages exist for workers in normal industry, job creation programs for the handicapped are not obliged to obtain a waiver to pay less than the minimum, such as is required in the United States. Because it is common that four different minimum wage levels in competitive employment should be set by law, for men, women, boys, and girls, and still other variations of the minimum are permitted, flexibility is also possible in establishing minimum wages for those whose productivity is lower than average.

The internal structure of Dutch wages on created jobs recognizes four main wage classes with 5 percent differences, according to the level and importance of the work. Different rates are also specified for adult men, adult women, young men, and young women. In addition, modifications of wages are made for variations in the cost-of-living in different areas and for those receiving disability pensions. But this is not the end of the differentiation. Each of the four wage classes has three steps which constitute a merit rating scheme allowing the worker at the top to earn 20 percent more than the worker at the first step. Each worker is judged regularly by two persons on five points: the quantity of work; the quality of work; the devotion to and interest in the job; the attitude toward colleagues, management, and regulations regarding the job; the care for materials, machinery, tools and buildings. The standard of judgment is that used in open industry.

Other countries have bonus schemes to reward extra effort, but the Dutch system is the most elaborate. It is considered an important tool in the process of rehabilitation for competitive employment and is generally accepted in Holland, although it may be difficult or impossible to apply on particular projects or jobs. In 1959 the Dordrecht workshop, a pioneer, criticized the complexity of the system, the difficulty of giving objective ratings, and the problem of worker dissatisfaction with different ratings and wages each week. Recently, official instructions have indicated that ratings need not be made so frequently.

A reading of the official guide, however, leaves no doubt that this is an extremely difficult system to administer. Nevertheless, its educative and incentive components seem to be fairly valuable. A Dutch worker not only can increase his earnings within his wage class, but he can also graduate to work in the higher wage classes. Such an upward movement has definitely occurred. From 1956 to 1967, workers in the lowest wage class decreased from 65 to 48 percent of all workers on created jobs, and those in the two highest wage classes increased from 1.5 to 16.1 percent of the total. It is possible that changes in the composition of the created jobs or eased standards of grading are factors, along with individual achievement. Some Dutch workers earn more on created jobs than they might initially in competitive employment, but officials maintain that this factor does not affect their willingness to transfer if the opportunity arises.

Under the various wage systems, it is possible that a worker of low productivity with several dependents may be capable of earning no more from a created job, after taxes, than he would receive from unemployment insurance or assistance or public welfare. Potential candidates for created jobs may be discouraged if they can obtain virtually the same income without work. The taxation of wages from created jobs sometimes is the crucial difference which negates the formal establishment of minimum earnings on created jobs at a level above welfare payments. In Britain it is felt that many unemployed section 2 registered disabled would not respond to offers of sheltered work because the financial incentive would be lacking. Sweden and Holland not only make a strong point of the moral value of work, but they may also have more personal impact through local government administration of programs instead of mainly through central government, as in Britain. In principle, they are prepared to deny social benefits to someone who rejects a created job, but it has rarely been necessary.

A more challenging problem is presented by the recipients of disability or invalidity pensions who constitute a prime source of candidates for created jobs. In the Netherlands, those drawing pensions constituted 46.7 percent of all the handicapped on created jobs in 1962. An increase in the pension rates led to a decrease in the number and proportion of pensioners to 28.8 percent by 1967. The 1966 Invalidity Act provided that more facilities should be made available for rehabilitation and also that no reduction in pensions should be made until the pension plus wages on a created job exceeds 90 percent of the daily wage on which the pension was calculated.

There always will be a certain number of pensioners who will resist work if any part of their pension is deducted. Some students have suggested the outright withdrawal of pensions from those who are unwilling to work on created jobs, but such drastic action has little chance of legislative enactment. Moral suasion has been effective in some countries. The OECD examiners recommended that Holland should pay more attention to the fullest physical restoration of the pensioners' work capacity in order to minimize the number who may reject work.[18]

Specialized Personnel and Services

Despite the attempts to make created jobs resemble normal work, four important differences affect the type of personnel hired and the services offered on created jobs programs. First, the handicapped workers may not be physically or mentally capable of performing all of the tasks on their outdoor projects or in their workshops. This situation leads to the special hiring of workers who do not qualify for created jobs. When private contractors conduct outdoor projects, as has been indicated, these workers may not appear on the employment rolls.

[18] OECD, *Manpower and Social Policy in the Netherlands*, Paris, 1967, p. 206.

Sheltered workshops which attempt to parallel factory methods or which employ particularly disabled persons are apt to take on some nondisabled workers. Fit employees are used in jobs which are not suitable for the severely disabled or for which they lack the qualifications. For example, in October 1967 the British Remploy network of 90 factories had a total of 9,449 workers and staff, of whom 6,979 were subsidized section 2 referrals of the severely disabled. If production workers alone are considered, the nondisabled employees of Remploy constituted 8.4 percent of the total. This is well below the agreed-on 15 percent; other workshops in Britain use a higher proportion of able workers than Remploy.[19] No comparable figures are available for Sweden or Holland, but they also permit the use of fit workers in order to make the productive process more efficient, to set a pace for the handicapped workers, and to perform special tasks. So long as the number of fit workers is controlled, the danger that the disabled will be deprived of jobs in the interests of profitability can be averted.

The second difference from ordinary industry involves the number, qualifications, training, and method of selecting the administrative and supervisory personnel. As experience has grown and job programs have become more sophisticated in the most advanced countries, certain trends have appeared. Reductions have occurred in the ratio of supervisory personnel to handicapped workers; people with medical or social work training have been supplanted by technical-management men in the top administrative posts; professional men have taken over from philanthropic ladies; and technical foremen have replaced nurses, therapists, etc.

In some cases, especially shops connected with psychiatric hospitals, the medical supervision runs in tandem with the business personnel. Others have trained their nurses to be technical foremen. But the main thrust is toward giving special government and private courses or training to suitable and sympathetic men with business and industrial experience so that they may become familiar with the particular problems of their handicapped workers.

The management of a workshop or outdoors project is consid-

[19] Bertram J. Black, *Industrial Therapy for the Mentally Ill in Western Europe*, New York, 1966, p. 30.

ered to have three aspects—technical, commercial, and rehabilitative. Normally the staff consists of a manager or director, an assistant manager who directs the daily routine, and foremen who direct individual departments or groups. A good technical man who can devise expedients or jigs to simplify the productive process is an asset. The overhead personnel tend to follow the lines of ordinary industry, but there is usually less specialization.

The willingness of successful men to devote themselves to managing created jobs for the handicapped is partially attributable to the fact that their earnings usually are not decreased by the transfer. Great Britain has found that retired or disabled officers of the Armed Services, especially those with industrial experience, are a good source of managers. A Dutch statement of the qualities needed by a manager is typical:

they should have technical capacities as well as psychological insight and, moreover, they should have the personal qualities required for the realization of the objects of the scheme. The task of the leader is not confined to the technical execution of activities, but he should also have an open eye for the difficulties confronting those working under his guidance. Furthermore he should be able to activate the zest for work of those concerned and to favourably influence their state of mind.[20]

A British statement calls on the manager to deal "sympathetically but if necessary firmly, with the numerous daily human problems and tensions encountered which are in many cases peculiar to the disabled worker and which often bear no relation to the circumstances of his employment." [21] To supervise mentally handicapped persons, exceptionally capable managers and staff are required. A Dutch expert prescribed the following qualities as crucial: ability to instruct, technical skill, and insight into the behavior of the mentally retarded. Additional desirable qualities are: independence, ability to make contacts, authority, patience, emotional stability and stamina, an understanding of rehabilitation, technical imagi-

[20] The Netherlands, Ministry of Social Affairs and Public Health, *Sheltered Employment in the Netherlands,* second edition.

[21] A. P. Curran, "Ten Years Follow-up of Employees in a Sheltered Workshop," *Rehabilitation,* July–September 1961, p. 49.

nation, a sense of economy. In Holland foremen are recruited among skilled industrial workers, men and women trained in the care of the retarded, and teachers and others in the educational field. Two-year training courses are available, as they are for managers.

Sweden regards the selection of the manager and foreman so seriously that a condition of obtaining the state subsidy toward their salaries is that each individual be approved by the Labour Market Board. The additional need for trained personnel in Sweden was recognized in several new course offerings in 1967–68. The personnel in sheltered workshops for the mentally retarded, an expanding area, were given instruction by the County Councils which are responsible for the early schooling and other needs of the retarded. Courses were arranged for managers and foremen of ordinary sheltered workshops and staff seminars were organized for supervisors and assistants on the special outdoor projects for alcoholics and delinquents to acquaint them with the characteristics of their workers and the services available from the Employment Service.

A third difference is the presence of auxiliary personnel to deal with the more intense medicosocial problems of those on created jobs. The number and type of such personnel vary from country to country and within a country, according to the practices in normal industry and the type of handicapped being served. In the Netherlands and Sweden, for example, large firms in competitive business employ social or welfare workers, and it is not surprising that workplaces for created jobs should follow suit. Social workers in every type of business assist workers not only with work adjustments but also with outside problems regarding family, housing, transport, and leisure activities. In those Dutch workshops where the mentally retarded are numerous, social workers help to regulate the workers' saving, expenditures, tax payments, living arrangements, and personal lives.

A physician specializing in industrial medicine and rehabilitation may be shared by several workshops. Psychiatrists, psychologists, physiotherapists, vocational rehabilitation specialists, and occupational therapists may be present in a staff or advisory capacity, according to the circumstances of the individual project or workshop and the traditions of the nation. Sweden's "contact man" looks after those on created jobs who have come from social institutions such as prisons or alcoholic care centers. The need of these groups for supervision on and off the job calls for extra personnel on their projects.

The final difference in the type of personnel and services offered to those on created jobs arises in countries which make a great point of the importance of transfers to competitive employment. Since a concern for the rehabilitation and improved performance of workers on created jobs may exist apart from the effort to transfer them to work in the open market, some of the specialized personnel may be employed in any case, but more of their time is needed if transfer to competitive jobs is the aim. And some additional specialists may be required as well.

The Swedish tripartite committee on labor market policy recommended in 1965 that outdoor projects for the handicapped as well as job programs for white-collar workers and musicians, which had been notably sluggish in transferring workers to competitive jobs, should be revised to emphasize training and rehabilitative aspects. These projects should

to the greatest possible extent . . . serve as a preparation for employment on the open market. . . . As is the case in municipal workshops for handicapped workers, [those in outdoor projects] should be observed by a team consisting of a vocational rehabilitation officer, a physician, the site manager and a welfare officer.

The *Riksdag* not only accepted this proposal in 1966 but also added the provision that each major outdoor project should have its own placement officer from the Employment Service on full-time duty.[22]

The Swedish belief in the power of extra personnel to effect transfers to open employment remains to be tested. Records of

[22] National Labour Market Board, *Modern Swedish Labour Market Policy*, pp. 40, 98.

outdoor projects for alcoholics and ex-prisoners prior to 1966 showed that only a small proportion returned to competitive jobs and that the returns occurred through the workers' own initiative more often than from efforts of the Employment Service or welfare officer. Sheltered workshops, which already had the additional specialists, succeeded in transferring only 484 out of 6,630 persons in sheltered work during 1965, or 7.3 percent. (A higher percentage can be achieved by choosing the number remaining in sheltered workshops at the end of the year as the denominator, but this method is not used in other countries.) While the rate of transfers was higher in sheltered workshops than in archive work (less than 3 percent in 1963) or outdoor projects, the difference is not impressive. Moreover, when the demand for labor slackened, the number of placements of sheltered workers in competitive jobs fell to 404 in 1966 and 374 in 1967, although the total number of potential candidates having some sheltered work experience rose to 7,486 in 1966 and 8,844 in 1967.[23]

Not only a recession period but also the secular growth of job creation programs tends to reduce the proportion which returns to open market employment. Thus, the Dutch program in the first half of 1953 reported a transfer rate of 40 percent among 1,727 persons. By the mid-1960s, when over 25,000 people were involved, the transfer rate was about 5 percent, despite the same attention to rehabilitation procedures. It is questionable whether the situation will be changed by a "revaluation of procedures and services . . . to assure the maximum proportion of re-entries into the regular labour market," as the OECD examiners recommended.

Finally, the experience of Britain's Remploy and other workshops which make no special effort to transfer workers must be considered. Year after year, about 200 to 250 severely disabled workers leave Remploy to take regular jobs. Would many more have made the move if specialized personnel had been employed to concentrate on this goal? And would the extra placements have justified the additional costs? The answers are difficult to determine even

[23] Arbetsvårdnytt, 1965, 1966, 1967, *Arbetsmarknadsinformation,* V, no. 2, 1966; V, no. 4, 1967; V, no. 4, 1968.

when the goals are agreed upon, but in this case, Britain does not share the view of Sweden and Holland that extra resources should be applied in order to facilitate a maximum return to competitive employment.

From this survey of the issues which affect created job programs in general, we proceed to the conditions and problems which are peculiar to the individual varieties of job creation: sheltered workshops, homework, outdoor projects, and white-collar job creation.

SHELTERED WORKSHOPS

The sheltered or social workshops enter into complex cooperative and competitive relationships with the private business sector, although their primary purpose is not to produce goods and services or to seek profitable operations, but to provide a steady flow of work with a suitable variety of jobs at good pay for the maximum number of handicapped workers at the minimum annual subsidy per worker.

If all suitable government contracts could be reserved and awarded to sheltered workshops, as some have recommended, and if sheltered workshops had not evolved as manufacturers of products for commercial sale, it might be possible for public authorities to provide the entire work load, as is done for outdoor projects. As it is, sheltered workshops have relied on several means of creating jobs: manufacture of their own products, execution of subcontracts for industry, and filling of government orders. The expansion of workshop employment and the more active role of governments in their finance and supervision have led to a rejection of the traditional broom and basket type of product, which often was sold at above-market prices through an appeal to the purchasers' charitable instincts. Another equally objectionable pattern was the sale of workshop products at prices well below the commercial cost of production, usually because costing, accounting, and management procedures were nonexistent or inadequate.

In place of the earlier practices, the new emphasis is on matching the products and procedures of competitive industry, both in the direct manufacture of workshop products and in the performance of contract work. Attention has been given both to improving the performance of the backward workshops and to the more difficult task of establishing guidelines for optimum operations.

How do trade unions and employers view the expansion of workshop employment and the competition with ordinary industry? As long as full employment prevails, price and wage levels are respected, and the workshops have only a small share of the market, the sale of workshop products occasions little adverse reaction. Even less conflict arises when subcontracts from industry are accepted. Holland's workshops have been aided by the fact that a large proportion of their output is for export. The practice of including union and employer representatives in the administration of sheltered workshops contributes to good relationships.

If there should be a severe recession in these countries, the favorable situation might be altered because private firms would compete for the smaller volume of subcontract business. It is reassuring that Sweden and Holland were able to find work for a substantially increased number of workers in sheltered shops during the recession of 1966–68. A survey in July 1967 by the Dutch authorities showed that existing subcontracts were adequate to carry 52 percent of the workers for six months and 78 percent for 2 months. While this was a less satisfactory position than would exist in times of great labor shortage, an encouraging aspect was the maintenance of the same type of work for 83 percent of the workshop workers as they had in 1966. Only 8 percent were working at a distinctly lower level of work and 9 percent had achieved an improved level.

A marked feature of government participation in the financing of sheltered workshops is a growing concern with improved performance. An extreme case of outmoded procedures was exhibited by the long-established British workshops for the blind which continued in the handicrafts of brooms and baskets. Compared with Remploy, Ltd., they appeared backward with regard to production, marketing, wage systems, accounting, and personnel. As a result of the Report of the Working Party on Workshops for the Blind in November 1962, a series of recommendations leading to modernization, mixing of disabilities, consolidation of shops, and improved efficiency were proposed. Their implementation was through the creation of the Industrial Advisers to the Blind, Ltd., a nonprofit corporation subsidized by the Department of Employment and Productivity and composed primarily of specialists with industrial experience. Two workshops in Bradford and Glasgow were chosen as pilots to experiment with new products and methods and serve as models for change elsewhere. Reports were also published in the *IAB News* on developments at other workshops which might be useful to the remaining shops. Although the workshops are under no compulsion to make cost-saving changes, their need for subsidies is a powerful prod.

In 1965 the British Department of Employment and Productivity appointed inspectors for all sheltered workshops who, among other duties, advise on efficient operation. National Labour Market technicians in Sweden and representatives of the Complementary Social Employment Provisions Division in Holland serve these functions.

One indicator of efficiency is the size of workshops, measured by the number of employees. Some are clearly so small as to be uneconomic. But the larger ones in some countries may be deceptive because several small units with different operations are housed under one roof. Still, economies in management, obtaining contracts, purchasing, and marketing may be achieved by such joint operations. Remploy accomplishes these by central administration. Small independent workshops secure the advantages by combining forces for certain outside negotiations. In Holland federations of workshops are organized on a provincial or interprovincial basis to avoid competition among workshops, coordinate price policies, regulate sales, canvass for contracts, and advise of general policy issues. Some Swedish County Councils achieve the same ends by taking overall responsibility for all workshops in their area.

Table IX.3 shows the distribution of workers in workshops by size in the Netherlands, Great Britain, and Sweden. The Netherlands has the greatest concentration of workers in workshops with 100 or more employees among the three countries. It also has relatively fewer small-scale workshops than the manufacturing industry of Holland as a whole, according to the business census of 1963. Because of the large number of one-man and small manufacturing firms in Holland, workers in firms with fewer than ten employees constituted 15.2 percent of the total, against 0.2 percent in the workshops.[24]

TABLE IX.3. Employment in Sheltered Workshops by Size of Shop, the Netherlands, Great Britain, Sweden, 1965–1966

	The Netherlands (30 June 1965) [a]	Great Britain (31 October 1966) [b]			Sweden (December 1966) [c]
		Total Number of Workers			
		Remploy	Blind	Other	
Size of Shop (Number of Employees)	20,337	6,505	3,704	1,732	6,257
	Percentage Distribution of Workers by Size of Shop				
	100.0	100.0	100.0	100.0	100.0
1–10	0.2	0.0	0.8	4.7	1.2
11–25	1.2	0.0	8.4	15.1	28.2
26–49	4.1	8.5	12.7	34.5	21.5
50–99	29.3	57.8	44.5	37.4	24.8
100+	65.2	33.6	33.7	8.4	24.3

[a] Data from Social Assistance and Complementary Employment Provisions Section, Ministry of Social Affairs and Public Health.

[b] Data from Disabled Persons' Branch, Department of Employment and Productivity.

[c] Data from Vocational Rehabilitation Division, National Labour Market Board.

The British workshops vary considerably according to type. Remploy has no shops with 25 or fewer workers and has a heavy concentration in the 50-99 class. Over one-third of blind workers are in shops with 100 or more workers. The shops operated for other severely disabled workers by voluntary agencies and local

[24] The Netherlands, Central Bureau of Statistics, *Maandschrift,* February 1968, p. 129.

authorities are the smallest. British manufacturing industry in general is on a considerably larger scale than the sheltered workshops. In comparison with the other two countries, the Swedish workshops are small. From the data presented on the three countries, it appears that only the Netherlands has organized its sheltered workshops in larger units than manufacturing industry as a whole.

Size of enterprise is only one factor in efficiency. Another measure is the degree of mechanization in relation to the standard in normal industry. Yet, sheltered workshops must favor labor-intensive methods if they wish to maximize employment. One solution is to employ more than one shift of workers on expensive machinery, but this is not usually possible with handicapped workers. It is also clear that sheltered workshops have to modify industrial practices to suit their workers' needs and that the more advanced the country's technology, the more careful must the workshops be in their choice of products and subcontracts. The difficulty was explained by the director of Rotterdam's workshops, a man with industrial experience who was hired by the city to manage its largest shop and advise all the other shops on methods of improving their performance. He found that the most modern shop and the least modern shop paid the same level of wages and had the same deficit per worker at the end of the year. Unless it can be shown that the modern shop was not operating at its greatest efficiency, the economic case for introducing the most up-to-date machinery may not be the same as in profit-seeking industry, although the rehabilitation aim may favor it.

While the optimum conditions have not yet been determined, progress has been made in eliminating the obviously inefficient procedures; one trend is toward a preference for subcontracts over production for sale. Dutch workshops used to be established close to where workers lived, but in recent years the shops have been set up near suitable factories in order to minimize storage and transport costs on subcontracts. Sweden also stresses the subcontract function of sheltered workshops as a complement to the industrial structure. Remploy and the Industrial Advisers to the

Blind in Great Britain cite the financial and organizational advantages of subcontracts over production for direct sale, which requires a large staff of nonhandicapped to advertise, sell, and conduct the business side and also requires that valuable floor space be devoted to storing materials and finished goods.

Some subcontractors supply and deliver materials, machinery, and instructors and pick up finished products. Sometimes workers from the workshops are borrowed temporarily by the factory. Factories which are short of space or workers welcome the opportunity to turn over some production to workshops. Remploy calls this "sponsorship." In Holland the writer saw sheltered workers assembling typewriters and making automobile accessories for well-known American companies and wondered whether the same companies would award such subcontracts in the United States. Both technological and social factors might militate against it.

HOMEWORK

Most authorities agree that homework should be limited to those who are unable to come to a workshop and should be assigned sparingly in industrialized countries. Homework encourages social and psychological isolation, may entail low-grade work, is difficult to organize, and is subject to the abuses of low pay and possible performance of the work by others in the family. If sheltered workshops are numerous in relation to a country's area and population, transportation is available, and climate and topography are not problems, as in the Netherlands, homework can become a negligible feature of job creation for the severely handicapped. About 200 homeworkers are supported through shelterd workshops and are included in Holland's workshop employment figure (Table IX.1). Sweden which has organized homework for over 1000 persons through sheltered workshops and homework centers is satisfied with their operation. Vocational training is given to some homeworkers. In Britain a few homeworkers are employed through the Remploy factories and a much larger group of blind homeworkers continues a traditional pattern. It is likely that this form of job creation will remain as a last resort.

OUTDOOR PROJECTS

Created jobs for the severely handicapped on open-air projects are arranged entirely by government agencies and usually yield no products for sale or income. Exceptions are found in the Dutch horticultural projects which sell their vegetables and herbs and in Swedish timber-cutting on contract with farmers and large lumber companies. In general, the projects add to the community or general welfare by undertaking tasks which regular government departments will not do at all or plan to do later and which have not been undertaken by the Special Public Works projects for the cyclically, structurally, regionally, and seasonally unemployed.

The establishment of separate outdoor projects for the handicapped has made it possible for the Special Public Works programs to limit their acceptance of handicapped workers. Thus, some 500 Dutch handicapped men, on the average, were employed on Special Public Works projects in 1956, but by 1965 the average was down to 70. Sweden also has shifted the handicapped to their own projects.

Among the advantages of outdoor projects in comparison with sheltered workshops are the ease of providing labor-intensive jobs, the rapidity with which projects can be established, the low capital investment per worker, the absence of conflict with the private economy, and the ability to establish separate workplaces for different disability groups. The chief disadvantages are the low level of the jobs, the poor preparation for transfer to the competitive labor market, and the unsuitability of the work for certain groups.

Table IX.4 shows three important aspects of the Swedish program: the large number of government agencies which provide work, the wide range of activities conducted by project workers, and the existence of separate projects for individual disability groups. Most jobs were provided by the National Forestry Administration and local governments (*Stako*), with the National Labor

TABLE IX.4. Job Creation for the Handicapped
on Outdoor Projects, Sweden, 1965

	Man-years Worked	Man-day Cost Sw. Kr.
Total	3099.5	125
Forestry care and lumbering	1405.0	96
Labour Market Board—For special categories: alcoholics, criminals, delinquents, mentally ill	374.4	107
Forestry Administration—For physically handicapped	1028.1	93
Forestry Administration—Day work for patients in mental hospitals	2.5	63
Nature work and Landscaping—Forestry Administration for physically and mentally handicapped	164.6	77
Roads—Physically disabled on Labour Market Board Special Public Works	297.6	443
Water and Sewerage—Labour Market Board for special categories	14.4	269
State Railroads—Labour Market Board for special categories	10.8	351
Care of Monuments, etc.—Central Board for Conservation of Antiquities	3.8	163
Projects for the hard-to-place	1203.3	81
Local Government (Stako) (T-works)	1095.3	82
Central Government	90.4	70
Army	6.9	74
Central Board for Conservation of Antiquities	6.0	121
Road Administration	4.7	100

Source: National Labour Market Board Technical Division

Market Board in third place in 1965. The projects range from isolated forest locations where the workers live in camps to clean-up
jobs in the heart of the cities and towns. Workers usually travel no
more than 60 km. (37 miles) round trip in buses provided by the
projects. In the north in particular, where population is sparsely
settled and projects are concentrated in the few larger towns, many
workers live in simple dormitories during the week and go home at
the weekends.

The geographical distribution of workers in a Swedish project
for the handicapped shows a disproportionate share in the seven
northern counties, but to a lesser extent than on the Special Public
Works projects. In 1965 and 1966, the monthly records showed
that from one-third to one-half of those on outdoor projects for the
handicapped lived in the north, although the area includes only 17
percent of the total population. More than two-thirds of the workers
were over 45 and one-fourth were over 60 in 1966. In 1965 and
1966, 4 to 5 percent were youths under 24 and some were as young
as 16. Handicapped youths were considered in need of more workplaces. Few women were employed on outdoor projects. In May
1966, they accounted for only 9 out of 3,668 workers and in
December 1967, 81 out of 6,773. Alternative forms of job creation
are urged for women, as the unsuitability of outdoor projects is generally conceded.

Sweden's outdoor projects for the handicapped cater to several groups. The first consists of those who are about to be discharged from various institutions: for the mentally ill, alcoholics,
criminals, and youthful offenders, plus some mental patients able
to do day-work away from the hospital. Each handicap group usually has its separate camp and work site and its tasks are likely
to be performed away from population centers. A bridge toward
normal living as well as a work experience is provided, with social
workers and other personnel to assist in adjustments. The great
importance of open-air projects as a work solution for alcoholics
is indicated by the records of the Vocational Rehabilitation Division.
In 1964, when 3,900 alcoholics (including 30 females) were placed
in some form of created work, 3,723 were assigned to outdoor proj-

ects, 115 were placed in sheltered workshops, 3 performed home-work, and 45 were given created white-collar jobs. A recommenda-tion of the tripartite committee on labor market policy called for an increase in sheltered workplaces for alcoholics and others in the spe-cial categories. Now "work centers" are being established which offer a variety of jobs, instead of the usual single project camp devoted to forestry work or roadwork. Projects are conducted either by private contractors through bids or by government units directly. Private contractors must take workers, with certain exceptions, from the Employment Service.

The physically handicapped also have their camps and work sites. A recent addition on projects are workers who live in isolated areas with few employment opportunities. This group accounts for much of the expansion since 1965 in the numbers of workers on outdoor projects. In the northern countries where they are relatively numer-ous such workers may be as skilled and productive as employed workers elsewhere, but their age and immobility makes it doubtful that they will work in competitive jobs again. To the extent that those on Special Public Works are younger, trainable, and mobile, they are not handicapped in the labor market as are the older proj-ect workers.

A third group consists of the hard-to-place who work for reduced wage rates, usually 15 percent below the hourly rates set by collec-tive agreement for municipal workers. Their work is centrally lo-cated and is organized mainly by the municipalities.

The jobs called "T-works," which Swedish local governments create for the hard-to-place with a state subsidy, are of particular interest because of their variety. Seven broad work categories are listed with 55 specific types of work. Because a high proportion of recreation facilities are publicly owned in Sweden, many of the tasks involve their care and maintenance. For example, project workers clean up and improve childrens' camp colonies, camping grounds, skating rinks, ski and bobsled slopes, bicycle and hiking paths, min-iature golf courses, sports stadia, ball fields, sports cottages in the mountains, summer homes at the shore, beaches and swimming pools, and playgrounds and sports fields around schools and parks.

Another group of jobs centers around public parks and ceme-
teries and includes ten specific types of jobs which each municipality follows in its assignments. The category of nature work includes such jobs as burning leaves, cleaning lakes, rivers, and
brooks, and preserving wild areas with rare trees and plants. Those
who are assigned to work around historical monuments and museums engage in such specific tasks as excavating old buildings,
moving and installing old walls, aiding in museums, cleaning and
maintaining tombs, and restoring old country homes and buildings
for public display of earlier modes of living.

The portion of "T-works" called "Diverse Works" has the largest number of subheads and is most closely related to urban improvement. These workers aid in snow removal and cleaning public
streets, open areas, and industrial grounds. They tidy garbage
dumps, storage places for gravel and sand, and other storage areas.
They mend fences and tend garden areas and create water supply
ponds for fire-fighting.

In Holland the range of activities on outdoor projects for the
severely handicapped is somewhat narrower because the terrain of
the country does not permit forestry works, the population is dense,
and the municipalities place most of the created jobs within their
own jurisdictions. In mid-1965 there were 1,068 separate outdoor
projects employing 6,493 handicapped workers. The vast majority
of the projects (87.7 percent) had 10 or fewer workers, while another 9.7 percent had 11 to 25 workers. Only 1 percent of the
projects had 50 to 200 workers, and none had more. Thus, outdoor projects are definitely a small-scale operation, especially in
contrast with Dutch sheltered workshops (Table IX.3). Many projects are turned over to private contractors who have their own basic
staff. They hire unemployed handicapped persons referred to them
by the Employment Service. These workers lay out and maintain
public gardens, parks, bicycle roads, footpaths, and playgrounds.
Published "before" and "after" photographs show the same sort
of block improvement that has been recommended for the American urban ghetto.

The age distribution of those on Dutch outdoor projects indicates a slightly more important role for older handicapped workers than in Sweden. From 1959 through 1965, those aged 56 to 65 constituted no less than 40 percent of the total and in some years as much as 47 percent. The next lower age bracket, 46 to 55, accounted for over 25 percent each year. Older workers, those over 45, are a higher proportion on Dutch outdoor projects than in Dutch sheltered workshops. It was the intention of the Dutch program in its early days to draw in "teddy boys," youths under 18 who seemed to be in social or moral danger. But the boys had so many other opportunities to earn money that they could not be recruited.[25] Young people under 23 have constituted from under 2 percent to over 3 percent of the total number on outdoor projects in each year from 1959 to 1965.

Women have had few of the jobs; in 1959 only 27 of the 9,765 on outdoor projects were female. In that year only 1,238 women were employed on all created jobs for the handicapped. Although the number of women has increased in later years, the proportion of women assigned to outdoor projects has not kept pace with the rise in the total number. It must be borne in mind that women have a low participation rate in the labor force in the Netherlands and that outdoor work would be particularly inappropriate for most of the eligible handicapped women.

Dutch outdoor projects offer relatively more places to the socially handicapped than sheltered workshops. In 1965 over 31 percent of those on outdoor projects, but less than 12 percent in sheltered workshops, had a character or social problem as their primary work handicap. Although the physically handicapped usually constitute the largest single group on outdoor projects, about one-fourth of the total in 1965 was primarily mentally handicapped. On the other hand, the outdoor projects take relatively few of the "B" workers, those with less than one-third of normal work capacity.

The recent increase in the numbers on outdoor projects for the handicapped in both Sweden and Holland is paralleled in other

[25] European Seminar on Sheltered Employment, The Hague, 1959, p. 29.

northern European countries. It is clearly a useful program in countries which prefer to give the handicapped created employment rather than maintain them in idleness.

WHITE-COLLAR JOB CREATION

In 1953 the Netherlands established a Social Employment Program for White-Collar Workers (*Sociale Werkvoorzieningsregeling voor Hoofarbeiders:* S.W.H.). Its objective, according to an official statement, was to provide "appropriate work for brainworkers who cannot obtain suitable work under normal conditions of employment and for whom training and retraining is not desirable or possible, in order thus to enhance, maintain or restore their fitness for work." Although the term "brainworkers" is used, a wide variety of nonmanual hard-to-place unemployed was encompassed from the outset. The range is from the lowest clerical to academics in research work. Displaced shopkeepers, forced out of business by the encroachment of new housing developments, also have been given these jobs.

A special scheme to aid artists is auxiliary to the S.W.H. program. Artists who demonstrate financial need may submit their works for purchase by the municipality, which acts with the advice of a local committee. Purchased works are placed in municipal buildings, and some artists are said to live entirely on the proceeds of sales to the municipalities. Some 600 artists have benefited annually in recent years. Discussions have been held on the possibilities of extending a similar plan to writers and musicians.

Sweden's program, called archive work (*Arkivarbete*), evolved from the designation of some Special Public Works jobs for unemployed professional and technical workers. Later, the program furnished created jobs for those who were deemed handicapped in the labor market and unsuited to Special Public Works projects because of their previous professions, special qualifications, age, or personal circumstances.

The range of beneficiaries on archive work is much the same as in Holland. A Swedish survey of archive workers in December 1960 according to their former occupation and amount of education showed that half came from professional, technical, administrative, and business jobs, while another 15 percent had been self-employed. As might be expected, the proportion who had completed higher education and technical or professional training was relatively high. These findings were renewed in December 1966.

Sweden has also made a particular point of giving created jobs to refugees and others of foreign birth whose unfamiliarity with the Swedish language prevents them from following their former occupations. Matching the Dutch concern for artists is the Swedish job creation program for unemployed musicians (*Musikerhjälp*); the jobs consist of work with amateur orchestras and other non-professional musical organizations.

Table IX.1 shows that the Dutch program for white-collar workers has grown more slowly than the Swedish. In Sweden, a considerable further expansion is expected partly because changes in the labor market are increasingly affecting white-collar workers who are handicapped, older, or immobile. However, the number of Swedish musicians on jobs has remained fairly constant and usually is less than 100.

The definition of suitable jobs for nonmanual workers and the actual establishment of openings offer a constant challenge to the responsible authorities. In the Netherlands appropriate work originally was defined as that "which would not be carried out but for the subsidies provided under the scheme. Tasks which are part of the ordinary activities of an institution or public department . . . fall outside the scope of this scheme." Some activities recommended to the municipalities in 1953, provided they were additional to the normal functions of public or nonprofit organizations, were:

1.) drawing up of questionnaires and compiling and arranging the results;
2.) collecting, compiling, and arranging statistical data;
3.) activities on behalf of libraries, museums, and collections;
4.) filing;

5.) activities connected with scientific research (in or outside of universities);

6.) activities connected with disasters (floods, etc.);

7.) clerical work of various kinds.

A more recent addition has been the subcontracting of work from private enterprise, along the lines developed by sheltered workshops. Another trend is a departure from the earlier practice of assigning each worker to his own project. Groups have been established under the direction of a S.W.H. supervisor. They serve as administrative service bureaus which take subcontracts from municipal agencies or private enterprise. For example, Caltex subcontracted the distribution of all of its promotional literature and materials to a S.W.H. group of 10 to 15 workers. The new element is that S.W.H. groups execute work which is part of the normal activity of a business or governmental organization. Under full employment conditions, the fears of competition with normal workers have subsided.

In February 1967, the largest S.W.H. group was in Amsterdam and had 118 workers. However, the individual project must still be quite common because as late as February 1967, the 2,300 S.W.H. workers were employed on 876 separate projects, an average of less than 3 workers per project.

Some projects visited by the writer in Holland show the range of activities possible for severely handicapped persons. In Rotterdam a leader and seven men occupied space in various nooks and crannies of a municipal office, next to regular civil servants. Half of the S.W.H. group had physical disabilities and half were mentally disabled. Their task was to address postcards to every adult resident of Rotterdam telling when to appear at the appropriate medical center for a free chest X-ray.

About 95 percent of the residents responded to the first postcard, but those who failed to answer were followed up by the S.W.H. group and given a second appointment. If this S.W.H. group were not arranging specific appointments, the municipality would simply resort to general posters and other advertising announcing the free tests. The medical centers would not have as steady a utilization of their X-ray equipment, and possibly some residents would skip the tests.

Another S.W.H. group did work of historical and legal interest. In the municipal archives they made and arranged card files, listing and dating every resident of the city and other family data. They drew on ancient and decaying papers and their new lists represent a preservation of records which might otherwise have been lost.

Swedish archive works are similar to the Dutch created jobs for nonmanual handicapped workers, except that private enterprise has not been tapped for contracts. However, some Swedish sheltered workshops do such white-collar jobs for industry. In December 1966, 2,917 archive workers were assigned as follows: 336 in museums, 681 in universities and high schools, 339 in libraries and archives, 793 in government offices and workplaces, 373 in nonprofit organizations, 122 in hospitals, and the remainder in miscellaneous posts. In 1960 some 56 percent were doing clerical work, 19 percent were engaged in archive tasks, and 10 percent were in library, laboratory, and related jobs; the rest had a variety of tasks. These workers do routine office work, typing, checking, simple cataloging, preserving, sorting, and bundling documents, clipping newspapers, marking museum specimens, packing and labeling objects, simple printing and bookbinding. Physical labor such as transporting documents or moving historical objects may be part of the job. Qualified professionals are assigned to research or scientific activities.

In 1967–68, 1,416 Swedish establishments provided jobs for 4,130 workers, an average of under 3 workers per establishment. About 85 percent of the establishments were central government agencies and the remainder were local government bodies. It is proposed that about 200 archive workers with at least five years on a project and a good work record should be absorbed by the agencies to which they have been assigned as regular workers at normal rates of pay. This transfer will relieve the Labor Market Board of some expense, benefit the workers financially and socially, and prevent agencies from using archive workers for normal operations.

Some examples of jobs in Stockholm included an Estonian minister in his 80s whose job was the organization and conducting of religious services for other Estonians in their own language. Other men were assisting in the creation of a national monument of a sunken warship which had been raised in Stockholm harbor after several hundred years of submersion. The preservation of antiquities provides many employment opportunities for archive workers. As in Holland, there has been recent concern about nonmanual workers with severe work handicaps and low skills who need supervision on archive projects. The Swedish office work centers, established by the county labor market boards, have been a partial answer to this problem. In 1967–68, 23 centers had a total of 379 places and planned to expand considerably. Both Sweden and Holland stress the need for a variety of jobs calling for a wide range of skills.

Older people predominate in the created jobs for nonmanual workers. A Swedish survey in December 1960 indicated that 58 was the average age among the 1,530 persons on archive work. In December 1966, 56 percent were over 60. Sweden permits such employment to continue beyond the retirement age of 67 if the person does not receive an old age pension or other income. West Germany's program is located chiefly in West Berlin and is specifically for older clerical workers whose employment opportunities have been severely limited by the transfer of the federal capital to Bonn. In Holland, where 64 is the upper age limit for entrance to the program and workers are terminated on their 65th birthday, older workers are also disproportionately represented.

The program for nonmanual workers, like sheltered workshops, offers opportunities for women. In Sweden, where married and older women have high labor force participation rates, about one-third of the archive workers have been female; in December 1965 and May 1966 the ratio was about 40 percent.

Swedish archive work has been highly concentrated in Stockholm and environs because most jobs are created directly by central government authorities. The 1960 survey showed that 53 percent of all jobs were in Stockholm, but in 1967–68 the proportion dropped to about 30 percent, in keeping with the recommendations of the tripartite labor market policy committee in 1965 that the municipalities sponsor a greater share of archive work and that the central government raise its subsidy for wages on municipal projects. In 1966 the subsidy was increased from 20 to 33 percent. The "archive works centers" operated by the County Labour Boards also help to decentralize from Stockholm. In Holland the program is conducted entirely by the municipalities or designated foundations and appears to be well-distributed geographically.

The administrative structure which implements the Dutch S.W.H. program is the same as for the manual workers (G.S.W.). Sweden places authority over archive work initiated in central government bodies in the Vocational Rehabilitation Division of the National Labour Market Board. Municipalities, through their unemployment relief committees, apply to the County Labour Boards for approval of projects and state subsidies. Workers must be referred by the local Employment Service office and are usually assigned to jobs for a fixed period, with a maximum of six months. Repeat assignments are possible and trial placements for short periods are also used.

In Sweden and elsewhere it may be anticipated that handicapped white-collar and professional workers will constitute an increasing proportion of all on created jobs for the handicapped. The planning of individual and group projects may become more difficult as the numbers increase.

This chapter has explored the reactions of northwestern European countries to the postwar view that government has a responsibility to create special jobs for all who need a sheltered environment. According to this view, jobs should be provided as a right, not as charity, and should be part of the commitment to full employment. The experience of Holland and Sweden has been cited most frequently because these countries have come closest to the ideal in conception and performance; the rapid expansion of their programs during the recent recession is noteworthy. A general European trend is also visible in the improvement of established programs in Denmark, Norway, and Great Britain and the implementation of legislation in France and Belgium. West Germany, long doubtful, also recognized the need for extensive job creation for the hard-to-employ in 1967.[26] Switzerland, however, remains apart, resembling the United States in its reliance on voluntary agencies to aid specific groups.

Since Holland and Sweden have gone farthest in offering created work as an alternative to idleness and dependency amongst marginal groups, some of the elements which have contributed to their successful operation may be cited, omitting the general factors of attitudes and organization which were listed at the conclusion of Chapter VIII.

A prime asset has been the cooperation of employers and trade unions. They in turn have responded well because of long periods of full employment and active government policies to combat departures from high prosperity. Another important factor has been the willingness of men trained in business enterprise to become managers and foremen on projects employing handicapped workers. The transfers are eased by the rough equivalence of salaries in the two fields as well as a degree of social acceptance of careers for men in social welfare activities. Solid accomplishment and public respect are generated by the avoidance of crash programs, the provision of long training periods for personnel, relative security with regard to financing from year to year, a sense of permanence, and a careful refusal to promise more than the programs can be expected to achieve.

It would be misleading to conclude that the programs are free of problems or that they operate at top efficiency. Over-all methods of assessing the performance of the various workshops and projects have not been devised. Financial results are important, but they are only one criterion. Problems remain concerning the importance which should be attached to transfers to the competitive labor market and in particular how much personnel and time should be de-

[26] G. Rehn, "Manpower Policy and European Unemployment," *OECD Observer*, December 1967, p. 18; Dr. Rolf Weber, "The Problem of Special Groups Vulnerable to Employment Difficulties in a Balanced Economy," OECD: Paris, February 1969, pp. 4, 12–14.

voted to achieving this objective. Excessive turnover on some projects is a continuing administrative problem and cost.

But the existence of problems does not mean that these countries would be prepared to discard these programs if an economist's cost/benefit analysis showed that it would cost the taxpayer less to pay the handicapped a maintenance allowance than to create jobs. The high social value placed on participating in the society through work, the human benefits even unto the unborn generations, and the potential for re-entering the competitive labor market are factors which would turn the balance in any acceptable analysis.[27]

[27] Neil W. Chamberlain ("Some Second Thoughts on the Concept of Human Capital," *Proceedings of the Industrial Relations Research Association,* Washington, December 1967, pp. 1–13) presents an interesting challenge of the American passion for immediate quantitative and pecuniary measurement to the neglect of the longer-range and broader objectives of a society.

X | Restraints on Dismissals of the Hard-to-Reemploy

The earlier chapters have dealt with the hard-to-employ who are out of work. Another group merits attention—those who are currently working but would become hard-to-employ if they lost their present jobs. Most frequently these are older workers, often with a long and good work history with one employer. Younger employed workers also may be counted as hard-to-reemploy if they have physical, mental, social, or skill handicaps which have not been overcome but rather have been tolerated in existing jobs. Whether dismissal occurs because of personal performance, the fortunes of the firm, the decline of a region or industry, technological and managerial advances, or the level of operations of the economy, these people are likely to become placement problems. Others who are likely to become hard-to-employ are displaced self-employed businessmen and farmers.

In the past decade the demand for labor has been strong at most times in the countries of northwestern Europe at the same time that the domestic labor supply has not grown rapidly. As a result, a substantial part of the marginal or hard-to-employ population has found employment. The proportion of employed workers who are over 50 years of age has been rising recently in several countries in western Europe and in important industries.[1] Large numbers at

[1] European Coal and Steel Community, (ECSC), High Authority, *14e Rapport général sur l'activité de la Communauté. . .* , Luxembourg, 1966, pp. 305, 308; Organization for Economic Cooperation and Development,

work might be considered hard-to-reemploy if they lost their jobs.

In surveying the attitudes, institutions, programs, and legislation which affect the hard-to-reemploy in western European countries, one cannot limit the discussion to the few measures which specifically single out the hard-to-reemploy. There is in addition the special impact on the hard-to-reemploy of general manpower policies directed toward all workers.

At the present time, three parallel and sometimes simultaneous approaches which affect the hard to-reemploy are followed in western European countries. Each approach is not used in every country and the emphasis varies from country to country. First, there are attempts to maintain continuity of employment in the same firm and in the same job. Second, there are programs to speed reemployment. To act before workers actually become unemployed, to take preventive measures, is one of the most significant innovations of manpower policy in the advanced western European nations. Increasingly, workers who are about to lose their jobs are of equal concern to manpower authorities as the relatively few who already are unemployed. Third, there are efforts to compensate for loss of employment by financial awards in addition to ordinary unemployment benefits.

Those western European countries in which a particular emphasis is placed on measures to maintain continuity of employment are characterized by a great fear of unemployment and considerable resistance to change. The rigid lines of apprenticeship, crafts, and education in some of these countries contribute to the uneasiness. A spirit prevails which is more reminiscent of the lean 1930s than the fat 1960s.[2] Many Europeans concede that fears of change and un-

(OECD), Manpower and Social Affairs Committee, *Annual Reports, Germany, 1963*, MO(63) 17/01 p. 14; OECD, *Age and Employment*, Paris, 1962, p. 19; International Labour Office, (ILO), *Report of the Director-General, Part 1: Older People*, Geneva, 1962, pp. 17–22; OECD, Regional Seminar, The Employment of Older Workers, *Final Report*, Paris, 1966, pp. 5–14, 33–36; Irvin Sobel and Richard C. Wilcock, *Placement Techniques*, OECD: Paris, 1966, pp. 17–30.

[2] For a brief summary of trade union attitudes, see, ILO, *International Differences in Factors Affecting Labour Mobility*, AUT/DOC/7, Geneva,

employment are excessive but, they say, memories die hard and the wonder is that Americans have not displayed an equal or greater reaction against the even higher rates of unemployment in the United States.

The persistence of old attitudes is suggested by Jacques Chazelle, former Director-General of the Labour and Employment Department of the French Ministry of Labour. Describing the changes in approach required to implement an active manpower policy, Chazelle declared that the worker "must stop considering change as synonymous with catastrophe, and he must discard outdated ways of thinking which saw business modernization as the desire to raise profits to the employee's disadvantage. . . . He must recognize that he can no longer work his entire life in the same place, or even at the same occupation. . . ." [3]

But a French trade union leader has indicated why anxiety persists among workers in spite of the establishment of various government programs to cope with structural change. Not only is the assistance offered to workers inadequate and difficult to obtain, but also the displaced worker is exposed to special hardships at the very time that national prosperity is elevating his neighbor's consumption habits and living standards. "In particular, it may be necessary, as a last resort, to uproot oneself from the place where one has friends and memories, and it also means facing an undeserved ordeal, which is more frightening for the older worker." [4] In many

---

1965, pp. 192–95; Jack Stieber, "Manpower Adjustments to Automation and Technological Change in Western Europe," in the *Report of the Commission on Technology, Automation and Economic Progress,* Washington, 1966, App. Vol. III, pp. 51, 58, 95, 116; "Labour Mobility: The Role of the Ministry of Labour," *British Journal of Industrial Relations,* July 1965, p. 149; Geoffrey Gorer, "What's the Matter with Britain," *New York Times Magazine,* December 31, 1967.

[3] Ambassade de France, Service de Presse et d'Information, *French Affairs,* No. 179, New York, June 1965, p. 11. See also, ECSC, *13 années d'actions sociales de la Haute Autorité de la CECA,* Luxembourg, 1966, p. 13.

[4] L. Lucas, in OECD, International Trade Union Seminar on Active Manpower Policy, *Supplement to the Final Report,* Paris, 1964, p. 27; Jack Stieber, "Manpower Adjustments. . . ," pp. 55, 58.

European countries workers are concerned about an inequitable distribution of the burdens and rewards of economic progress.

A conspicuous exception to these attitudes is found in Sweden, where unions, employers, and government are in remarkable agreement on labor market policy. At its discussions of labor market policy in 1966, the Swedish Parliament declared that Swedish workers did not regard changes in the economy as a threat to employment but rather as an opportunity to improve their jobs and earnings. Trade union representatives confirm the view that the worker's positive attitude is based on the knowledge that growth will benefit the whole country because society will minimize the economic hardships on those directly affected and will distribute the burdens fairly.

Because of Sweden's slow growth of population and chronic labor shortages, rationalization and structural transformation have aroused little concern until quite recently. The director of the Swedish Institute for Labour, at an international conference on automation, warned that "a policy of promoting rationalization and efficiency should not be pursued beyond the point where national manpower [policy, ed.] is no longer able to provide employment for the redundant manpower." [5]

In those countries where attempts are made to maintain continuity of employment within an enterprise, the chief forms are restraints on dismissals, sharing the work, maintenance of demand for the products and services of existing firms, and retention of a work force through reconversion and retraining within the enterprise. These measures have particular significance for those who would be hard-to-reemploy. In the present chapter, the legal restraints on dismissals are discussed.

The first step is to minimize the number to be dismissed. An American has observed that "West European employers differ from

[5] Interviews with officers of the Swedish National Labour Market Board; Sweden, National Labour Market Board, *Modern Swedish Labour Market Policy,* Stockholm, 1966, p. 75; Gösta Rehn, "Manpower Policy and European Unemployment," *OECD Observer,* December 1967, p. 34; Rudolf Meidner, in *Proceedings of the International Conference on Automation, Full Employment, and a Balanced Economy,* (Rome), New York, 1967; Trevor Evans and Margaret Stewart, *Pathway to Tomorrow,* London, 1967, pp. 68–69, 71, 108–109; Jack Stieber, "Manpower Adjustments. . . ," pp. 101–102.

274 | *Restraints on Dismissals of the Hard-to-Reemploy*

their American counterparts in assuming a greater social obligation for providing continuous employment for their workers. This may extend to continuing to employ, or delaying dismissal of, workers who are no longer needed. . . ." [6] European firms, and especially the nationalized industries, have achieved substantial reductions in employment without resorting to dismissals. Through advance planning which may take five to ten years, the companies are able to reach the desired labor force size by relying on normal attrition and turnover, the encouragement of voluntary leaving or early retirement, and the cessation of recruitment. The last measure, if practiced for many years, will produce an undesirable age structure in the firm or industry, and it may also limit the opportunities of new entrants. Trade unions have not opposed such restrictions so long as general employment conditions have been good. The particular industries affected—coal mines, railroads, shipyards—have not been attractive to new entrants in any case.

In order to avoid dismissals, European employers, often under the prodding of trade unions, transfer surplus or disabled workers within a plant or office, usually with a wage guarantee at the same

[6] Jack Stieber, "Manpower Adjustments. . . ," pp. 122, 59–62, 90, 116; ILO, *International Differences. . .* , pp. 221–22, 244–45, 253–54; ECSC, High Authority, *Mesures de réadaptation appliquées en République Fédérale d'Allemagne, en Belgique et en France, Bilan et resultats, 1960–1965,* Luxembourg, 1966, pp. 20, 39; Frederic Meyers, *Ownership of Jobs: A Comparative Study,* Los Angeles, 1964, pp. 15, 65, 71, 106–12; Arnold R. Weber, "Variety in Adaptation to Technological Change; The Contribution of Collective Bargaining," in OECD, International Seminar on the Requirements of Automated Jobs, *Supplement to the Final Report,* Paris, 1965, pp. 205–18; Günter Friedrichs, "Planning Social Adjustment to Technological Change at the Level of the Undertaking," *International Labour Review,* August 1965, pp. 91–105; Clinton E. Jencks, "British Coal: Labor Relations Since Nationalization," *Industrial Relations,* October 1966, pp. 101–102; A. D. Smith, *Redundancy Practices in Four Industries,* OECD: Paris, 1966; ILO, *Manpower Adjustment Programmes: I. France, Federal Republic of Germany, United Kingdom,* Labour and Automation, Bull. no. 4, Geneva, 1967, pp. 19–22, 94–96, 148–52; Solomon Barkin, ed., *Technical Change and Manpower Planning,* OECD: Paris, 1967; Dorothy Wedderburn, *Enterprise Planning for Change,* OECD: Paris, 1968.

or a slightly reduced wage for less demanding work. In Sweden internal transfers of this kind are said to be generally unfavorable to the workers. In 1966 the Labour Market Board conducted a survey among all industrial firms with 500 or more workers to discover what their practices were with regard to their own hard-to-place employees. Dismissal was used in cases involving blue-collar workers by 34 percent of the firms, while 92 percent of the firms reported that they tried to find another suitable post in the firm. Some 63 percent also devised light tasks such as those of a sweeper or watchman for employees with physical handicaps, while 27 percent did the same for the mentally handicapped. The proportions were lower in each case for supervisory and administrative employees. Dismissals were most common in the textile and related industries, in firms regardless of industry whose total employment was decreasing by more than 10 percent and in firms where technical or organizational change was occurring without an expansion of employment.

Transfers to other locations are a common practice in nationalized industries and large corporations. Costs of moving, new housing, and other expenses are often borne by the companies. In some industries, French textiles, for example, employers have the obligation under collective bargaining agreements to find places for their surplus workers in other firms or even other industries. When dismissals are necessary, phasing of the discharges is generally planned so that the numbers coming on the local labor market will be controlled.

Another approach, especially satisfactory in the case of surplus older workers, is to retrain and place them at their previous or higher levels of skill and earnings. Great Britain's Employment Service provides a training instructor or will give instruction to supervisors so that they can train older workers. It is also urged that employers should redesign jobs, adapt work places, and in other ways make it possible to return older workers to productive and well-paid posts. Employers facing labor shortages are better candidates for these approaches than those who are seeking to reduce their work force. The Swedish survey of large industrial firms previously mentioned inquired whether employees who had become disabled or hard-to-place were offered retraining within the firm. Some 54 percent of the firms provided retraining for blue-collar workers and 37 percent offered it to supervisory and administrative personnel. In both cases, the proportions were highest for enterprises undergoing technical or organizational change and expanding employment. Almost three-fourths of such firms gave blue-collar workers an opportunity to retrain, while just over half had such courses for supervisory and administrative personnel. At the other extreme, firms which were not changing technically and had stable or declining employment offered retraining to only 24 percent of blue-collar and 18 percent of white-collar employees.[7]

These practices and attitudes of western European employers toward continuity of employment, while not universal, are so widespread that legislative restrictions on an employer's right to dismiss his own employees have been enacted and accepted in a few countries. Some of the legal provisions refer to specific individuals who would be considered hard-to-reemploy, while other laws pertain to dismissals in general, but have special meaning for the hard-to-reemploy.

RESTRAINTS ON DISMISSALS OF SPECIFIC INDIVIDUALS

The dismissal laws may protect the jobs of particular hard-to-reemploy persons. In West Germany, for example, "a termination must be regarded as unjustifiable from the social point of view,"

[7] Sweden, National Labour Market Board, "Anpassningsåtgärder för Svårplacerad Arbetskraft inom Större Industriföretag," *Arbetsmarknadsinformation*, M, 1, 1967, p. 17; ILO, *Redundancy Procedures in Selected Western European Countries*, Geneva, 1966, pp. 63–64, 78–87, 156–157, 161–162; Rudolf Meidner, *Proceedings. . . ,* p. 5; ILO, *Manpower Adjustment Programmes: II. Sweden, U.S.S.R., United States*, Labour and Automation, Bull. no. 6., Geneva, 1967, pp. 22–23; Interviews in Great Britain; Stephen Griew, *Job Re-design*, OECD: Paris, 1964; G. Marbach, *Job Redesign for Older Workers*, OECD: Paris, 1968; OECD, *Promoting the Placement of Older Workers*, Paris, 1967, pp. 91–93; Solomon Barkin, ed., *Technical Change and Manpower Planning*, pp. 47–255.

says an official publication, "if it is not characterized by urgent internal requirements preventing the continued employment of the employee in the undertaking concerned." Furthermore, the dismissal will be "regarded as unjustified from the social point of view if the employer in choosing the employee who is to be given notice did not pay due attention to the social aspect of a case or did not do so adequately." However, an ILO report on Termination of Employment in 1962 suggested that operational considerations actually have had priority over social considerations in the Federal Republic. As a consequence of the recession of 1967, the law was amended in order to strengthen the powers of the labor court to declare certain changes in the employment situation of individuals as "socially unjustified" and therefore invalid in law.

An employee who feels that he has been dismissed without due attention to the social circumstances may take his case to court and, if successful, can win an award of up to a year's pay. A court interpretation in one case declared that "in regard to an employee who has been working for the enterprise for a long time and whose capacity is diminishing because of increasing age, the employer will first have to try to give him an easier job." [8]

This view is in accord with the practice of many employers and statutory provisions in other western European countries. The Netherlands dismissal law of 1945 has been interpreted to forbid the dismissal of workers where the consequences of termination will be more serious for the employee than the employer. Dutch employers recognize social reasons for maintaining employment and will not often submit the name of a hard-to-employ person to the Employment Service for individual dismissal. Instead, employers reassign these workers to light or menial tasks such as those of watchman, errand boy, or sweeper. These solutions may be preferable to unem-

[8] Federal Ministry of Labour and the Social Structure, *Notice of Dismissal and Protection against Dismissal*, Monongraph 13, Social Policy in Germany, Essen, 1963, p. 13; "Dismissal Procedures, IV: Federal Republic of Germany," *International Labour Review*, September 1959, pp. 266–67; ILO, *Report of the Director-General, Part I: Older People*, p. 43; ILO, *Redundancy Procedures. . .* , p. 97.

ployment, but they fall short of the practice of the most socially-minded European firms where job redesign, special equipment, or sheltered conditions are provided for employees who have grown old or incapacitated while in the service of the company.[9]

Legal provisions, supplemented by social practice, also prevent the dismissal of specific types of persons who would become hard-to-reemploy. Disabled workers are a major example. The very existence of a quota system for employing disabled persons is in itself a restraint on the dismissal of disabled workers because employers may thus fall below their quota. In Britain, it is a legal offense to discharge without reasonable cause a registered disabled person if the discharge would leave the employer under his quota; however, in practice, every attempt is made to persuade employers to comply with their obligations, and legal proceedings are rare. Collective agreement provisions with regard to dismissal procedures in Britain are subject to the overriding statutory provisions which protect registered disabled people in employment.[10]

The West German law requires that a seriously disabled person (a legal definition) shall not be terminated without the approval of the Chief Welfare Authority (*Hauptfürsorgestelle*) and that a minimum of four weeks notice be given to the worker. Even disabled persons whose employers are not under legal obligation to employ them or who are employed in excess of the obligatory quota have protection against dismissal. An employer's request for dismissal must be formal, in writing, and in duplicate and it must be approved by the Labour Office, the Works Council, and the government's spe-

[9] Interviews with the Netherlands Ministry of Social Affairs and Public Health; ILO, *Manpower Adjustment Programmes: I. . .* , pp. 95–96; OECD, *Manpower Problems and Policies in the Netherlands,* MO(66)18, p. 111; OECD, Manpower ad Social Affairs Committee, *Annual Reports, Germany, 1964,* MO(64)10/01, p. 24; OECD, International Trade Union Seminar on an Active Manpower Policy, *Supplement to the Final Report,* p. 24; Alfred L. Green, *Manpower and the Public Employment Service in Europe,* 1966, p. 55; ILO, *International Differences. . .* , p. 239; Jack Stieber, "Manpower Adjustments . . . ," pp. 59–61, 90–93, 105; OECD, Regional Seminar, The Employment of Older Workers, *Final Report,* pp. 7, 29, 42–43.

[10] "Dismissal Procedures, V: United Kingdom," *International Labour Review,* October 1959, pp. 354, 358.

cial representative for disabled persons assigned to the particular workplace. Action on a favorable decision cannot be taken until four weeks have passed, and the Chief Welfare Authority has four weeks in which to make his decision; thus several months may pass before a disabled worker actually loses his job.

Even an employer who is closing his business is not relieved of his obligations to disabled workers unless he gives the employees notice three months before the final wage or salary is paid. Approval of dismissals in a business undergoing more than temporary retrenchment is contingent on an employer's giving the minimum period of three months notice and the retention of a sufficient number of disabled in employment to meet the legal quota. Dismissal may be approved if the number of disabled persons is in excess of an employer's quota, or the workers are assured of other appropriate employment, or they are over 65 and have adequate financial support. Disabled persons participating in industrial disputes have reinstatement rights beyond those of ordinary workers. Others given similar specific protection against dismissal in Germany are repatriated prisoners of war, victims of National Socialism, and disabled miners.[11]

Despite the legal protection of the job rights of severely disabled persons, a significant increase in unemployment among such workers occurred from 1965 through 1967 when a general recession affected West Germany. In the overfull employment conditions of 1965, only 5,000 severely disabled persons were listed as unemployed, but by 1967 the average stood at 13,000. As economic activity revived in 1968 the severely disabled unemployed began to decline, reaching 9,000 in October 1968. While the dismissal law had not given absolute protection to disabled employees, it had kept the number of dismissals down to the minimum consistent with the survival of individual firms. Since those who were dismissed were mainly the seriously handicapped, many required special counseling or training before they could be reemployed when business conditions improved.

In the Netherlands, the 1947 law requiring employers to maintain

[11] Federal Ministry of Labour and the Social Structure, *The Employment of Seriously Disabled Persons,* Monograph 4, Social Policy in Germany, Essen, 1965, pp. 20–23.

a 2 percent quota of disabled workers has never been enforced, but the mere citation of the law to employers by the Employment Office may cause the withdrawal of requests for the discharge of disabled employees. Dutch law also forbids the discharge for two years of workers who become ill and are on sickness insurance.

GENERAL RESTRICTIONS ON DISMISSALS

Beyond the protection against dismissal offered to particular categories of workers, some European countries have enacted general legislation restricting the employer's rights with regard to termination of employment of groups of workers for economic reasons. The laws of France and the Netherlands have their origins in the postwar dislocation, while the German dismissal act is more recent. These statutes supplement other laws, civil codes, and decrees which regulate contracts of employment, periods of notice, and dismissal procedures in the case of individuals. Italy's law of 1966 forbids dismissals of individuals without "sufficient grounds" and puts the onus of proof on the employer.

Any legal restriction on the total numbers who may be dismissed for economic reasons could assist the hard-to-reemploy. However, such dismissal laws could also inhibit employers from hiring the least able workers because it might be difficult later on to discharge them. In periods of labor shortage, employers have not been deterred by such considerations, as surveys of individual countries indicate.

West Germany

In West Germany, the reaction against Nazi labor controls led to a mild law on collective dismissals. The law requires only that an employer inform the Employment Service in writing when he contemplates a mass dismissal, which is defined according to the size of the firm and includes only workers over 20 with six months' service.

Although the Employment Service does not review the employer's economic need to dismiss workers, the notification requirement is considered an inhibiting factor on dismissals, particularly since the employer's notice must be accompanied by the comments of the firm's Works Council which represents the workers and usually is influenced by the trade unions. By law, the employer must discuss with the Works Council "the nature and extent of the proposed mass dismissals as well as the avoidance of hardships arising as a result of such dismissals." In the public service sector, which is equally covered, "the staff council has the right to participate in the winding-up, curtailment, removal, or fusion of authorities or important parts of them." Dismissals do not become effective for four weeks to two months after the employer sends in his notice.

In explaining why this indirect approach is taken to the regulation of mass dismissals, an official publication of the Federal Ministry of Labour and the Social Structure declared:

Prohibition of the dismissals would in the long run fail its object, since a prevention of dismissals justified by economic necessity would eventually endanger the enterprise as such and thus the employment of the other employees. It is not up to the individual enterprise to counter the risk of unemployment.[12]

The West German restraints on dismissals for economic reasons are weak compared with those of other western European countries, as described below. Nevertheless, in the winter of 1966–67, when credit restrictions sharply reduced economic activity, many German employers felt that a delay of even one month in the effective date of mass dismissals was too heavy a burden. Evasions of the law occurred in several directions. Works Councils played a passive role in some cases, either not entering discussions of dismissals or feebly asserting themselves. Employers dismissed at one time only

[12] Federal Ministry of Labour and the Social Structure, *Notice of Dismissal and Protection against Dismissal,* pp. 10–12, 17; Reports from U.S. Embassy, Bonn; Jack Stieber, "Manpower Adjustments . . . ," pp. 92–93; Italy, Act no. 604 to issue rules for the dismissal of individual employees, July 15, 1966.

as many workers as was just below the number which would require notification to the Employment Service of a mass dismissal.

For example, an employer of 500 workers must notify the Service and then wait for one month if he plans to fire 50 workers within four weeks; but if he makes 49 dismissals he is free of both the notification requirement and the one-month delay until the dismissals become effective. Instead, the employer can give each individual worker the minimum notice required by his contract, which is usually two weeks, but may be as little as a day or a week. The metallurgical industry particularly was charged with evasion of the mass dismissal rules. Moreover, in some industries and areas (the Ruhr specifically) young people under 20 were adversely affected because the mass dismissal law excluded them from protection.

The overfull employment in Germany after 1960 resulted in the employment and retention of many marginal workers. When the labor market became looser in the fall of 1966 many employers seized the opportunity to discharge the workers considered less productive. The general dismissal law offered little protection to the hard-to-reemploy unless they had specific legal protection.

The experience during the recession led to several changes in the law. No worker was to be given less than two weeks notice of termination, and those with long service or workers over 45 were to receive up to three months notice. To discourage the dismissal of older workers, employers were required to pay them lump sum compensation of up to 18 months pay. Employers who fail to give adequate notice of dismissal due to reorganization of a firm may be required to pay for the loss of wages during retraining courses; otherwise, this compensation is paid by the unemployment insurance fund. To protect youths, coverage was begun at 18 instead of 20. Executive employees, previously exempt from dismissal notice provisions, were also brought into the scheme.

The Netherlands

The Netherlands has a far more stringent dismissal law with much greater protection for the hard-to-reemploy than West Germany. The Extraordinary Labour Relations Decree of 1945 was introduced as an emergency postwar measure to regulate labor turnover and wages. One of its chief purposes was to obtain reemployment for the "worker of Netherlands nationality, whose labour relationship ended after May 9, 1940 . . . in connection with the conditions prevailing under the occupation, otherwise than of his free will, or whose labour relationship was terminated on account of the fact that he was called up in active service before that date."

Employers were required to rehire for full-time work at prevailing conditions all who had previously worked for them for at least ninety days, including those who were unable to perform their work because of illness; the latter went directly on Sickness Insurance benefits. "Employer" was broadly defined to include one who had replaced or succeeded a previous employer. Workers were given one month to take up their former jobs after notification by an employer, while employers were required to rehire promptly after receiving an application from a qualified worker. No reemployment rights were reserved to wartime members or supporters of the National Socialists or similar organizations in the Netherlands or to any unpatriotic person.

This sweeping attempt to restore the prewar employment situation was very beneficial to many hard-to-place unemployed. The decree applied to most of the economy; specifically excluded were government and public workers, teachers, members and employees of certain religious groups, domestic workers in households, and other designated groups, such as workers on probation and corporate directors.

Accompanying the provisions regarding reemployment, which had to be fulfilled within a short time period, were a set of parallel regulations with indefinite duration regarding any future termination of a contract of employment either by the employer or the worker. With some modification in 1963, these 1945 restrictions on dismissal have continued in force, supplementing civil law limitations on the termination of contracts which were originally introduced in 1907. The civil law provides that employers, apart from those in the construction industry, must give advance notification of dismissal equal to one week for each year of service after age 21, with a maximum notice period of 13 weeks, except where serious misconduct or neglect of duty has occurred. Cash payments may be made in lieu of notice. Both individual dismissals and shutdowns or slack period lay-offs are covered in the civil law, as are procedures for legal suit.

The 1945 Emergency Decree stipulated that the civil law termination of employment by either party is not legal until the permission of the Director of the Regional Employment Office is granted, unless it is established that mutual consent or a justifiable cause of termination exists. A statutory control over mobility of every kind in most industries was thus instituted and it was linked to other sections of the Decree which aimed to restrain wage and price increases.

In practice, the Employment Office passes only on disputed cases where a worker opposes his dismissal or an employer contests a worker's desire to leave. Advice is given by a committee representing employers and employees as well as by representatives of the Labour Inspectorate and special panels of advisers for particular industries. Guidelines are also prepared by the Directorate-General for Manpower. Frequently the Director of the Regional Employment Office finds a compromise solution other than simple termination. While law suits are possible under civil law, in fact they are rare.

In making his decision, the Director of the Regional Employment Office is guided by the state of the labor market and the alternatives open to employers and workers; the latter criterion is certain to favor the hard-to-reemploy. Although it is relatively difficult to dismiss Dutch workers, especially the hard-to-reemploy, the hiring of marginal workers by Dutch employers has been as active as in any western European country. The chief consideration has been the tightness of the labor supply and the quality of the alternative candidates available; at a certain point of labor scarcity, foreign workers may be preferred to the residual unemployed.

After so long a period of government control over dismissal procedures in Holland, employers simply accept the system and compliance is good. It is said that employers sometimes overstate their dismissal plans in order to compromise on a number closer to their real intentions. At the end of 1966, when unemployment began to rise, some protests were voiced against mass dismissals which did not conform to all of the legal conditions; however, individual instances would not have aroused attention if evasion of the regulations had been general or long-standing.

The requirement that workers as well as employers obtain approval to leave a job is an unusual feature of the Dutch law. Workers seeking better jobs and higher pay under the labor stringency which has prevailed during most of the past decade have been responsible for a larger number of requests for termination of employment than employers in eight of the ten years, 1956–65.

As Table X.1 shows, the total number of cases initiated by employers and workers varies with fluctuations in the unemployment

TABLE X.1. Requests for Termination of Employment, the Netherlands, 1956–1965

Year	Unemployment Rate	Requests Initiated by Employers		Requests Initiated by Workers	
		Total Number Male and Female	Male Workers	Total Number Male and Female	Male Workers
1956	0.9	15,305	12,641	26,308	20,879
1957	1.2	18,028	14,999	21,578	16,836
1958	2.3	57,231	50,277	7,260	4,887
1959	1.8	31,538	27,170	12,510	9,132
1960	1.1	17,774	14,243	21,413	17,389
1961	0.8	13,390	10,670	30,336	25,314
1962	0.7	16,839	13,082	29,422	24,833
1963	0.7	13,405	10,236	23,344	19,898
1964	0.7	14,460	11,393	25,518	21,842
1965	0.8	14,853	11,958	18,716	15,467

Source: The Netherlands, Ministry of Social Affairs and Public Health; OECD, *Manpower Statistics, 1950–1962*, Paris 1963: OECD, *Manpower Statistics, 1954–1964*, Paris, 1965; OECD, *Economic Growth 1960–1970*, Paris, 1966, p. 26.

rate. In poor business years, such as 1958 and 1959, employers greatly increased their requests for termination while workers sharply reduced theirs; the reverse took place when the labor market became tight. The over-all annual volume of termination requests and decisions does not appear to be large in relation to the number of workers covered by the dismissal provisions or total turnover data. Women figure less frequently in the termination requests brought by employers than they do in total employment or in termination cases initiated by workers. Also, from year to year the total number of cases involving women fluctuates less than that of male workers.[13]

The operations of the Dutch dismissal system appear to be a reasonable response to economic pressures in the labor market. As Table X.2 shows, the most frequent decision was to grant the re-

TABLE X.2. Decisions on Requests for Termination of Employment, the Netherlands, 1956–1965

	Initiated by Employer	Initiated by Workers
Total Number of Cases 1956–1965	212,823	216,405
Percentage Distribution	100.0	100.0
Request Granted	59.6	45.2
Request Denied	5.4	24.6
Settled by Mutual Agreement	8.6	9.7
Request Withdrawn	26.4	20.4

Source: The Netherlands, Ministry of Social Affairs and Public Health.

quest for termination of employment. Employers' requests were approved relatively more often than workers', an indication that job changes to obtain inflationary wage boosts were occasionally resisted, while the discharge of surplus workers was permitted almost

[13] The Netherlands, Ministry of Social Affairs and Public Health, *Arbeidsmarktbeschrijving,* annual; for some comparative data on the U.S.A., France, West Germany, Sweden, and Italy, see ILO, *International Differences. . . ,* pp. 90–120.

uniformly. The proportion of dismissal requests finally settled by mutual agreement was low for both employers and workers, while cases which involved the withdrawal of the request because another solution had been found were somewhat more important on the employers' side.[14]

A recent assessment of Dutch dismissal procedures by the head of the personnel department of Unilever in the Netherlands gives them high marks:

Although this statutory regulation gives the impression of seriously encroaching upon the freedom of the parties, in practice it has contributed toward peace on the labour market, without materially affecting normal conditions. Representatives of employers and workers as well as the labour inspection board are consulted when an application for dismissal has to be judged. The interests of employer and employee are carefully weighed against each other. In the case of genuine redundancy employers are not obliged to keep employees in service, nor are the latter kept on against their personal wishes. On the other hand, excessive turnover as a result of the tight labour market is curbed (the regulation has a preventive effect), and at the same time employers are restrained from rash action in the matter of dismissal. Moreover, the procedure does much to promote the employment service's task of mediation. Nevertheless, one may ask whether this statutory regulation, however useful it may have proved in practice, is not assailable in principle.

The Dutch trade unions have sought the repeal of this law in their drive to obtain unregulated wage increases. Moreover, the OECD examiners of Dutch manpower policy suggested a tripartite study and recommended that "changes in this programme be considered as part of a total system of policies and practices dealing with redundancies and dismissals. . . ."[15] If legal restraints are re-

[14] Interviews and information from the Netherlands Ministry of Social Affairs and Public Health and U. S. Embassy, The Hague; Martin P. Dettinger, "Incomes Policy in the Netherlands Since 1945," Industrial Relations Research Association, *Proceedings*, December 1966, pp. 149–54.

[15] OECD, *Manpower and Social Policy in the Netherlands*, Paris, 1967, pp. 234–35; OECD, International Management Seminar on Active Manpower Policy, *Supplement to the Final Report*, Paris, 1965, p. 96; Jack Stieber, "Manpower Adjustments. . . ," pp. 116–17.

moved, the hard-to-reemploy would continue to rely on the employer's reluctance to dismiss hardship cases.

France

French provisions regarding dismissals caused by economic circumstances also are a continuation of a postwar control measure to mobilize manpower for priority rebuilding and development. An ordinance of May 24, 1945, is still in effect, although portions of it are applied only in the North and East. The ordinance and explanatory decrees require that employers inform the local Manpower Service whenever they wish to dismiss an individual or a group of workers. If the Manpower Service does not respond negatively in seven days, approval is assumed. Since the legislation is intended only to cover dismissals due to changes in the economic circumstances of the firm, ordinary disciplinary dismissals are not reviewed.

In practice, collective dismissals which threaten to create local difficulties are of major interest to the Manpower Service. A firm must demonstrate that a reduction in force is necessary because of a decrease in activity, a reorganization of the business, or a change in production techniques. The request is to be accompanied by the approval of the Works Council, a committee consisting of the head of the enterprise, elected worker delegates, and trade union advisors. A Works Council is required by law to be established in every enterprise with over 50 workers, and may exist in smaller enterprises which are unionized. Several collective agreements specify consultation with the Works Council. Since the Works Councils almost never concur in dismissal plans, they frequently have been ignored or by-passed by employers. The strongly organized textile industry is an exception. In July 1966, a renewed legislative effort was made to obtain employer compliance with the rule on consulting the Works Council.

Every enterprise employing 20 workers or more is required by law to establish internal rules governing the organization of work and discipline and to make general provisions, if the subject is not covered by a collective agreement, on the order of lay-off in case of group dismissals. The order of lay-off must give due attention to family responsibilities, seniority, and occupational qualifications. An examination of the work rules of a few companies indicates that seniority is treated as a combination of years of work and family responsibilities. Collective bargaining agreements tend to cover the same points as well as provide for severance pay, rehiring rights, and other matters.

The significant Employment Security Agreement of February 10, 1969, signed by the leading trade unions and two chief employer associations of France, made the Works Council or plant committee the focal point of consultation and policy decisions on an expanded range of employment and unemployment issues. The trade union aim is to promote job security and soften the impact of inevitable staff reductions by making its voice heard at the enterprise level. The 1969 agreement reflects labor's dissatisfaction with the behavior of employers and government manpower agencies.

The French Employment Service reviews a request by an employer to determine that the total number of dismissals is necessary and that the particular individuals are listed as the internal rules prescribe. Since dismissals may sometimes be in excess of a firm's needs or may single out particular workers punitively—for example trade union activists—a firm which builds up its staff after a collective dismissal is subject to review and may be asked to rehire some of the dismissed workers. West Germany, Italy, and other countries protect trade unionists and others against punitive dismissal.[16]

In spite of the elaborate procedures of the 1945 law, enforcement is weak when an employer persists in making dismissals which have been disapproved. As a trade union official analyzed it:

. . . the law, in spite of a few isolated Decrees, does not give a clear ruling on the consequences of a refusal to authorize dismissals. The fact of over-riding such a decision, does not *ipso facto* lay the firm con-

---

[16] France, *Réponse au questionnaire sur les systèmes de préavis à long terme,* ref. Doc. MO(64) du 26 novembre 1964 de l'OCDE; "Dismissal Procedures I: France," *International Labour Review,* June 1959, pp. 625–42; France, Act no. 66-427, to amend certain provisions of Ordinance 45-280 of 22 February 1945 to institute works committees, 18 June 1966; Frederic Meyers, *Ownership of Jobs. . .* , pp. 63–67, 69–70.

cerned open to sanctions, except in cases where special provisions have been made for workers' representatives and members of factory committees. In any case, however vigilant the Manpower Administration may be in weighing these economic criteria, it has in the last resort only powers of persuasion, since its rulings cannot, according to the law, cause an establishment "substantial, direct and special prejudice," without engaging the civil responsibility of the State.

Unless pressure is brought to bear at the highest levels, the employment situation in a region can hardly, under these conditions, be effectively invoked as an argument against plans for collective dismissals. A few rare courageous rulings by the courts during recent years have, however, reminded people that workers whose dismissal has been brought about through the inefficient management of the enterprise could also suffer "direct and special prejudice of sufficient gravity" to demand legal redress.[17]

Whether or not employers can be prevented by law from making dismissals, there is no doubt that employers in France are under considerable pressure to retain workers. As Kurt Braun has said, "prevailing French public opinion is inclined to regard the separated worker as a person being deprived of a vested interest in his employment" and "the employer is under a moral obligation to make great efforts to protect his workers from the hardships of temporary or final job loss, mass dismissals or layoffs." [18]

Some of the measures an employer is supposed to take in advance of dismissals would amaze an American employer. A French employer is expected to find new jobs for his workers, retrain them so that they can work elsewhere, seek out a purchaser for his building and equipment who will employ the former workers, postpone dismissals until new jobs are found, or take any other step which

[17] OECD, International Trade Union Seminar on an Active Manpower Policy, *Supplement to the Final Report,* pp. 13–14.

[18] Kurt Braun, "European Limitations on Employee Dismissal," *Monthly Labor Review,* January 1965, pp. 67–68; "Technical Progress and its Social Consequences in the French Textile Industry," *International Labour Review,* July 1965, pp. 61–62; *Labor Developments Abroad,* September 1966, p. 5; Stieber, "Manpower Adjustments. . . ," pp. 77–78; Meyers, *Ownership of Jobs. . . ,* pp. 63–66; ILO, *Manpower Adjustment Programmes: I. . . ,* p. 19.

will satisfy the trade unions, local politicians and political organizations, and the church, all of whom consider mass dismissals a matter of public concern, especially when reemployment is difficult. The labor inspectors also respond to social pressures, and may postpone, phase, or reduce the number of dismissals in order to facilitate the placement of the workers and satisfy public opinion. However, the number of labor inspectors is considered inadequate for the task of investigation.

A high official of the French Ministry of Labour has questioned the usefulness of such measures as the dismissal legislation of 1945, since it "cannot be called real protection unless it is supplemented by means for positive action." [19] Jacques Chazelle, then Director-General of the Labour and Employment Department of the Ministry of Labour, went on to say that "it appeared necessary to prevent these protective measures, insofar as they reduce or slow down technological changes, from conflicting with the objective requirements of economic progress, which involve transforming a business or sector and a corresponding reduction in manpower." He said, however, that employers must also be considerate of labor and recognize that it "is in no way a production factor that can be placed on the same level as capital or technology . . . the real interest of these men ultimately takes precedence over production imperatives. The result is that workers will have to be informed and consulted on business modernization projects more regularly and further in advance." But employers generally are slow to accept this view, and trade unions still cling to protective measures, though they regard the dismissal law as ineffective.

The dismissal procedures under the French regulations of 1945 have also been declared obsolete by a representative of the French Employers' Association (*Conseil National du Patronat Français*). Citing the need for substantial geographic and occupational mobility of workers in order to modernize and make French industry competitive, the spokesman questioned the usefulness of a procedure which tends to restrain dismissals. He further noted the need to re-

[19] Ambassade de France, Service de Presse et d'Information, *French Affairs*, No. 179, pp. 5, 11.

vise the 1945 regulations to take account of the increasing prevalence of national collective bargaining agreements which deal in detail with dismissals.[20]

It appears that collective dismissals for economic reasons have not assumed serious proportions in France and that reemployment has been rapid in most cases. The industries most involved have been textiles in the Vosges, mining in the Midi, shipbuilding and ship repairing at Nantes and Saint-Nazaire. More recently, the numbers dismissed have been larger as rationalization has been forced by competition within the Common Market and price stabilization efforts at home.

According to official figures, 857 firms reported in 1964 that they were planning to dismiss more than 20 workers at once; they had a total of 316,365 employees and planned to dismiss 40,876 workers. In 1965 the number of reporting firms rose to 951 and they planned to dismiss 49,548 of their 304,981 employees. The 1966 totals were somewhat lower, but in 1967 1,077 firms reported that they planned to dismiss 60,900 of their total of 295,600 employees, or over 20 percent. Actual dismissals tend to be fewer than the original announcements. The French data show that only a small portion of the dismissals are attributable to technological or organizational changes or geographic relocation and that ordinary business reverses remain the greatest enemy of stability and continuity of employment. If one adds the dismissals for economic reasons in French firms where under 20 workers are involved, the totals would rise considerably.

The existence of alternative employment opportunities, the pressures by trade unions, the efforts of employers, and the close working relations between the French Manpower Administration and the enterprise contemplating collective dismissals have minimized both

20 OECD, International Management Seminar on Active Manpower Policy, *Supplement to the Final Report*, pp. 43–44; OECD. Manpower and Social Affairs Committee, *Annual Reports, France, 1964*, MO(64)10/08, pp. 13–14; Meyers, *Ownership of Jobs. . .* , pp. 69–70; OECD, International Joint Seminar on Geographical and Occupational Mobility of Manpower, *Final Report*, Paris, 1964, pp. 74–83; *Labor Developments Abroad*, March 1968, pp. 5–8.

displacements of workers and subsequent unemployment. Older workers in France appear to benefit particularly from the protection afforded by trade unions and the dismissal legislation.[21]

We have seen that some western European countries offer hard-to-reemploy persons specific or general legal protection against dismissal. Day to day, the chief value of such laws is as an educational tool to convince employers not to discharge individuals who would have difficulty in obtaining reemployment. It is not often necessary to threaten employers or to invoke the laws. Nor are unreasonable demands made on employers. Some extra costs may be imposed on employers by the restrictions on dismissing certain categories of workers whose employment represents compliance with a quota system. But the numbers of workers involved are not so large as to raise prices or restrict exports. This is particularly likely to be true if the workers have achieved average productivity, as is the case with many of the physically and mentally handicapped on quota jobs.

The general legal constraints on dismissal are most highly developed in the Netherlands and France. But even where there are no dismissal laws, the pressures on private and public employers to minimize dismissals are severe. Great Britain, which has no legislation of this type, is the outstanding example. Similarly, without legal pressure, the nationalized industries in various countries have borne extra labor costs in order to phase out reductions in personnel with a minimum of displacement. They were able to finance this through subsidies from government, and it has been shown that the same sums could have been spent more advantageously in the retraining and relocation of the affected workers.[22]

Restraints on dismissals, whether legal or institutional, tend to favor the hard-to-reemploy when labor is scarce, when mass dismissals are discrete and isolated, or structural changes affect an entire

[21] ILO, *International Differences. . .* , p. 127; France, Ministère du Travail, *Rapport sur la situation de l'emploi . . . 1965,* Paris, 1965, p. 15; Ministères des Affaires Sociales, *Rapport sur la situation de l'emploi . . . 1966,* Paris, 1966, p. 21; idem, *Bulletin mensuel de Statistiques Sociales,* February 1968, p. 23; ILO, *Manpower Adjustment Programmes: I. . .* , pp. 20–23; ILO, *Redundancy Procedures. . .* , p. 150.

[22] ILO, *Redundancy Procedures. . .* , pp. 177–81.

industry. It is not clear, however, that dismissal laws or employers' favorable attitudes are effective in checking dismissals, particularly of the hard-to-reemploy, when economic activity slackens, as it did in 1966–68. But over the long postwar period of full and overfull employment, the maintenance of continuity of employment through restraints on dismissal, as provided by law, custom, and trade union activity, has had special importance for hard-to-reemploy European workers. The extra costs borne by employers have been considered heavy in some countries; and in Britain the phenomenon is called "disguised unemployment."

XI | Continuity of Employment: Other Measures

The maintenance of continuity of employment is attempted in ways other than by restraints on dismissals. Some methods involve the negative approach of preserving jobs without regard to the economic contribution of the workers or the additional costs imposed on the enterprise. Work-sharing, which is discussed first, may be of this character. The remainder of this chapter deals with positive attempts at the level of the firm to maintain continuity of employment for workers threatened by displacement. These approaches stress the maintenance of demand for the products of specific enterprises and the retraining of staff within firms which are changing their products, technology, or organizational practices.

SHARING THE WORK

In many western European countries, a strong preference exists for sharing the work, rather than resorting to dismissals or layoffs when work is slack. Since the normal European work-week is still well above 40 hours in many cases and overtime is prevalent in some industries, trade unions campaign actively for reductions in standard hours and endorse work-sharing as one method of reaching their goal. The worker's presumption of property rights in his job and the employer's feeling of responsibility toward his staff and his concern that workers may not be available when needed later have

lent support to work-sharing. Custom, collective bargaining agreements, and even legislation provide for the elimination of overtime,
reduction of hours, and extensions of vacations when a temporary
slowdown is foreseen. Se great have been the pressures for security
and stability that the concept of "temporary" slowdown has at times
been stretched to cover fairly permanent changes.

Work-sharing has received statutory approval in West Germany
as an alternative to "anti-social notice to terminate." The concept
goes back to 1920 legislation and was revived in the Federal Republic in 1951. Under the 1951 law, an employer "may be expected to
meet difficulties by an initial system of staggering work or by oc-
cupying in other departments of the enterprise, employees who
owing to a cut in production have become dispensable at their present place of work." [1] Partial unemployment of this type is compensated by a special scheme of unemployment insurance, separate
from insurance against total unemployment. Italy and France make
the same distinction.

Paternalism and the image of a "good" or "successful" employer
are reinforced by the desire of employers to hold their labor force
intact in slack periods, so that they can expand operations quickly.
As a spokesman for the German employers' confederation (BDA)
observed:

Compensation to short-time workers prevents such workers from being
fully unemployed and ensures that the workers remain on the firm's
payroll. This implies that the firm does not need to fear losing highly
skilled workers owing to the fact that they become unemployed due to
marketing or supply difficulties. The same applies to compensation, designed to avoid dismissals, for labour which has been laid off due to
temporary restrictions in the firm's activities owing to lack of fuel or
other essential supplies.[2]

[1] Federal Ministry of Labour and the Social Structure, *Notice of Dismissal
and Protection against Dismissal,* Monograph 13, Social Policy in Germany,
Essen, 1963, pp. 12–14; International Labour Office (ILO), *Redundancy
Procedures in Selected Western European Countries,* Geneva, 1966, pp. 60,
67–90, 162.

[2] Organization for Economic Cooperation and Development, (OECD),
Manpower and Social Affairs Directorate, International Management Sem-

It is only one step further to defend labor hoarding, which has been fairly general in boom and recession periods in several European countries. The recession of 1966–67 in a few European countries was different in that a genuine shakeout of labor occurred and employment declined more than output.[3]

In the Netherlands, legislative approval was expressed for work-sharing in the 1945 Decree on Extraordinary Labour Relations, parts of which remain in effect. It authorized employers to put employees on part-time rather than dismiss them and offered state financial assistance in some cases. In addition, under both the industry-worker financed "waiting benefits" and the government unemployment insurance system, a proportionate amount is paid for reduced hours of work. At times, management maintains workers in short-time employment even when the prospects for renewed full-time employment may not be good. The disadvantages of this practice, according to the OECD examiners of Dutch manpower policy, are that the worker may exhaust his unemployment benefits while on short-time and have no coverage for a subsequent period of full unemployment, and that the worker on short-time with poor future prospects may be inhibited from seeking another job by his satisfactory combination of wages and compensation.[4]

In France trade unions have strongly urged work-sharing. Ac-

inar on Active Manpower Policy, *Supplement to the Final Report,* Paris, 1965, p. 12; ILO, *Redundancy Procedures. . . ,* pp. 106–108.

[3] Kurt Braun, "European Limitations on Employee Dismissal," *Monthly Labor Review,* January 1965, pp. 67–68; *OECD Economic Outlook,* Paris, July 1967, p. 40; R. R. Nield, *Pricing and Employment in the Trade Cycle,* National Institute of Economic and Social Research Occasional Papers no. 21, Cambridge, Eng., 1963; Gladys Palmer, "Contrasts in Labor Market Behavior in Northern Europe and the United States," *Industrial and Labor Relations Review,* July 1960, pp. 519–32; Jack Stieber, "Manpower Adjustments to Automation and Technological Change in Western Europe," in the *Report of the Commission on Technology, Automation and Economic Progress,* Washington, 1966, App. Vol. III, pp. 51, 78; *OECD Economic Outlook,* December 1967, July 1968.

[4] The Netherlands, Decree of 1945, modified by the Act of June 20, 1963, sec. 10 subsec. 1; OECD, *Manpower and Social Policy in the Netherlands,* Paris, 1967, p. 231.

cording to a French trade union leader, "in the event of widespread unemployment, the rule is also to prescribe a general reduction in working hours before dismissing any workers in employment." If a firm has obtained permission to work overtime, which is required under a prewar French law, the labor inspector can revoke the permit in order to spread work and prevent dismissals. Some French legislation has provided for the extension of the provisions of specific collective agreements to entire areas and industries.

Government unemployment compensation for short-time work is supplemented in several countries by payments from employers under industry schemes. Together these have tended to be regarded as a guaranteed or minimum wage. Jacques Chazelle, then a high official of the French Ministry of Labour, called the work-sharing approach negative and "not enough to prevent job losses." The OECD also has remarked on the costs of protective and restrictive measures. In Britain this cause of a reduction in output and efficiency has been assailed, along with other restrictive practices.[5]

5 "Dismissal Procedures, V; United Kingdom," *International Labour Review,* October 1959, pp. 347–61; "Dismissal Procedures, I: France," *International Labour Review,* June 1959, pp. 625–42; Kurt Braun, "European Limitations. . ."; Ambassade de France, Service de Presse et d'Information, *French Affairs,* No. 179, p. 5; ILO, *International Differences in Factors Affecting Labour Mobility,* AUT/DOC/7, Geneva, 1965, n. 2, pp. 126–27; Gösta Rehn, "Trends and Perspectives in Manpower Policy," in Margaret S. Gordon, ed., *Poverty in America* San Francisco, 1965, pp. 214–15; OECD, International Joint Seminar on Geographical and Occupational Mobility of Manpower, *Supplement to the Final Report,* Paris, 1964, pp. 21–22; France, Ministère des Affaires Sociales, *Rapport sur la situation de l'emploi . . . 1966,* Paris, 1966, p. 54; Jack Stieber, "Manpower Adjustments. . . ," pp. 51, 59, 77–78, 122; Frederic Meyers, *Ownership of Jobs: A Comparative Study,* Los Angeles, 1964, pp. 64, 69–70; ILO, *Manpower Adjustment Programmes: I. France, Federal Republic of Germany, United Kingdom,* Labor and Automation, Bull. No. 4, Geneva, 1967, pp. 27, 149–50, 152; Arnold R. Weber, "Manpower Adjustments to Technological Change: An International Analysis," in Solomon Barkin and others, eds., *International Labor,* New York, 1967, pp. 139–40; ILO, *Redundancy Procedures. . . ,* pp. 106–109, 120–25, 162, 187–88; European Coal and Steel Community, (ECSC), *La protection des travailleurs en cas de perte de l'emploi,* Luxembourg, 1961; Solomon Barkin, ed., *Technical Change and Manpower Planning,* OECD: Paris, 1967.

Some indication of the extent of compensated work-sharing can be obtained from official unemployment compensation data. Since the exclusions from coverage are considerable in individual countries, a good deal more work-sharing occurs than is compensated. Most countries will not pay for partial unemployment which results from normal seasonal variations, internal problems, or reorganization of individual firms. In France a ministerial order is required to designate the industries and time periods for which workers may be compensated. Limits are set on the total number of compensated hours in a year and the total weekly amount of wages plus partial unemployment benefits. Several industries provide supplementary compensation for reduced hours of work in agreements negotiated through collective bargaining. In February 1968 a national agreement on partial unemployment benefits was signed by the leading trade unions and the main organizations representing employers.

In 1964 compensated partial unemployment in France cost about one-fourth as much as government assistance payments for total unemployment and almost 30 percent of the 1965 expenditure for total unemployment; in both years total unemployment rates had risen in response to anti-inflationary measures. The French industries which used compensated work-sharing to a great degree were textiles, clothing, metals, shoes and boots, and fur and leather products. The average monthly number of workers involved in compensated partial unemployment rose from 8,100 in 1963 to 29,600 in 1964, and 70,200 in 1965. By 1966 the average number of workers dropped to 15,767 and the indemnified days to 70,900. The 1967 average increased again to 46,785 workers and 211,100 days.[6]

In West Germany the average number of short-time workers took a sharp downturn after 1960, declining even more rapidly than total unemployment. Only about 6,000 workers were on compensated part-time in February 1966, an indication of the extent of "overemployment" then prevailing in West Germany. As unemployment began to rise at the end of 1966 due to controls on credit and other anti-inflationary measures, employers resorted to work-sharing as a

[6] France, Ministère des Affaires Sociales, *Rapport sur la situation de l'emploi . . . 1966*, pp. 19, 20, 43–45; idem, *Bulletin mensuel de Statistiques Sociales,* February 1968, p. 23.

means of postponing large-scale dismissals. By mid-December 1966, 90,000 workers were on compensated part-time; and a month later the number rose to 240,000, reaching 344,000 in February 1967, the highest level since 1948.

Union spokesmen reported, and the *Bundesanstalt,* the German Employment Service, agreed, that the numbers actually working part-time were considerably greater, since the official figures recorded only those eligible for unemployment compensation. The Metal Workers Union estimated that there were 329,000 metal workers alone on short-time in February 1967.

In view of the increased significance of work-sharing in recession periods, the administrative council of the *Bundesanstalt* (BAVAV) proposed that the maximum duration of short-time unemployment compensation, payable to eligibles who work less than five-sixths of their normal week, be extended from 26 weeks to 39 weeks. Data for the Netherlands, Belgium, and Italy also indicate that compensated work-sharing is likely to rise disproportionately as total unemployment increases seasonally, cyclically, or regionally.[7]

The extent to which private and public employers in western Europe actually resort to part-time or other job-saving arrangements in situations where American employers might resort to dismissal or lay-off cannot even be estimated. In periods of high over-all demand, American employers also avoid discharge of workers. Those American workers who are protected by strong unions may have as much job security as any European workers. But American employers appear to respond with lay-offs or dismissals much more rapidly than their western European counterparts when business circumstances or technological changes suggest a reduced need for manpower or a changed work force. Western Europe attitudes, practice, customs, and laws have a bias toward stability, and both unionized and nonunionized industries carry a larger payroll than might be tol-

[7] Information from U.S. Embassy, Bonn; U.S. Embassy, Rome; Belgium, Ministère de l'Emploi et du Travail, Office National de l'Emploi, (ONEM), *Rapport Général 1965,* Brussels, 1966, p. 5; the Netherlands, Central Bureau of Statistics, *Maandschrift,* April 1967, p. 344; *OECD Economic Outlook,* Paris, July 1967, p. 41; ILO, *Redundancy Procedures. . . ,* p. 106.

erated in American firms. It appears to add up to a somewhat more favorable situation for those who would be hard-to-reemploy than prevails in the United States.

ILO researchers have concluded that French workers would not be dismissed even if government and industry programs for compensated short-time did not exist. The "head-on collision with the trade unions and public opinion" and the fear that the skilled workers would be lost to the company would inhibit dismissals. Therefore, government and industry schemes to minimize the wage losses of work sharing are accepted. However, it is suggested that such programs should not be used to forestall adaptation to structural change and that over-all time limits on the payments might be imposed.[8]

The usual objections to work-sharing are that it is cost-raising and tends to postpone manpower and adjustments. But it is necessary to weigh all of the costs and benefits, private and social, of work-sharing, especially to consider compensated partial unemployment as an alternative to lay-off or total unemployment for some and employment for others. The complexity of the problem emerges fully when varying demand and supply conditions are posited for labor, and seasonal and regional immobilities are considered. No simple answer that work-sharing is always more costly than immediate dismissal can be given in all cases.

MAINTENANCE OF DEMAND FOR EXISTING FIRMS

If continuity of employment is threatened by a lack of orders in an industry or in certain firms, it is possible for government to intervene to sustain demand. This is a borderline area encompassing both general politicoeconomic policies and specific acts directed toward particular firms. It may involve the subsidization of uneconomic industries and firms as well as the stimulation of sound companies.

Maintenance of domestic employment may also be aided by pro-

[8] ILO, *Redundancy Procedures. . . ,* pp. 187–88.

tective policies which restrict imports or stimulate exports. Whether by customs duties, import licenses, consumption taxes, direct subsidies, tied gifts and loans, supported prices, tax rebates, loans, accelerated depreciation, or other means, most countries at one time or another have supported the volume of domestic demand and employment in given industries and firms. For example, such support on a national and Common Market level has enabled the European coal industry to close uneconomic mines very slowly and to retain a larger number of older miners than free trade in coal and other fuels would have permitted.[9]

These general economic policies, along with fiscal and monetary policies, must be distinguished from specific measures which influence employment directly. The placement of government orders, and particularly the timing of orders, has been used to maintain employment in industries or firms which otherwise might have to discharge workers or close. Sweden has developed this method to a high degree. Government demand for the products of such industries and firms is stimulated by indirect or direct placement of orders at an earlier date than they would otherwise be placed. Such selective boosting of demand is correlated with general monetary, fiscal, and trade policies in Sweden which influence demand and employment. But the selective measures are directed toward particular industries and firms and can be brought into play more rapidly and effectively than general measures. While Swedish policies to stimulate demand in specific firms are not designed to protect the jobs of any particular type of worker, they are apt to save the jobs of those who might otherwise become unemployed and hard-to-reemploy, as the tripartite committee on labor market policy acknowledged in its 1965 report.

The Swedish Labour Market Board is in charge of advance orders to the affected industries or firms. The Board can either obtain an increase in the regular appropriations of various government departments or, more quickly, place orders directly, using special funds available to the Labour Market Board for the purpose of supporting employment. The Board also may speed up the placing of contracts already authorized. Local authorities may be encouraged

[9] ILO, *Redundancy Procedures.* . . , pp. 49–54, 56–57, 175–80.

to place additional orders or to give orders in advance of schedule; under adverse employment conditions, the Labour Market Board, on authorization by the government, may subsidize orders by local authorities.

A full discussion of extra orders to industry as a stimulant to employment was conducted by the tripartite committee on labor market policy. The committee endorsed the use of extra orders to industry when there is a threat of permanent curtailment of production or actual shutdown of a plant. In such circumstances, the extra orders, finely calculated, would maintain employment until the Employment Service has time to place the workers in new jobs or enroll them in training programs. When a temporary cutback or stoppage threatens, the committee suggested that extra orders should be used to maintain the work force intact, ready to resume full activities. They cautioned, however, that these orders should not be used to prop up an uneconomic enterprise whose costs and other operations are not competitive.

If the threatened decline in demand is cyclical in origin, the extra orders should be placed with an entire sector of industry by means of competitive bids rather than with selected firms. To assure that sufficient orders are placed, the committee recommended that the share of the public investment reserve earmarked for government purchase of industrial products be increased and placed under the control of the Labour Market Board. They further recommended that an inventory of municipal orders which would be placed in advance be maintained and that the government subsidy of 20 percent to the municipalities be used to induce the municipalities to place advance orders.

In the ensuing discussion, an objection to the committee's views on extra orders to industry was voiced by the National Institute of Economic Research, which urged that extra orders be denied to firms preparing for permanent closure; instead, the Employment Service should be improved so that it could act on shorter notice. The Institute also opposed extra orders in any circumstances where they tend to perpetuate uneconomic operations.

However, the government accepted the committee's recommendations almost *in toto* and the Parliament approved them in the spring of 1966. Jurisdiction over extra orders to a whole sector remains with the government, rather than with the Labour Market Board, and subsidies to municipalities are available only for orders involving whole sectors.

While the use of advance orders to firms and industries is most dramatic during recessions, the Labour Market Board has funds at its disposal to provide advance orders or extra orders to individual firms at all times. During a recession, the Labour Market Board's share of government advance orders is quite small, but in good years it may be the sole source because extra orders are used only in special cases. From 1960 through 1965, the Labour Market Board spent a high of 13 million Sw. kr. in 1964 against a low in 1962 of 700,000 Sw. kr. In the recession of 1963, the total central and local government expenditure on these orders was 133 million crowns. During 1967–68, recession years, 50 million crowns was added to the Labour Market Board's 5 million crowns for extra orders to the textile, clothing, and engineering industries. Defense Ministry orders also were speeded up. An advisory service to assist businesses contemplating closure was established. The Labour Market Board recently reaffirmed its belief in the utility of advance orders and predicted that a fairly large need for them will continue even in boom periods.[10]

If an industry or a firm in Sweden is faced with an unusual decline in orders which threatens the level of employment, the National Labour Market Board, an agency with remarkably broad economic powers, has at its command several other means of increasing the demand for the products or services of the affected industry or firm. Government or, upon its authorization, the Labour Market Board may approve the release of investment reserve funds, which Swedish firms build up individually. These funds are used for specific invest-

[10] *Arbetsmarknadspolitik,* pp. 185–99; National Labour Market Board, *Modern Swedish Labour Market Policy,* pp. 36–37, 48, 65, 95–96; OECD, Manpower and Social Affairs Committee, *Annual Reports, Sweden, 1963,* MO(64) 10/18, p. 9; Sweden, *AMS Statistik till Husbehov,* 1966, p. 6; interviews with National Labor Market Board; Gunnar Eliasson, *Investment Funds in Operation,* pp. 100–106, *Arbetsmarknadspolitiken 1969–70,* p. 26.

ments, purchases of equipment, or the replenishment of inventories from the affected industry or firms. Conditions are usually set as to the amount and timing of such releases of investment reserve funds. In both the 1958–59 and 1962–63 recessions, the release of investment reserve funds was used to good effect, though the timing of build-up and curtailment was held to be superior in the latter period.

The operation of these alternatives is illustrated by the experience of the Swedish engineering industry, which includes the manufacture of machinery, vehicles, ships, etc. Early in the winter of 1962–63, a reduction of employment was foreseen in this industry. The first step, taken in November 1962, was the release of investment reserve funds to firms which undertook to place orders before April 30, 1963, for the heavy equipment manufactured by Swedish or foreign engineering firms. Applications from some 262 firms were approved for the expenditure of 308 million Swedish crowns (about $60 million), with about 30 percent going for foreign equipment, a proportion in keeping with normal practice in this industry.

Further assistance to the engineering industry came from the placing by government agencies of orders worth 50 million Sw. kr. in the spring of 1963, although they had been scheduled for the following fiscal year. Moreover, a national subsidy of 20 percent was granted to municipalities which speeded up their orders; 80 million Sw.kr. (about $15 million) was spent on orders in this way. While these sums are not a large proportion of the total sales of the engineering industry, a considerable number of jobs were saved and created during 1963 through these measures. In the recession of 1967–68, the authorization to draw on investment reserve funds was estimated to have saved or created 14,100 jobs as of February–March 1968, while advance orders to industry were credited with saving 3,300 jobs. During 1967 companies withdrew 1.8 billion Sw.kr. from their investment funds, but less interest was shown in 1968.[11]

[11] *Arbetsmarknadspolitik,* pp. 157–70. Investment reserves are a Swedish innovation which bridges general and special employment-creating measures. For fuller information, see Gunnar Eliasson, *Investment Funds in Opera-*

The construction industry may need to be stimulated because of circumstances in the industry or a downturn in the whole economy. When the latter situation prevails, the government can release additional housing credits, speed up government projects, exempt non-priority construction from taxes, and plan new construction. It can also permit firms to draw upon their investment reserve funds for construction. In the recessions of 1958–59 and 1962–63, substantial withdrawals from investment reserves were approved for construction projects which were either speeded up or newly created. Beginning in May 1962 investment funds of over 600 million Sw. kr. (about $114 million) were released for projects slated to begin from July to November 1962 and to end by May 1963 when it was expected that a seasonal upturn would carry employment forward without special stimulus. As the date for completion of the projects approached, the Labour Market Board, realizing that some projects would remain unfinished, authorized the resumption of such projects after the summer rise in employment—from November 1963 to the end of March 1964. Some 858 projects giving work to a high of 10,000 in February 1963, and creating an average of 3,900 new jobs, operated in the recession of 1962–63. In 1967–68, the public construction of schools, hospitals, and old people's homes was speeded up to save or create 5,600 jobs as of February 1968.[12]

---

tion, National Institute of Economic Research, Stockholm, 1965, pp. 7–32; Krister Wickman, *The Swedish Investment Reserve System,* The Swedish Institute, Stockholm, 1963. Martin Schnitzer, "Unemployment Programs in Sweden," Economic Policies and Practices, Paper no. 5, Joint Economic Committee, U.S. Congress, 88th Cong., 2nd sess., Washington, 1964, pp. 29–42; U.S. Department of Labor, *Manpower Policy and Programs in Five Western European Countries,* Manpower Research, Bulletin 11, July 1966, p. 50. *Labor Developments Abroad,* January 1968, p. 15; ILO, *Redundancy Procedures. . . ,* pp. 54–55; Sweden, National Labour Market Board, *Arbetsmarknadspolitiken 1969/70,* Stockholm, 1968, pp. 26–27; Svenska Handelsbanken, *Economic Review,* Index, No, 10, 1968.

[12] Gunnar Eliasson, *Investment Funds in Operation,* pp. 65–99; Bertil Olsson, "Employment Policy in Sweden," *International Labour Review,* May 1963, pp. 20–21; Schnitzer, "Unemployment Programs. . . ," p. 48; OECD, *Annual Reports, Sweden, 1963,* MO(63) 17/18, p. 6; *Arbetsmarknadspolitik,* pp. 157–62; *Labor Developments Abroad,* January 1968, p. 15; *Arbetsmarknadspolitiken 1969/70,* p. 27.

Increases in housing and other construction to counter seasonal and cyclical unemployment create new jobs directly and have important secondary employment effects on the economy. They are a means of maintaining continuity of employment for the labor force of the industry, including the hard-to-reemploy. Other countries also offer subsidies and grants to firms undertaking construction during the winter months.[13]

These interesting Swedish measures to stimulate demand in particular industries and firms are part of a highly developed and rational labor market policy in which the uneconomic maintenance of employment continuity or preservation of particular jobs is rejected. On the whole, Swedish policies assume and prepare for job changes and adjustments by workers, and rely on adequate social and private action to ease the necessary transfers.

RECONVERSION AND RETRAINING WITHIN THE FIRM

Even the most dedicated efforts to maintain a work force intact in an undisturbed environment have had to yield before the tides of change sweeping over Europe. Competition within and outside of the Common Market has altered production methods, labor requirements, and output. To encourage acceptance of change by workers and assure a maximum of job continuity, several western European governments and international bodies sponsor subsidies to employers who retain and, if necessary, retrain within the plant their own underemployed or laid-off employees while the enterprise undergoes reconversion. The workers involved earn nearly normal weekly wages.

The inclination of several individual countries to experiment with such measures is stimulated by the readiness of both the European Economic Community, through its Social Fund, and the High Authority of the European Coal and Steel Community to give financial support to those member countries which establish programs for re-

[13] Jan Wittrock, *Reducing Seasonal Unemployment in the Construction Industry,* OECD: Paris, 1967.

conversion or retraining within the firm conforming to principles approved in Brussels or Luxembourg.[14]

The scope and activities of the Social Fund of the European Economic Community are limited by article 125 of the Treaty of Rome. Financial assistance may be granted by the Fund to a member country for enterprises in which workers are on short-time or are unemployed because the firm is undergoing reconversion. But aid can be granted only after the country has submitted a reconversion plan, obtained approval from the European Commission in advance of making changes, and after it has shown that the workers resumed employment in the enterprise for at least six months after reconversion was completed. The Fund's contribution cannot exceed 50 percent of the cost of keeping workers idle for six months.

Furthermore, the treaty's definition of "conversion" is fairly strict in order to eliminate claims on the Fund for industrial changes which should properly be borne by the enterprise itself. "Conversion" is defined as the permanent cessation of an existing output and replacement by new products. Few requests have been made by member countries thus far and none had been granted in the first years of operation of the Fund. The limitations on the authority of the Fund have been cited by other bodies within the European Economic Community as the cause of its inactivity in this area.[15]

The European Coal and Steel Community, now incorporated in the European Economic Community, also will make grants to mem-

---

[14] Mark J. Fitzgerald, *The Common Market's Labor Programs,* Notre Dame, 1966, p. 172; Margaret S. Gordon, *Retraining and Labor Market Adjustment in Western Europe,* Washington, 1965, pp. 181–82; National Labour Market Board, *Modern Swedish Labour Market Policy,* pp. 25–26, 80; ILO, *Redundancy Procedures. . . ,* p. 150.

[15] J. Muilwijk, "The European Social Fund of the European Economic Community," reprinted from *Labour Law in Europe,* Supplementary Publication no. 5 of the *International and Comparative Law Quarterly,* 1962, pp. 76–77, 81; European Economic Community, *General Report on the Activities of the Community,* annual, Brussels, 1963–1967; OECD, International Trade Union Seminar on an Active Manpower Policy, *Supplement to the Final Report,* Paris, 1964, pp. 101–102; Mark J. Fitzgerald, *The Common Market's Labor Programs,* pp. 19–21, 29.

ber countries when they assist firms in the coal, iron, and steel industries to pay their work force during enforced idleness in a reconversion. This is one of a group of employment measures which have been authorized, first under section 23 of the annex to the main treaty, and, since 1960, under article 56 as amended. The EEC may make nonrepayable grants to support wages during a reconversion, but the recipient country must in turn make a special contribution which at least equals the sum granted.

The detailed reports on the activities of the ECSC under article 56 mention the provision for paying workers during reconversion, but none of the official data on beneficiaries and grants separate out this item. It is likely that it was a minor form of aid in view of the large number of direct transfers of coal miners to other mines belonging to the same company and the speedy reemployment of the majority of dismissed workers.[16]

Only a few programs of individual countries deal explicitly with reconversion or retraining of existing employees within the firm. Where the programs do not distinguish clearly between retraining the incumbent employees and new workers, it is difficult to assess the effects on job continuity. This is the case in Sweden and Italy. To the extent that only a portion of an existing work force is retrained, the hard-to-reemploy among them are less likely to be chosen than the younger, more able workers.

In Belgium a government program was introduced early in 1961 to maintain the wages of workers temporarily laid off or working part-time while their firms reconverted for the manufacture of new products. The government and the firms were to share equally the maintenance of wages at 90 percent of former gross earnings and pay all contributions on behalf of workers to insurance and pension plans for six months. At the end of that period, workers were to be taken back into employment. Few employers have applied for this aid. In 1964 an automobile assembly plant near Antwerp was granted help for 820 workers at a cost to the government of 20.5

[16] ECSC, *Mesures de réadaptation appliquées en République Fédérale d'Allemagne, en Belgique et en France*, Luxembourg, 1966, pp. 19–21, 29–30, 39–41.

million Belgian francs (about $411,000); no new requests were reported in 1965 or 1966.[17]

France has offered financial aid to firms which as a result of concentration, specialization, conversion, or decentralization wish to train their own staffs for new jobs. This activity has been part of a program sponsored by the Economic and Social Development Fund (FDES), which also authorized training within firms of workers dismissed by other firms. Therefore, the total accounts of this scheme are not an accurate reflection of the numbers of workers whose continuity of employment was maintained by means of FDES subsidized training. From 1955 through 1967 the FDES aided a total of 118,427 workers at an expenditure of over 90 million francs (over $18 million). In many of the years the regions having the largest number of retrained workers were the Loire and Brittany, and the three industries for which more than three-fourths of the total were trained were metallurgy, electrical and electronics work, and textiles.

An amendment at the end of 1966 (Act 66–892) to the law establishing the National Employment Fund (63–1246) permits the Fund to give financial assistance to firms which retrain their own workers, either for new kinds of jobs with the reconverted firm or with new firms.

The AFPA (*Association pour la formation professionelle des adultes*), the most important source of training courses in France, also supports training to assist workers to remain in their old firms. However, one should note the comment on actual procedures made in 1963 by Laurent Lucas, Deputy Secretary General of the French Confederation of Christian Workers (CFTC):

Whether in oil, ship-building or the footwear industry, job transformations carried out by the firms have often sharply divided the workers most capable of adjusting themselves to the new technological conditions from the rest, even when the firms signed an undertaking, which

[17] OECD, International Trade Union Seminar on Active Manpower Policy, *Supplement to the Final Report*, p. 121; Belgium, ONEM, *Rapport Annuel, 1965*, Brussels, 1966, Ch. III, p. 5; *idem, Rapport Annuel, 1966*, Brussels, 1967; *idem, Rapport Annuel, 1967*, Brussels, 1968.

was never put into practice, to give preference to staff already in the firm over specialized workers recruited from outside.[18]

In Sweden, subsidized retraining on the job of redundant workers is concentrated in the northern development areas, but it is also available elsewhere. Employers and the Labour Market Board are under strong pressure to minimize dismissals through the provision of retraining facilities and new jobs for redundant workers in their own factories. So deep is this commitment that the government has on occasion purchased industrial facilities and operated them in order to maintain continuity of employment. A case in point is the government's purchase of two small private machine-tool companies and part of a third company in order to provide employment for workers at a terminating government facility in Västeras. The newly-formed government machine-tool company became the largest in the industry and it was hoped that, over and above its saving of jobs, it would be more efficient and profitable than its individual components had been.

Great Britain favors firms in development areas over others as regards subsidized retraining of workers who might otherwise lose their jobs. Retraining subsidies are offered to firms in development areas which "can establish that retraining is needed to avoid a substantial reduction in the size of the labour force, e.g., a danger of closure of the factory or a part of it. The retraining must also form part of general measures such as major reorganization of the factory or a part of it." [19]

[18] OECD, International Trade Union Seminar on Active Manpower Policy, *Supplement to the Final Report,* p. 24; Margaret S. Gordon, *Retraininng and Labor Market Adjustment in Western Europe,* pp. 179–82; ILO, *International Differences. . . ,* pp. 220–21; OECD, International Management Seminar on Active Manpower Policy, *Supplement to the Final Report,* pp. 57–58; France, Ministère des Affaires Sociales, *Rapport . . . 1966,* pp. 33–34; Ministère du Travail, *Rapport . . . 1965,* pp. 28–29; OECD, International Joint Seminar on Geographical and Occupational Mobility, *Final Report,* pp. 77–79, 80; ILO, *Manpower Adjustment Programmes: I. . . ,* pp. 21, 37, 40, 57, 60.

[19] Great Britain, Ministry of Labour, *Assistance with Industrial Training for Firms in Development Areas,* London, October 1967; ILO, *Manpower*

The data are insufficient to permit solid conclusions, but it appears that the programs to assist employers to retrain their own workers or maintain them during reconversion of plants have not been used to the same extent as the more general labor market measures.

This chapter and the previous one have dealt with a group that may be largely invisible when unemployment is low—those older and marginal workers who have jobs under full employment conditions but become hard-to-reemploy if they lose their jobs. Their great interest is in the maintenance of continuity of employment until they retire or withdraw from the labor market. In exploring western European laws, customs, and attitudes affecting the hard-to-reemploy, we have surveyed such negative measures as restraining dismissals and sharing the work and such positive measures as maintaining demand for existing firms and giving assistance to firms attempting to retain or retrain their labor force while converting their production.

In terms of numbers, the negative methods may offer the most significant protection for older workers when general employment levels are high. These methods are quite ineffective in periods of mounting unemployment, although the hard-to-reemploy may find temporary protection through the special safeguards which various countries impose on the dismissal of specific individuals. Before the conclusion is drawn that all such measures are inherently and uniformly uneconomic, a full consideration should be given to all of the relevant social and private costs and benefits. The difficulties of calculating the effects on employment-creation of such positive measures as Sweden's advance and extra orders to industry should serve as a reminder of the even greater complexities which surround an analysis of the negative measures.[20]

Adjustment Programmes: II. Sweden, U.S.S.R., United States, Geneva, 1967, pp. 22–23; *Modern Swedish Labour Market Policy,* pp. 25–26, 64, 80; *Sweden Now,* December 1968, p. 20.

[20] For an excellent statement of the problems of measurement, see Gunnar Eliasson, *Investment Funds in Operation,* Stockholm, 1965, pp. 33–64. See also, A. D. Smith, "Active Manpower and Redundancy Policies: Their Costs and Benefits," *International Labour Review,* January–February 1967, pp. 49–60.

The high value placed on job security by most European workers and trade unions reflects a belief that the burdens of economic change will fall inequitably upon them and that the gains will be garnered by others. However, the essentially negative method of relying on the enterprise to maintain employment is beginning to yield to positive public and private manpower policies which aim to transfer surplus workers to new jobs with a minimum of displacement and unemployment.

XII | Speeding Reemployment

Efforts to maintain continuity of employment by one means or another cannot protect indefinitely all of those who would be hard-to-reemploy. For those who do face loss of work, the most urgent need is a satisfactory new job, preferably without an intervening period of unemployment. In a full employment economy, increasing attention can be paid to those still in employment but threatened by unemployment. The importance of anticipatory action has been emphasized in Sweden because of the substantial reemployment difficulties of redundant older and disabled workers, particularly women whose tendency to retire from the labor market under adverse conditions may mask their differential hardship. The reemployment problems of older workers, particularly in closures of firms, arise from a combination of factors, of which the most important are inadequate prior education and training, difficulty in adapting to a faster work tempo, and restricted occupational or geographical mobility due to physical, psychological, or social handicaps connected with aging.[1]

The smooth transition from one job to another or from terminating employment to training course is one of the newer concerns of

[1] Rudolf Meidner, "The Employment Problems of Individuals and Groups," *International Conference on Automation, Full Employment and a Balanced Economy*, (Rome), New York, 1967, pp. 2–6; International Labour Office, *(ILO), Manpower Adjustment Programmes: II. Sweden, U.S.S.R., United States*, Labor and Automation, Bull. no. 6, Geneva, 1967, pp. 41–42.

the most advanced labor market policies in western Europe. The aim is to aid the economy as well as the workers who are about to be displaced. Measures to facilitate reemployment of those about to lose their jobs or occupations are not designed specifically for the hard-to-reemploy, but the latter stand to benefit particularly if they are included in anticipatory programs.

While those involved in mass dismissals are most often and most easily treated in advance of discharge, cases of individual displacement also have been and can be so handled. The emphasis in this chapter is on public measures directed toward those still in employment. Manpower programs which are designed primarily for the unemployed are not considered here unless they include special arrangements for those who are about to be displaced.

ADVANCE WARNING OF DISMISSALS

Clearly, foreknowledge of impending dismissals is valuable to the manpower agencies charged with the task of finding new jobs for workers before the old ones terminate. Historically, employers first had to be persuaded or forced to give workers and their representatives advance notice; this has been a long-standing issue in collective bargaining negotiations. Over the years, employers have been compelled to give reasonable advance notice of dismissal to the affected workers through collective bargaining agreements, civil codes, and specific laws in many western European countries. France has one of the most generous legal provisions for workers with some length of service.[2]

Valuable as it is to give workers and Works Councils advance notification of dismissal, this by itself is an inadequate labor market measure. The significant improvement in the postwar period has

[2] ILO, *Termination of Employment (Dismissal and Lay-off)*, Report VII (1), Geneva, 1962; ILO, *Redundancy Procedures in Selected Western European Countries,* Geneva, 1966, pp. 91–92, 110–14, 181; Frederic Meyers, *Ownership of Jobs: A Comparative Study,* Los Angeles, 1964, pp. 40–43, 66–67.

been the adoption by several countries of compulsory or voluntary schemes whereby each employer planning the dismissal of a stated number of workers for economic reasons gives considerable advance notice to the Employment Service. The latter then prepares for the reemployment of the redundant workers while they are still at work.

An excellent statement of the advantages of advance notice of dismissal has been provided by the Swedish Labour Market Board:

The advance warning system is regarded as an important part of the general labour market policy, because such measures as employment service, training, industrial location, etc. will require time in order to be successfully implemented. To keep the employees well informed about planned close downs etc. and about the measures undertaken to cope with the situation, makes the situation less dramatic and simplifies the readjustments on the labour market which are necessary for economic progress. . . .

The employment service gathers information about the work force, makes clear which employees can immediately be placed in other work and analyses obstacles to placement in other cases. Measures to remedy such obstacles may be vocational training or economic aid to facilitate removal to some other place. Preparations are made for public emergency work projects, if such projects should be required, and other measures to raise local employment may also be undertaken. One solution may be the location of new industry to the locality in question. The routine includes i.a. the attaining of a schedule for dismissals which is liable to facilitate replacements without unnecessary hardships for the employees concerned. The establishment of a temporary employment office within the undertaking has often proved to be useful. It is regarded as important that the joint action thus undertaken is not just aiming at general solutions but also at the problems of individuals.[3]

In western Europe, early notification of mass dismissals to the Employment Service has been established with varying degrees of compulsion and compliance. West Germany has the most formal

[3] Sweden, National Labour Market Board, *Answers to OECD questionnaire on advance warning systems,* MO (64) 22, pp. 2–3; Arnold R. Weber, "Manpower Adjustments to Technological Change: An International Analysis," in Solomon Barkin and others, eds., *International Labor,* New York, 1967, pp. 137–39.

and comprehensive provision. According to the German Law on Safeguards in Respect of Notice to Terminate of August 1951, a mass dismissal occurs when, within a period of four weeks, an employer normally having 21 to 49 workers plans to dismiss more than five workers; an employer with a normal staff of 50 to 499 workers plans to dismiss 10 percent, or more than 25 workers; and an employer of 500 employees or more plans to dismiss 50 or more. Employees are defined as those with at least six months' service who are 18 years old at dismissal time. The law applies to all enterprises and bodies covered by private law as well as to public service enterprises. Dismissals on building sites due to inclement weather and in other seasonally affected enterprises are not covered, nor are discharges connected with industrial disputes or disagreements at high levels of the organization.

The employer's notice to the Employment Service must be given a minimum of one month before dismissals are made. It serves, in part, to provide "information concerning any possible saturation of the labour market," according to a representative of the German Employers' Confederation (BDA), and "facilitates the work of the placement service in finding other situations for the workers dismissed and provides a breathing space during which any special features of the firm concerned having repercussions on the labour market situation can be taken into account." [4]

Officials of the Federal Institute of Labour Placement and Unemployment Insurance, now the Labor Office, stated that under ordinary circumstances compliance with this law has been satisfactory. Moreover, some covered employers report dismissals in advance when fewer workers are involved than is legally stipulated, and

[4] Organization for Economic Cooperation and Development, (OECD), Manpower and Social Affairs Directorate, International Management Seminar on Active Manpower Policy, *Supplement to the Final Report,* Paris, 1965, p. 12; Federal Ministry of Labour and the Social Structure, *Notice of Dismissal and Protection against Dismissal,* Monograph 13, Social Policy in Germany, Essen, 1963, pp. 17–18; Interviews with BAVAV officials in Nürnberg; U.S. Embassy, Bonn; ILO, *Manpower Adjustment Programmes: I, France, Federal Republic of Germany, United Kingdom,* Labour and Automation, Bull. no. 4, Geneva, 1967, pp. 91–94, 105–106.

many small employers not covered by the law tend to notify the Employment Service. However, as we have seen earlier, the recession of 1966–68 produced some evasion of the law.

Norway also has a law on advance warning which provides two months' notice, with the full agreement of employers' organizations. Italy's law requires approval of dismissals by the local employment office, thus providing a form of advance notice. Belgium relies on the indirect knowledge obtained from applications for aid for industrial development or notice of closure of firms in connection with severance pay.

The French manpower authorities have many means of obtaining information about dismissals. Individual dismissals are reportable under the Ordinance of 24 May 1945. In addition, every firm which discharges twenty or more workers is required to report, citing the cause of dismissal. These are, however, not advance reports. Firms are also supposed to report one month in advance when they intend to dismiss 20 or more workers. But a French official response to an OECD questionnaire on advance warning indicated that in 1964 only about 50 percent of the enterprises expecting to discharge twenty workers or more actually gave a month's advance notice to the manpower service of the Ministry. The compliance was reported to be better in the provinces than in Paris, but suitable reemployment was relatively easy in the capital. Employers were said to be much less favorable than the trade unions to advance notice or open discussions of possible curtailment of work. Employers claimed that revelation of such plans might lead to financial difficulties for the firm, either on the stock market or by cancellation of orders, while production schedules might be hindered by workers' strikes or resignations. A major concession was made by employers in the national collective bargaining agreement of February 1969. They agreed to notify the Works Council or plant committee in writing of any planned reduction of staff and to discuss the causes and remedies available. In a mass layoff due to economic conditions, the plant committee is to be given advance notice of eight days if 10 to 49 workers are involved, 15 days for 50 to 99 workers, and one month for 100 or more workers. If a merger or reorganization is to take place, the required advance notice concerning mass layoffs is longer. While the National Employment Agency, created in December 1968, need not be notified at the same time, it may be assumed that they will hear about mass layoffs which are notified to plant committees.

French manpower authorities do not rely exclusively on reports from employers to discover where future trouble spots may emerge. Many other programs enable them to engage in advance planning and active intervention in almost all collective dismissals occurring in areas where reemployment opportunities are limited. They also can compensate for a lack of advance notice by withholding permission for dismissals for up to four months and they can arrange for the phasing of dismissals over a long period.[5] Yet, a formal advance notification system with a high degree of compliance is considered superior to *ad hoc* arrangements. This point was made by the OECD examiners of the Netherlands manpower policy, who stated that the Dutch dismissal law was no substitute for a system of advance warning.

Until the end of 1965, Great Britain depended entirely upon informal and voluntary advance notification of redundancies to the Employment Service. Nationalized industries gave long advance warning both to the trade unions and Employment Service, but other employers were less cooperative. Rumors of a forthcoming closure or reduced operations of an enterprise might circulate in a community for months before the event, but unless the enterprise chose to inform the manager of the local employment exchange, no official action could be taken.

Advance warning of a few weeks or a month was given most frequently where the relations between the manager of the local employment exchange and the enterprise were close and cordial or an employer's redundancy policy included such notice. Employers were

[5] France, *Réponse au questionnaire sur les systèmes de préavis à long terme,* Référence: document MO(64)22, 26 Novembre 1964 de l'OCDE, 10 pp.; OECD, *Age and Employment,* Paris, 1962, pp. 36–45; ILO, *Manpower Adjustment Programmes: I. . . ,* pp. 19, 20, 30–31; European Coal and Steel Community, (ECSC), High Authority, *Mesures de réadaptation appliquées en République fédérale d'Allemagne, en Belgique et en France,* Luxembourg, 1966, p. 39.

said to be reluctant to announce their intentions in advance because of possible adverse effects on their ability to conduct business. Their competitors and customers might take advantage of the situation, and their position might be abruptly worsened by the premature departure of workers facing dismissal.

The British Redundancy Payments Act of 1965 introduced compulsory advance notification of impending dismissals, largely as an administrative measure connected with making redundancy payments. In any redundancy involving more than ten workers who have been with a firm for at least two years, an employer must give the employment exchange 21 days advance notice or forfeit the reimbursement due him from the national redundancy fund. Partially as a result of their legal obligations, some large employers have given long advance notice, invited the Employment Service to establish an office on the premises, and offered redundant workers extra "retention pay" in order that production should not be disrupted and the phasing of dismissals should be preserved. As an extra protection for dismissed workers the General Electric Company agreed to pay special unemployment pay to those who remained out of work for some time.[6]

By this time the reader has come to expect that Sweden will be a leader in advanced labor market measures. The noteworthy feature here is the completely voluntary character of Sweden's early warning system. Begun in 1945, the present advance-notice scheme was firmly established in March 1952 when the National Labour Market Board concluded agreements with the leading federations of employers in industry and commerce (the Federation of Swedish Industries, the Swedish Employers Confederation, the Commercial Employers Association, and the Collective Bargaining Organization of the Cooperative Movement).

In 1954 all agencies of the national government were directed to inform the labor market authorities whenever civilian personnel

[6] Interviews with Ministry of Labour Officials; *Ministry of Labour Gazette*, February 1963, pp. 50–55; ILO, *Manpower Adjustment Programmes: I. . . ,* pp. 165–67; *The Times* (London), January 30, 1969; *The Guardian* (Manchester), January 31, 1969.

were to receive notices of termination of employment. In 1963 the employers' organizations in the important forestry sector came into the scheme. Municipal authorities and private employers not covered by formal agreements also cooperate in giving advance notice. The major exclusion is the construction industry, for which other measures have been devised.

In accordance with their voluntary agreements, Swedish employers must give advance warning under a variety of circumstances: definite closures or stoppages lasting more than fourteen days; cutbacks in production of significance to the local labor market; temporary lay-offs of up to two weeks; short-time working hours affecting a considerable portion of the employees; lay-off or dismissal of seasonal labor. In 1966 notice of planned increases of employment was added.

The Swedish system of advance warning adopted in 1952 required employers to give two-months notice to the Labour Market Board in most cases, a longer period than is asked in other countries. In considering suggestions that the notice period should be lengthened, the tripartite committee on labor market policy reported in 1965 that formal action was unnecessary since many firms planning large-scale lay-offs already gave six to twelve-months notice and the trend appeared to be toward even longer periods of voluntary notice. However, the structural changes in the Swedish economy and the rising unemployment of 1966–68 led to a revision of the 1952 agreement in 1967–68. The period of advance notice was increased to three months in cases where dismissals affect more than 50 workers and to four months if a planned closure will affect more than 100 workers. It also was provided that advance warnings should be given as soon as possible in cases involving the dismissal, lay-off, or partial unemployment of five or more employees of an enterprise; formerly, such notifications had been required only when ten or more workers were affected.

The period of notice is, however, not the only problem in making the advance notice system effective. The tripartite committee on labor market policy observed in 1965 that it would be valuable to expand the agreements to cover all the labor market. Many small

322 | Speeding Reemployment

enterprises are not obliged to give advance notice to the Employment Service. Studies of the registered unemployed indicated that those who had received dismissal notices constituted only 24 percent of all registered unemployed in December 1966, 18 percent in May 1967, and 31 percent in May 1968.[7] More employers must be drawn in, if the advance notice system is to cover the majority of workers who are affected by planned reductions of the labor force. Of course, a fair proportion of the unemployed will always consist of individuals who have voluntarily left their jobs or have been dismissed for personal reasons.

Several sources, including representatives of employers, confirm that covered Swedish employers are satisfied with the advance notice system and do not regard it as a restriction on their freedom of action. Some firms which had given three to four years notice or longer had no complaints about the effects on key staff, but occasionally a firm has found that its operations were hampered by premature departures of key workers. A suggestion has been made that a staying-on allowance be given to workers to assure continuity of operations after dismissal notices are given. Another sort of problem arises when workers on advance notice hesitate to accept new jobs for fear of losing their severance pay.

A firm's request that its dismissal intentions be kept confidential is honored, and the Labour Market Board does not view an occasional premature release of information "as a serious argument against advance warnings." "If the firm considers it imperative to observe special discretion, it can instead go outside official channels to contact the county labour director personally," a spokesman for employers explained. Although the Works Council is supposed to be notified by the employer as early as possible and not later than the public authorities are informed, in special cases when secrecy is deemed advisable to protect the interests of the enterprise, notice to

[7] Secretariat for Economic Planning of the Ministry of Finance and the National Institute of Economic Research, *The Swedish Economy,* Preliminary National Budget 1968, p. 87, Revised National Budget 1968, p. 79; "Arbetslösa i Maj 1968 PGA Företagsnedläggelse eller Driftsändring Sedan i Januari 1967," *Arbetsmarknadsstatistik,* no. 11B, 1968.

the Works Council may be delayed. The revised agreement of 1967–68 stipulated precise rules governing the confidential aspects of dismissal plans.

So well accepted is the advance warning system in Sweden that "failure of individual firms to notify planned staff reductions in accordance with the agreements is liable to give rise to certain publicity in at least the more important cases." The Employers' Confederation has established a special internal agency called the Industrial Bureau of Employment Questions which advises member firms on how to explain dismissal plans to workers, the public authorities, and the press. It also advises on matters of pensions, severance pay, and other compensation to workers. Another important function is the establishment of liaison between firms and the Labour Market Board. "These frequent and informal contacts between employers and labour market agencies appear to be helpful in seeing that matters of notice are flexibly and satisfactorily dealt with." Swedish opinion holds that a voluntary advance warning system is more effective than a compulsory one.[8]

The number of workers involved in advance notices of dismissal in Sweden over a period of years is shown in Table XII.1. A high proportion of all notices emanates from the metals and textiles industries, but the engineering, mining, and paper and pulp industries have also been prominent recently. The numbers dismissed with advance notice are only a fraction of the total number of employees in covered firms; in manufacturing firms the 1961–66 annual average was 1.0 percent. The textile industry had the highest ratio, with 6.1 percent of its covered employees receiving notices of dismissal in 1966. A survey in December 1966 of the 3,274 workers still un-

[8] Sweden, National Labour Market Board, *Answers to OECD questionnaire on advance warning systems,* MO(64)22; OECD, International Management Seminar on an Active Manpower Policy, *Supplement to the Final Report,* pp. 112–13; OECD, International Management Seminar on the Public Employment Services and Management, *Supplement to the Final Report,* Paris, 1966, pp. 48, 219–21; *Arbetsmarknadspolitik,* SOU 1965; 9, Stockholm, 1965, pp. 480–84; Trevor Evans and Margaret Stewart, *Pathway to Tomorrow,* London, 1967, pp. 38–39.

TABLE XII.1. Advance Notice of Dismissal, Sweden, 1958–1968

| Year | Unemployment Rate [a] | Number of Advance Notices | Number of Workers Dismissed | | | Number on Short-time |
			All Industries	Metal Industry	Textile Industry	
1958	2.5		26,800			15,500
1959	2.0	270	8,900			3,700
1960	1.4	134	6,732	955	2,718	950
1961	1.2	197	8,271	1,856	2,571	1,100
1962	1.3	222	9,993	4,255	1,204	500
1963	1.4	205	8,108	3,623	608	400
1964	1.1	126	4,312	1,287	578	0
1965	1.1	189	8,900	2,012	2,773	600
1966–67 [b]	1.5	687	25,200	10,783	3,464	2,600 [c]
1967–68 [b]	1.9	622	24,700	10,202	3,357	1,900

[a] Unemployed members of Unemployment Insurance Funds registered at Employment Service offices. Slightly higher rates are shown in the quarterly labor force surveys.
[b] For budget years.
[c] For calendar year 1966.
Source: National Labour Market Board

employed among the 20,700 who had received dismissal notices during 1966 showed that the residual group was comprised disproportionately of disabled and older workers. A hard core of 10 to 20 percent who became hard-to-reemploy was observed in each shutdown.[9] Clearly, the existence of an advance warning system does not in itself assure that reemployment of the displaced workers will be swift or complete. But it can be argued that their position would have been still worse without advance warning.

In some countries, the Employment Service may not have the staff, the ability, and the programs to take advantage of the early notice of dismissals. It was suggested at an international OECD conference on the public employment services that it might be desirable to justify the advance notice period by a demonstration that much more effective handling of cases resulted, perhaps with some attempt at measurements of costs and benefits.[10] We therefore turn to a consideration of the measures used to speed the reemployment of those about to lose their jobs, with special attention to the hard-to-reemploy.

MEASURES TO PROVIDE NEW JOBS

One of the common procedures in a collective dismissal is to set up a special Employment Service office in the affected plant; personnel usually are borrowed from nearby employment offices. Wider contacts are established to locate jobs outside the local area. In Sweden special committees are formed in difficult cases, consisting of representatives of the enterprise, trade unions, Employment Service, and municipal authorities. The new agreement on advance notice of closures provides for establishing such coordinating committees

[9] Meidner, "The Employment Problems of Individuals and Groups," pp. 3, 4, OECD, Council, *Implementation of Recommendation on Active Manpower Policy,* C(67) 106, Paris, 6 November 1967, p. 76.

[10] OECD, International Management Seminar on the Public Employment Services and Management, *Supplement to the Final Report,* p. 221; Sweden, Kungl Arbetsmarknadsstyrelsen, *Arbetsmarknadsstatistik,* no. 56, Stockholm, March 15, 1967.

whenever a plant is to shut down. The increase in lay-offs and shut-downs in Sweden in 1967 led to a strengthened and more systematic cooperation between the vocational guidance service and the placement officers in order to aid the newly displaced. Some local Employment Service offices were enlarged by adding permanent vocational guidance sections and the mobile vocational guidance services were expanded.[11] France in 1967 provided for the formation of *ad hoc* local labor market committees which could bring to bear on each local dismissal a variety of labor market measures to suit the particular situation.[12] The February 1969 national collective bargaining agreement reinforced all governmental arrangements to deal with mass layoffs. The network of employer-trade union committees, starting at plant level and rising to interindustry committees for the various regions, is to initiate training and relocation programs in cooperation with the official agencies.

Workers are more likely to register at an Employment Service office which is established on the work premises than at the regular local office, particularly in countries where the penetration rate of the Employment Service is low and workers customarily use other channels to obtain work. Repeated experience with mass dismissals appears to improve the performance of the Employment Service. One example is the contrast between the weak handling by the British Employment Service of the numerous redundancies in the motorcar industry in Birmingham in mid-1956 and the carefully planned supervision of the closure in 1964 of a factory producing refrigerators and washing machines in which over 1,400 workers were made redundant.[13] Further improvement in the procedures for

[11] Meidner, "The Employment Problems of Individuals and Groups," p. 7; Sweden National Labour Market Board, *Berättelse Angående Verksamheten under Budgetåret 1967–1968*, Stockholm, 1968, p. 86; *idem, Berättelse Angående. . .* , 1966–1967, p. 128.

[12] Law 67-48201.

[13] Hilda R. Kahn, *Repercussions of Redundancy*, London, 1964, pp. 100–110; OECD, International Management Seminar on the Public Employment Services and Management, *Supplement to the Final Report*, pp. 201–203; *Labor Developments Abroad*, February, 1967, p. 7; Ministère des Affaires Sociales, *Rapport sur la situation de l'emploi . . . 1966*, Paris, 1966, p. 36; ILO, *Manpower Adjustment Programmes: I. . .* , pp. 31–34, 106–107, 167.

handling mass dismissals have been made and are expected from the Manpower and Productivity Service which was established in 1968 in the Department of Employment and Productivity.

In dealing with workers who are about to become unemployed, whether individually or in groups, the Employment Service or other responsible manpower agencies strive first to find job vacancies, preferably those which permit a transfer without intervening unemployment and without any reduction in status or earnings. One of the most interesting innovations in western Europe has been the payment of a wage supplement for a stated period in order to permit a redundant worker to take a job at a lower wage rate with little loss in total income.

Older dismissed workers, the core of the hard-to-reemploy, often discover that under high full employment their problem is not a lack of new jobs as such, but rather unattractive pay and status in available jobs. Swedish surveys among trade union members have shown that almost one-fourth who voluntarily left their jobs had a drop in earnings, 16 percent suffered a reduction of other fringe benefits, and 15 percent lost promotion opportunities. Much larger percentages of workers experienced such losses among the redundant workers in major Swedish plant closures which were studied in detail.[14]

As yet, the supplementation of wages for job changers exists in just a few countries for particular kinds of workers and is used only in mass dismissals. The development of such a supplement for coal, iron, and steel workers, called an *indemnité de réemploi,* owes much to the financial support of the High Authority of the European Coal and Steel Community, now merged in the European Economic Community. In 1968, following the ECSC lead, Belgium introduced wage supplements for all workers involved in complete closures of firms which had employed at least 25 workers.

Members of EEC who establish their own schemes to enable redundant coal and iron miners and steel workers to take jobs at lower pay outside of their industries may obtain about 50 percent of the cost from the EEC. Each country sets its own terms of eligibility

[14] Meidner, "The Employment Problems of Individuals and Groups," pp. 4–5.

and payment, but there is a trend toward uniformity. The government pays the dismissed worker any difference between his new wage and, usually, 90 to 100 percent of his old wage, subject to a maximum wage base and a maximum period of payment of one to two years. While the Netherlands and Italy first adopted such schemes in 1965 and Luxembourg made its agreement in 1966, France, Belgium, and West Germany have had such programs for several years. The latter countries have used the wage supplement to some degree. Of some 70,900 workers, mostly coal miners, affected by closures of mines and steel works in Belgium, France, and West Germany from 1960 through 1965, about 75 percent of the Belgian, 60 percent of the French, but only 4 to 5 percent of the West German workers received the supplemental wage payment for one or more months (*indemnité de réemploi*). Many received the wage supplement after a period of receiving the waiting or tide-over allowance (*indemnité d'attente*), described below in the chapter on financial compensation for the displaced.

An analysis of the 8,287 recipients of wage supplements in Belgium showed that their age distribution was much the same as that of the entire group of 10,590 dismissed workers. Therefore, older miners did not utilize the wage supplement scheme disproportionately, although they may have received a larger average supplement than the younger workers. A higher proportion of dismissed foreign miners (83 percent) than of native-born (72 percent) received the wage supplement in Belgium, indicating that inferior jobs were available to the foreign miners. The latter tended to be both much younger and much more rapidly reemployed than the Belgians. It is noteworthy that the scheme, administered by the Belgian government, fully covers dismissed foreign workers.

In France 62 percent of a sample group of dismissed miners and steel workers received the wage supplement. Together with other earnings, these workers achieved 90 percent of their former wage, on a then maximum base of 1200 F.f. a month ($240). In the Centre-Midi, a difficult area for reemployment, the benefit could be received for a maximum of two years. In other areas where the allowance was paid for no more than one year, workers were able to give up the allowance after 5 to 6 months, except in the iron mines of the French Pyréneés, where 9 to 10 months was the usual duration. Those who relinquished the allowance before it expired are assumed to have brought their new earnings up to 90 percent of their former base wage.

The wage supplement was used to a minor extent by West German coal miners because of two factors: the direct transfer of dismissed miners to other operating workplaces owned by the same company, and the relatively high proportion of older and over-age miners who retired on early pensions or other arrangements. Dismissed German steel workers made relatively more use of the wage supplement.

It appears that few of the displaced miners and steel workers who received the wage supplement went directly to lower-paid jobs. Most took the adequate waiting allowance first, presumably in order to exhaust the possibilities of finding jobs which would pay as well or better than their old jobs. After a while, when they found that their best alternative opportunity demanded some decline in earnings, the existence of the wage supplement induced them to accept such work. From the somewhat limited French evidence, it appears that for many the decline in earnings did not last even through the year. This suggests that permanent decreases in wage levels were not involved, but rather training periods for new work.

The ECSC and EEC have been exceptionally alert to the problem of reemployment for older or handicapped redundant miners and steel workers. In recent revisions of its agreements with its member countries, several special provisions were added for these groups. The effect is to lengthen the period of benefit and raise the percentage of previous earnings available as a wage supplement. In the Dutch mines, a supplement to earnings is offered when miners take lower-paid work in the mines, as well as in other industries.

The European Economic Community also supports a measure in Belgium by which employers' wage payments and social security contributions may be subsidized if older and handicapped displaced miners or steel workers are hired. The program was approved in 1965 by the High Authority because Belgium had established a similar subsidy in 1963 for other workers (see Chapter VII). The ECSC has taken an individualized approach to each country and shown flexibility and imagination in responding to the needs of particular groups, especially the hard-to-reemploy.[15]

France adopted the wage supplement for other dismissed workers, in addition to miners and steel workers, in 1963 when the National Employment Fund was established. Influenced directly by the ECSC plan, the French program provides a guarantee of 90 percent of a worker's former wage for the first six months and 75 percent for the next six months if he takes a new job which pays less than his previous wage. This allowance can be given only if employers make contractual and financial arrangements on behalf of a group of dismissed workers involved in actual or impending unemployment in a difficult region or occupation.

The program, called les allocations temporaires dégressives, resulted in seven contracts in 1964 and 1965 which theoretically could have benefited almost 1,500 workers. But the actual beneficiaries were only about one-tenth of the theoretical number, according to the 1966 report on the activities of the Fund. Speculating on the causes of the infrequent requests for this allowance, Ministry officials cited the possibility that most dismissed workers find new jobs at wages which are high enough to disqualify them for the allowance. Certain practical difficulties also were observed. The determination of the base salary on which the size of the allowance depends is complicated and not clearly defined. New employers, learning that the dismissed workers might obtain a wage supplement,

[15] Interviews with Belgian manpower officials; interviews in Luxembourg with officials of the European Coal and Steel Community; ECSC, *Mesures de réadaptation.* . . , pp. 8, 10, 16, 17, 25–26, 35–36; ECSC, *15e Rapport général sur l'activité de la Communauté.* . . , Luxembourg, 1967, pars. 388–407; ECSC, Direction Générale, Problèmes du Travail, Assainissement et Reconversion, *Les actions sociales de la C.E.C.A. pendannt l'annee 1966,* Luxembourg, 1967, pp. 32–35; ECSC, *Aides spécifiques dont peuvent bénéficier les travailleurs âgés touchés par les fermetures,* Doc. No. 5558/1/66F, Luxembourg, 1966, pp. 3, 9, 16; France, Ministère des Affaires Sociales, *Rapport . . . 1966,* p. 48; Belgium, *Revue du Travail,* August 1968, pp. 1120–38.

were tempted to offer unduly low wages. Finally, it proved difficult to obtain financial and other cooperation from the former employers and, legally, the program could not be instituted without their participation.

To remedy the situation, it was suggested that consideration be given to the substitution of a lump severance payment for the wage supplement and that the requirement of a formal agreement with the discharging employer be removed. However, eligibility would still depend on the dismissed worker's association with an occupation and region having a marked lack of alternative employment opportunities.[16] Only two new conventions were concluded with employers in 1966. In 1967 the F.N.E. (*Fonds National de l'Emploi*) had a new potential clientele for the wage supplement—some 8,000 dismissed employees under 60 years of age who had worked for NATO before the bases were removed from France. Almost 2,000 other workers were theoretically eligible for wage supplements under twelve conventions signed in the recession of 1967, but the number actually taking advantage of the wage supplement is not known.

These initial reactions of the French authorities indicate doubts about a type of measure which has been successfully applied to miners and steel workers. However, under the ECSC approved plans, it is not necessary to have the financial support of the employer making the dismissals, and apparently the calculation of the base salary does not constitute a special problem.

The wage supplement as an approach to smoothing reemployment for groups of workers discharged from declining industries has not been tried long enough nor investigated sufficiently to determine whether it merits more general application. In principle, a wage supplement program can ease the transition for those hard-to-reemploy whose long period of steady employment has left them unprepared for the harsh realities of their future job prospects. However, the experience to date does not indicate whether the hard-to-reemploy have in fact particularly benefited from wage supplements.

When suitable jobs are not available in the local area for those

[16] Ministère du Travail, *Rapport sur la situation de l'emploi . . . 1965*, p. 23; Ministère des Affaires Sociales, *Rapport . . . 1966*, pp. 28–29, 36.

who are about to lose their jobs, the manpower agency seeks other measures to avoid unemployment. A counseling and guidance service which pays attention to the special problems of the hard-to-reemploy is useful. Training or retraining courses and mobility allowances have been opened in several countries to those who still have jobs or are self-employed. A trend toward widening the access by the employed to such programs may be discerned. The Swedish Parliament, laying down the guidelines for labor market policy in 1966, affirmed that those facing a risk of unemployment should be eligible for government-financed training, and also urged a liberal interpretation of risk of unemployment. Thus, paid training in a new field may be offered to those whose long-run prospects in their present occupations are unfavorable. In 1967 France made training allowances available to employed workers who are willing to be trained for shortage occupations.

Various forms of subsidized training permit those who are about to lose their jobs to by-pass unemployment. Employers may be subsidized to retrain their own redundant workers for other enterprises or to take on redundant workers from other firms for retraining and new employment. However, observers have noted that European employers "are little inclined to train employees discharged by other firms whom they do not want to hire or who may leave after completing a course. Substantial government assistance has been necessary to overcome this kind of employer reluctance." [17]

Governments have stimulated adult training within firms by loans, grants, subsidies, tax rebates, and exemptions. Employers may be reimbursed for the use of materials and equipment, the loss of working time, instructors' salaries, trainees' allowances, and the difference between the productivity of trainees and ordinary workers. In some countries, West Germany and Italy, for example, adult training is financed in whole or part by unemployment insurance funds. Pressure to utilize training facilities and complete training courses is placed on workers, with penalties and rewards as incentives.[18]

Nonfinancial incentives to employers include exemptions from the

[17] *Labor Developments Abroad*, May 1968, p. 7.
[18] *Ibid.*, pp. 7–9.

provisions of labor laws which would increase the costs of training. Firms also are allowed to offer training allowances which are below the statutory or contractual minimum wage; however, the trend is toward liberal training allowances and maintenance of the income of trainees. Governments also offer advice and guidance to firms in the planning and operation of training courses.

Training which is particularly directed toward those about to be dismissed has been sponsored by the ECSC, the European Social Fund, the French National Employment Fund, and the French Economic and Social Development Fund. Allowances for trainees tend to be fairly close to former earnings under the newer programs. Workers do not feel that they are unemployed, but rather that they are temporarily at a reduced training wage and may move on to even better earnings than they formerly had.

In Italy the ECSC supports a program which gives workers on the waiting allowance a higher proportion of former wages if they elect to attend a training course. Belgium, with ECSC aid, has paid particular attention to prompt retraining for displaced miners, especially older miners with physical or occupational handicaps. In 1966 over 1,000 miners were enrolled in government training centers, training programs run jointly by government and industry, or individual training within a firm. Some 261 men, mostly older miners or problem cases, had first spent up to eight weeks in "observation centers" where their needs and capacities were analyzed; 202 of the 261 were subsequently placed in training programs.

The French Government, on the basis of an agreement with the steel industry in July 1966, passed a decree in August 1967 which extended aid to dismissed workers in other ECSC industries, coal and iron mining. This considerably improved financial support for those undergoing retraining; the benefits were made retroactive to July 1966. The ECSC accepted its 50 percent share of costs for training allowances of longer duration, higher maximum ceilings for computing allowances, enlarged eligibility for higher paid workers, and bonuses for those completing more advanced courses or obtaining diplomas or certificates. The effects of the new regulations were shown in the increase of retrainees to 379 in 1967, compared with only 80 in 1966 when the total number of dismissals had been larger. Special introductory courses were established by the mining companies, under the direction of the official training agency, the A.F.P.A., to encourage the iron miners of Lorraine who were hesitant about entering retraining. These courses were judged a success in acclimating the miners to the idea of retraining and helping them to choose specific courses.

However, retraining generally has not been sought by older miners and underground workers, who tend to be highly skilled and attached to their specialty. Retraining also carries the danger that the new trade may suffer a slump, as happened in 1967 when West German miners who had been retrained as steel workers faced the prospect of further retraining to qualify for vacancies in office work and civil service jobs. In November 1967 the West German government announced a new plan to alleviate the effects of unemployment among miners in the Ruhr Basin, where uneconomic mines are being shut down; an improved retraining program was one of the points of the program.

In most countries, the hard-to-reemploy are not prime candidates for retraining; Sweden is among the exceptions. But the opportunity to obtain training and retraining seems to be better when the hard-to-reemploy are part of a collective dismissal rather than when they are displaced individually.[19]

Mobility programs which are directed toward those who face a loss of employment as well as those actually unemployed are provided by the French National Employment Fund, the ECSC, and the

[19] Sweden, National Labour Market Board, *Modern Swedish Labour Market Policy*, pp. 78–80; Margaret S. Gordon, *Retraining and Labor Market Adjustment in Western Europe*, Washington, 1965, pp. 60–61, 85–87, 179–82; ECSC, *Mesures de réadaptation. . .* , pp. 8, 27, 37–38; ECSC, *14e Raport général sur l'activité de la Communauté. . .* , Luxembourg, March 1966, p. 321; ECSC, *15e Rapport général. . .* , pp. 265, 266; ILO, *Manpower Adjustment Programmes: I. . .* , pp. 34–41, 100, 109, 118, 168, 180; *Labor Developments Abroad*, January 1968, pp. 15–16; ILO, *Redundancy Procedures. . .* , pp. 150–51; Belgium, Office National de l'Emploi, (ONEM), *Rapport Annuel, 1966*, Brussels 1967, pp. 88–89; *Labor Developments Abroad*, May 1968, pp. 7–9.

British scheme of miners' transfer allowances among others. The ECSC supports housing construction in nonmining areas in connection with its mobility allowances in order to encourage redundant miners to take up new occupations in other areas. Mobility allowances have proved to be relatively insignificant in ECSC-supported programs in France, Belgium, and West Germany. From 1960 through 1965, about 3,600 dismissed miners and steel workers, out of a total of 70,900, received mobility allowances in order to take new work. The number was somewhat larger in 1966.[20]

The recent Swedish decision to consider applications for mobility allowances from employed persons followed recommendations by the tripartite committee on labor market policy. The committee felt that grants to employed persons, whether or not threatened by unemployment, should be made during a trial period and should be limited to workers in sectors with declining employment whose employers approve their transfer. Some of the employers' organizations voiced their concern that difficulties might arise in individual cases and urged that employers' views should be given much weight.

In approving the policy, the Parliament stated that such transfer allowances could become important in areas with high and persistent unemployment, since those in jobs might be able to move more easily than the unemployed or those threatened with unemployment. The hope was expressed that the vacancies created by the subsidized movement of the employed might be filled by the local unemployed who found it difficult to move.

As with training and retraining courses, the hard-to-reemploy, because of age and other circumstances, frequently are less interested in and less acceptable for mobility allowances than younger, able workers. An interesting Swedish idea under discussion is the variation of mobility allowances according to age, in order to encourage older workers. The extension of opportunities to enter retraining courses and receive mobility allowances to those displaced from independent farming and other self-employment is another trend.

[20] ECSC, *Mesures de réadaptation. . . ,* p. 10; ILO, *Manpower Adjustment Programmes: I. . . ,* pp. 38–44, 111–13, 170. OECD, *Government Financial Aids to Geographical Mobility in OECD Countries,* Paris, 1967.

Small farmers can obtain special compensation if they sell their farms and take up another occupation.[21]

An alternative measure to mobility allowances in general favor in western European countries is the attempt to bring new industry into areas where substantial unemployment exists or is anticipated. The reluctance of displaced workers and farmers to move from familiar surroundings is strong and it is reinforced by housing shortages in the expanding areas. As a result, employers as well as governments are expected to go to great lengths to provide new jobs when old ones are disappearing and local reemployment prospects are dim. A German trade union leader put it this way: "Firms which make considerable investments for rationalization purposes must also make the appropriate investments to ensure that new jobs are found for workers who become redundant owing to such rationalization." [22]

The social outlook of European trade unionists leads to the position that it is more desirable to create new enterprises in depressed areas than to expect workers to move.[23]

An account of the general efforts to create jobs in development areas is beyond the scope of this study. Such programs have absorbed some of the hard-to-employ and have provided alternative jobs for the hard-to-reemploy in declining industries. But, as has been indicated earlier, employers who move to areas of surplus labor can hire housewives who previously have not worked, workers

[21] National Labour Market Board, *Modern Swedish Labour Market Policy,* pp. 29, 64, 82; Meidner, "The Unemployment Problems of Individuals and Groups," p. 7; OECD, Council, *Implementation of Recommendation on Active Manpower Policy,* p. 76; Ministry of Finance, *The Swedish Budget 1969/70,* p. 51.

[22] OECD, International Trade Union Seminar on Active Manpower Policy, *Final Report,* Paris, 1964, p. 152; Mark J. Fitzgerald, *The Common Market's Labor Programs,* Notre Dame, 1966, pp. 171–73; Graham L. Reid and Lawrence C. Hunter, *Industrial Worker Mobility,* OECD; Paris, 1966, pp. 133–40.

[23] OECD, International Joint Seminar on Geographical and Occupational Mobility of Manpower, *Final Report,* Paris, 1964, pp. 27, 56–61, 66, 138ff., 190.

from other firms, or workers from labor-short areas. The situation actually may be disadvantageous to the hard-to-reemploy, unless subsidized employers in development areas are required to absorb some part of the labor supply released by declining industries.

Sweden, whose northern counties have experienced a sharp contraction of employment in forestry and agriculture, has found large numbers of hard-to-reemploy accumulating in these areas despite the well-publicized and financed mobility program, regional development assistance, retraining measures, and special job creation. As a result of the sweeping victory by the Labour Party in the 1968 elections, it is anticipated that the government may play a more active role in owning and operating industrial enterprises, in determining the location of private investment, in supervising structural rationalization to meet international competition, and in maintaining companies to provide employment in the north. The government owns and operates two important enterprises in the north, a steel company and a forestry-products company, which run at a loss but are defended because of the employment they provide. The employment needs of the north may lead to further government enterprise in these areas through the intervention of the newly-created state Development Bank. A sacrifice of profitability and growth in favor of the social and economic needs of the people may result, but the hope in government circles is that a conflict of this sort can be avoided.[24]

The High Authority of the European Coal and Steel Community and now the EEC sponsored a form of job creation by private enterprise which directly favors the reemployment of dismissed miners and steel workers, including the hard-to-reemploy among them. Member countries which have passed suitable legislation and have submitted plans showing an orderly cutting back of production, staggering of dismissals of miners and steel workers, and establishment of training courses, may request the EEC to grant low-interest loans to new enterprises. These firms must set up plants in the affected area, give promise of economic viability, and undertake to employ

[24] David Jenkins, "Business and Finance," *Sweden Now*, December 1968, p. 20.

the dismissed workers on a priority basis, as a percentage of the whole staff, or on some other basis. This measure favors the hard-to-reemploy directly. In South Limburg, Holland, retrained coal miners have been successfully absorbed by such firms, but the employers have been disturbed by their inability to seek employees among nonminers and juveniles.[25]

A CASE STUDY FROM FRANCE

A description in some detail of a single case where the combined efforts of a private enterprise, various branches of the French government, and the High Authority of the ECSC resulted in an extremely successful transfer of redundant French steel workers to newly introduced companies may show the interrelationships of the various measures which have been described in this chapter.

In December 1961 a large French corporation employing about 17,000 workers, the *Compagnie des Ateliers et Forges de la Loire* (CAFL), decided after a considered investigation that it should close an unprofitable subsidiary company, a steel works in Boucau on the southwest coast of France, near Bayonne and the Spanish border. Annual losses attributable to the subsidiary ran as high as 10 million francs a year.

The subsidiary, known as *Forges de l'Adour*, had been built in 1880 and provided employment for about 1,700, with a higher than average number of older and handicapped workers. Boucau itself had a population of 4,500 and a large proportion of its working

[25] ECSC, *13 années d'actions sociales de la Haute Autorité de la CECA*, Luxembourg, 1966, pp. 19–20; interviews in Luxembourg; ILO, *Manpower Adjustment Programmes: I. . .* , p. 43–44, 128, 180–81. ILO, *Redundancy Procedures. . .* , pp. 135–44, 151–53; *Labor Developments Abroad*, January 1968, pp. 15–16; OECD, *Manpower and Social Policy in the Netherlands*, Paris, 1967, pp. 149, 211–13; ECSC, *15th General Report on the Activities of the Community*, Luxembourg, 1967, pp. 275-87; Communauté Européenne du Charbon et de l'Acier, Communauté Economique Européenne, Communauté Européenne de l'Energie Atomique, (ECSC, EEC, EAEC), *Premier rapport général sur l'activité des Communautés en 1967*, Brussels-Luxembourg, 1968, pp. 272–76; Reports from Dutch mine officials.

people as well as that of the surrounding villages was employed by the steel works. In all, some 6,000 persons may have been directly dependent on the steel works.

The area had experienced other closures recently, had little alternative industrial or other employment, and had recently assumed financial burdens in order to improve the port of Bayonne, a move calculated to assist the steel company's operations. If the implementation of the government's development plan for the region had not lagged, some new jobs might have been available. As it was, the only immediate source of jobs was the construction industry, which might have absorbed about 200 workers. But neither the type of work nor the pay would have suited the steel workers, one-third of whom were over 50 years old.

The decision to close the steel works was kept secret from the community for several months, although the government was informed. When the community learned the news, its reaction was to insist that the steel plant remain in operation. Great hostility was shown to all efforts to make other arrangements, even to those which aimed to keep the workers in the same location and employed at equal or better jobs. Two years after the announcement of the impending closure, protest meetings were still being called. Prominent local figures lent their support to the highly organized steel workers, who were both Basque and rural homeowners, a potent combination against mobility. By the end of 1964, three years after the initial closure decision, only eight workers had taken advantage of the steel corporation's offer to transfer them to company plants in other parts of France, and a mere 25 steel workers had accepted government mobility allowances.

Because of the community attitude and the existence of a regional development plan, all proposed solutions had to center on the introduction of new industries which would provide a suitable type and number of jobs for the displaced steel workers. The steel company itself played a major role in the subsequent effort to make a smooth transition to new employment. The story of what it did, through an agreement with the Ministry of Finance and Industry and on its own initiative, is a remarkable record of social responsibility.

For almost a year after the announced closure, the company continued in full operation while the agreement with the Ministry of Finance and Industry was worked out. Signed in October 1962, the agreement obliged the company not to dismiss workers for several years and to close down the plant by slow stages. At the end of 1964 the company still carried 1,114 employees, of whom 912 were engaged in operating the steel works; the remainder were in retraining courses set up by the company or in special status.

The most important commitment made by the company was its undertaking to create an industrial park and to attract firms which would provide the necessary employment at acceptable wages. Governmental long-term loans, bonuses, tax relief, and industrial conversion grants were available for the construction of overhead facilities and new plants. The ECSC also agreed to contribute toward the costs of conversion.

However, the red tape of obtaining official approval resulted in the loss of some prospective firms. According to a director of the parent corporation who wrote an account of the company's efforts to attract new employers for the steel workers, it was a far more difficult task than would appear from a summary of the successful outcome. From April 1963 to January 1965, the CAFL, the parent company, succeeded in signing agreements with ten companies providing for 1,540 jobs at good wage rates, with the majority of jobs reserved for the redundant steel workers. But during the same period the CAFL had unsuccessfully negotiated with as many as sixty companies, actually concluding thirteen contracts before it obtained its ten final agreements. Each agreement stipulated that the age pyramid of the workers in the new factories should be the same as in the former steel works. Several of the contracts were feasible only because the CAFL shared in furnishing the risk capital for the new ventures.

Reflecting on its experience with reconversion, the director of the CAFL suggested that the facilities available for a particular plant were less important than the resources and capabilities of the area as a whole. He attached great importance to finding vigorous and imaginative entrepreneurs who were not averse to risk-taking. In underdeveloped and poor areas such as southwest France, the establishment of a local development corporation might assist prospective firms which otherwise would find the obstacles too great.

A variety of industries was drawn to the region by the efforts of the CAFL: metallurgical, machinery, cement, wood products, and chemical. An addition to a chemical plant, planned for 1966, was partially financed by the High Authority of the European Coal and Steel Community through a loan of 12.4 million francs (about $2.5 million). The new companies ranged in size from three employing 25 to 35 workers to one with 600 places.

The third obligation placed upon the CAFL was to assist the Ministry of Labor to retrain the workers of Boucau. Because of opposition to the closure of the plant, the workers showed great resistance to training courses. They had to be persuaded that the steel works would close and that they could improve their situation by training for new jobs. To give the workers assurance, the company agreed to maintain them on the payroll while they went to training courses, provided space for some training courses in the works, and shared the expense with the French government and the ECSC of special allowances to trainees who traveled a long distance daily or maintained two homes.

The Ministry of Labour began training courses in advance of the actual signing of contracts, which proved to be a wise move, since some companies decided to establish in the area because of the promised availability of trained workers. After several new firms agreed to open by the beginning of 1964, workers' responses to training offers improved and the trade unions began to cooperate. Adapting training centers and courses to the special situation and calling upon both private companies and the several well-organized training organizations for adults which exist in France, the Ministry was able to train 362 workers in centers and 300 on the job by the end of 1964, with others still in training after the plant closed in mid-1965. Training ranged from simple instruction for 150 workers slated to go to the new cement factory to advanced metallurgical courses. The ECSC gave financial support to those in retraining. All observers remarked on the outstanding success in retraining older workers, those over 40 and even over 50. Many were able to secure jobs as metal workers which paid more and had better status than steel work.

At the beginning of 1966 only 40 of the original 1,673 workers remained without a promise of employment. These were truly hard-to-place cases. When the steel works was closed in mid-1965 almost 600 workers had already left; some had died or reached normal retirement age, 114 had accepted prepension at age 60 or over (arranged through the National Employment Fund), a few had moved away, and the rest were employed in the new factories. Most of the remainder were in training courses or were about to be absorbed by the new factories. Another 184 had firm promises of employment that would materialize in 1966 or 1967. The addition to the chemical plant, under construction with an ECSC loan, was to employ about 175 workers, with the majority of positions suitable for older or unskilled workers. Those who were waiting for promised employment received the ECSC-supported tide-over allowance, and they could also receive the wage supplement if their new wages were below 90 percent of the old.[26]

Praising the entire operation, the High Authority of the ECSC commented: "The success of so large an operation appears all the more remarkable because the employees of the Forges de l'Adour consisted in large part of older or physically handicapped workers."[27]

The over-all experience of the countries aided by the ECSC has not been quite so favorable as that of the French steel works at

[26] Jean Quesnel, "La reconversion du Boucau," *Revue Française du Travail,* January–March 1965, pp. 57–69; Jean Cassou, "Les problèmes de la reconversion du personnel des Forges de l'Adour," *ibid.,* pp. 71–79; France, *Réponse au questionnaire sur les systèmes de préavis à long terme,* document MO(64)22, 26 Novembre 1964 de l'OCDE, p. 10; Ministère des Affaires Sociales, *Rapport . . . 1966,* pp. 48–49; European Coal and Steel Community, *Mesures de réadaptation. . . ,* pp. 37, 40; ECSC, *14e Rapport général. . . ,* pp. 330, 339–40; ECSC, Cahiers de reconversion industrielle, no. 9., *Le bâtiment industriel dans la politique de développement régional en France,* Luxembourg, 1965, pp. 18–35; ILO, *Manpower Adjustment Programmes: I. . . ,* pp. 41–43, 71; ILO, *Redundancy Procedures. . . ,* pp. 152, 163–66.

[27] ECSC, *14e Rapport général. . . ,* p. 340; *15e Rapport général. . . ,* par. 429.

Boucau in regard to the absorption of the hard-to-reemploy. However, the total number of hard-to-reemploy miners and steel workers who were placed in jobs through programs sponsored by the ECSC probably has been considerably greater than it would have been in the absence of such measures as the generous waiting allowance, the wage supplement, the training allowance, the several mobility and separation allowances, the special provisions for older and handicapped workers, the lump-sum payment to older or handicapped miners and steel workers (Germany), the subsidy to employers who hire the older or handicapped miners and steel workers (Belgium), the subsidies to employers who retain their workers during reconversion, subsidized housing, and the loans and aid to employers in other industries who take on redundant miners and steel workers. From 1954 to the end of 1967, 333,705 workers were given one or more kinds of ECSC financial assistance.[28]

This is an impressive kit of tools which has been used to forestall and limit unemployment among those about to lose their jobs, and it has given particular attention to the hard-to-reemploy. Of course, the rapid reemployment of the dismissed miners and steel workers owes a great deal to high levels of employment and transfers within large companies, as in West German coal mines. Problems arise even under the best programs when general unemployment increases.

The High Authority of the ECSC is not content even with its small core of hard-to-reemploy. After a detailed examination of the experience of the workers dismissed from 1960 to 1965 in France, Belgium, and West Germany, the High Authority concluded that "the presence of a large majority of older or handicapped workers among the wage earners who remain unemployed for a long time leads the High Authority to accord particular attention to the problems posed by the reemployment of such workers." [29] Although in theory the ECSC must wait for member governments to suggest pro-

[28] ECSC, EEC, EAEC, *Exposé sur l'évolution de la situation sociale dans la Communauté,* Brussels-Luxembourg, 1968, p. 28.

[29] ECSC, *14e Rapport général. . . ,* pp. 326–27, 331; ECSC, *Mesures de réadaptation. . . ,* pp. 11, 18–19, 27–28, 38–39; ECSC, *15e Rapport général. . . ,* pars. 394, 397, 398.

grams to aid redundant miners and steel workers, in practice the ECSC is able to stimulate the adoption by member countries of desired measures and of fairly uniform approaches to reemployment by conducting studies, sending consultants to member countries, and announcing the availability of certain kinds of grants and loans.

Similar cases of reemployment, perhaps not so drawn out or ultimately so successful as that of Boucau, both in keeping the workers in their home town and placing the hard-to-reemploy, can be cited from the experience of other countries, not members of ECSC. In Sweden, for example, the chief difference in procedures is that comprehensive manpower measures are available for individual discharges as well as mass dismissals, less use is made of such financial incentives as waiting allowances and wage supplements, and more resort is made to emergency public works and mobility allowances. The degree of government intervention and methods of keeping a declining enterprise in business in Sweden also differ from French practice, since detailed economic planning and government controls are more firmly established in France.

In this chapter public manpower programs in western Europe have been described which are essentially anticipatory as regards the hard-to-reemploy. In general, the hard-to-reemploy fare better when over-all public manpower policies and agencies are well developed and have considerable scope. Special programs for the hard-to-reemploy are not necessarily more beneficial than effective general manpower measures with selective attention to the difficult cases. One of the significant developments observed in western Europe is the increased proportion of former earnings granted to those in retraining courses and new jobs at lower pay.

When mass dismissals, which may be serious in their concentrated impact, occur, the hard-to-reemploy appear to benefit considerably from being treated as part of a larger group of dismissed workers of average employability. Special efforts to speed reemployment through an advance warning system, the opening of training and mobility allowance programs to those who are not yet unemployed, and job creation programs connected with regional development and national economic planning can minimize unemployment among the hard-to-reemploy.

For the hard-to-reemploy whose threatened loss of employment is an individual matter, it is valuable to have a wide range of manpower programs which can be used to deal selectively with each case, preferably before the worker loses his job. It is significant that Sweden has found recently that about 15 to 20 percent, at a minimum, of those who lose their jobs in mass dismissals or closures of firms are hard-to-reemploy and require the services of the Vocational Rehabilitation Service, described in earlier chapters. Some will be capable of work only in a sheltered environment. The success of all manpower policies for the hard-to-reemploy as for the hard-to-place unemployed, rests heavily on a strong demand for labor relative to supply. Without it, the chief recourse is to develop direct job creation by government and nonprofit institutions, outside of the competitive framework, as described in Chapters VIII and IX. The new Swedish industrial workshops for displaced older workers are particularly relevant.

XIII | Financial Compensation to the Displaced

Despite the efforts to assure reemployment for those about to lose their jobs in western European countries, displacements and unemployment due to technological and market factors have become a normal occurrence. Unemployment has also increased in periods when "overheated" economies have been cooled off by general deflationary measures; areas of above-average unemployment have been relatively hard hit by dismissals at such times. Therefore, a search has been made for additional methods of protection for workers. One result, potentially beneficial to certain types of hard-to-reemploy workers, has been the growth of new programs to provide financial compensation for a loss of employment or livelihood which is attributable to economic conditions.

Three types of public financial compensation for loss of employment have assumed increased importance in western Europe. The first offers some groups better income maintenance during unemployment than has heretofore been available; in form, the new provisions are either supplementary or substitute unemployment benefit schemes. Improvement of traditional unemployment insurance and assistance schemes has also been attempted in several countries.

In the second type of financial compensation, the payment is purely for the loss of property rights in the job, usually as a lump-sum payment, and carries no obligation to report to an employment office or show availability for work. Such severance or redundancy payments, originally introduced under collective agreements, now are provided also by governments and through international organizations. The final type of compensation, a pre-pension payment, encourages retirement from work at an earlier age or on better terms than are stipulated by standard old-age pension systems.

SUPPLEMENTARY AND SUBSTITUTE UNEMPLOYMENT BENEFITS

The years of sustained full employment in many countries of western Europe have not led to indifference about the maintenance of income for the small numbers who do become unemployed. When full employment is assumed as a norm, departures from it can be seen as a brief, unavoidable waiting period between jobs during which a worker should receive a high percentage of his normal income, whether he is idle, in a training course, or in a job created for him. While this enlarged view is not yet general, there is decreasing concern about unemployment allowances which closely approach former earnings. One aim is to offset the workers' resistance to change. The recent period of increased unemployment associated with deflationary credit restrictions has been especially conducive to new legislation.

Until 1959 France had relied on inadequate local government unemployment assistance payments which were limited to claimants with incomes below a specified level and excluded some areas of the nation. In 1958 an agreement to establish industry unemployment insurance funds was signed by the most important employer associations and confederations of trade unions; the negotiations were accompanied by strong government encouragement and approval. Statutes made the coverage of this agreement more general in 1959 and almost universal in 1967. This legal device of generalizing or extending the provisions of a specific collective bargaining agreement to a much wider population, used frequently in France, confers a maximum of government approval and requires a minimum of government administration or financial support.

It is curious that France, a nation which has used governmental authority liberally, should have chosen to provide for unemployment insurance, generally recognized as a state function, through joint industry-trade union action, an underdeveloped area of French life. The government's desire to save money or, more charitably, to use its funds for active manpower policies is as reasonable an explanation of the somewhat unorthodox development as one is likely to find. While the industry funds (ASSEDIC) are nominally independent of government, at times government has pressed for modifications and adaptations of the scheme which have increased the obligations of the funds.

The new French unemployment insurance system is financed entirely by employers and workers (the lowest-paid workers make no contribution). Workers covered by the scheme may receive 40.25 percent for the first 91 days and then 35 percent of their average daily wage for the rest of their eligibility period. Their unemployment insurance payments may be supplemented by government-financed unemployment assistance, provided the total does not exceed 80 to 95 percent of the former wage, according to the worker's individual situation. Since September 1967 the two benefits are paid simultaneously. The duration of the insurance benefits is variable, with longer periods for older workers (over 50). In recent years both the unemployment assistance and the unemployment insurance programs have been broadened and improved. One of the chief amendments of 1965 permits unemployed workers who are still in receipt of insurance benefits eight months after their 61st birthday to continue to receive benefits until they reach 65, at which time the regular old-age pension begins. In October 1967 the national government assumed financial responsibility for unemployment assistance; place of residence was disregarded and the income limits were liberalized.

French workers who are covered by the supplementary unemployment insurance system are considerably better off now than under the sole protection of the meager unemployment assistance scheme. But other countries have done as well or better for their workers under unemployment insurance alone. Great Britain, which has had a flat-rate unemployment insurance system, introduced a supplementary benefit which is earnings-related. The supplement which may be paid for six months of unemployment or sickness, plus the flat-rate benefit and dependents' allowances may reach a maximum of 85 percent of a worker's previous average weekly earnings. The maximum duration of the flat-rate unemployment benefit has now been standardized to 312 working days for all, in recognition of the fact that the extra days previously awarded to those with larger numbers of contributions were an unfair discrimination against those in less stable industries and less prosperous regions.

It was intended that the changes should reduce the numbers of unemployed who have in the past been compelled to apply for means-test assistance, but critics maintain that the earnings-related supplementary insurance benefit will not give enough support to men with low earnings and large families. Under the previous arrangements, as Adrian Sinfield's unpublished study shows in some detail for Shields, a northeastern town, those whose earnings and employment were most precarious had the least security when unemployed. Further measures for these groups were promised by the government.

It is significant that between 1948 and 1963 only one-third of those who have been insured against unemployment had ever claimed any benefit at all. If only a minority of the labor force uses the insurance program under full employment, it may be necessary to rethink both the amount of support offered to the most disadvantaged unemployed and the possibility of using insurance funds for labor market programs, as the German system does.

An improvement in Italian unemployment benefits in 1966 and 1968 raised the basic amounts and lengthened their duration, and also increased the dependents' allowances to the same amounts as employed workers receive as family allowances. An extra daily benefit was provided in 1968 for unemployed industrial workers who participate in retraining courses. In addition, one of the two 1968 laws on unemployment benefits introduced a special allowance for unemployed men and women a few years short of pension age (60 for men and 55 for women). These differential unemployment benefits for older workers are appearing in a number of countries and are leading, as we shall see, to pre-pensions for selected individuals among the older unemployed.

Belgium has established supplementary benefits which are paid by the "livelihood guarantee funds" of various industries. By Royal Order the agreements to set up funds, which are reached by national joint committees of employers and workers in an occupational sector, are made binding on all firms in a given industry or branch. Qualified workers in covered industries who become unemployed for economic reasons are entitled to special allowances, usually for no more than 40 days a year. These allowances, payable in addition to ordinary unemployment benefits, are financed by the employers through an industry payroll tax which varies from 3.6 to 10.5 percent of the wage bill.

In West Germany unemployment insurance coverage was broadened and benefits were raised as of April 1, 1967. The average increase was 15 percent, giving a single person about 62.5 percent of earnings and a married worker with two children up to 80 percent. Moreover, an unemployed worker with three or more children who receives unemployment allowances for his dependents will also continue to receive the standard children's allowances paid to those who are employed. The unemployed with fewer than three children can receive whichever dependent's allowance is more favorable.

Adjustments have also been made in the benefits paid to partially unemployed German workers, those whose plants are on temporary shutdown, and recipients of bad-weather allowances in the construction industry; they may now receive up to 62.5 percent of their net earnings. Unemployment assistance has been improved too, allowing 52.5 percent of previous net earnings to those who have exhausted unemployment insurance and have met the means test.[1]

[1] International Labour Office, (ILO), *Manpower Adjustment Programmes: I. France, Federal Republic of Germany, United Kingdom,* Labour and Automation, Bull. no. 4, Geneva, 1967, pp. 25–28, 97–100, 156–59; Frederic Meyers, "The Role of Collective Bargaining in France: The Case of Unemployment Insurance," *British Journal of Industrial Relations,* November 1965, pp. 363–91; Organization for Economic Cooperation and Development, (OECD), Manpower and Social Affairs Committee, *Annual Reports, France, 1964,* Mo (64) 10/08, pp. 14, 15; France Ministère des Affaires Sociales, *Rapport sur la situation de l'emploi . . . 1966,* Paris, 1966, pp. 37–41; U.S. Joint Economic Committee, *European Social Security Systems,* Paper no. 7, 80 Congress, 1st sess., Washington, 1965; *Labor Developments Abroad,*

Sweden has never had compulsory government unemployment insurance, relying instead on government-subsidized and supervised trade union funds in the industries most subject to unemployment. In addition, lay-off pay for a limited period is provided through a 1964 agreement between the leading employers' and workers' organizations. These benefits, financed by employers, compensate qualified nonterminated workers during periods of temporary cuts in production. For some, the lay-off benefits cover the uncompensated waiting period under unemployment insurance. The worker is not obliged to return to the same employer if the lay-off exceeds one full work week (five or six days) or notice to return to work is not given in good time.

At the end of June 1968 there were 43 approved unemployment insurance funds with 1,689,000 members, about half of the total number of employed persons in Sweden. The excluded groups are largely those with job security, such as government employees, or workers who are not seriously affected by unemployment, such as married women in part-time work. Nevertheless, some of the unemployed are needy and have no recourse except to the modest municipal cash assistance programs in the ten larger towns. These programs, however, have largely become complementary to public welfare assistance for persons with reduced or no work capacity. As a result, some workers have either borne the financial burden of unemployment themselves or have felt pressed to accept new work quickly, without giving the Employment Service time to develop suitable job plans.

The committee on labor market policy recommended an expansion of Sweden's municipal unemployment assistance programs, an adjustment of the municipal regulations to conform with those of

February 1967, p. 6; Information from U.S. Embassy, Bonn; ILO, *Redundancy Procedures in Western Europe*, Geneva, 1966, pp. 101–105, 114–19, 182–83; France, Ordinance No. 67-580, Income Guarantees for the Unemployed; "New Employment and Unemployment Legislation in France," *International Labour Review*, March 1968, pp. 307–11; *Labor Developments Abroad*, July 1969, p. 6; France, Ministère des Affaires Sociales, *Rapport . . . 1968*, Paris, 1968, pp. 45–51.

the unemployment insurance funds, a transfer of administrative authority from the local unemployment committees to the executive of the municipality, and a change in the national government's grants-in-aid to the municipalities from a variable amount with a 20 percent minimum to a fixed 50 percent to all municipalities.

When the recommendations were discussed, they drew criticism. The National Labour Market Board opposed the proposals because they favored a national rather than a municipal system, while the main trade union federation (LO) objected because it feared that the principle of providing work for the unemployed might suffer and that minimal cash support would be offered instead. The government's guidelines on this issue at the parliamentary session in 1966 stressed that the employment principle should continue to receive priority, but recognized that cash assistance is required in some cases in order to give the unemployed worker and the Employment Service time to effect a good placement. Rather than endorse the committee's proposals, the government decided to appoint a special committee to study the question of improved protection during unemployment, while retaining the existing system unaltered and fixing the government subsidy to the municipalities at 20 percent.[2]

More recently, Swedish discussions and action have been influenced by the mounting number of displacements due to the rationalization of Swedish industry in the face of international competition and the higher general unemployment in 1966–68. Income guarantees during transition periods or labor market insurance against a loss of income were suggested by the Commission on Cash Support and were supported in trade union circles which earlier had stressed only jobs. In July 1968 older unemployed workers, those over 60 or over 55 in special cases, were given two differential benefits through

[2] Sweden, National Labour Market Board, *Modern Swedish Labour Market Policy*, Stockholm, 1966, pp. 41–43, 65–66, 99–100, 117–18; Sweden, *Arbetsmarknadspolitik*, SOU 1965: 9, Stockholm, 1965, pp. 254–73; Carl G. Uhr, *Sweden's Social Security System*, U.S. Dept. of Health, Education and Welfare, Social Security Admin., Research Report no. 14, Washington, 1966, pp. 92–105; International Labour Office, *Manpower Adjustment Programmes: II. Sweden, U.S.S.R., United States*, Labour and Automation, Bull. no. 6, Geneva, 1967.

government subsidies. Those who are entitled to unemployment benefits and have difficulty in finding work can receive unemployment benefits for 450 to 500 days instead of 150 to 200 days. And thereafter, until the old-age pension becomes payable at 67, they may receive a special adjustment grant of 800 Sw.kr. per month which is taxable. Those who are not entitled to unemployment benefits also may obtain the adjustment grant if their age and difficulty in obtaining employment qualify them. In mid-June 1969, 4,900 persons, 20 percent of the registered unemployed, were receiving either prolonged benefit or the special adjustment allowance. In the first year of operation, certain trends appeared in the utilization of the new forms of assistance. Increasing proportions of all older unemployed workers drew each kind of benefit, even as over-all unemployment declined. The growth in the number of recipients of adjustment allowances was more rapid than in the number receiving extended unemployment benefits; the rising participation of those who did not belong to unemployment insurance funds was the chief cause. Extended unemployment benefits were claimed increasingly by workers between 55 and 60 years old. A disproportionate share of the recipients of adjustment allowances have been from the seven northern forestry counties. Unemployed older women constituted over one-fourth of the recipients of extended unemployed benefits in both January and June 1969 and slightly less than one-fourth of the recipients of adjustment allowances in May and June 1969; women thus appear to have a fair share of the new programs. The number receiving municipal cash assistance also has been somewhat reduced as a result of the new measures. Sweden, under the pressure of recession, has modified its earlier view that jobs can be created for virtually all of the hard-to-employ.[3]

[3] Rudolf Meidner, "The Employment Problems of Individuals and Groups," in *International Conference on Automation, Full Employment, and a Balanced Economy,* (Rome), New York, 1967, p. 7; *New York Times,* January 15, 1968, "Sweden is Honing Competitive Edge;" National Labour Market Board, *Arbetsmarknadspolitiken 1969–70,* Stockholm 1968, pp. 34–36; Ministry of Finance, *The Swedish Budget 1968/69,* Stockholm, 1968, p. 39; National Labour Market Board, "Äldrestödet I Januari 1969," *Arbetsmarknadsstatistik,* no. 6B, 1969; *Arbetsmarknadsstatistik,* no. 12B, 1969.

Almost everywhere else there has also been an effort to increase and improve the financial support of unemployed workers. Gösta Rehn, the Director for Manpower and Social Affairs of the OECD, has suggested some new approaches toward income maintenance during initial periods of unemployment. These programs "would give the individual income security over time but . . . would not require him to submit to those continuous controls which make unemployment periods, even if covered with very good insurance benefits, a rather awkward and destructive experience." Another advantage of such a buffer is its ability to absorb "the first impact of some of the variations in the demand for labor," reducing "the need for hasty, costly, and sometimes inflationary measures to stimulate local creation of employment and manpower relocation." [4]

Some moves in the direction suggested by Mr. Rehn are discernible in western Europe. The European Coal and Steel Community was responsible for the introduction in several member countries of a "waiting or tide-over allowance" (*indemnité d'attente*) designed for redundant coal and iron miners and steel workers who need income support until they obtain new employment. The assumption is that these workers should get better benefits than unemployment insurance affords. Even the stigma of unemployment is to be removed by calling the benefits "waiting allowances."

Each country which seeks to provide such benefits to its miners and steel workers must pass appropriate legislation and must bear half of the costs, drawing the remainder from the High Authority of the ECSC, now merged in the European Economic Community. France, Germany, and Belgium have been making such payments for several years, while Italy and the Netherlands first claimed the benefits of the amended article 56 of the ECSC Treaty in 1965, and Luxembourg, the remaining member, submitted its first case in 1966.

[4] Gösta Rehn, "Trends and Perspectives in Manpower Policy," in Margaret S. Gordon, ed., *Poverty in America*, San Francisco, 1965, p. 217; see also, A. D. Smith, "Active Manpower and Redundancy Policies: Their Costs and Benefits," *International Labour Review*, January–February 1967, pp. 49–60.

The EEC supports a member country's program if there has been a particularly heavy drop in permanent labor requirements in the coal, steel, or iron industries due to technological or marketing changes. By a liberal interpretation of its functions, the EEC holds that the reduced labor requirements need not arise solely from the introduction of the Common Market to qualify the member country for aid. While the EEC sets general conditions for the waiting allowance, the specific terms vary from country to country. The outstanding feature is the high proportion of previous wages which is paid.

In general, a waiting allowance can be paid for up to one year of unemployment. However, the new Italian plan called for a maximum of 15 months, while Holland provided a maximum ranging from 12 to 30 months, depending on the age and seniority of the unemployed miner or steel worker, and specifically favoring the hard-to-reemploy. Adjustments are made from time to time to meet the situation in particular countries and the needs of special groups, such as disabled or older miners and steel workers.

The ECSC High Authority agreement with West Germany contains a provision for public reimbursement of 50 percent of an unemployment payment made by a private or state coal or iron mine or steel works to its older or handicapped workers who are unemployed for over a year. If the enterprise pays the unemployed workers, the government will reimburse half of the payment, to a fixed maximum, from the 13th month of unemployment through the 36th; the ECSC bears half of the government's share. Even if the private enterprise does not make the payment, the government, with ECSC aid, will pay its half to the unemployed worker.

In all countries, the amount of the waiting allowance declines as the period of unemployment lengthens. Thus, the Italian plan starts by granting during the first three months a maximum of 85 percent of previous normal salary (with a maximum base amount), and descends by steps to 55 percent in the last six months.

In Belgium 100 percent of former wages can be paid in the first four months, dropping to 80 percent in the second four months, and to 60 percent in the last four months. Older and handicapped miners and steel workers who remain unemployed after receiving 365 days of benefits may be granted an extension of 183 days at 60 percent of the former wage. The categories eligible for the extended benefit are: blue-collar workers who are more than 50 years old; white-collar workers who are more than 40 years old; underground and surface miners with twenty years of underground work who are over 45; workers with a physical handicap of at least 30 percent or a mental handicap of 20 percent at the time of their dismissal.

Regular unemployment compensation payments, other social benefits, and occasional earnings are deducted from the monthly waiting allowance in most countries. Several plans call for the payment of additional cash to miners who formerly received free coal for household use from their companies.

These waiting allowances are superior in most cases to the benefits under ordinary unemployment insurance schemes. In any event, reemployment opportunities, including transfers within very large companies in these industries, have been so good that relatively little use has been made of the waiting allowance.

In Germany, for example, an analysis was made of 20,435 workers dismissed from 24 coal mines, 16 iron mines, and two steel mills from 1961 to 1963. Only slightly more than half, 11,016 cases, required any assistance from programs supported by ECSC. Of these, 1,434 received only the waiting allowance; the number would be larger if one included those who subsequently received another type of ECSC benefit during the year of eligibilty. In Belgium and France, relatively large numbers began with waiting allowances but during the year transferred to the wage supplement (*indemnité de réemploi*), which was designed to compensate workers when they accept employment which pays less than their former jobs.

Like unemployment insurance, the waiting allowance is predicated on the worker's availability for employment. In Belgium, for example, ineligibility for a waiting allowance arises from any of three circumstances: if a worker is unavailable for employment; if he is totally incapacitated or unable to perform any work; or if he refuses or abandons suitable employment or a training course.

Some countries have embellished the generous waiting allowance with a feature which is rarely found in unemployment insurance. This is an additional cash payment to those who accept employment before their waiting allowance runs out. The Netherlands wrote such a bonus into its new waiting allowance program, hoping to reduce the period of joblessness. The Belgian plan was not approved for subsidy by ECSC because the graduated bonus is largest for those who find work within the first month after receiving their waiting allowance and it decreases as the period of unemployment lengthens. By this arrangement the Belgian government has given the greatest financial inducement to those best able to find jobs quickly. As it happens, according to Belgian officials, 80 percent of the recipients of the bonus have been young, foreign workers. The ECSC would prefer a bonus plan which gives the highest percentages to older and handicapped workers.[5]

Programs to supplement unemployment benefits were established by nationalized industries in Great Britain. In the coal industry, the Coal Board made a weekly payment to men whose dismissals were due to closures and concentration of coal mines. Men of any age up to 65 were eligible for the special payment, but the maximum pe-

[5] European Coal and Steel Community, (ECSC), High Authority, *14e Rapport général sur l'activité de la Communauté. . .* , Luxembourg, 1966, pp. 320–31; *15e Rapport général. . .* , Luxembourg, 1967, pars. 388–407; ECSC, *Mesures de réadaptation appliquées en République Fédérale d'Allemagne, en Belgique et en France,* Luxembourg, 1966, pp. 9–11, 16–17, 25–26, 36–37; Belgium, Office National de l'Emploi, *Les aides accordées aux travailleurs licenciés des industries du charbon et de l'acier,* Brussels, pp. 6–13; Kurt Braun, "Labor Market Policies of the European Coal and Steel Community," *Lessons from Foreign Labor Market Policies,* vol. 4, *Selected Readings on Employment and Manpower,* Subcommittee on Employment and Manpower Committee on Labor and Public Welfare, U.S. Senate, 88th. Cong. 2nd. sess. Washington, 1964, pp. 1403–08; Interviews in Luxembourg with officials of ECSC; ILO, *International Differences in Factors Affecting Labour Mobility,* AUT/DOC/7, Geneva, 1965, pp. 244–45; Interviews with Belgium manpower officials; ECSC, Direction générale, Problèmes du Travail, Assainissement et Reconversion, *Aides spécifiques dont peuvent bénéficier les travailleurs âgés touchés par les fermetures,* Doc. No. 5558/1/66F, Luxembourg, October 1966; ILO, *Redundancy Procedures. . .* , pp. 137–41; Belgium, *Revue du Travail,* August 1968, pp. 1120–38.

riod was six months for men up to 59 years of age and it declined sharply above that age; only three weeks' pay was given to men over 64 because early pensions were also available to the older miners. The amount of the payment was equal to two-thirds of the standard grade rate for the man's former job, minus the unemployment benefit available to a single man. These weekly payments continued until a job was obtained, a reasonable offer of work was refused, or the benefit period ran out. To be eligible, a miner had to register at the employment exchange or be in receipt of sickness benefit. Since the end of 1965, the miner's weekly payment scheme has been superseded by the National Redundancy Payments Act.[6]

A distinct trend may be observed in western European countries toward making more adequate financial provision for unemployed workers, both in the percentage of former earnings allowed and in the duration of benefits. The hard-to-reemploy unemployed benefit from the general improvements as well as the special provisions which some countries have made for them alone. Perhaps the most significant and subtle alteration of attitude toward unemployment is the use of the term "waiting allowance" to describe the unemployment benefits which displaced coal and iron miners and steel workers receive in the Common Market countries. In 1968 Belgium extended this type of benefit to all workers in enterprises employing at least 25 workers, and government absorbed the entire cost.

REDUNDANCY PAYMENTS

The income support measures described above are supplemented by various arrangements to pay dismissed workers lump sums as compensation for their loss of job. Such severance or redundancy payments are made in addition to unemployment insurance and involve no obligation to seek work or training. A strong sense of property rights in the job has pervaded trade union discussions of redundancy payments, while arguments for social justice and sharing the burdens of progress have predominated in government, aca-

[6] Interviews and reports from the National Coal Board of Great Britain.

demic, and employer circles. The sense of urgency about making financial provision for those facing mass dismissals has been unaffected by the fact that relatively few displaced workers have had difficulty in securing new jobs promptly. The payments are seen realistically as a method of obtaining trade union acceptance of massive changes in job structures.

Severance payments were first developed privately through collective agreements, employer programs, and the payment of wages in lieu of statutory dismissal notices. Various nationalized industries in western European countries also adopted severance payments as they modernized equipment, closed down uneconomic operations, and made other adjustments in the postwar period which altered their manpower requirements.[7] What is new is the entry of government into the field and the imposition of compulsory schemes on employers.

Great Britain has the most highly developed redundancy measures which the nationalized coal, gas, electricity, transport, and atomic energy industries pioneered.[8] The nationalized coal industry, for example, made its own redundancy lump-sum payments for several years before it came under the national scheme at the end of 1965. In 1959, when no fixed retirement age existed in coal mining, the demand for coal had decreased markedly, leading to a dismissal of surplus workers, the imposition of compulsory retirement at 65, and the payment of a lump sum of up to £200 to each redundant miner. Men under 65 received smaller amounts, depending on age and years of service. During the year ending September 30, 1965,

[7] ILO, *Redundancy Procedures. . .* , pp. 125–32; ILO, *Manpower Adjustment Programmes: II. . .* , pp. 30–31.

[8] *Ministry of Labour Gazette*, February 1967, p. 130; July 1966, pp. 414–15, 381; February 1963, pp. 50–55; Ministry of Labour, *The Redundancy Payments Scheme*, London, 1965, 32pp.; OECD, International Trade Union Seminar on an Active Manpower Policy, *Supplement to the Final Report*, Paris, 1964, pp. 46–48; Interviews and Information from the British National Coal Board; *Labor Developments Abroad*, February 1967, p. 6; Frederic Meyers, *Ownership of Jobs: A Comparative Study*, Los Angeles, 1964, pp. 33–40; *Financial Times*, London, June 21, 1966; *The Times* (London), 1967, 1968, 1969, *passim*.

the Coal Board authorized lump-sum redundancy payments of £553,058 ($1,548,562) to 28,964 miners, of whom 27,581 were below the compulsory retirement age.

In other British industries the trade unions blazed the way by obtaining agreements stipulating lump-sum severance payments to those dismissed for economic causes. The trade unions at first held the view that redundancy payments should be sought only through voluntary collective agreements, but later they supported a compulsory statutory system, provided that it could be augmented by voluntary agreements which established higher rates of payment. A precedent for government action had been set by the Cotton Industry Act of 1959; among other purposes, the government's financial support to the contracting industry was used to compensate redundant workers. In the 1960s increasing numbers of private firms introduced voluntary redundancy payments schemes.

The British Redundancy Payments Act of 1965 gives a large number of workers the right to claim financial compensation from their employers if they are dismissed because their employers no longer conduct business at a given place or do not need the particular employee's type of work. Redundancy payments may be made to any worker under contract who has had at least two years' service with a particular employer, who customarily works at least 21 hours a week, and who is under 65 (male) or 60 (female) at the time of dismissal. Persistent short-time work or periods of lay-off which the employer cannot justify also qualify the worker for redundancy payments. The specific exceptions are such groups as registered dock workers, share fishermen, Crown servants, and employees in the National Health Service, employees with fixed-term contracts, close relatives of the employer. Some of these groups have their own redundancy compensation plans.

Redundancy is defined broadly. The worker's position is well protected by the statute and by tribunal and court interpretations. Termination of a contract by the employer or failure to renew an expiring contract constitutes dismissal, but a worker may leave during the period of obligatory dismissal notice without forfeiting his right to redundancy pay unless his employer contests his leaving. He must, however, wait for a dismissal notice before leaving if redundancy pay is to be claimed. In a dispute over the cause of dismissal, the onus lies on the employer to show that the employee was not discharged as redundant. Unreasonable refusal of an employer's offer of renewal of contract or of suitable alternative work prevents a worker from receiving redundancy pay.

However, workers who declined to move to a new job 120 miles away were awarded redundancy pay by the Court of Appeal. The Coal Board has complained that its manpower is being depleted by the availability of redundancy pay to dismissed miners who refuse a job in another area. A shipyard welder who rejected a new pay and productivity contract which would have required him to work without a mate was upheld by the High Court in his claim for redundancy pay. Thus, the interpretations of "unreasonable refusal" of alternative work have been favorable to individual workers but somewhat negative on encouraging labor mobility, the removal of restrictive labor practices, transfer of firms, and rational manpower utilization. Nevertheless, the government maintains that the existence of redundancy payments has made it possible to reduce staffs without industrial friction. Little effect has been seen on decisions to institute labor-saving devices and methods.

Some anomalies have appeared as a result of the broad coverage of the law. Workers have received redundancy pay when their firms were sold to new owners, even though the workers were retained in their old jobs. Dismissed workers who have been rehired for their old jobs within a month or two have qualified for redundancy pay. When the Rootes Group of automobile factories discharged 400 men in December 1966 and rehired 180 the next month, the trade unions maintained that the reduced work load should have been handled by work-sharing instead of dismissal. But management claimed that the favorable reception of the new car models in January could not have been predicted. When a company discharges workers as redundant and soon afterward advertises for workers of the same category, the government may investigate. But, as the law is written, there is nothing intrinsically wrong in such action.

Disputed cases have been numerous. In 1967 there were some

10,000 cases of which 7,223 were settled by industrial tribunals and 2,425 were disposed of without a hearing. About three months was required to process applications to the tribunals because of a shortage of chairmen.

The redundancy payment is a lump-sum, tax-free amount calculated on the basis of years of service with the last employer, age at dismissal, and the last weekly pay (with a maximum allowable base). The initial payment schedule gave a redundant worker one-half week's wages for each year of service performed between 18 and 21 years of age, one week's wages for each year between 22 and 40 and thereafter one and one-half week's wages for each year. Entitlement to redundancy pay is gradually reduced for men when they reach 63 until it ends at 65 when the old-age pension begins. At most, a redundancy payment could provide 30 week's pay with a total maximum payment of £1,200.

Employers who provide lump-sum payments or pensions within a stipulated period after dismissal under private redundancy plans may, under certain conditions, offset them against the government program. If voluntary agreements offer superior terms, the firms concerned may secure exemption from the national scheme, but they may in no case pay less than the statute provides. A survey by the British Institute of Management in 1968 indicated that 50 percent of the firms paid more than the Redundancy Act provides. Workers do not lose any part of their unemployment insurance rights nor is the waiting period for benefits changed when they receive redundancy pay.

The financing of the redundancy payments scheme has proved to be troublesome in the first years of operation. Although the government legislated the program, it provided that employers bear the entire cost. As deficits have mounted, government has resisted suggestions that it assist the Redundancy Fund. In this uncharted area, it has been difficult to forecast the amount required to compensate all claims. About twice as many redundancy payments have been made as was anticipated and the average payment has been larger than was expected, partially because wage rates have been rising and partially because workers with long service have been prominent among the redundant.

The Redundancy Fund is financed by a flat-rate contribution by employers for each employee, with a different rate for men and women; the rate for male employees has been at least twice that for women. Employers who make redundancy payments to dismissed employees apply to the Redundancy Fund for rebates which cover a portion of the employer's costs. In February 1969 the employer's rebates were decreased to 50 percent of his payment and a uniform rebate rate was introduced for all years of a worker's service in an effort to meet the Fund's deficit of £17 million and to discourage the firing of older men which had been less costly to the employer under the original differential rebate system. Employers have been uneasy about the repeated increases in their contributions and the decrease in their rebates, but their proposals to curtail workers' benefits as a means of meeting the Fund's deficit were rejected. As of early 1969 this part of the formula was as stated in the 1965 Act.

Between December 1965 and October 1968, 587,000 redundancy payments were made at a total cost of $295.2 millions. The average payment has been £150 to £250 at various periods in the first three years. The industrial distribution of the redundancy payments indicates that the industries with the largest number of employees tend to have the most redundancies, but the conformity is far from per-

Redundancy Payments 1966

Industry	Number of Recipients	Rank of Industry in Number of Employees June 1966
Construction	19,200	5
Engineering, elec.	16,200	3
Distributive trades	15,000	1
Vehicles	11,900	8
Misc. Services	8,400	4
Transport & Commun.	8,200	6
Textiles	7,300	10
Paper, printing, publ.	6,100	11
Food, drink, tobacco	5,900	9

Source: Ministry of Labour Gazette, February 1967, pp. 102–103, 130.

fect. The nine industries with the greatest number of redundancy payments in 1966 were among the top eleven in terms of the number of employees (employed and unemployed) in June 1966. Two industries which do not appear on this list offer more than average security to their employees, who tend to be service rather than production workers. They are the second largest industry in terms of employees—financial, professional, and scientific services—and the seventh—public administration services. The 1967 and 1968 records are fairly similar to that for 1966, but in 1968 mining and quarrying was among the leaders.

The ratio of the annual number of redundancy payments to the cumulative total of workers becoming unemployed in each industry would be an even better measure of the industrial incidence of redundancy payments, but such data are unavailable. It is likely that the larger redundancy payments go disproportionately to skilled and nonmanual workers in the more prosperous areas. Adrian Sinfield's study of unemployment in Shields, a northeastern depressed town, showed that only a small proportion of his sample would have qualified for redundancy payments.

Certain firms may use the Redundancy Fund to a greater extent than is customary in their industry. Employers and their organizations have asked for studies to discover which enterprises are passing some of the costs of poor management and personnel practices on to the Redundancy Fund.

Concern has also been expressed that the redundancy payments scheme has fostered early retirement among men who are able to work until 65. Employers may be tempted to discharge older workers who have been retained out of a sense of obligation, if they are able to obtain substantial redundancy payments. Men nearing retirement age may choose to leave before they become 63 in order to get the maximum redundancy payment. They may be further encouraged by the availability of unemployment insurance benefits and private pension plans. Surveys show that employers claim to be using the principle of "last in-first out" in establishing redundancy lists, but the Redundancy Fund reported that 70 percent of its beneficiaries in 1968 were over 41 years old.

Outright collusion to give redundancy payments to younger workers has been charged, but the government denies that any number of cases can be found. The redundancy payments have been credited with an effect on the labor market, giving dismissed workers the freedom to shop around for new jobs. However, the official records show that one-third of the workers receiving redundancy payments find new work immediately and another third are settled in four or five weeks. It also is claimed that workers who know they are to be dismissed do not look for or accept new work until they actually receive their discharge notice because of the possible loss of redundancy pay.[9] The OECD examiners of British manpower policy questioned whether the relatively large amounts of redundancy pay were in balance with the lesser amounts provided for such positive labor market activities as retraining and geographical mobility.

From the outset, the basic principles of the British redundancy legislation have been criticized. Cash payments without provision for training or reemployment are said to inhibit the adaptation of workers to economic change. And, it is said, if the object of redundancy payments is to compensate for income deficiencies and inequalities, such payments are less effective than other economic policies. Finally, while it may be suitable that compensation for loss of property rights in a job should be negotiated by trade unions, such measures should not be legislated by government. John Pardoe, a Liberal M.P., repeated some of these points and added some new ones in an evaluation at the end of 1968. He suggested differential charges on employers on a similar basis to experience rating in the unemployment compensation systems of American states. He opposed the lump-sum grant and urged a reform of all unemployment legislation in order to provide an income guarantee of at least two-thirds of a worker's normal earnings during unemployment, rising to 100 percent while a worker is in an approved training program.[10]

[9] *The Times* (London), 1967, 1968, 1969, *passim.*

[10] Jack Wiseman and Keith Hartley, "Redundancy and Public Policy," *Moorgate and Wall Street,* Spring 1965, pp. 45–66; *The Times* (London) December 30, 1968; *Monthly Labor Review,* April 1969, p. 63; *OECD Observer,* August 1969, p. 17.

Despite these strictures, other countries have been legislating redundancy payments. In 1966 Belgium strengthened and formalized earlier legislation of 1960 which had provided a temporary scheme. The new law affects firms which employed an average of at least 50 workers during the previous year and are closing down completely. Under the act, a firm is defined as a "technical working unit" and a closing occurs when "on the final cessation of the principal activity of the undertaking, or any department of the undertaking, the number of workers falls below one-quarter of the average number of workers employed there over the calendar year preceding the year in which the closure occurs."

Workers with five years of service at the time of closure are eligible for compensation for the loss of their jobs if their dismissal occurs within twelve months before or after the closure and their employer does not immediately find them alternative employment which lasts at least six minths at their same wage rate and seniority. Workers actually involved in the closure procedures can apply for dismissal compensation as long as three years after the closure. The Belgian scheme is generally more limited than the British, which covers individual and group dismissals as well as closures.

Compensation is payable at the rate of 1000 B.fr. ($20) for each year of service to a maximum of 20,000 B.fr. ($400), with periodic adjustment to changes in the retail price index. The redundancy payment is additional to any unemployment benefit or payment in lieu of notice that may be made. Each employer is responsible for his own payments. If the employer fails to make the closure payment out of his own funds within fifteen days of the cessation of a worker's contract, a Fund administered by the National Employment Office and based on additional contributions by employers to either the National Security Office or the National Mineworkers' Retirement Fund will compensate the workers.

Unlike the British redundancy payments scheme, the Belgian Fund does not cover any of the costs, but merely pays for defaulting or delinquent employers who are expected to make reimbursement. From June 1960 through 1966, the Belgian Fund paid out 33,945,986 B.fr. on behalf of 69 enterprises which closed down and failed to pay their workers. In this period only 1,529,201 B.fr. had been recovered from the delinquent employers, over half of whom had been engaged in textile manufacturing and construction activities. In 1967 alone, the fund paid out 22,990,475 B.fr. on behalf of defaulting employers. The total number of Belgian workers who have benefited from dismissal payments is not known.

Sweden established fairly general severance payments in 1964 through an agreement between the leading confederations of employers and trade unions. Specifically intended to aid older workers who are released as a result of shutdowns or major cutbacks, the severance payments are confined to workers over 50 with ten years' service or more with the same employer, or those whose age plus years of service total 65 or more. Workers over 62 need not be unemployed to qualify for severance payments, and those who obtain casual, short-term, or much lower-paid work also can qualify while at work. But, in general, the severance payments are given to dismissed workers who are unemployed. Eligibility continues for five years after dismissal, enabling those whose employment situation deteriorates later on to claim compensation.

The payments are made out of a single nation-wide fund financed entirely by employers' contributions of 0.1 percent of their annual wage bill. The maximum possible severance payment is estimated to be 11,000 Sw. kr. for a worker of 62 with many years of service. A fixed amount is paid for each year of service, supplemented by a variable amount according to the age of the redundant worker. Little used in the first years, the severance payments scheme proved to be of great value from 1967 on, as the number of plant closures, mergers, and reorganizations mounted.

In France severance pay has been provided in an increasing number of collective agreements, but usually for salaried staff. By an ordinance of July 1967, the provisions were extended to all wage earners in covered industries if they had over two years' service in the firm.[11]

[11] Belgium, Office National de l'Emploi, (ONEM), *Rapport Annuel, 1965,* Brussels, 1966, p. 25; *Rapport Annuel, 1966,* Brussels, 1967, p. 43; *Moniteur Belge-Belgisch Staatsblad,* 2 July 1966, No. 127, p. 6879; Italy, Act. No.

Italy passed dismissal legislation in 1965 concerning individuals; the law provides that "every employee whose contract of employment has been terminated shall be entitled to a length-of-service bonus." Collective dismissals in cases of staff reductions, retrenchment, or redundancy were specifically excluded from the law. For a quarter of a century Italy has had a generous scheme under the Civil Code for compensating dismissal and voluntary leaving. The amount of the payments are determined by collective agreements, with a minimum set by law or the courts. It has been said that the generosity of these dismissal payments has held back the development of adequate unemployment insurance benefits.[12]

West Germany has introduced the beginnings of a redundancy payments program with its statutory provision that employers who terminate the contract of workers over 45 must pay them a lump sum amount of up to 18 months pay.

The High Authority of the European Coal and Steel Community and now the EEC give financial support to member countries which provide a lump-sum payment as compensation for loss of employment in the mines or steel works. This payment (*indemnité forfaitaire*) is designed to aid older or handicapped miners and those living in areas in which it is difficult to obtain reemployment. In West Germany, the chief user of this type of benefit, the payment usually is made in conjunction with special miners' pensions provided through German social legislation.

The High Authority also supported a French program in 1962 to give severance pay to dismissed coal miners from the Centre-Midi region. For miners who were leaving the industry for good, a flat sum of three months' to six months' pay was granted, depending on the man's length of service; a small bonus for service at the coal face was added. While the ECSC paid only on behalf of miners with at least ten years of service, the French program offered redundancy

604, July 15, 1966; ILO, *Manpower Adjustment Programmes: I.* . . , pp. 28–29; France, Ordinance on Employment 67/581, July 1967; ILO, *Redundancy Procedures.* . . , pp. 98–99, 166–67; ILO, *Manpower Adjustment Programmes: II.* . . , pp. 30–31.

[12] ILO, *Redundancy Procedures.* . . , pp. 99–100, 181, 182.

pay to all who lost their jobs in these mines and who would not become coal miners elsewhere.[13] Similar provisions were made for other dismissed coal miners whose jobs were permanently destroyed.

The growth of programs to provide lump-sum redundancy payments has led to some theorizing about the effects on management practices. While conceding that generous severance pay, along with other financial benefits, induces workers to accept the need for mobility, Charles P. Kindleberger raised the possibility that employers facing high severance costs would be encouraged to substitute machinery for labor, resort to overtime rather than new hirings, and hoard rather than dismiss surplus labor.[14] No country's redundancy payments have been either so generous or prolonged to permit a test of the theory.

It is likely that the lump-sum redundancy payment will continue to win support and will appear increasingly in governmental programs as well as in collective bargaining contracts and the formal and informal policies of employers. The hard-to-reemploy have a particular interest in and need for such additional financial support. If the granting of redundancy payments should ever be tied to enrollment for retraining or registration for employment—a distant prospect at present—the hard-to-reemploy might require special treatment. The integration of redundancy payments with manpower policy objectives remains an open issue.

EARLY RETIREMENT PENSIONS

Even when labor shortages are acute and the demand for labor of all kinds is high, some older workers who are about to lose their

[13] ECSC, *15e Rapport général*, Luxembourg, 1967, para. 268; ECSC, *Mesures de réadaptation*. . . , pp. 9, 10, 17; ECSC, Direction générale, Problèmes du Travail, Assainissement et Reconversion, *Aides spécifiques dont peuvent bénéficier les travailleurs âgés touchés par les fermetures*, pp. 3, 13, 14; ILO, *Manpower Adjustment Programmes: I*. . . , pp. 24, 101; ILO, *Redundancy Procedures*. . . , pp. 166–67.

[14] Charles P. Kindleberger, *Europe's Postwar Growth*, Cambridge, Mass., 1967, p. 169.

jobs may realistically be judged unlikely to obtain work again before they reach retirement age. The problems of advancing age may be complicated by residence in a region of declining industries, low or out-moded educational attainment and work skills, and physical or mental disabilities.

As yet, the approach to this problem in western Europe has been highly selective and divorced from general old-age pension programs. Any suggestion to lower the standard retirement age in national pension schemes is generally opposed, although most countries permit optional early retirement at reduced pension rates in certain circumstances.

In countries which have had labor shortages in recent years, the emphasis has been on retaining those about to retire and encouraging the return to work of old-age pensioners. This is done by various means: offering a higher deferred pension to those who work past retirement age, making the pension independent of retirement or income, exempting entirely or increasing the amount of earnings or days of work permitted without reduction of old-age pensions, exempting employers from making contributions to the pension fund on behalf of employed pensioners, and permitting voluntary exclusion from social security contributions by part-time workers.

Germany has established the occupational disability pension (*Berufsunfähigkeitsrente*), which enables partially disabled workers to be reemployed without loss of pension; the regular disability pension (*Erwerbsunfähigkeitsrente*) would be forfeited if the recipient obtained a regular job. Denmark, which in 1937 had reduced the general pension age to 60 years because of heavy unemployment, raised it again in 1956 to 67 years; the pensionable age in Norway was set at 70 in the 1966 National Insurance Act. All general pension action is in the direction of encouraging older people to continue at work.[15]

[15] Sven O. Hydén, *Flexible Retirement Age,* OECD: Paris, 1966; OECD, Regional Seminar, The Employment of Older Workers, *Final Report,* Paris, 1966, pp. 5–6, 9, 33; OECD, Manpower and Social Affairs Committee, *Annual Reports, Belgium, 1964,* MO (64) 10/03, p. 33; *Germany, 1964,* MO (64) 10/01, p. 32; *Germany 1965* MO (65) 16/01, p. 4; Detlev Zöllner,

Sweden had been opposed to early pensions other than as a voluntary choice by individuals who elect to retire on reduced pensions. The tripartite committee on labor market policy, reporting in 1965 to the Swedish Parliament, discussed the introduction of early retirement pensions for older workers who are just short of the pensionable age, become unemployed in sparsely populated areas, and are not likely to benefit from mobility grants or industrial location activities. Even emergency public works are limited in such areas because of the difficulty of finding economically acceptable projects. The committee therefore recommended that a special inquiry be launched on the subject of improved insurance protection and early retirement pensions for older workers in sparsely populated areas.

In subsequent discussions of the committee's report and in the government's statement on labor market policy, the subject of early pensions did not reappear. Instead, in conformity with basic Swedish views, emphasis was placed on the provision of jobs for everyone who wished and was able to work.[16] But as unemployment began to increase in 1966, Swedish trade unions (LO) and others raised the issue again, requesting "improved opportunities for pre-

Social Legislation in the Federal Republic of Germany, Bad Godesberg, 1964, pp. 36, 47; Kirsten Rudfeld, *Welfare of the Aged in Denmark,* Copenhagen, 1963, pp. 37–39; OECD, Manpower and Social Affairs Committee, *Manpower Problems and Policies in the Netherlands,* MO (66) 18, Paris, 1966, p. 106; Carl G. Uhr, *Sweden's Social Security System,* U.S. Department of Health, Education and Welfare, Social Security Administration, Research Report no. 14, Washington, 1966, p. 44; Norway, National Insurance Act no. 12, 17 June 1966; ILO, *Manpower Adjustment Programmes: I. . . ,* p. 163; Juanita M. Kreps, *Lifetime Allocation of Work and Leisure,* U.S. Department of Health, Education and Welfare, Social Security Administration, Research Report no. 22, Washington, 1968, pp. 29–33; ILO, *Redundancy Procedures. . . ,* pp. 69–70.

[16] Sweden, *Arbetsmarknandspolitik,* pp. 413–16; National Labour Market Board, *Modern Swedish Labour Market Policy,* pp. 42, 66, 88–89; interviews with manpower officials in Sweden, France, Belgium, and West Germany; OECD, *Age and Employment,* Paris, 1962, pp. 11–13; Jack Stieber, "Manpower Adjustments to Automation and Technological Change in Western Europe," in *Adjusting to Change,* Appendix vol. III, Technology and the American Economy, Washington, 1966, pp. 79, 90–93, 105.

retirement pensions" for redundant workers. While a formal system has not been introduced, the special adjustment allowance introduced in 1968 and described above as unemployment benefits, may mark the beginning of a selective pre-pension program.[17]

Despite a general reluctance to lower the pensionable age, specific measures have been developed in individual countries to assist the early retirement of workers under special circumstances. West Germany grants old-age pensions to men of 60 who have registered as unemployed for the previous full year; the rate of pension is determined by the number of years of contribution.

In several countries coal miners are singled out for special early pensions because of the heavy incidence of injuries and illness and the secular decline of manpower needs in the wake of technological changes, competition from other fuels, and market shifts. Early retirement on pension for miners is particularly well developed for West German miners. Since the age structure of workers in the German coal mines has been much more heavily weighted by older workers than, for example, in the French or Belgian industries, German provision of early retirement is especially valuable to hard-to-reemploy miners.

German mineowners are said to follow a deliberate policy of dismissing older workers in order to reduce the average age in the mines. Table XIII.1 shows the relative importance of dismissals of older miners in Germany, compared with France and Belgium. Significantly, even after substantial numbers of older coal miners had been dismissed in Germany, the proportion of employed workers over 50 was higher in 1964 than in 1957, and was about twice the ratio in France and Belgium in both years.

Belgium is known for heavy unemployment among older workers, but the age distribution of its dismissed coal miners seems to belie this generalization. The low percentage of older workers among the dismissed Belgian coal miners is explained by the heavy concentra-

[17] Meidner, "The Employment Problems of Individuals and Groups," p. 7; The Swedish Institute, *The Status of Women in Sweden,* Stockholm, 1968, p. 81; National Labour Market Board, *Arbetsmarknadspolitiken 1969–70,* Stockholm, 1968, pp. 34–36.

TABLE XIII.1. Employment and Dismissal of Older Workers in Coal, Iron, and Steel: West Germany, France and Belgium, 1960–1965

	Total Number of Workers (Sept. 30, 1965)	Numbers Dismissed Under ECSC Coverage [a]	Percent of Dismissed over 50 Years old	Percent of Employed Workers 50 or over (1957)	Percent of Employed Workers 50 or over (1964)	Foreign Workers as Percent Total Workers (Sept. 30, 1965)
Coal Mines	538,000	42,412	—	15.0 [b]	15.7 [b]	—
W. Germany	315,300	30,851	46.0	15.4 / 19.4	15.5 Ruhr / 16.2 Saar	6.9
France	153,600	1,476	9.1	7.1 / 7.1	8.8 Lorraine / 7.5 Centre-Midi	19.8
Belgium	69,100	10,085	13.4	6.3	7.6 South	48.9
Iron Mines	23,400	6,768	—	n.a.	n.a.	n.a.
W. Germany	6,700	4,560	29.0	n.a.	n.a.	n.a.
France	16,700	2,208	13.0	n.a.	n.a.	n.a.
Belgium	—	—	—	—	—	—
Steel Works	381,200	3,858	—	23.9 [b]	(1963) 24.1 [b]	—
W. Germany	203,500	2,829	38.0	24.8	25.7	7.2
France	126,300	524	19.5	23.0	21.3	27.3
Belgium	51,400	505	41.6	26.7	27.1	22.4

373

[a] Time period covered varies. The longest period covered is 1960–64.
[b] For the entire European Coal and Steel Community.

Source: European Coal and Steel Community, High Authority, Mesures de réadaptation appliquées en République Fédérale d'Allemagne, en Belgique et en France, Luxembourg, 1966, pp. 14, 24, 34; European Coal and Steel Community, High Authority, 14e Rapport général sur l'activité de la Communauté. . . , Luxembourg, 1966, pp. 302–309, 459.

tion of young, foreign workers in the Belgian coal mines. About 55 percent of the dismissed Belgian coal miners were foreigners, against less than 2 percent in Germany and about 11 percent in France. However, the proportion of foreigners retained in the Belgian coal mines was almost the same as their dismissal rate; the Belgian dismissals therefore did not reflect discrimination against foreign workers. But, taking account of the youth of Belgian coal miners, the dismissals cannot be considered favorable to older workers. In the Belgian steel industry, where 500 of the 505 dismissed workers were Belgians, 41.6 percent were over 50 years old, a higher ratio than in either France or Germany.

The comparatively low percentage of older dismissed workers in France may be a reflection of the strong attitudes on continuity of employment which have been described earlier. In the French steel industry, workers over 50 actually seem to be a lower proportion among the dismissed than among the employed.[18]

The large number of older workers who have been dismissed from the German coal mines is both the cause and consequence of German provision for early retirement. Under the Miner's Special Scheme (*Knappschaft*), early retirement on pension can occur under varying conditions and ages: 40 to 50, at 50, at 55, and at 60. A miner who becomes physically unfit for underground work at any age gets an additional pension (*Bergmannsrente*) above the usual disability pension. The same arrangement is made for a miner over 50 years old who has worked for 25 years, of which at least 15 years were at the coal face.

In 1963 a new benefit was introduced for able-bodied miners over 55 with a prescribed qualifying period of work. If they were forced to end their work in the mines for any economic reason, but in particular because of rationalization, they were to get a benefit (*Knappschaftsausgleichsleistung*) equal in amount to the miners' occupational disability pension (*Berufsunfähigkeitsrente*). A miner of

[18] ECSC, *Mesures de réadaptation*. . . , pp. 14–17, 24–34; ILO, *Manpower Adjustment Programmes: I*. . . , p. 24; *Labor Developments Abroad*, January 1968, pp. 15–16; ILO, *Redundancy Procedures*. . . , p. 70; ILO, *Manpower Adjustment Programmes: II*. . . , pp. 31–33.

60 who has been unemployed for a full year and has 25 years of qualifying work, 15 of them at the coal face, is also eligible to receive an early old-age pension. In 1966, to speed the retirement of additional older miners men of 55 or more who voluntarily left coal mining after a stipulated number of years were also entitled to the early retirement pension. [19]

These benefits are sufficiently attractive to older miners and reemployment is sufficiently difficult to encourage many German miners to retire from the labor market when they become redundant. In order to assist those who would be eligible for early pensions, the European Coal and Steel Community shares the costs of providing a lump-sum redundancy payment, previously described. The extent to which dismissed German miners have accepted early pensions rather than unemployment allowances can be seen from ECSC data. About twice as many dismissed German miners received the lump-sum payment as received both the unemployment waiting allowance and the reemployment allowance. In 1963 and early 1964, 75 percent of total German expenditures on programs supported by ECSC were for lump-sum payments to miners planning early retirement.[20]

The British early retirement pension scheme for miners permits men aged 60 or over with 10 years of qualifying work to receive an immediate pension of £1 per week for life; at 65 the national old-age pension is added. At the end of 1965, 1,855 miners were receiving an early retirement pension, compared with 90,699 regular pensioners over 65. Miners aged 55 to 59 can retire with a deferred pension, payable at 65 when their regular old-age pension is payable. These early pensions are not revoked if the coal miner finds work outside of the nationalized industry, but if he returns to em-

[19] ILO, *Manpower Adjustment Programmes: I. . .* , pp. 102–103; OECD, Manpower and Social Affairs Committee, *Annual Reports, Germany, 1964,* MO (64) 10/01, p. 33; Zöllner, *Social Legislation in the Federal Republic of Germany,* pp. 36–38; ECSC, *Mesures de réadaptation. . .* , pp. 17, 19, 20; Interviews with officials of the Federal Institute for Labor Placement and Unemployment Insurance (BAVAV); ECSC, *Aides spécifiques. . .* , pp. 1, 2.

[20] ECSC, *Aides spécifiques. . .* , pp. 16, 17; OECD, Manpower and Social Affairs Committee, *Annual Reports, Germany, 1964,* MO (64) 10/01, p. 19.

ployment with the Coal Board, he forfeits his early pension. At the end of September 1965, 29,430 miners received deferred pensions, a very substantial increase over the previous year. Some miners who receive redundancy payments may elect to receive early pensions after they have exhausted their unemployment benefits.[21]

In several other countries, early retirement pensions are available to coal miners, railwaymen, and others through social legislation which the ECSC may support. In Italy workers may retire at 55 from mines, quarries, and peat bogs, provided that they have had a certain number of qualifying years of employment and currently have no gainful occupation. France grants early retirement pensions to miners with 30 years' service in certain coal fields in the Centre-Midi. Many private companies also have such provisions.[22]

A more generalized approach to early retirement is taken by the French National Employment Fund, established by law in December 1963. The Fund is not an operating agency, but its resources are used for specific purposes. The Fund provides several types of allowances, some similar to those originated by the European Coal and Steel Community but without limitations on the industries which qualify. With regard to early retirement, the French National Employment Fund supports pre-pensions for some workers over 60, generally 62 or more. The workers must be involved in mass dismissals which occur in regions or occupations with unemployment problems, and the older workers must be personally unsuitable for retraining or placement.

These workers cannot receive the early retirement benefits unless their employer initiates a request and signs a contract with the National Employment Fund. While individual enterprises sign the con-

[21] Interviews with officials of the British National Coal Board, June 1966; Great Britain, National Coal Board, *Reports and Accounts,* 1964–65, Mineworkers' Pension, Industrial Injuries, Supplementary Benefits and Special Fatal Accident Schemes, pp. 6, 8, 9.

[22] Margaret S. Gordon, *Retraining annd Labor Adjustment in Western Europe,* Washington, 1965, p. 98; OECD, *Manpower Problems and Policies in the Netherlands,* MO (66) 18, p. 39; ECSC, *Aides spécifiques. . . ,* pp. 2, 14, 16; ILO, *Manpower Adjustment Programmes: I. . . ,* pp. 24, 103–104, 163–64; ILO, *Redundancy Procedures. . . ,* pp. 70–71, 81–85, 87.

tracts, they generally follow the draft form developed by the employers' federations. The trade unions are also apprised of the progress of the contract negotiations.

The contract covers the financial responsibilities of the various parties which may include, besides the government and the firm, the bipartite (industry-trade union) Association for Employment in Industry and Commerce (ASSEDIC) which operates the unemployment insurance system, and, occasionally, the National Interprofessional Union for Employment in Commerce and Industry (UNEDIC) which coordinates the fifty or so ASSEDIC units and assures the financial security of the units. The obligation of the UNEDIC to contribute toward pre-pensions has been contested by that organization. In addition, the contributions on behalf of the worker and employer to the supplementary old-age pension scheme are paid by the National Employment Fund. The requirement of a contract is to insure that the enterprise will bear part of the cost of the pre-pension and will not "abuse the fund's facilities in order to lay off large numbers of workers with a light heart."

For those who do become eligible for the pre-pension, the amount may not be lower than the unemployment allowances otherwise payable and an attempt is made to maintain income at 75 to 95 percent of the former wage (based on a 40-hour week). The pre-pension is paid until the worker reaches 65 years and three months or goes on regular old-age pension. It is a distinct advantage that pre-pensioners are no longer required to register at the employment office and are not considered available for work.

Some calculations of the shares borne by the various parties indicate that for unskilled workers, the government, ASSEDIC, and firm divide the costs of the pre-pension almost equally, but that government pays a relatively small share for highly-paid workers. The financial burden on firms, such as those in the textile industry, has deterred some from concluding agreements to establish pre-pensions.

Since firms which are going out of business are among those making contracts with the National Employment Fund, the Fund has arranged that such firms make lump-sum payments before their dissolution. The 1966 annual report of the Fund pointed with some pride to the fact that a contract had been made with a Chamber of Commerce in one case where the member firm was bankrupt; the acceptance of financial responsibility by the Chamber for the pre-pensions of a member's employees was cited as an admirable spirit of solidarity.

In its first year of operation, 1964, the National Employment Fund spent about 264,000 F.f. ($52,800) for its share of pre-pension payments to 1,222 workers. Some 4,000 workers were involved in the mass dismissals, which ultimately yielded 1,335 beneficiaries of pre-pensions under the eleven agreements signed in 1964. In seven of the eleven agreements, over fifty workers were involved in each dismissal. The industries most severely affected were naval shipbuilding installations along the Atlantic coast, particularly in southern Brittany at Nantes and Saint-Nazaire, where alternative employment is scarce.

The second year of operations produced a somewhat smaller total number of pre-pensioners. But these 968 pre-pensioners excluded persons covered by seven agreements which were in course of negotiation at the end of the year and whose conclusion was expected to yield about the same total number of pre-pensioners as in 1964 under 22 separate agreements. The predominance of naval shipbuilding in the dismissals leading to pre-pensions continued, but metallurgy and textiles contributed some cases, giving a wider geographic distribution to the program. Increased use of the program in 1966 and 1967 was associated with a rising total number of dismissals under the jurisdiction of the National Employment Fund. In 1966, 36 agreements provided pre-pensions for 3,086 of the 8,000 dismissed workers in the covered firms. The 96 agreements in 1967 designated 6,595 pre-pensioners out of 28,995 dismissed workers. A substantial portion of the agreements in 1967 concerned dismissed workers over 60 from the Allied Bases of NATO which were removed from France. Over the first four years, heavy industry was responsible for about one-third of all agreements, reflecting the older labor force in these industries and their reduced labor needs.

Even though nongovernmental sources contribute to the pre-pensions, the government's manpower officials review dismissal plans with great care and, during the negotiations which precede signing of contracts attempt, with frequent success, to convince an enterprise to retain a certain number of workers over 60, to maintain at their old jobs workers between 50 and 60 who would be hard-to-reemploy, and to give larger severance payments to the displaced older workers than are provided by collective agreements.

On the basis of the early experience with French pre-pensions, one might conclude that an insignificant number of workers would qualify each year. However, the program has found great favor with the trade unions, and the demand for retirement at 60 figured prominently in the nation-wide disputes of 1968. It has been justified by others for depressed areas and industries.[23] If the definition of "region or occupation of severe unemployment" is stretched or removed, pre-pensions might become general. In that event, many thousands of new pre-pensioners might be created each year. This would be contrary to the original intention of the National Employment Fund that early retirement, a negative labor market policy, should be secondary to the other positive measures promoted by the Fund.

The possibility that pre-pensions under the National Employment Fund may become widespread makes more serious the various criticisms of the scheme voiced by high manpower officials in France. They pointed out that an unfair discrimination is made between victims of mass dismissals who are eligible for pre-pensions and other older workers whose individual dismissals at 60 may be equally or more burdensome. Thus far each mass dismissal qualifying for a pre-pension contract has involved at least twenty workers, but in some cases as few as four of those dismissed have been candidates for the pre-pension, according to the detailed listing of pre-pension agreements of the National Employment Fund in 1964 and 1965.

Another criticism is that the rate of pre-pension is considerably higher than the reduced pension available to a worker who voluntarily retires at age 60 under the national old-age pension scheme. The fear of manpower officials is that the remedy for these defects will

[23] ILO, *Redundancy Procedures.* . . , p. 71.

be in the direction of encouraging early retirement throughout the country by liberalizing the 60–65 pension in the regular old-age plan as well as by extensions of the pre-pension of the National Employment Fund.[24]

The basic idea of the French pre-pension is attractive—that there should be a national scheme, possibly outside the regular old-age pension system, to provide adequately for those older workers who are truly unable to find new employment, but have not reached the age for full retirement. The idea should be particularly appealing in a country whose labor supply is growing rapidly enough to avoid concern about losses of manpower through early retirement.

Even in countries where manpower shortages lead to general emphasis on drawing upon older workers, some of the older unemployed are not likely to find new jobs, and they must rely upon a variety of income supplementation programs until they reach the standard retirement age. A selective pre-pension scheme covering all industries could accept only those older workers who are unlikely to find work but are not eligible for disability benefits. It could provide more adequate benefits than a reduced regular pension, maintain full eligibility for the regular old-age pension, and eliminate the discouraging and painful requirement of weekly registration at the employment office which must be fulfilled by those in France or Germany who are on extended unemployment benefits or in Belgium on unlimited unemployment insurance payments.

Quite another kind of encouragement to early retirement is found in a few western European countries with regard to farmers who

[24] Ministère du Travail, *Rapport sur la situation de l'emploi . . . 1965,* Paris, 1965, pp. 18–19, 23–24; Ministère des Affaires Sociales, *Rapport sur la situation de l'emploi . . . 1966,* Paris, 1966, pp. 29–31; Ambassade de France, Service de Presse et d'Information, *French Affaires,* no. 179, 1965, pp. 8, 11; Gordon, *Retraining. . . ,* pp. 182–85; Interviews with officials of the Manpower Directorate and Commissariat du Plan in France; ECSC, *Aides spécifiques. . . ,* pp. 10–13; F. Meyers, "The Role of Collective Bargaining in France. . . ," *British Journal of Industrial Relations,* November 1965, pp. 385–87; ILO, *Manpower Adjustment Programmes: I. . . ,* pp. 23–24; ILO, *Redundancy Procedures. . . ,* pp. 71, 132–34, 184–86.

have grown too old either to work their farms or transfer to industry, and who find it difficult to sell out because of the decline of values in their farming area or for other economic reasons. Their farms may be purchased by the government under regional development or land-use plans. This is important to farmers who are covered by some sort of retirement pension, as in the German Green Plan, as well as to those who rely chiefly on the proceeds of the sale of their farms to carry them through retirement.

Since 1964 the Netherlands has offered owner/operators of small farms who wish to withdraw from active farming a termination allowance. A monthly payment, starting at 50 years and rising in amount to 64, serves as an inducement to retirement from farming and perhaps from the labor force as well. The amount is sharply reduced at 65 when the old-age pension presumably supplements the farming termination allowance. In 1966 a single termination allowance was introduced which is paid regardless of age; this is more in the nature of a redundancy payment than an early retirement allowance. The Dutch program for reducing the number of uneconomic farms has attracted several thousand applications from farmers, many of whom will use their termination allowances to retire from work.

Another group for which the Dutch have recently made special financial provision is that of small retail shopkeepers and independent craftsmen over 50 years of age. This area of economic activity is also declining, and it is estimated that one-third of the 300,000 operators of these businesses do not earn even the legal minimum wage. About 2,000 stores close every year at present; perhaps half because of old age or illness and another 20 percent because of bankruptcy, emigration, or housing redevelopement which eliminates the shop. The termination allowance, payable monthly after age 50, would be available to some 1,500 persons a year. Whether they retire from all work or enter the labor market to work for others depends, as with farmers, on personal desires and circumstances and the success of the various guidance and training programs which are offered to these displaced individuals by the labor market authorities. The termination payments at age 50 or above are an inducement to early retirement, even though they carry no restrictions on alternative gainful employment.[25]

In this chapter we have reviewed the trend in western Europe toward more generous public financial support for displaced workers and we have examined the impact on the hard-to-reemploy. Among the most noteworthy developments in recent years is the ECSC conception of unemployment benefits as a "waiting allowance" which guarantees nearly full earnings between jobs. Another discernible trend is the provision through governments of redundancy or severance payments, over and above the arrangments in collective bargaining agreements. Finally, early retirement pensions are increasingly available to older workers who are unlikely to be reemployed.

For the hard-to-reemploy who are not retained in their old jobs and will not find new jobs quickly or at all, financial compensation for loss of employment is a matter of prime importance. The form most suited to the needs of the older hard-to-reemploy workers is the pre-pension which leads into the standard old-age pension. A generous unemployment benefit or waiting allowance, in the newer concept, is useful to younger workers who need only time to be placed.

Redundancy payments are valuable as a supplement, but not as the sole source of social income for the hard-to-reemploy. When redundancy payments are made to workers who are about to leave the labor market in any case, the arguments against this form of benefit which have appeared in Great Britain have little validity. However, some of the hard-to-reemploy who receive redundancy payments may be deterred from seeking new jobs. In this sense, redundancy payments have yet to be assimilated into an active manpower policy. In general, income maintenance during periods of unemployment has received increased attention in western Europe.

[25] OECD, *Manpower and Social Policy in the Netherlands,* Paris, 1967, pp. 183–84.

XIV | The Issues in European Perspective

When one explores the programs of another country for relevance to American problems, it is helpful but not essential if conditions in the foreign nation are closely comparable to ours in nature and scope. We can learn about programs for the integration of minority groups, for example, from countries where minorities are a much smaller part of the population than they are in the United States. And we should not offer our larger and more complicated problems as an excuse for a troublesome backlog of unresolved issues. All the more reason to have initiated earlier and greater preventive and remedial action! A confrontation with alternative sets of values and priorities or with different national styles provides the opportunity to reassess features of one's own country which are generally regarded as fixed and immutable.

The choice of the countries of northwestern Europe as exemplars in a discussion of programs for the hard-to-employ follows a clear but not always acknowledged American pattern. European leadership in social policy, notably in social insurance, has long provided models for the United States. Although our programs have been adopted piecemeal after considerable debate and passage of time, and we have added our own modifications and distinctive features, our debt to western Europe has been great. Since World War II northwestern Europe also has pioneered in the recognition and assistance of the hard-to-employ. While each country has its own strengths and specialties, Sweden's experience commands the greatest attention, not only for its specific programs but also for its supporting institutions and policies.

The experience of western Europe strongly suggests that the maintenance of over-all unemployment rates at 2 percent or less for years at a time may be the single most important factor in minimizing the number of hard-to-employ and motivating a program to seek out the residual group who might appear unemployable in the United States at 4 percent unemployment. From this point of view, American unemployment rates of 3 to 4 percent, though inflationary, may not be low enough, especially if account is taken of the absorption by the armed forces of large numbers of youths who otherwise might have been jobless.

It also should be recognized that much of what has been celebrated as the social effort of American business to absorb the hardcore unemployed has been a response to high turnover and labor shortages created by the demands of the war in Vietnam plus a booming civilian economy. Complacency about the decline in American unemployment rates during the 1960s seems unwarranted. In the longer run, the gap between western European and American unemployment rates may widen still more in the absence of a substantial American military involvement.

While the reasons for the European ability to achieve much lower unemployment rates than the United States are complex, part of the explanation lies in the deliberate and effective European programs to smooth seasonal and regional variations in employment, resulting in lower over-all unemployment rates and having an anti-inflationary influence as well. The United States has far to go in these fields.

Differential unemployment rates, such as those for youths, are also less marked in Europe than in the United States, in part because European institutional arrangements and standards afford an easier transition from school to work. After 8 to 10 years of basic schooling, European youths are accepted directly for training which can lead to skilled status, but those who remain in unskilled jobs are not regarded as deprived. The issue is complicated in the United States by high expectations based on long stays in school, the view that all jobs should have promotional possibilities, and the growing reluctance of youths from the minority groups to accept employment in the low-prestige and low-paid service occupations.

Moreover, the unemployment situation does not permit the United States to import foreign workers for the menial jobs, as labor-short northern Europe has done, thereby upgrading opportunities for its domestic labor force. In light of our difficulties in achieving full employment, especially for teenagers, promises to achieve a full realization of human potential in the 1970s may, in the words of Arthur M. Ross, former Commissioner of Labor Statistics, be an indulgence in "the flatulent rhetoric and moral overcommitment to which Americans are notoriously addicted."

Under the pressure of labor shortages and the guidance of advanced social policies, several western European nations have forestalled unemployment and the development of hard-to-employ groups by aiding rural people to adapt to an urban environment and helping foreign workers to adjust to a new country. General manpower programs to match workers and jobs, to train and upgrade the whole labor force, and to aid mobility have reduced unemployment and promoted the placement of the hard-to-employ. Naturally, these efforts are most effective when the demand for labor is strong. By European standards, American programs to date have been underdeveloped and too reliant on private enterprise and nonprofit organizations.

The commitment to full employment is put to a severe test when demand slackens or balance-of-payments problems threaten employment. Unlike some of the other European countries, Sweden continues to give "the individual's right to make a meaningful contribution to production . . . decisive importance for the shaping of policy." Even price and cost stability are secondary objectives so long as international competitiveness and domestic equity can be maintained by productivity gains, taxation policy, and other means.

As unemployment rises, specific measures are initiated in Sweden to maintain or increase employment in the private and public sectors. The Swedish innovation of "investment reserve funds" for private firms is used in such a period. The government's own contracts and orders to private firms are increased by advancing the schedule

386 | *The Issues in European Perspective*

for placing such orders. In this connection, the United States has only scratched the surface of the possibilities for utilizing government contracts to influence employment. Not only deliberate timing of contracts, but also purposive geographical distribution and the potential for aiding specific groups of workers should be explored fully. Sweden also uses its extensive public construction program to influence the volume, location, and timing of employment. Schools and homes for the aged which are scheduled for later construction are started up sooner if the over-all employment situation or the state of the construction industry are weak. These measures to maintain employment are supplemented by the enlargement of existing programs to train workers and offer created jobs of a public works type.

In February-March 1968, it is estimated that about 125,000 Swedish workers were saved from unemployment by these measures; in terms of an American labor force twenty times larger, this would be 2,500,000 persons who otherwise might have swelled the unemployment rolls. Actual unemployment in February 1968, according to the Swedish quarterly labor force sample surveys, was 102,000, or 2,040,000 in the U.S. equivalent. Since seasonally adjusted American unemployment in that month was 2,941,000, it appears that the Swedish countermeasures held the deepest unemployment of their recession at a lower figure than the U.S. did at its full employment level.

While it is difficult in a discussion of the hard-to-employ to overemphasize the importance of a high demand for labor relative to the supply, it should be noted that the proportion of the population which is hard-to-employ, especially through functional illiteracy, poor motivation, or alienation, is sharply affected by the social standards of the society. If a high place is given to the welfare of all children, if only a narrow gap is permitted between the minimum and the average levels of housing, education, nutrition, health care, social services and recreational facilities, and if equality is sought in legal and civil rights and income distribution, then the proportion who are hard-to-employ for social reasons is apt to be relatively low.

The western European countries which care most about the human and social aspects, Holland and the Scandinavian countries, have found that a large public role is necessary to achieve these objectives and to provide the required personnel and facilities. Some functions may be farmed out to private enterprise or nonprofit agencies, but planning and supervision are retained in public hands. The augmentation of low incomes by transfer payments is not regarded as a substitute for providing adequate public services and facilities. These countries are impressed with the obstacles to expansion of certain services and facilities if they are left to the forces of private demand.

The question arises of how these social measures are financed. An international comparison in 1966 of the proportion of gross national product represented by taxes of every kind shows Sweden with 41.1 percent and the United States with only 28.2 percent; Sweden's per capita GNP is second highest in the world after the United States. Of the eleven European nations in the comparison compiled by the Swedish Ministry of Finance, only Switzerland had a lower proportion of GNP in taxes than the United States.

Not only is the share of GNP taken by government greater in Sweden than in the United States, but the share of governmental expenditures devoted to social programs in Sweden is also larger than in the United States. The central government in Sweden supports social programs both by direct expenditures and by grants-in-aid to the municipal governments which have primary responsibility in some areas. Grants-in-aid constitute about one-sixth of central government expenditures and one-fourth of municipal expenditures, higher proportions than in the United States.

These financial facts underlie the national priorities which Sweden has been quite successful in meeting. But Sweden and other countries in Europe do not share the American faith in the power of money alone or the efficacy of crash programs. Time, careful planning, and long periods for training personnel are allowed. Gradual improvements and expansions of programs are acceptable and they are geared to the possibilities of delivering services.

A combination of tight labor market and effective social programs in several European countries has tended to hold down the number of hard-to-employ, but the variety of types has not diminished. Every kind of difficulty found among the American hard-core can be duplicated in European countries, but in relatively small numbers. In Sweden alcoholics, narcotics addicts, refugees, gypsies, released prisoners, school dropouts, youths from reform schools, and older workers are the main categories of the socially handicapped. Their total number is not staggering, though Sweden uses methods of outreach which few countries can equal.

The motives for assisting the hard-to-employ have undergone some change since World War II. The earlier humanitarian interest in the physically and mentally disabled has been enlarged by a commitment to full employment which extends to those intermittently or permanently outside the labor force. These societies place a very high value on work as a means of participating in the community and achieving self-respect and status. By comparison, the American dedication to full employment is half-hearted and sporadic.

Another motive for assisting the hard-to-employ to find work has been persistent labor shortages. As part of an active manpower policy which seeks to reduce excessive turnover and inflationary pressures on wage rates by filling vacancies, the programs for the hard-to-employ can contribute toward the goals of rapid economic growth, price stability, and full employment. Only Sweden has developed this aspect of an active manpower policy in an integrated fashion. Particularly notable is Sweden's use of periods of slack demand for labor to expand retraining courses which fit the hard-to-employ for work when demand revives.

A final motive is the desire to hold down the costs of providing pensions and public assistance by reclaiming those who could become self-supporting. Workers who are receiving disability or invalidity pensions have weak incentives to work if they must forfeit part or all of their pensions. This "pension neurosis" is a more important problem in many western European countries than are employables on unemployment insurance benefits, unemployment assistance, or public welfare who resist taking jobs.

European public assistance programs avoid several of the problems which beset the American system. First, since the eligibility rules for public assistance are the same from place to place within most European countries and the amounts granted vary only with regional differences in the cost of living, those who depend on public support are not inclined to migrate; the housing shortage is a barrier in any case.

Second, the combined income from work plus family allowances in European countries generally is larger than public assistance. In the United States net earnings may be less favorable than welfare payments when family allowances are not available to bolster low wages and the costs of child care are an extra burden for women who head households. The recent American innovation of permitting a certain portion of earnings to be retained by welfare recipients, strictly forbidden in most European countries, may shift the balance toward work.

Third, the European countries provide unemployment assistance or general welfare to jobless men who have exhausted or never had a claim to unemployment insurance benefits, thus reducing their temptation to desert or pretend to desert their families. (If they do the latter, public assistance is being used as a supplement to low wages, much as family allowances would be.)

In spite of lower unemployment rates and a wider variety of social insurance and pension programs than in the United States, the European countries have found a continuing need for public assistance for some employables. Sweden regards the offer of jobs and the availability of manpower programs as the responsibility of government and the only effective method of testing willingness to work. In several countries the work-shy on public assistance tend to be single men, often drifters or recluses, who have physical or psychological problems. Rehabilitation and work experience centers have recorded some success with the long-term unemployed and occasionally a threat of cutting off assistance is used to induce a search for work. Britain has found that some men with large families may be as well off on public assistance as on unskilled jobs, but their apparent disinclination to work can be changed by a chance at skilled employment.

Women with young children are recognized in Europe as a genuine welfare category, and no pressure is placed on them to seek work. Children are not listed as primary relief recipients, as in the United States, but as dependents of the adults, and as a result the total numbers on welfare are not so frightening. By European standards the United States provides inadequate coverage in every category of public assistance; accordingly, no contradiction necessarily exists between rising welfare rolls and declining unemployment.

While the taxpayers' complaint that some employables live on public funds may be heard almost anywhere in western Europe, this is a minor theme among the motives for assisting the hard-to-employ to find jobs. Humanitarian views, the commitment to full employment, the high value placed on work for the individual and society, and the pressure of labor shortages are more important factors in shaping programs for the hard-to-employ who remain even when full employment prevails and social programs are highly developed.

Sweden, whose program is most integrated and comprehensive as to coverage, organization, and services, defines the hard-to-employ as "persons who, due to physical or mental defects or social deficiencies, have, or expect to have, more difficulties than others to obtain and hold gainful employment." This broad definition was urged on the U.S. Rehabilitation Services Administration by the National Citizens Advisory Council on Vocational Rehabilitation. Under such a definition, all of the hard-core unemployed could be aided.

Much of the strength of Sweden's program for the hard-to-employ derives from its integral relation to other manpower programs and its administration through the National Labour Market Board, a semiautonomous agency with broad financial and policy powers. The Vocational Rehabilitation Division at the national level and special officers of the Employment Service in each county supervise the more difficult cases, while ordinary placement officers and their supervisors in the local Employment Service offices deal with less complicated cases. As well organized as the Swedish system is, some failures of communication have been observed between the two main operating divisions, the placement section and the vocational rehabilitation officers. But the sort of division that has grown up in New York City between the State Employment Service and the Human Resources Administration would not be tolerated in Sweden.

In many ways the Rehabilitation Services Administration is the most suitable American agency to direct a permanent program for the hard-to-employ. But the location of the R.S.A. in the Department of Health, Education and Welfare, its own reluctant attitudes, the difficulties of establishing organizational and programmatic connections with the Employment Service (which already has a stake in this area and logically should play a key role), the competing claims of community programs financed by the Office of Economic Opportunity, and the scattered efforts of business corporations make it doubtful that conflict, overlapping, and duplication will soon be ended.

The initial elements of the most advanced European programs for the hard-to-employ are the interviewing and screening process and the provision of guidance and counseling services, including the advice of various specialists. A selected group may be sent to other institutions for psychotechnical tests, an assessment of vocational capacity, work experience, vocational training, or further education. The attempt to make placements in the competitive labor market is the culmination of the earlier efforts, and it proceeds either by intensified or special techniques or by approaches to prospective employers through legal compulsion or financial incentives. Finally, those who cannot be placed in open employment may be provided with created jobs outside the usual enterprise structures.

Since many of the European measures exist to some degree in the United States, the novelty is not in their content but in their widespread application throughout a country under uniform standards. It may be easier to bring together the European experience than to collect and present the diverse American practices. Hardly a day goes by but that some American demonstration project, announced as breathtakingly revolutionary, tries out a program which has been well-established in a European country for some time. Some translation of the scope of European programs into American dimensions will be attempted, along with reflections on the aspects of European policy which are suited to American conditions.

Intake procedures are a clue to a program's ability to reach those who need its services. One evidence of success in Sweden is the large number of registrants at the Vocational Rehabilitation Service. The total is approaching 100,000 new cases annually; in terms of an American population 25 times larger, this would be 2.5 million cases handled in a single year. It should be contrasted with the U.S. Rehabilitation Services Administration's report that over 200,000 persons were rehabilitated into employment or self-employment in 1968 and that a backlog of 4 million people in the United States with physical and mental disabilities need rehabilitation services; 450,000 more become disabled each year.

If the millions of socially handicapped who need rehabilitation services are added, the size of the problem emerges, even if it is restricted to the portion requiring vocational rehabilitation only. In Sweden disabled homemakers are eligible for the vocational rehabilitation program and are taught to manage at home with little or no assistance. Adaptation of appliances and surroundings to the disability is part of the service.

To be effective, a program for the hard-to-employ must maintain intimate working relations with medical, social work, psychiatric, corrective, educational, and other social services. In the best circumstances people are referred to the manpower agency, having already been given preparatory care. But most countries have a two-way flow, since many of the hard-to-employ who come to the attention of the Employment Service need remedial treatment and supportive services before or while they are groomed for jobs. Permanent, specialized remedial agencies are needed in the United States to serve the Employment Service and other placement agencies which have been attempting to do some of the corrective work themselves. Employers who have experimental programs for the hard-core unemployed also could benefit from a network of remedial agencies. Such remedial agencies need not be government operated, but there should be central direction and supervision and uniform standards.

Sweden is able to rely on institutional referrals for the vast majority of its vocational rehabilitation cases. Hospitals, sanitariums, doctors, special schools, prisons, alcoholic and narcotics care centers, reform schools, and other welfare agencies are alerted to send on those who are ready for vocational rehabilitation beyond that offered in their institutions. It took some years for these institutions to respond fully to the outreach efforts of the Vocational Rehabilitation Service, even though the latter is aided by "contact men," employees of the Employment Service who serve as liaison with all of the medical and social institutions. The contact men assist people while they are institutionalized and after they are discharged so that they can resume a place in the labor force.

The Swedish Employment Service has established new procedures to facilitate the discovery and care of hard-to-employ cases. By reducing the amount of time its placement officers spend with applicants who are chiefly searching for information, the Employment Service freed its officers to give more attention to the 30 percent of registrants who needed the personal contact. This solution is particularly effective where funds or personnel cannot be expanded rapidly.

Guidance and counseling may be offered to the hard-to-employ by placement officers or counselors who have no placing functions. They may act alone or after conferences with psychologists, psychiatrists, social workers, doctors, vocational guidance specialists, technical advisers, and others who are on the staff or serve as consultants. Whether the counselor refers the worker directly for placement or suggests that further services are desirable, the usefulness of the personal contact and interest of a counselor is gaining acceptance. Counseling of the hard-core has made rapid strides in the United States, particularly in experimental programs. The task is to make the best practices general and expand the number who receive counseling.

If workers are not ready for placement and there is doubt about their capacities, they may be sent for psychotechnical testing, vocational assessment, or work experience. These services are available in the United States in some areas and for some groups. The distinctive feature in the most advanced European countries is that these services are provided on a permanent basis in a network of government financed and supervised institutions which may be initiated and operated by local authorities or nonprofit agencies. They cover the entire country, serve every type of handicap, provide a uniform level of service from unit to unit, test a variety of occupations, and are integrated with the counseling and placement services.

The total number of places available for performing these services in the United States may be proportionately greater than in Britain, Denmark, or Sweden, but in terms of accessibility and maintenance of standards, the publicly-organized services of the European countries probably contribute more. If the nucleus of high-standard non-profit agencies which furnish these services in the United States could be induced and financed to direct a great expansion, both geographically and in the clientele served, the semblance of a national system might appear. Those agencies that offer work experience should be differentiated from the sheltered workshops or, at a minimum, separate sections should be established, as in European practice.

A national system would help to maintain the steady flow of clients needed to minimize underutilization of staff and facilities. A waiting list may be desirable because illness and other difficulties cause a high rate of dropouts. In fact, the European experience suggests that a low rate of completion of courses should be expected if the services are offered to those who are truly hard-to-employ.

A special word should be said about the work experience centers or Industrial Rehabilitation Units, as the British named them. They have enormous potential usefulness for the United States as a means of preparing people for work, increasing their punctuality and work pace, and simulating the conditions of work. The voluntary efforts of American business to fill this void are inadequate on several counts: the total number of places supplied is unlikely to meet the total need, the worker is readied for whatever work the particular employer happens to be engaged in without regard to the worker's own inclinations and abilities, and the quality of the supervision cannot be verified.

European employers have shown little interest in offering preemployment remedial education or social services to prospective native-born employees, although they have supported government enthusiastically as the proper authority for this activity. Those who have been counting on American employers for these preparatory services must explain why corporations are suited to the work or should bear the expense on a large scale. Employers' efforts probably should be confined to disadvantaged workers who are motivated already to work. The creation of adequate public facilities to serve the large numbers who need and will need assistance has been sidetracked by the reliance on industry. The contribution of business should be viewed as a small supplementary measure, although there is great value in the location of a center in or near a factory and in the promise of jobs afterward.

Vocational retraining for the hard-to-employ is most highly developed in Sweden, where over 50 percent of all trainees are disadvantaged in the labor market. Since Sweden's total retraining effort is impressive—2 percent of the labor force annually are retrained at present—the large share of the hard-to-employ is particularly significant. Moreover, high proportions of all retrainees obtain jobs in the occupation for which they trained and at higher wages than they earned previously. In this as in other spheres, the hard-to-employ benefit from the concurrent programs to retrain, upgrade, and improve the utilization of the entire labor force. The substantial increase in the numbers in retraining during the winter months of the 1967–68 recession especially benefited the Swedish hard-to-employ, and is one of the countercyclical policies that bear exploration in the United States.

Since there is considerable interest in skill training within industry for the hard core in the United States, the European experience should be examined. In spite of acceptance of a more active role for employers in the formal training of youth in Europe than in America, European employers have not responded well to subsidies for training the hard-to-employ. Retraining in industry in Sweden has constituted about 15 percent of the total, excluding informal on-the-job training which is not counted in Europe. Employers are a useful source of training in certain occupations, but public courses have had to supply the bulk of the retraining places. A disappointing aspect of training within industry has been the very small fraction of trainees retained by the company as employees. American results should be reviewed after a few years to see whether the European pattern is repeated.

Placement is the objective of all the services for the hard-to-employ. Probably every special technique known in Europe has been used in some part of the United States, at least in an experimental or pilot program. One American experiment, genuinely innovative, and which has not been tried in Europe, has been the banding together of corporation representatives to pledge themselves to hire the hard-to-employ out of a sense of social responsibility. When the public relations smoke has cleared, it may be possible to estimate how many vacancies would have been available in any case and how many of those hired might have been chosen without a campaign. Comparisons should be made between participating and nonparticipating firms. To test such a program properly it should be conducted in a period of steady or slack demand and attention should be given to the effects on those just above the hard-core level.

In some European countries, the placement of the hard-to-employ in competitive markets has been promoted by two methods not in fashion in the United States: wage subsidies and legal compulsion. Employers have reacted very poorly to the offer of wage supplements as an inducement to hire the hard-to-employ referred by the Employment Service. There is no requirement that training be given. In Belgium and Sweden, only a few hundred workers are employed under this system, but Sweden has hopes of swelling the number of semisheltered workers, as they call them, to 5,000. Employers seem disinclined to submit to the reporting and supervision involved in obtaining the subsidy.

Legal compulsion on private and public employers to provide jobs for the physically or mentally disabled exists in the larger western European countries. It has been well accepted by employers in Great Britain and West Germany because the quotas are reasonable, active rehabilitation programs are in effect, and specialized officers of the Employment Service make careful placements. In American terms, about 1,500,000 workers would be on the quota system if the proportion in Britain and West Germany prevailed.

Many of those on quota employment in Europe would obtain

jobs without legal support, especially when there is a strong demand for labor. For those who might not obtain work and for those who might be the first to be fired, the legal backing is valuable. To the extent that employers create more jobs under the quota than they would otherwise offer, and to the extent that quota workers earn standard wages for lower-than-average output, employers and consumers are absorbing some of the costs that would otherwise be borne by the workers in question and public programs. The quota system in West Germany may provide a job for the kind of severely disabled worker who would not be accepted by Swedish or Dutch employers, but this is difficult to test, as is the quality of the jobs under the quota.

Even if a law to establish a quota system seems a remote possibility, some use of the idea could be made in the United States, perhaps under the Rehabilitation Services Administration. On a voluntary basis, the acceptance of a given quota of referred disabled persons or hard-core unemployed could be proposed to government agencies at all levels and to government contractors. If it proved successful, private employers could be enlisted with credit given for the disabled or hard-core already employed by given firms. The Philadelphia Plan for the employment of minority workers by government contractors is an example of this approach, although the term "quota" is resisted by officials.

Another group which has received attention in western Europe is that we call the hard-to-reemploy. Some employed older workers who never had difficulty in obtaining or keeping jobs would have difficulties if they lost their jobs. Others who are at work have such serious handicaps that they would surely be hard-to-employ if their present jobs ended. The interest of these groups is to maintain continuity of employment, and various kinds of general manpower measures influence their position. In West Germany, Holland, and France the hard-to-reemploy are aided by general and specific legislation which restricts the freedom of employers to dismiss their workers. Legislation in some countries also provides for work-sharing instead of dismissals, supplementing and reinforcing custom, and trade union agreements.

The general laws concerning dismissals and work-sharing cannot prevent but may delay reductions of staff when an industry-wide or nation-wide slump occurs. The hard-to-reemploy tend to be dismissed first under such conditions, unless they have specific protection under special dismissal laws, which usually are enacted in connection with the quota system for employing the physically or mentally handicapped.

When, as in the United States, strenuous efforts have been made to obtain employment for the handicapped or hard-core unemployed, the entire project may be nullified if the disadvantaged workers are the first to be laid off. But it is doubtful that legislation on dismissals or work-sharing will be enacted in the United States, since there would be severe conflict with trade union seniority rules on lay-off. For informal arrangements, the greatest hope lies in making compensated lay-off so attractive to workers with seniority that they will not object to the hard-core workers being retained.

An unintended and negative use of the dismissal and work-sharing laws has been to support the uneconomic retention of surplus employees when a firm suffers a loss of business or introduces technical or organizational changes which call for a smaller or different type of labor force. The hard-to-reemploy benefit particularly at such times because many of them would suffer prolonged unemployment or fail to find new jobs even when manpower policies are highly developed. Yet, this use of dismissal laws cannot be recommended.

Positive inducements to workers to cooperate when their firms are changing production methods or products have been offered by several European governments and through the Social Fund of the European Economic Community and the High Authority of the Coal and Steel Community. Subsidies make it possible for employers to pay workers a high proportion of wages while they are laid off and are waiting to resume work. A measure which bears copying by the United States is the retraining allowance paid to employers who keep their labor force intact while instructing them in the new positions they will hold.

Another positive measure to maintain continuity of employment, developed by Sweden and with potential for the United States, is the selective letting of government contracts in an accelerated way, and to specific firms or industries which are threatened with a loss of orders and a need to dismiss workers. Other Swedish devices which tend to maintain jobs for the hard-to-reemploy and may create jobs for some unemployed are the release of "investment reserve" funds, the initiation of new private construction, and the speeding up of public construction projects.

But continuity of employment cannot be maintained indefinitely for all. In a dynamic economy a certain amount of worker displacement is necessary and inevitable. Those who are about to be displaced benefit from manpower programs which try to obtain new positions before the workers actually lose their old jobs. Advance notice to the Employment Service through formal or legal arrangements, direct transfers from jobs to training programs or new jobs, and introduction of new enterprises in an area where displaced workers are immobile are some techniques worth copying on a national scale. They are most effective when vacancies are plentiful or the means of creating additional employment opportunities exist.

Special services and specific programs to aid the hard-to-reemploy may reach some who do not benefit from the general measures. A notable addition to policy is the payment of a wage supplement for a time to workers who accept lower-paid jobs. In the United States there is room for the reinforcement of the private plans of some corporations and trade unions by public action to aid displaced workers whose employers are unlikely to provide such benefits.

Periods of unemployment may occur even when manpower measures are numerous and effective. The improvement of unemployment benefits reflects the belief that unemployment should be regarded as a brief period between jobs. The Coal and Steel Community even calls its benefits for miners and steel workers "waiting allowances." Some older workers who become unemployed in certain industries and certain countries are now permitted to remain indefinitely on unemployment benefits until their governmental old-age pensions begin. Another innovation which frees some older unemployed workers from the obligation to register as unemployed or seek work is the pre-pension. Its introduction in the United States would be a valuable extension of Social Security to those who are 55 or 60 years old and have little prospect of ever working again.

Still another novelty is the public program to pay a lump-sum severance or "redundancy" payment to dismissed workers, presumably for their loss of property rights in their jobs. This benefit has been most highly developed in Great Britain, but shows a tendency to spread in Europe. Open to criticism on several grounds, public severance payments in revised form may eventually gain consideration in the United States.

Continuity of employment serves the needs of the hard-to-reemploy best. Next in importance are measures which anticipate impending unemployment, minimize the period of unemployment, give financial security, and assist in new placements. Finally, programs to ease or speed retirement from the labor force may be the best solution for some of the hard-to-reemploy. The European innovations in these fields are worthy of close study.

A final area in which European experience is valuable is that of special job creation for those who temporarily or permanently have difficulty in obtaining or holding employment in the competitive labor market. This activity, which in the United States is called "Government as Employer of Last Resort," has much the same status in Europe; it is suggested only after all other placement possibilities have been considered. Holland and Sweden have developed job creation most extensively and elaborately, but virtually every western European country has some form in operation. However, none would be considered guaranteed employment.

Two main programs for special job creation are found, differentiated by the type of workers who are eligible. The first, which we have called Special Public Works in this study, has been concerned with workers of average capacity whose location and occupation subject them to periods of unemployment even when labor markets are extremely tight. This method of countering regional and seasonal unemployment is seen as a bridge between jobs at normal wage rates particularly for older unskilled and immobile men. The former role of the job creation program as a countercyclical measure has been reduced; for example, in the recession of 1966–68, the expansion of the program could be disproportionately small in relation to the increase in unemployment because several other approaches were taken toward stimulating employment.

Under European conditions, the job creation programs appear to be free of stigma on the workers or "leaf-raking" charges, perhaps as a result of using private contractors to execute all projects in Holland and considerable numbers in Sweden. A small portion of the projects are carried out on private property, with the owners paying a portion of the costs. These aspects may be important for the United States, where the old image of the WPA and fears of creeping socialism and the undeserving poor may threaten any program entirely operated by government. However, over-all direction and maintenance of standards is a responsibility which government cannot shirk. In any case, a strengthened Employment Service is needed to assist whatever agency is chosen to create the jobs.

Certain differences in American conditions may make it possible to initiate a job creation program which avoids some of the structural limitations noted in an earlier chapter. An American program would not need to be tied so closely to outdoors work on roads and land improvement but could emphasize supplementary public services which are in short supply in many communities. Opportunities as subprofessional aides could be provided for women, for white-collar workers, and for some who might find outdoors work demeaning.

The public service jobs also have a greater possibility for upgrading than outdoor work. At the same time, these are at present labor-intensive jobs, in contrast to road building and other construction work which is more efficiently done with machinery and skilled workers who do not need created jobs. The problem of bringing created jobs to the workers in areas where economic development is at a standstill or is declining also can be eased if the emphasis is on supplementary public services, housing, and urban rehabilitation.

An American job creation program would be based on the substantial residual unemployment and the high differential rates among certain groups. It would have a year-round character in the central cities. Therefore, the need to make rapid seasonal adjustments in project employment levels, a difficult task for the European programs, would be of less consequence in the United States.

On the other hand, an American program might face some pressures of its own. If employed part-time and full-time workers whose earnings are below those available on full-time created jobs should seek these new jobs, the size and cost of the program could become prohibitive. At a minimum, great pressure would be exerted on low wages in jobs not subject to the federal minimum wage. To be efficient and acceptable, a job creation program should not promise too much or expand too rapidly. Some limitations on eligibility may be necessary, even if guaranteed employment is the ultimate goal.

The second type of job creation under the auspices of government in western Europe makes work opportunities for those who are able to work but require a sheltered environment. In mid-1968 the Netherlands had 42,039 persons in created jobs for the severely handicapped, distributed among sheltered workshops, outdoor projects, and special jobs for white-collar, technical, and professional workers. If the same proportion of the population were provided with such jobs in the United States, close to 700,000 positions would be needed. Even then it is likely that the American unmet need would be greater than the Dutch. The incidence of birth defects, accidents and illness, and social disabilities is lower in the Netherlands, and their preventive and remedial programs are more developed in spite of the fact that the Dutch per capita GNP is less than half that of the United States.

For long-run manpower and social planning in the United States it would be desirable to consider such a job creation program. But in view of the higher priority of the job creation described above as Special Public Works, the public expansion of existing sheltered work in the United States might be deferred. Since all available public service and public works projects should be offered first to the disadvantaged, this type of job would be in limited supply for the handicapped. Furthermore, a substantial expansion of sheltered workshops which can offer workers a reasonable income and good working conditions rests on the desire of the private business sector to subcontract work due to acute shortages of labor and factory space, such as western Europe has experienced.

Instead of working toward substantial expansion of American sheltered workshops, which now have about 100,000 persons in some form of work experience or sheltered employment, the Rehabilitation Services Administration should use its good offices and financial influence to help modernize existing workshops, to broaden their admission policies, and to form the base on which a greatly expanded system can someday be built.

In reviewing the specific factors associated with the most successful programs for the hard-to-employ, such as Sweden's, we must give a high place to the formal recognition of a variety of types of hard-to-employ persons as a single category for whom it is necessary to have permanent, comprehensive, well-financed and administered programs in both tight and loose labor markets. These programs are initiated by government because so many of the hard-to-employ have no contact with internal labor markets. Local governments play an important role in executing general policy, while nonprofit agencies and private enterprise also assume part of the task.

General acceptance of government agencies and their programs is fostered by the use of tripartite and multipartite policymaking, advisory, and administrative bodies which draw management and labor organization into day-to-day issues. A strong Employment Service and an integration of programs for the hard-to-employ with other manpower and social programs are sources of strength. Each case is treated individually and the most suitable services are selected from an array of possible actions.

The European countries which have been most advanced in serving the hard-to-employ have been small and homogeneous in population. They are ruled by central governments under a parliamentary system and have effective local governments serving relatively small populations. To these advantages, which are not reproducible, must be added some attitudes which assist the implementation of programs for the hard-to-employ: the acceptance of a large measure of economic planning in a private enterprise setting, the actual fulfillment of social goals, a high valuation of work, the refusal to allow financial and budget procedures to determine the social priorities or interfere with the continuity of social programs.

There is a national style which permeates the whole structure of social action, and it reveals itself particularly in the willingness of people to accept direction and interference in their lives which might be resented in other countries. At the same time the personnel take a somewhat paternalistic attitude toward those they serve. Some subtle influences are exerted on the programs which are not measured by numbers of cases or money spent.

If American interest in or acceptance of European programs for the hard-to-employ depended upon a demonstration that they achieved their objectives at minimum cost or that the best alternatives always were chosen, or that benefits exceeded costs, the whole subject would have to be abandoned. The data needed for such analyses are lacking in most instances, and attempts to engage in such calculations have been rare. By American standards, the research output of European government and academic authorities in these fields is meager.

The most advanced European countries do not match the United States in the collection and analysis of manpower data, basic manpower research, and evaluation of programs. Yet, the foreign visitor is impressed by the intimate acquaintance of high officials with the details of operations at the local level and their quick response to changes in the employment situation. Sweden has recently become concerned with the setting of priorities in its labor market measures and the introduction of cost-effectiveness studies. Taken together with the modest and self-critical approaches of Swedish manpower officials, the new procedures should keep Sweden in the forefront.

Despite the admirable aspects, there are limitations, even in Sweden. No country has fully realized the OECD's goal in terms of an active manpower policy to achieve a full utilization of marginal human resources and to give all individuals an opportunity to work and participate fully in society. Even Sweden has permitted the hard-to-employ among others to work at menial, low-paying, and dead-end jobs. But over-all, the best European programs command respect and imitation for their treatment of hard to-employ persons as well as for their efforts to minimize the numbers who require the special services.

Index

Adult training, *see* Training and retraining programs

Advisory Committee for Supplementary Employment (Holland), 187

Agricultural Wages Act (Britain), 125

Alcoholics, 43, 48, 65, 75, 76, 88, 116T, 210, 237, 258-59

Algerians in France, 49

Archive work (Sweden), 262 ff.

Artists (Dutch): job creation for, 262

Assessment clinics (Sweden), 64-65

Association for Employment in Industry and Commerce (ASSEDIC: France), 348, 377

Association pour la formation professionelle des adultes (AFPA), 310, 334

BAVAV, *see* Federal Institute for Labor Placement and Unemployment Insurance

Becker, H. J.: quoted, 149, 170

Belgium: surveys of unemployment, 14-17; comprehensive approach to program for h-t-e, 40; medicopsychotechnical testing centers, 63; work adjustment and experience centers, 66-67; placement of h-t-e, 102, 118; quota employment, 120-21, 122; subsidized employment, 163-68, 164T; Special Public Works, 185, 186, 196T; job creation, 268; wage maintenance during reconversion, 309; information on dismissals, 318; wage supplements for displaced miners and steel workers, 327, 328 ff.; unemployment benefits, 14, 67, 163, 349-50; redundancy payments, 366-67; employment and dismissal of older workers in coal, iron, and steel, 372 ff., 373T

Blind, 88, 103, 123, 222, 232, 251-52, 253T, 254-55

Board of Education (Sweden), 88, 97

Board of Trade (Britain): factories built by, 171

Bradford, England: workshop for the blind, 252

Braun, Kurt: quoted, 290

British Institute of Management, 362

Caseloads: in Sweden, 44 ff., 75; in Germany, 44 ff.; differentials, Sweden and U.S., 392

Maladjusted, socially, 43, 59, 65, 75, 88, 97 ff., 116T, 210, 236-38, 261
Manchester, England: Counselling Project (OECD), 26-27
Mangum, Garth L.: quoted, 34
Manpower and Productivity Service (Britain), 327
Manpower policies, role of: as social concern, 30-37, 385 ff.; OECD's "active manpower policy," 32-34, 80, 404; in programs for h-t-e, 38 ff.; in Employment Service, 41 ff.; for disadvantaged minority groups, 49 ff.; on-the-job training, 90; quota systems, 161; special job creation, 180 ff.; attitudes toward unemployment, 270 ff.; programs for hard-to-reemploy, 271, 315 ff., 344-45; concern with job security, 313; redundancy payments, 365
—*Belgian*, 14-17
—*British*, 21-27, 138-42
—*Dutch*, 17-21, 297, 282-88, 285T, 287T
—*French*, 288-93
—*German*, 150
—*Swedish*, 12 ff., 40, 42 ff., 80
Manpower Service (France): role in dismissals, 288
Medical examinations (British): for unemployed, 55, 127
Meidner, Rudolph: quoted, 31, 273
Mentally ill and retarded, 43, 45, 48, 49, 50, 54, 69, 70, 72, 88, 97 ff., 113, 114, 116T, 122, 126, 210, 219-20, 222, 245, 257T, 258
Michanek, Ernst: quoted, 31
Minder geschikten (Holland), *see* Hard-to-employ
Minder validen (Holland), *see* Hard-to-employ
Miners, *see* Coal miners

Ministry of Labour, *see* Department of Employment and Productivity (Britain)
Ministry of Social Affairs and Public Health (Holland), 224
Mobility of labor force, 2; in Britain, 24; in Sweden, 100-01, 190 ff.; transfers by nationalized industries and corporations, 275; transfer of redundant workers, 334-36, 339
Musicians, Swedish; job creation program for unemployed, 263

National Advisory Committee on the Employment of Older Men and Women (Britain), 121
National Assistance Board, *see* Supplementary Benefits Commission (Britain)
National Board of Private Forestry (Sweden), 88
National Citizens Advisory Council on Vocational Rehabilitation (United States), 390
National Coal Board (Britain), 82, 357
National Employment Fund (France), 330-31, 333, 342, 376 ff.
National Forestry Administration (Sweden), 257
National Fund for the Handicapped (Belgium), 166
National Institute for Social Welfare (Italy), 153
National Institute for War Disabled (Italy), 153
National Institute of Economic Research (Sweden), 303
National Insurance Act (1966; Norway), 370

Refugee groups: aid to, 50, 154, 263

Regional Employment Premium (Britain), 177

Registration as disabled person (Britain), 123 ff.: *see also* Disabled Persons Register (Britain)

Rehabilitation: programs for, 39 ff., 43 ff.; linking of medical and vocational, 65; within sheltered workshop, 218; *see also* Social services; Vocational rehabilitation

Rehabilitation Centers (Denmark), 55

Rehabilitation Services Administration (United States), 34, 390, 391, 392

Rehn, Gösta, 354

Remploy, Ltd. (Britain), 216, 222, 227 ff., 230T, 234, 239-40, 241, 245, 249, 251, 252, 253T

Repatriates to Belgium, 165

Report of the Working Party on Workshops for the Blind (1962; Britain), 252

Report on Racial Discrimination (PEP), 25

Research: on impact and long-range effects of rehabilitation programs, 38 ff.

Reserved employment: Britain, 142-43; Germany, 152; France, 156-59

Resettlement clinics (Britain), 48

Retirement pensions, early: problems of older workers, 369 ff., 399-400; selected national programs, 370-82; as aid to farmers, 380-81

Retraining programs, *see* Training and retraining programs

Road construction: as Special Public Works program, in Sweden, 201 ff., 204T

Ross, Arthur M.: quoted, 385

Rotterdam, Holland: Counselling Project (OECD), 20

Scandinavia: income distribution aim, 7, 387; work attitudes, 8; diversity of rehabilitative programs, 41; attitudes toward on-the-job training, 90; range of vocational rehabilitation, 114-15; opposition to principle of quota employment, 120 ff.

Screening services, 47, 52 ff.

Selective Employment Tax (Britain), 177

Self-employment, subsidized: European programs, 173-76

Severance payments, *see* Redundancy payments

Sheltered workshops, 250 ff; in Holland and Belgium, 66-67, 213, 219 ff., 221T, 226 ff., 230T, 253T; in Sweden, 74, 168 ff., 213 ff., 219 ff., 221T, 226 ff., 230T, 253T; in Britain, 216 ff., 230T, 253T; *see also* Industrial workshops; Remploy, Ltd.; Social Employment program (Holland)

Sinfield, Adrian, 24, 25, 113, 115, 127, 138, 349, 363

Social Employment program for blue-collar workers (Holland), 210-13, 218-20, 221T, 225, 235-36, 249, 251, 253T, 255, 260-61

Social Employment Program for White-Collar Workers (Holland), 210, 221T, 262, 263-65, 266-67

Social Fund (EEC), *see* European Economic Community

Social-pedagogic Service (Holland), 113